INSTRUCTIONAL TECHNOLOGY

INSTRUCTIONAL TECHNOLOGY
Its Nature and Use

Sixth Edition

WALTER A. WITTICH
Professor Emeritus, University of Hawaii at Manoa

CHARLES F. SCHULLER
Professor Emeritus, Michigan State University

HARPER & ROW, PUBLISHERS
New York Hagerstown Philadelphia San Francisco London

Sponsoring Editor: George A. Middendorf
Project Editor: H. Detgen
Designer: T. R. Funderburk
Production Manager: Marion A. Palen
Compositor: American Stratford–Graphic Services, Inc.
Printer and Binder: Halliday Lithograph Corporation
Art Studio: J&R Technical Services, Inc.

INSTRUCTIONAL TECHNOLOGY: ITS NATURE AND USE, SIXTH EDITION

Library of Congress Cataloging in Publication Data

Wittich, Walter Arno, Date–
Instructional technology, its nature and use.

Includes bibliographical references and index.
1. Audio-visual education. I. Schuller, Charles Francis, joint author. II. Title.
LB1043.W58 1979 371.33 78-12812
ISBN 0-06-047169-7

Acknowledgments

THE AUTHORS wish to express their appreciation to the following companies, individuals, and institutions for their valuable assistance in supplying the fine photographs and other visual materials on which this book so heavily depends. All photographs and diagrams not credited in this list were supplied by the authors.

Figure 1.1 Comsat / 1.2*a–b* Enrich, Inc., Palo Alto, Calif. / 1.5 Oakland Public Schools, Oakland, Calif. / 1.6 Hawaiian Curriculum Center, Honolulu / 1.10 J. Herbert Klausmeier and Richard E. Ripple, *Learning and Human Abilities: Educational Psychology,* 3rd ed. (New York: Harper & Row, 1971), fig. 6.2, p. 197 / 1.11 Pecos National Monument Photo, Pecos, N. Mex. / 1.16 Apple Valley School, Yakima, Wash. (Edward H. Marble & Assoc., Architects, A.I.A.)

2.1 Children's Television Workshop / 2.2 Eastman Kodak Company / 2.3 Michigan State University / 2.4*c* Eastman Kodak Company / 2.5 Rand McNally / 2.6 Charles Beseler Company / 2.7 Coronet Instructional Films / 2.8*a* National Film Board of Canada / 2.8*b* Michigan State University / 2.9 NASA / 2.10*a–b* Eastman Kodak Company / 2.11 Michigan State University / 2.12 Ray Atkeson / 2.13 National Park Service / 2.14*a–b* Michigan State University / 2.15*a–b;* 2.16*a–d* Michigan State University Graphics / 2.17 Michigan State University / 2.18*a–d;* 2.19*a–d* Michigan State University Graphics / 2.20 © by The New York Times Company. Reprinted by permission. / 2.21 *Educational Technology Magazine* / 2.22 © 1974 United Feature Syndicate, Inc. / 2.23*a–c;* 2.24; 2.25; 2.26 Michigan State University Graphics

3.1 Fisher Scientific Co. / 3.2 Society for Visual Education / 3.3 Michigan State University / 3.4*a* University of Wisconsin / 3.4*b–c* University of Hawaii / 3.5 Denoyer-Geppert Co. / 3.6 Camera-Craft, Inc., Seattle, Wash. / 3.7 Long Beach Unified School District, Long Beach, Calif. / 3.8 Denoyer-Geppert Co. / 3.9 Los Angeles City Schools, Audio-Visual Section / 3.10 Robert C. Ragsdale, Toronto / 3.11 Singer, Link Division / 3.12 Michigan State University / 3.13*a* Oregon Museum of Science and Industry / 3.13*b* Bloomfield Hills Public Schools, Bloomfield Hills, Mich. / 3.14; 3.15*a–c* Michigan State University Graphics / 3.16*a, c* Mexican National Tourist Council / 3.16*b* Museo National de Antropología, Mexico City / 3.17 © Walt Disney Productions / 3.18 Museum of Art, Science & Industry, Bridgeport, Conn. / 3.19 Detroit Science Center / 3.20 Oregon Museum of Science & Industry / 3.21 The Southern New England Telephone Company, Public Relations Dept.

4.1 Adlai E. Stevenson High School, Prairie View, Ill. / 4.2 Hays from Monkmeyer / 4.3 *Nation's Schools* / 4.4 Tim Kantor, Rapho Guillumette, photographers / 4.5 Foxfire project, Eliot Wigginton, director / 4.6 BOCES / 4.7 Blue Water Marine Laboratory, Dept. of Marine Programs, University of Hawaii / 4.8*a–b* Humboldt County Schools, Office of Environmental Education, William Gaffaney and R. Brett Matzke, photographers / 4.9*a* Honolulu Newspaper Assc. Library / 4.9*b* Honolulu Newspaper Assc., John Titchen, photographer / 4.10*a–c* American Telephone & Telegraph Co. / 4.11*a–b* Milwaukee Public Schools / 4.12*a–b* Three Rivers Commercial, and Lamphere Schools, Madison Heights, Mich.

5.1 John Reeves / 5.2*a* Alex Gray / 5.2*b* E. F. Hauserman Co. / 5.3 Seattle Public School System and Camera-Craft, Inc. / 5.4 Robert C. Ragsdale, Toronto / 5.5 Hans Geerling Photography / .5.6 *a–b* Milton B. Conhaim, Inc. / 5.7; 5.10*a–b* University of Wisconsin / 5.11 Educational Aids, Inc. / 5.12–5.14 Michigan State University / 5.15*a–d* Michigan State University / 5.16*a–b* Ben Kann

6.3*a* Newcomb Audio Products and W. Roy Watson / 6.3*b* Minnesota Mining & Mfg. Co. / 6.3*c* Viewlex Audio Visuals, Inc. / 6.3*d* Califone International, Inc. / 6.4 Norelco / 6.5 North American Philips Corporation / 6.6 Shure Brothers, Inc. / 6.7*a* Califone International, Inc. / 6.7*b* Bell & Howell / 6.7*c* Audiotronic / 6.8*a* Electronic Futures, Inc. / 6.9*a* Lexicon, Inc. / 6.10*a* Newcomb Audio Products and W. Roy Watson / 6.10*b* Califone, Inc. / 6.11*a* AVEK Audiovisual Electronic Keyboards / 6.11*b* Newcomb Audio Products and W. Roy Watson / 6.13 The Australia Correspondence School of the Air / 6.14; 6.20*a* Chicago Public Schools / 6.20*b* University of Wisconsin—La Crosse / 6.20*c* Educational Equipment

7.1 Eastman Kodak Company / 7.2 Society for Visual Education / 7.3 Sawyer's Inc. / 7.4*a* Michigan State University / 7.5 Department of Education, San Diego County, California / 7.6*a, d, h* Society for Visual Education / 7.6*c* Encyclopaedia Britannica Corporation / 7.6*b, c, e, f, i* McGraw-Hill / 7.7*a* Instructional Materials Center, Los Angeles / 7.7*b* Viewlex / 7.7*c* Standard Projector & Equipment Co., Inc. / 7.8 Eastman Kodak Company / 7.9 Michigan State University / 7.10*a* Charles Beseler Company / 7.10*b* Viewlex / 7.10*c* Singer and Campbell Photos, Inc. / 7.11 Courtesy—American Optical Corporation / 7.12*a–b* Charles Beseler Company / 7.12*c* 3M Company / 7.13 A. J. Nystrom & Company / 7.14 Realistic Visual Aids / 7.15 Charles Beseler Company / 7.16 Los Angeles Public Schools / 7.17 DuKane / 7.18; 7.19 National Cash Register Co. / 7.20 Michigan State University / 7.21 Califone / 7.22 Michigan State University / 7.23 Young America Films, Inc. / 7.24 Hudson Photographic Industries / 7.25*a* Viewlex / 7.25*b* Graflex, Inc. / 7.25*c* Hudson Photographic Industries / 7.26*a* Eastman Kodak Company / 7.26*b* Sawyer's / 7.27*a–b*; 7.28*a–b* Charles Beseler Company / 7.27*c* American Optical Corporation / 7.28*c* Standard Projector & Equipment Co. / 7.29 Michigan State University

8.1*a–b* Atomic Energy Commission / 8.1*c–e* NASA / 8.2*a* Viewlex / 8.2*b* Eiki International / 8.2*c* Bell & Howell / 8.2*d* Viewlex / 8.2*e* Fairchild Industrial Products / 8.2*f–g* Charles Beseler Company / 8.4*a* *Kentucky Pioneers,* Encyclopaedia Britannica Educational Corporation / 8.4*b* Doubleday Multimedia / 8.4*c* International Film Foundation / 8.4*d* Film Communicators / 8.4*e* International Film Foundation / 8.5*a* Coronet Instructional Films / 8.5*b* *Seed Dispersal,* 3rd ed., Encyclopaedia Britannica Educational Corporation / 8.6*a* Dr. H. E. Edgerton / 8.6*b* Moody Institute of Science / 8.7*a* From the film *Microscopic Life: The World of the Invisible,* distributed by Encyclopedia Britannica Films, Inc. / 8.7*b* Coronet Instructional Films / 8.7*c* Dimension Films / 8.8*a–b* Coronet Instructional Films / 8.9*a–b* Weston Woods Studios / 8.10*a–b* Australian Commonwealth Film Unit / 8.11 W. A. Wittich & J. G. Fowlkes, *Audio-Visual Paths to Learning* (New York: Harper & Row, 1946) / 8.15*a–b* Eastman Kodak Company / 8.16*a–d* Iolani School, Honolulu, Hawaii

9.1 Children's Television Workshop / 9.2*a* *Zoom,* WGBH, Boston / 9.2*b* Bilingual Children's Television, Inc., 2150 Valdez St., Oakland, Ca. 94612 / 9.3*a–e* Agency for Instructional Television / 9.5*a* The Public Television Library / 9.5*b* Sony Corp. of America / 9.6 Sony Corp. of America / 9.7*b* Punahou Schools / 9.7*c* Great Plains National Instructional Television Library / 9.8 Denver Public Schools / 9.9*a–b* Donald J. Cyr / 9.10 *Educational Television Magazine,* the Clark School for the Deaf, and Gordon Daniels / 9.11 *Educational Television Magazine* and H. Eugene Hollicks

10.1–10.2 American Telephone and Telegraph Corporation / 10.3 Waterford Township, Michigan, School District / 10.4 University of Hawaii / 10.5 Wff'N Proof—Learning Games Associates, Christine Allen, photographer

11.1*a–d* WNET—Public Broadcasting Station 13, New York / 11.2*a–j* Hawaii English Project / 11.4 National Special Media Institutes, USOE / 11.8; 11.10 Michigan State University

Contents

Foreword

The pleasant task of introducing this excellent new edition of a standard textbook has set me thinking back over some meaningful anniversaries.

This is written almost exactly on the thirtieth anniversary of the invention of the transistor. Without this remarkable little instrument many of our modern instructional media would not exist. Without it we could not have had such educational experiences as television from the moon and the first color pictures of the Blue Planet spinning in space. So familiar and pervasive has this device become that it sometimes seems to us as though we have always had transistors, and it comes almost as a surprise to recall they came into existence for the first time, in the Bell Telephone Laboratories, in 1947.

This is the twenty-second anniversary of the publication of Fred Skinner's *Verbal Behavior* and *Schedules of Reinforcement* (with C. B. Ferster) . These set down much of the thinking behind Skinner's 1954 article "The Science of Learning and the Art of Teaching," which stimulated the great flurry of activity in programmed instruction just getting under way twenty years ago, that has since meant so much for our understanding of the objectives and events of instruction and for the practice of formative research on the materials of instruction. Twenty years ago Bloom's notable taxonomy of instructional objectives was entering into the design of instruction, and educators were reading May and Lumsdaine's *Learning from Film*. And 1957 was the first full year of instructional television at Hagerstown.

Twelve years ago, in 1967, the first edition of Gagné's important and influential book *The Conditions of Learning* was in the hands of scholars and educators. It was a time of a great stirring of interest in computerized instruction. The first ATS satellite was sitting 22,300 miles above the Pacific, challenging educators to use it. And in 1967 the British government appointed an official committee to plan the Open University.

In just ten years, the ATS-1 has come to look tiny beside the ATS-6 and still more powerful relays. *Conditions of Learning* is in its third edition. The Open University has nearly 30,000 graduates.

In thirty years the pace has never slackened. Physical and instructional technology have seemed to race each other. The unbelievably swift rate of change is hard for us who have lived through those decades to comprehend until we look back and note how the language of the field has changed in three decades from audiovisual aids to audiovisual instruction to instructional technology, each change indicating a broadening and deepening of the concepts involved.

As I have reviewed in my mind these last thirty years, I have thought how difficult it must be to keep a widely used textbook like *Instructional Technology: Its Nature and Use* marching with developments. A book of this kind must do at least two things for its readers. It must keep them up to date with current understanding of the media as instruments of teaching and learning. Secondly, it must offer its readers a workable method for selecting media and using them as a part of a system of instruction. Professors Wittich and Schuller, drawing on their long experience in preparing students to work in this field and advising major universities on their use of instructional media, have always done this second task in an eminently practical and down-to-earth manner. The characteristic of this edition that is especially likely to please its users, however, is what the authors have done to keep the book abreast of theoretical advances. This book was first published in 1953. For the first twenty years of its life it was called *Audiovisual Materials*. The change to *Instructional Technology* in the fifth edition (1973) was a reflection of changing times and a changing field. This sixth edition goes farther in building a framework for the new title. For example, it begins with the perception of instructional materials. This is truly forward-looking, because it is in the field of perception that we are most likely in the coming decade to find the insights we so badly need into the differences between learning from print and from the electronic and pictorial media. This combination of the practical and the theoretical, understanding and doing, cannot but recommend this book to any user who is preparing to work in the field.

Wilbur Schramm
Distinguished Researcher
East–West Center
Hawaii, U.S.A.

Preface

The pace of innovation in education has stepped up considerably since the fifth edition of *Instructional Technology* was published in 1973. One indication of this is the some 500 school systems, both here and abroad, that have conducted Instructional Development Institutes (IDI's) since that time. IDI's train school staffs to use systems principles to find solutions to teaching and learning problems—solutions that frequently involve innovative media uses.

Hundreds of community and junior colleges have incorporated sophisticated instructional technology in their systems of instruction, and many colleges and universities have established offices of instructional design and development. From elementary through higher levels of education, there is evidence of the acceptance of media and technology as an integral part of the educational scene.

The North Central Association of Colleges and Schools provides the following definition of instructional technology:

> Instructional technology is the combination of human and nonhuman resources employed in a systematic way in the design, implementation, and evaluation of the total process of learning and teaching. . . . It links the human resources of specialists in curriculum and instructional design, evaluation, and media with the nonhuman resources of instruction/information networks which include materials and machines for print, audiovisual media, television and radio, amplified telephone, learning laboratories, the computer, games and simulation, and teaching machines.[1]

The sixth edition of our book retains much of the content, though in thoroughly updated and revised form, and the convenient organization and methods of treatment that helped make earlier editions highly successful. In addition, there are substantial sections on visual literacy, multimedia applications, outdoor laboratories, computers, simulation, and games. All are presented within the broad context of instructional technology as a practical and effective means of improving teaching and learning.

[1] Inventory of Policy and Programs for Instructional Technology by Ad Hoc Committee on Instructional Technology, Commission on Research and Service, North Central Association of Colleges and Schools, 1975.

Much insight has been gained in instructional development (ID) since the last edition as new learning materials and strategies have been developed, field tested, evaluated, and refined under the aegis of the *University Consortium for Instructional Development and Technology.* In preparing this edition of *Instructional Technology,* we have drawn on tested and effective ID principles and emphasized those most useful to teachers and learners in classroom situations. Pertinent ID principles are incorporated throughout the book, and readers are encouraged in the suggested activities at the end of each chapter to begin early to apply these progressively to their own teaching-learning situations. By the end of the term, they should not only be more competent to handle the various media per se, but to incorporate them, as appropriate, in more effective and systematic planning.

Specific features of the book are intended to be helpful to both instructors and students. Each chapter is preceded by a set of objectives and concluded with a summary, suggested development activities, lists of relevant source materials, and selected references.

A separate supplement, the *Student Production Guide,* prepared in collaboration with David W. Hessler of the University of Michigan and Jay C. Smith of the University of Oklahoma, is designed to give students further opportunities to apply the information they have gained from using this book. The guide, which is action oriented, includes detailed and well-illustrated directions for producing simple and inexpensive teaching materials; directions for operating and maintaining projection, TV, and sound equipment commonly found in schools; and lists of sources for production equipment and materials.

The materials, both in the *Student Production Guide* and in the text have been field tested, revised, and evaluated with the help of colleagues, graduate students, and hundreds of students of education in our several institutions. We wish to extend our thanks to them and to the friends, professional colleagues, and prepublication reviewers who have been of inestimable assistance to us in preparing this sixth edition. We wish to thank particularly Professors Shinye Gima and Lillian Lum for introducing materials used in the fifth and sixth editions in the classroom and evaluating them under actual teaching conditions. Thanks are also due to Professors Lucius Butler, Richard Sanderson, Paul Snipes, Lore F. Fujimoto, and Geoffrey Kucera of the University of Hawaii and to Professors Bruce Miles, Wilfred Veenendaal, James Page, Donald Wilkening, Kent Gustafson, and Paul Witt of Michigan State University for their helpful suggestions during preparation of the manuscript. Particular appreciation is due Ruth Murphy, former Executive Assistant at Michigan State University, for her dedicated and invaluable assistance on this and the preceding editions.

Walter A. Wittich
Charles F. Schuller

To the Student

Our concern for the effective use of instructional technology is based on the principle that information and ideas can best be communicated by a proper combination of materials and methods rather than by the printed and spoken word alone. The teacher is the vital force in the selection and use of instructional media, as the one person in a position to evaluate constantly the interaction of learners with them. It is the teacher who sees the extent to which individual goals and needs are being met by whatever materials and techniques are being used.

Several other underlying assumptions will become apparent to you as you use this book.

First, learners must be given the opportunity to prepare themselves to enter a society outside the school in which there is a wide range of communication alternatives, by exposing them to instruction, where appropriate, through the use of comparable alternatives.

Second, learners should have the opportunity to select and use appropriate print and nonprint materials in exploring their own interests and needs, and should have access to such materials when they need them, and for whatever time they need them, either individually or in groups.

Third, learners should be given the opportunity to acquire skill in using a variety of media to help communicate ideas. They should be given a chance to acquire facility in handling not only the written and spoken word, but also the languages of graphics, photography, audio and video recordings, models, simulations, games, and the like.

In this book, you will be introduced to the nature and uses of instructional technology and also to a basic instructional development plan. Properly followed, that plan can help you acquire initial skills in defining learning problems, developing specific objectives, systematically selecting appropriate media and instructional strategies, and evaluating both the process and the learning results as you go along.

A basic instructional development plan is introduced at the end of Chapter 1. In subsequent chapters, alternative learning materials and instructional strategies are introduced. At the end of each chapter, you are asked to consider these materials and strategies and, where appropriate, to incorporate them into your own instructional plans. This will remind you that instructional development is open ended. You should constantly reevaluate your use of materials, keeping in mind both your own and your students' learning goals.

As a final note, we would urge all who are not already familiar with it to become acquainted with the professional association of the field, the Association for Educational Communications and Technology (AECT). AECT offers many benefits and services to professionals and students in instructional technology and is the key source for publications and R & D information in the field. For information, address the Executive Director, AECT, at 1126 16th Street, N.W., Washington, D.C. 20036.

We wish you good reading, enjoyable research, and insightful involvement with instructional technology as you explore its nature and uses.

W.A.W.
C.F.S.

1 The Teacher and Instructional Technology

Objectives

To enable you to do the following:

1. Identify at least four social, curricular, and technological changes that have influenced the nature and use of learning media.
2. Explain the basic processes of communication and some factors that affect it in teaching-learning situations.
3. Explain briefly six tenets of educational psychology related to the selection and use of instructional media.
4. Construct a general instructional development plan, based on the systematic use and evaluation of a wide variety of learning media.

Day in and day out, riding in fixed orbits 22,240 miles above the Atlantic, Indian, and Pacific oceans, communications satellites absorb and transmit information. News, business reports, educational material, and social and economic data pass through their sensors to be relayed to a wide network of earth stations below. Instantaneously, mass media pick up messages intended for the public.

In the industrialized world the influence of the mass media is overwhelming. Television and radio, films, books, newspapers, and magazines compete relentlessly for our attention. They provide a constant flow of facts and fantasies, words and images, goodies labeled "Eat me" and "Drink me" that can make us shrink or grow. The information explosion prompted by instantaneous electronic communication has radically altered the human environment. It has given us a multifaceted view of a rapidly changing world that itself accelerates the pace of change.

This is the world our children are born into. It makes them, in many cases, well informed, aware of events at large, and skilled in receiving and interpreting visual messages. They are at home with at least one electronic medium, television, from an early age; as a result, they are uniquely able to benefit from multimedia instruction and the new instructional technology.

CHALLENGES AND ALTERNATIVES FOR TEACHERS

Most instructional functions can be performed by a variety of media. Teachers, printed materials, films, even computers, may do equally well at explaining, illustrating, or testing a student's knowledge of a phenomenon, a concept, or a rule. All may have a hand in teaching students the one thing that is crucial in a rapidly changing environment—how to think for themselves. This has produced a shift in the teacher's role. The teacher's chief task has become not the dissemination of information that may or may not be useful in later life, but the provision of a wide variety of learning experiences and the nurturing of creative responses to instruction. Print and electronic media have become not merely tools, but the building blocks of a more efficient and interesting learning environment.

When more information is communicated by learning media, teachers can give more attention to the uniquely human aspects of education, to understanding the needs of individual students, helping them to set and realize goals, and stimulating them to *use* the information available from educational media. In spite of all the information bombarding us, we learn only that to which we actively respond. Producing this type of learner response is the goal of the educational process.

Like instruction, learner responses can be more exciting when a variety of media is used. In addition to giving their ideas verbally and in written reports, students can learn to plan and produce slide presentations, take photographs, create graphics, write filmscripts, record their ideas on videotape, make mockups, set up three-dimensional exhibits, plan and produce television programs, and play educational games. (See Figure 1.3.) Unlike most mass media, instructional media can be used for two-way communication.

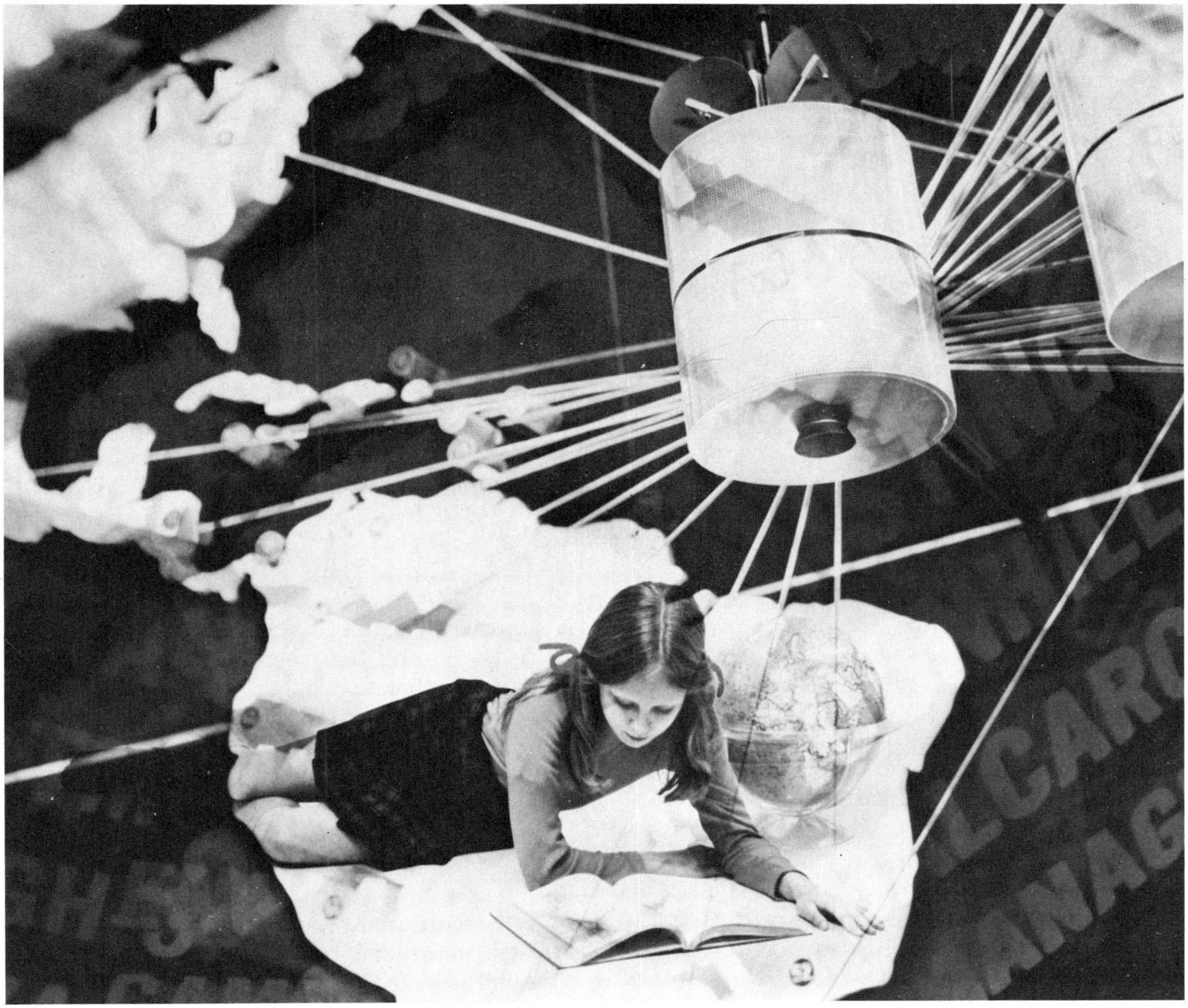

Figure 1.1 Global communications occur instantly as audio, computer, and television messages are transmitted between earth stations and floating (orbiting but stationary) satellites positioned above the world's oceans. Today's young people must learn to cope with the information generated by these and other products of modern technology. How does all this affect your role as a teacher?

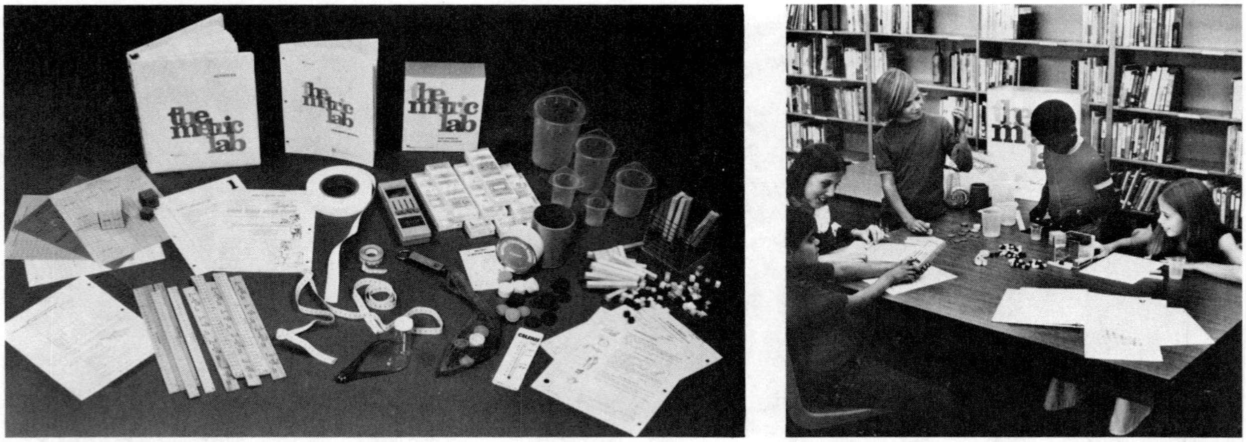

(a) (b)

Figure 1.2 Learning media can be highly effective in "backstopping" teachers who must assume new instructional tasks. (*a*) A multimedia learning package such as this one designed to teach students about the metric system is created by the combined efforts of experts on a subject and media innovators. (b) What influence might materials such as these have on your own teaching strategies?

New Instructional Strategies

Flexible scheduling, interest in individualized and self-paced instruction, and the increasing availability of well-planned and well-produced learning materials have all contributed to changes in instructional strategies.

The inquiry method. Science teachers have used a student-centered teaching method called the *inquiry method* for some time. This approach to instruction helps learners to grow intellectually by developing their ability to ask questions, to analyze information, and to find creative ways of solving problems.

The inquiry method works best when learners have a chance to respond to many kinds of learning experiences—direct observation of an environment, laboratory experiments, films, audiotapes, work with actual specimens, graphics and diagrams, and so on. When learning resources are properly used, three advantages of the inquiry method become apparent:

1. Learners are more likely to become interested in developing their own ideas or hypotheses about a subject.
2. Learners show more creativity in posing questions and setting objectives of their own.
3. Learners demonstrate more initiative in using a variety of learning media as they attempt to test their ideas, satisfy their curiosity, and find answers to their questions.

As a result, many social studies and language arts teachers have become interested in using this method. In one high school, for example, social studies teachers encourage individual students and teams of students to develop their own "research questions." Pupils have flexible schedules that give them time to go to the social studies learning resources center (Figure 1.4) to examine the school's collection of films, filmstrips, and audiotapes for useful data. In addition, they are encouraged to seek useful "real-life" experiences that will help them find answers to their questions.

(a)

(b)

Figure 1.3 Communication is a two-way event. Teachers have already learned to use many media to bring learning experience to students. The next step is to help learners use alternative media to respond creatively to instruction. This teacher has taught her pupils (*a*) how to use a portable videotape recorder and (*b*) how to take still photographs and use them to tell a story. The result will be sent to friends with whom the youngsters have been corresponding. (*c*) This girl is learning French vocabulary from self-study modules. (*d*) She and some of her classmates have also created vocabulary games to make learning words more interesting.

What cognitions and skills do such activities demand of learners? Why do some students choose such activities? What kinds of responsibilities have their teachers chosen to assume? What are some of the payoffs?

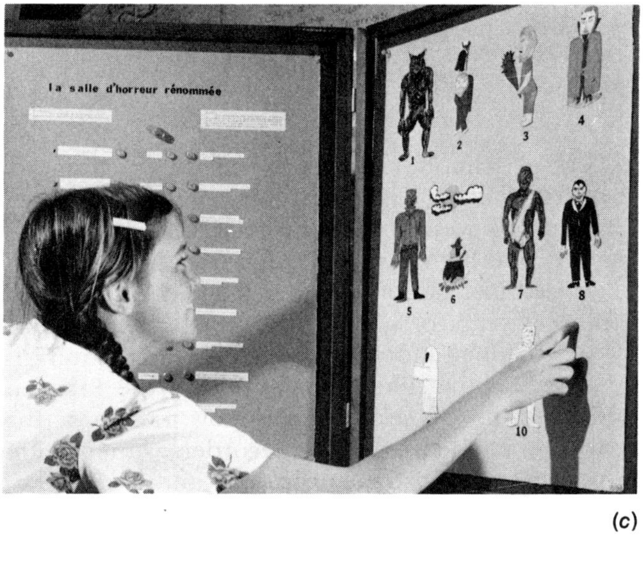

(c)

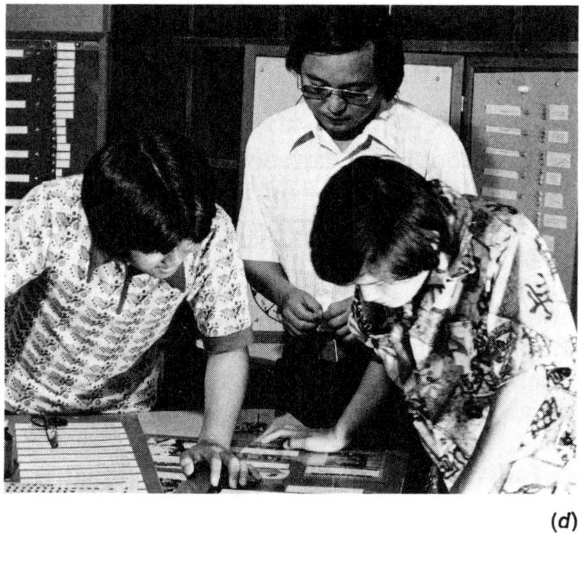

(d)

Figure 1.4 During the time schedules for independent study in this high school, students are free to come to the learning resource center to examine learning media that will help them find answers to research questions they have posed for themselves. How do such facilities compensate for a lack of homogeneity among students? What opportunities do you see for both slow and gifted learners when they work in an environment like this? What effect may it have on their progress and on the role of their teachers?

At the Sobrante Park School in Oakland, California, students carry on individual research in a library that has been expanded to include a wide variety of new equipment and materials (Figure 1.5). In this library pupils can consult not only traditional reference books, but maps, audiotapes, picture sets, films, filmstrips, and the like. They are encouraged to borrow these materials just as they would library books.

Individualized instruction. Individualized instruction is being emphasized in increasing numbers of schools. This approach to teaching requires that students have easy access to a large variety of preselected learning materials.

In one highly successful program of individualized instruction, nearly 90,000 children from 4 to 9 years old have progressed at their own pace through more than 2000 learning materials (Figure 1.6). The children spend the first ten days to three weeks learning how to operate the equipment—cassette tape recorders, super-8 film projectors, filmstrip projectors, audiocard readers, even an electric typewriter. Their activities

Figure 1.5 Students at the Sobrante Park School in Oakland, California, have unlimited access to all kinds of learning media. This teacher is helping pupils locate materials on questions brought up during class discussions. Would you consider such efforts part of your role as a teacher? How much "help" would you give your students in this regard?

are guided by a teacher who has attended a summer training session on the techniques used in the project. Once the children are familiar with the equipment, they gather for a daily planning period, during which they report their progress from charts they themselves keep up (under the teacher's supervision) and decide which skills they will work on and what media they will use. Periodically, they call on the teacher or their peers to check their progress. They progress at their own pace, soon become adept at helping one another, and not only make

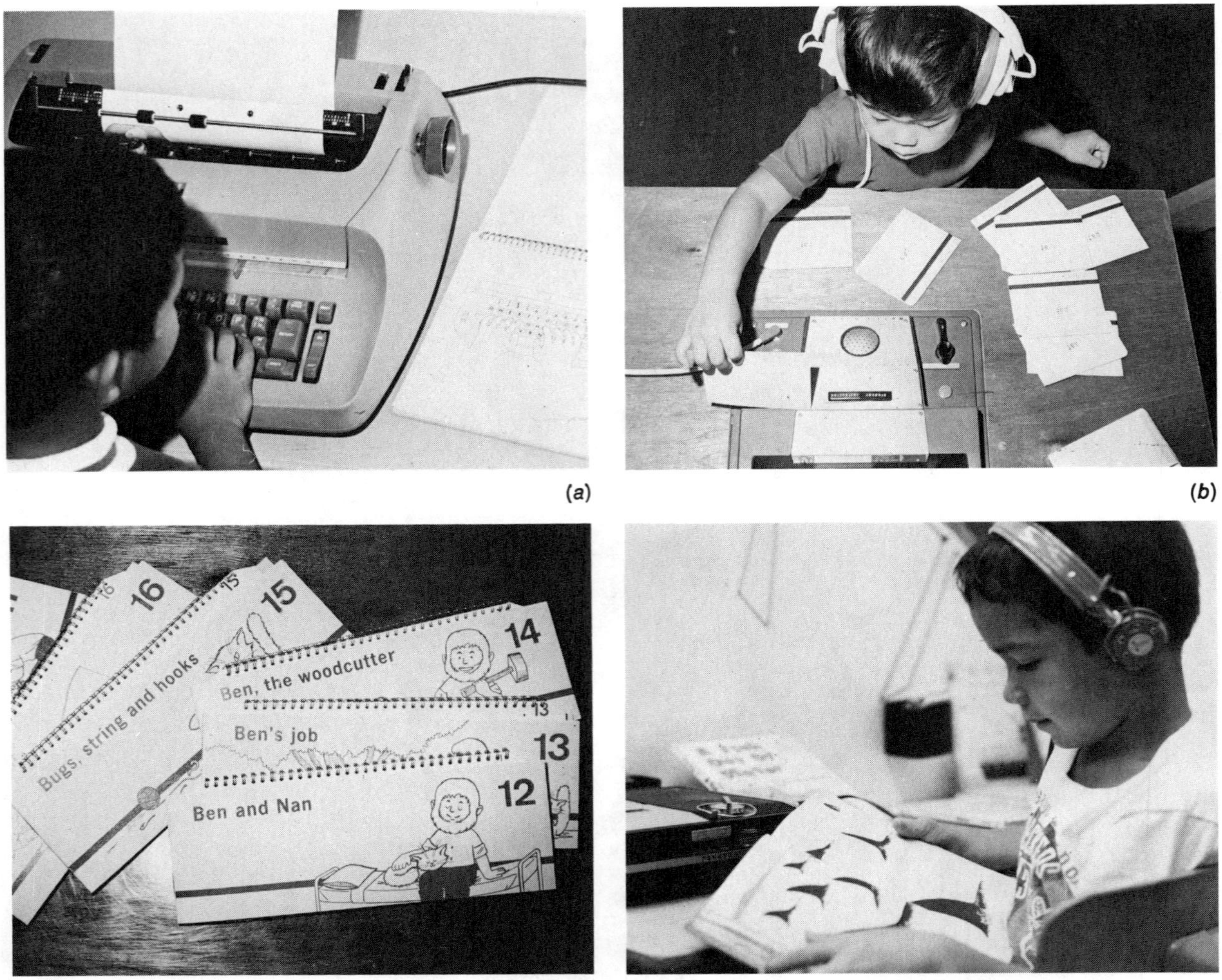

(a) (b) (c) (d)

Figure 1.6 These children aged 5 to 8 easily master the use of a variety of self-teaching equipment. (*a*) This child is independently mastering typing skills. He begins typing even before he knows how to read, following visual cues from the manual next to him. (*b*) This child is using a magnetic card reader to identify simple word families. He begins by identifying families of similar short words, then moves on to short phrases and finally to simple sentences. As his language skills grow, he will also help others in class to learn. (*c*) Children also use the card reader to listen to simple stories written phrase by phrase on illustrated cards. (*d*) A child reads a book, previously recorded on tape, matching what he hears to what he sees. To allow children to work in this fashion, classrooms are reorganized to provide semiprivate work-study areas for individuals and small groups. Note the absorption of the children in these pictures as they work. What advantages would there be in more widespread use of this kind of instruction? What role would you as a teacher play?

faster progress than children taught by traditional methods, but, more important, show increased interest in school and schoolwork.

Multimedia Communication

As we have already pointed out, the use of media to communicate information and skills frees teachers to play a new and exciting role: helping students to understand themselves and their goals and to recognize and use the most effective means of reaching those goals. Today's teachers should know how to organize a learning environment that includes a wide variety of learning media. The right audiovisual materials can communicate information, teach skills, and provide general cultural experiences learners need.

Learning media should also reinforce one another. If they do not, learners can be overwhelmed by a kaleidoscope of experiences without clear goals.

ORGANIZING A LEARNING ENVIRONMENT

One of the responsibilities of teachers is to understand the nature and needs of learners and attempt to organize the kind of environment that will elicit the greatest response from them. As one educator points out,

> Motivation to learn in school is in part a function of what resides within the individual and in part a function of the external world he encounters. Some positively motivated youngsters seem to draw most heavily upon forces located within themselves to enhance their learning. They believe in learning and knowledge, for example, and the new and novel excite them. Ambiguity and uncertainty intrigue them.
>
> Other students, equally well motivated, seem to be most positively affected by the quality and quantity of stimuli which they experience in school. Exciting lectures, fascinating movies, vivid illustrations, and intense discussions are likely to spark these students' efforts.
>
> In terms of the intake-output dimension, some students seem moved to consume the learning world around them, while others are producers. Students who are avid readers and thoughtful listeners—who seek information in every way—are "intake" types. They are consumers of information and experiences of every kind. Other students are "output" people. They write. They talk a lot. They generate ideas and concepts. Their motivations propel them to active rather than passive learning roles.[1]

The careful selection of materials and their wise use can go far toward motivating learners to respond to instruction.

The Act of Communication

In order to know the world, one should, ideally, experience it firsthand. But as the world becomes more complex it becomes increasingly difficult to provide children with firsthand experience of its many aspects. Obviously, some compromise in the form of substitute experiences must be developed to teach them to understand their environment. This is what communication is all about.

To select appropriate media through which substitute experiences may be provided, we must understand what is involved in the process of communication. A basic model of this process is shown in Figure 1.7. Messages, information, and reactions to information travel from the sender toward the receiver. The route along which they travel may be thought of as a *communications channel,* or a stimulus-response channel. A message (*stimulus*) may consist of a statement made by a student or a teacher, or it

[1] Jack R. Frymier, "Motivating Students to Learn," *National Education Association Journal* (February 1968).

Figure 1.7 A basic communications model. What influences the channel of messages?

may come from a film, chart, picture, or chalkboard illustration. The receiver of this stimulus will generally react in some way—by listening, looking, touching, tasting. These reactions lead to other responses. A question may lead to an answer; examination of a film, a specimen, or an object may lead to a verbal observation or a smile. A message communicated by a teacher may bring forth interested responses from some pupils and nothing from others. Ideally, a communication channel carries both messages and countermessages. Information is given, received, and responded to.

The communications channel between teachers and pupils must be kept wide open so that valid insights can be transmitted and received. In an ideal learning environment messages travel along a channel clear of any interference. In the real world, out-of-school communications media often make a greater impact on students than teachers and school media. (See Figure 1.8.) In addition, some formidable barriers to effective communication—psychological ones—originate in the classroom itself.

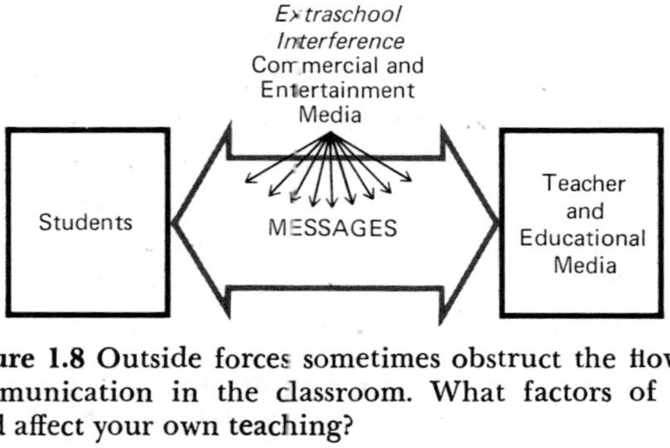

Figure 1.8 Outside forces sometimes obstruct the flow of communication in the classroom. What factors of this kind affect your own teaching?

Psychological Barriers to Communication

Some psychological barriers to communication between teachers and pupils are caused by conditions outside of school, but others arise from conditions in the classroom itself. Teachers must always be alert for interference that prevents them from reaching students. They must not only recognize possible sources of interference, but also know how clear channels of communication can be established and maintained. Generally, the clear reception of messages depends on the avoidance of five barriers to effective classroom communication: too much verbalization, confusion about referents, daydreaming, perceptual problems, and actual physical discomfort. (See Figure 1.9.)

Too much verbalization. The human organism is remarkable in the way it automatically sets up defenses against annoying stimuli. It is amazingly simple to shut out what we do not want to hear. We simply concentrate on some-

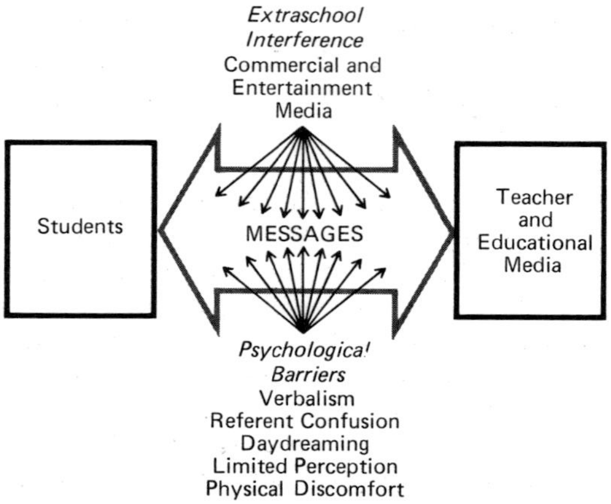

Figure 1.9 Psychological barriers also obstruct the flow of communication in a classroom. What experience have you had with these barriers?

thing else. Students find it very easy to tune teachers out when their teaching approach is too repetitious and thus uninteresting. Experienced teachers report that the continued use of any one kind of teaching device results in a decrease in its efficiency. Certainly the effectiveness of words declines as pupils sit through lecture after lecture. Interest and attention decrease in the face of a seemingly endless barrage of words. As one teacher reports,

During the first five or six weeks of school, pupils listen to me. They seem very interested in my descriptions and directions. Then comes a curious change. As week follows week and more words follow more words, interest lags and finally even I realize that it is time for a change, a change in the methods I use to get [ideas] across. . . .

To overcome this problem, teachers of language arts, social studies, science, and mathematics may draw on a wide variety of instructional materials that use modern communications techniques to transmit information. Most public schools already have much of the equipment and materials needed by teachers who wish to improve their effectiveness.

Confusion over referents. It is natural for people, children and adults alike, to turn automatically to seemingly related experiences for help in understanding something new. When reference to previously learned material helps us comprehend new material, a *positive transfer* of insights is said to occur. Often, however, attempts to apply previously acquired insights to new problems result in what is called *referent confusion*. The experience a student draws on to deal with new material is not relevant.

Referent confusion is particularly likely in verbal communication, because differences in frames of reference make it possible for two people to use the same words to mean completely different things. Teachers can never be entirely sure that the words they choose to describe an idea or a process will be equally meaningful to every one of their students. Each student's background influences his or her understanding of what is being said in a unique way. The greater the abstractness or remoteness of the subject, the less similarity there is likely to be between the teacher's meaning and the pupil's understanding of it.

One way to overcome this kind of communication problem is to deliver messages that are highly graphic, visual, and unmistakable. The more graphic and visual a message is, the more understandable the stimuli received are. This is one of the principles of modern multimedia instruction.

Daydreaming. Another common yet avoidable obstacle to efficient communication is daydreaming. Many students are remarkably adept at it; some can even smile attentively at the teacher while their thoughts are far away. Alert teachers are aware of students who have a tendency to daydream. Rather than punishing them, however, they search for classroom-generated causes of such behavior. Often daydreaming can be lessened or eliminated by making lessons more interesting or easier to understand. Learning materials that appeal to the senses and require some kind of activity by the student are very useful in this regard.

Perceptual difficulties. A learner's store of information about the world is gained through the senses, largely through the eyes and ears but also through the mechanisms of smell, touch, and taste. Science has learned a great deal about the physical aspects of perception, but the psychological processes by which the brain receives and deals with messages are less clear. Both can have a tremendous effect on the learning process.

Individual variations in the efficiency of hearing, seeing, tasting, and so on, are common and obvious. Some children cannot see well and need glasses. Others have poor hearing. Some are verbal rather than visual learners. All these physiological differences affect their reactions to classroom experiences. Teachers should see that their students have hearing and vision tests at regular intervals. If children do have problems, corrective action should be taken promptly.

There is a great deal of evidence that the more concrete and clear the sensory messages presented to learners are, the more accurate their interpretation of those messages will be. Moreover, the greater the number of alternative learning experiences available to students, the more likely the effective communication of ideas is. Often learners can be taught to improve their rate of absorption and retention of sensory information. Most people can train themselves to increase their reading speed without decreasing their understanding of the material. Pupils' visual skills can be improved by teaching them to divide a field of observation into units. Airline pilots train themselves to make visual sweeps of their instruments, systematically focusing on each gadget in sequence. They may then transfer their glance to the sky in front of them, perhaps following a figure-eight line of sight so as to include areas above and below the horizon. They do this systematically and at calculated intervals. Bus drivers follow a similar routine.

When proper listening and viewing techniques are made as much a part of a student's education as consideration of the content of a lesson, there is a notable increase in the amount of information observed and understood.

Physical discomfort. We are all aware that our physical environment can have a favorable or an unfavorable effect on our emotions. Yet for decades little or no attention was given to the physical comfort of the student in the classroom. Learning was considered a painful process in the best of circumstances, and some discomfort was thought to be a salutory thing. Private industry has recognized for some time that comfortable working conditions have a definite economic value (witness the many new office buildings with striking interior decor, air conditioning, soundproofing, carpeting, and lighting systems that can be precisely controlled to supplement or replace natural illumination). The fact that comfortable physical surroundings are as desirable in classrooms as in business establishments has been generally acknowledged in recent years, and schools today are expected to provide a comfortable environment for learning. Classrooms have been remodeled for comfort and pleasantness. Air conditioning ensures greater physical comfort on hot days, and carpeted floors provide improved acoustical effects. Color is important and decor makes a notable difference to apathetic students.[2]

Classrooms should have controlled lighting systems that permit the use of projected materials, temperature controls that encourage mental alertness, and acoustics that deaden reverberations. The temperature and acoustics particularly should be automatically controlled.

Six Learning Tenets

The broad variety of learning media available today can offset a host of impediments to communication. But no matter how well devices seem to work from the teacher's point of view, it is their effectiveness from the learner's point of view that is crucial. In selecting and using media, a teacher must take into account some basic learning tenets:

1. Each learner is unique. Students' interests, their intelligence, the efficiency of their

[2] Frank Brum, Atlantic City Educations Seminar, Carnegie Corporation, reported in *Honolulu Advertiser* (February 27, 1965), p. B1.

senses, and the way they respond to instruction make them eternally different from one another.

2. Perception is the foundation of learning.
3. Learning requires involvement. Students must be aware of the reasons for their actions and must actively seek information, skills, and insights. They must also know what is expected of them.
4. The content of a lesson and the media used to communicate it must be suitable to the learner.
5. Teaching strategies must be appropriate.
6. Creativity is a goal of learning.

1. Each learner is unique. The traditional point of departure in considering the uniqueness of individual learners is intelligence. Because this area is so thoroughly studied in basic teacher education courses, only a brief reference will be made to it here.

In any ordinary classroom the intelligence of students varies greatly. Even if all the pupils are assumed to start the school year with an equal amount of knowledge, variations in intelligence will soon account for variations in progress. (See Figure 1.10.)

Learners also differ in the way they receive, internalize, and respond to stimuli. Figure 1.11 shows five stages in our physical response to visual and auditory stimuli where differences can occur. Not long ago a group of junior high school students made a tour of an automobile assembly plant. One of the goals of the trip was to give the students a chance to find answers to some questions they had asked about automobile manufacturing. They watched, fascinated, as an automobile frame was moved into place and the car body swung into position above it. They followed the advance and retreat of the automatic screw and bolt tighteners that secured the two together, caught up in

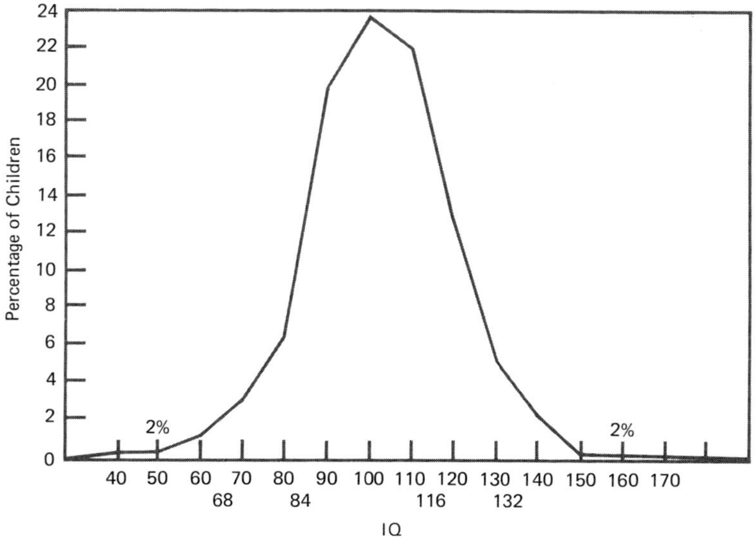

Figure 1.10 This diagram shows a normal distribution-of-intelligence curve. Can you place students with whom you work in their approximate positions on the curve? What provision have you been making for variations in intelligence in your use of learning media?

Figure 1.11 These children are observing the work of an Indian artisan. Can you trace the interactions of old and new cognitions that may bring about changes in their feelings or attitudes about Indians? Use Figure 1.14 to help you.

a flood of visual, auditory, and even olfactory stimuli. When the students returned to the classroom and were given an opportunity to discuss what they had seen, two things became evident. Not only did the children differ in how they interpreted the field study experiences, but there was an astonishing variation in what individual pupils had actually seen, thought they had seen, and had not seen.

The implications of such incidents are well known to most teachers. Wide variations in perception, cognition, conceptualization, and response may be expected from a group of students in any learning situation. It is foolish, therefore, to expect that learning experiences arranged for large groups of students will result in a uniform mastery of skills or uniform insights. Nor is it realistic to believe that such experiences will be of equal use to all students in solving related problems or attaining other learning goals. Nevertheless, teachers can achieve more control over the efficiency of learning experiences by following these suggestions:

a. Organize learning experiences that take into account individual differences. Introduce activities for individuals and small groups as well as for the traditional large classroom group.
b. Arrange for a variety of learning experiences. Give your students a choice of learning media that reinforce one another so that they can select those that have the most appeal for them.
c. Encourage individual responses that will reveal the nature and accuracy of a student's ideas about a subject.

2. Perception is the foundation of learning. Perception is the process by which learners become aware of themselves and events in the outside world. Perceptions are the product of that process, and they depend greatly on the kind of learning environment within and outside the classroom.

Learners' perceptions result in *cognitions,* or understandings of perceived events; these cognitions are the materials from which learners build *concepts,* which in turn are useful in building further concepts and solving problems.

As students grow, through perceptual experiences, in knowledge and understanding, they become more able to use cognitions in satisfying ways. They become more adept at recognizing or imagining linkages between cognitions and at dealing with abstract concepts.

Art teachers, for example, report that among pupils who have learned some basic art skills—how to work with charcoal, brushes, or clay—it is the children who have had a wide range of experiences, who have traveled, and who have observed a wide variety of people, places, and things firsthand who are most likely to use their new skills to produce truly creative drawings, murals, or ceramic pieces.

Similarly, language arts teachers report that the pupils most able to do creative writing (a form of conceptualization) are the ones whose heads teem with cognitions (understandings) gained from experience with many literary forms—dramas and comedies on the stage, on television, and in films; novels and short stories; biographies; and news reports—and from travel and intelligent observation of the communities in which they live.

How does a teacher develop awareness of a target concept among students? Let us take for an example the term *atoll.* We begin by defining the concept and supporting subconcepts.

DEFINING THE CONCEPT

An atoll is a broken-ring-shaped coral reef enclosing a lagoon. It may be thought of as a large, partly submerged saucer that usually has an inlet somewhere along its leeward side. The outside edge is alive with reef dwellers—coral polyps, shellfish, and marine plants. Colonies of coral grow outward to enlarge the atoll and trap sand as it is washed inshore. Atolls develop in shallow, warm waters—warm enough to support the life cycles of coral, shellfish, and plants. Their development is also affected by prevailing winds and ocean currents.

DEFINING RELATED SUBCONCEPTS

Coral: Details can be given of its size, shape, and color; the nutrients it requires; its method of reproduction; and the like.

Shellfish: Their characteristics and habits can also be explored.

Ocean currents: Their temperature, direction, and relationship to tides can be discussed.

Prevailing winds: Their nature and sources can be explored.

The number of related concepts explored can always be expanded, depending on the degree of interest students have in a subject.

The next step is to assemble interrelated learning media that will give students further opportunities to perceive the nature of atolls and their inhabitants. In doing this, the teacher should consider the needs of the students; if most of them have spent their lives inland, marine life, the ocean, lagoons, and atolls will be unknown quantities to them. Those who show a particular interest in the subject can be encouraged to search the learning resource center themselves for useful material. As usual, the teacher should lead the way.

Now let us examine some of the media that can be used: flat pictures of polyp colonies, specimens of coral skeletons, photographs from a neighbor who has taken a snorkling vacation in Micronesia, a set of filmstrips showing the formation and growth of atolls, a detailed map of an atoll, a videocassette showing underwater views of living coral, and films on aspects of reef growth.

Once students become truly involved in exploring a concept, their activities acquire a momentum of their own. A teacher described the situation this way: "Once we got started . . . I had all I could do to keep up." The eventual result, in this case, was a large relief model of an atoll surrounded by displays, maps, diagrams, and specimens, all created by students or groups of students.

In general, the more experienced students become at assimilating perceptions into cognitions, the more sophisticated they become as learners. As they acquire more cognitions, they accumulate more tools for conceptualization. They become more capable of reflective thinking.

Perception and thinking. One important goal of education has been reached when individuals have acquired a large enough store of cognitions and concepts to be able to think about and solve problems using symbols (words, numerals, and other cues), and without referring continually to the things for which the symbols stand. But without a sufficiently broad base of direct, or quasi-direct, experiences with the things of the world, this goal cannot be achieved.

Figure 1.12 shows how the transition from concrete to abstract learning takes place. The triangle at the left reveals how a pupil begins

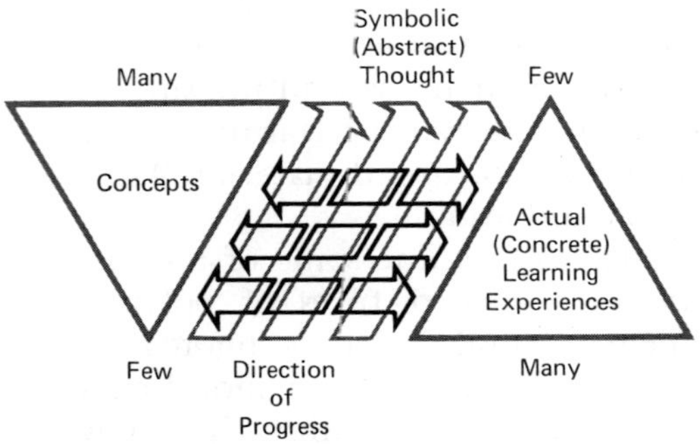

Figure 1.12 As our stock of cognitions grows, our dependence on concrete learning diminishes. How does this affect teaching procedures?

with a few primitive concepts or no true concepts and gradually builds up a large stock of complex and inclusive concepts. To see how the pupil acquires this learning we must move to the right-hand triangle. A large base of concrete and direct experiences enables him or her to build concepts. Gradually the pupil becomes less dependent on these experiences in acquiring new concepts. Finally, a stage is reached where he or she can expand understanding of the world through indirect experiences involving symbols.

Ideally, teachers will recognize that pupils who have relatively few concepts need a maximum of concrete learning experiences. As they acquire more concepts, more abstract and symbolic (or verbal) learning experiences may be appropriate. In their progress toward more abstract thinking, pupils may sometimes backtrack. This is not necessarily cause for alarm. Often students seem to be regressing when in fact they have only temporarily returned to basic, direct experiences to fill gaps in understanding.

An understanding of the relationship between known concept levels and the need for direct or increasingly sophisticated learning experiences enables a teacher to help a class move steadily toward the top of both the triangular scales in Figure 1.12. The goal is to use classroom plans, materials, and techniques that permit students to advance in this way. Those at the base of the right-hand triangle in Figure 1.12 will be most in need of basic, direct experiences with people, objects, and events. Those farther along will benefit from simulated first-hand experiences provided through films, recordings, and slides. Those still higher on the scale will be able to relate to semisymbolic media, such as graphs, diagrams, and charts (Figure 1.13). Finally, pupils should acquire a facility in working with symbols that have little visible relationship with their referents—numerals, math symbols, and words.

Perception and attitude formation. Attitudes are learned predispositions to react in a certain way to people, objects, events, or situations. They can be learned through orderly involvement in planned learning experiences that yield useful cognitions and concepts or through random involvement in social situations. In either case, they are based, ultimately, on our perceptions. (See Figure 1.14.) Teachers often have an opportunity to modify socially undesirable or unrealistic attitudes held by their pupils. Unfortunately, in too many cases they perpetuate and reinforce them instead.

3. Learning requires involvement. The idea that learners, to be successful, must interact with the elements of the learning environment is one of the central areas of agreement in educational psychology. Learners must know what they are expected to do. They should, whenever possible, have a hand in establishing the purposes of a learning experience and be given the opportunity to discover information on their own, at their own rate. Happily, many new instructional media make it feasible to do just that.

In using instructional media, three things should be considered:

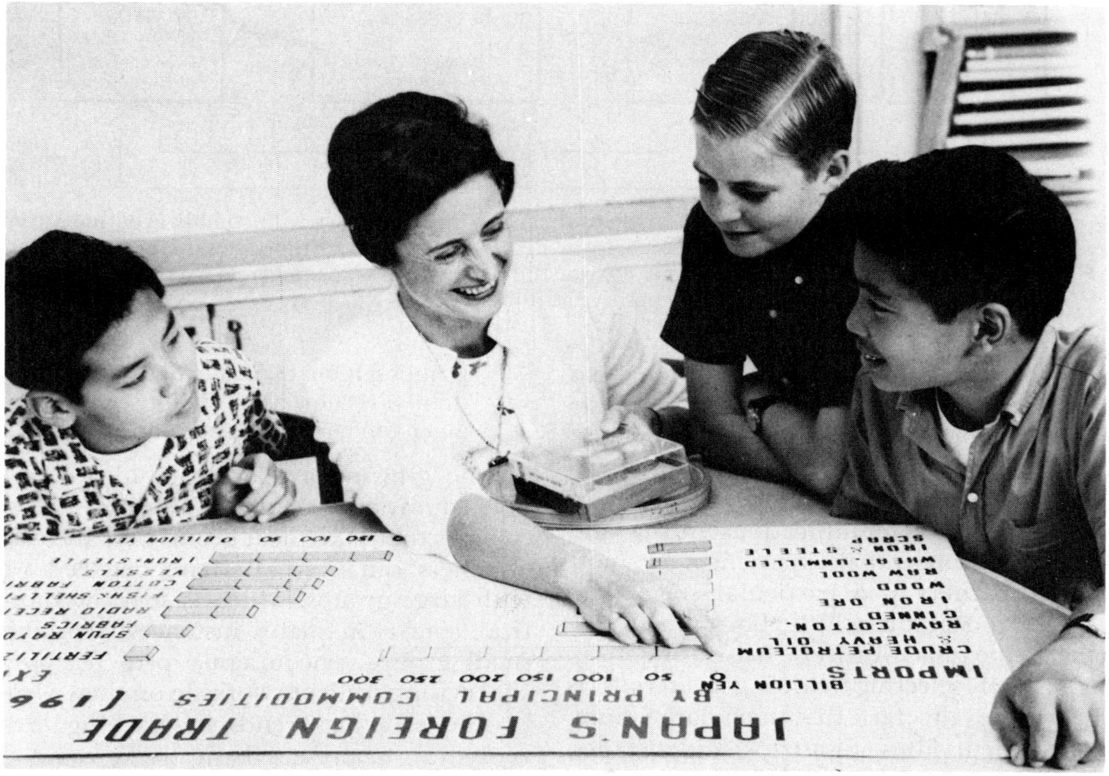

Figure 1.13 These pupils have constructed a graph of Japanese exports and imports. What learning activities do you think preceded the preparation of this graph? Where would you place these pupils on the scale in Figure 1.12?

a. Learners usually participate wholeheartedly in any activities they help to plan.

b. Learners are likely to become apathetic and "learn" to escape responsibility if they receive too much direction from teachers.

c. Learners' progress toward the completion of learning activities tends to depend on their own goals. Usually the more they have to do with setting the goals of such activities, the more they push themselves to achieve.[3]

[3] Based on Goodwin Watson, *What Psychology Can We Trust?* (New York: Columbia University Teachers College Press, 1961), p. 5.

Genuine pupil participation in planning learning activities should be encouraged whenever possible.

4. Learning experiences must be suitable. Learning materials should be used that are compatible with pupils' learning styles. Because learning styles have much to do with sensory preferences (whether one is a visual or verbal learner, for example), materials and teaching strategies should be selected with these in mind. Learning materials must also be appropriate to the stock of cognitions and concepts learners already have.

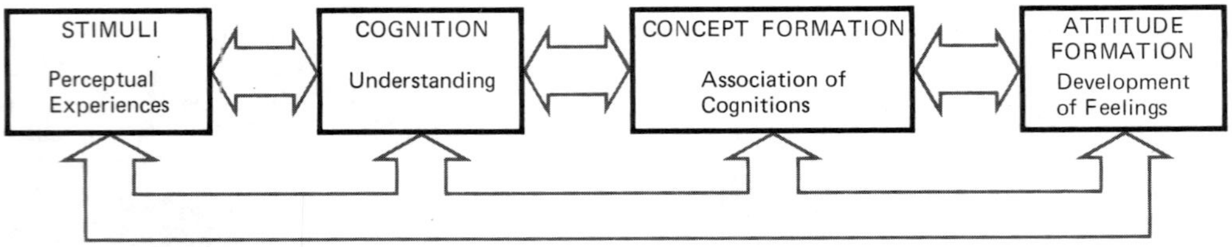

Figure 1.14 The interrelated events that occur as learners interact with stimuli. The use of appropriate learning media can help in developing useful attitudes toward peoples, places, and events. To what extent do you think that you as a teacher will be able to help your students acquire socially positive attitudes?

Teachers must know pupils well enough to assess their abilities, backgrounds, and interests —to understand when they are ready to handle particular materials and to adapt materials to their levels of readiness. Teachers must also understand which communications media and which concrete conceptual experiences are most suitable to learners at a particular stage. Material that is too simple will be boring, and material that is too difficult will be frustrating.

The task of selecting learning materials is complicated by the fact that such large numbers of excellent films, filmstrips, slides, tapes, models, specimens, charts, and flat pictures are available. This work need not be done by the teacher alone, however. It can become an integral part of pupil involvement in the learning process.

5. Teaching strategies must be appropriate. New instructional media have given birth to new teaching strategies. Traditional classes are composed of perhaps 30 or 35 students working under the direction of one teacher. However, the right size for the group always depends on the maturity of those in the group and the nature of the activity. (See Figure 1.15.) A psychologist points out that

> working, interacting groups seem to do best when composed of five to eight members. "If the group is large, some become performers and others spectators. At age six, spontaneous groups seldom exceed two, three, or four children. Sizes now accepted for school classes are much too large for good cooperative work."[4]

The growing availability and acceptance of new educational media has cleared the way for changes that take ideal group sizes into account. Teachers can now alternate between working with large groups, which is still the most practical course in many instances; working with small groups; encouraging peer teaching; and supervising students working on their own.

The evolving trends in teaching are essentially (a) to present basic background data to large groups of students; (b) to organize the large groups into smaller groups that actively discuss and use information rather than passively absorbing it; and (c) to give students as many opportunities as possible to work on their own, at their own pace, with appropriate learning materials. By using such strategies, students become involved in learning, regardless of individual differences.

6. Creativity is a goal of learning. Learning for learning's sake is not enough. Teachers who want their students to get the fullest benefit from print and nonprint materials should encourage them not to be satisfied until they have experimented with a variety of creative uses for new skills and information. Not only does this reinforce what has been learned, it produces a

[4] Watson, *What Psychology Can We Trust?*, p. 15.

(*a*)

(*b*)

Figure 1.15 This is the Social Studies Learning Resource Center at Kailua High School in Hawaii, shared by hundreds of students. Students are free to come to the center to work individually or in small groups. There they have easy access to all kinds of learning resources: filmstrips, recorded materials, films, pictures, newspaper files, books, pamphlets. (*a*) Students locate filmstrips. (*b*) They study the pictures, charts, and related data. (*c*) They meet to discuss their findings and to decide which other materials to consult. How do your learning resources facilities compare with these? What are your reactions?

(*c*)

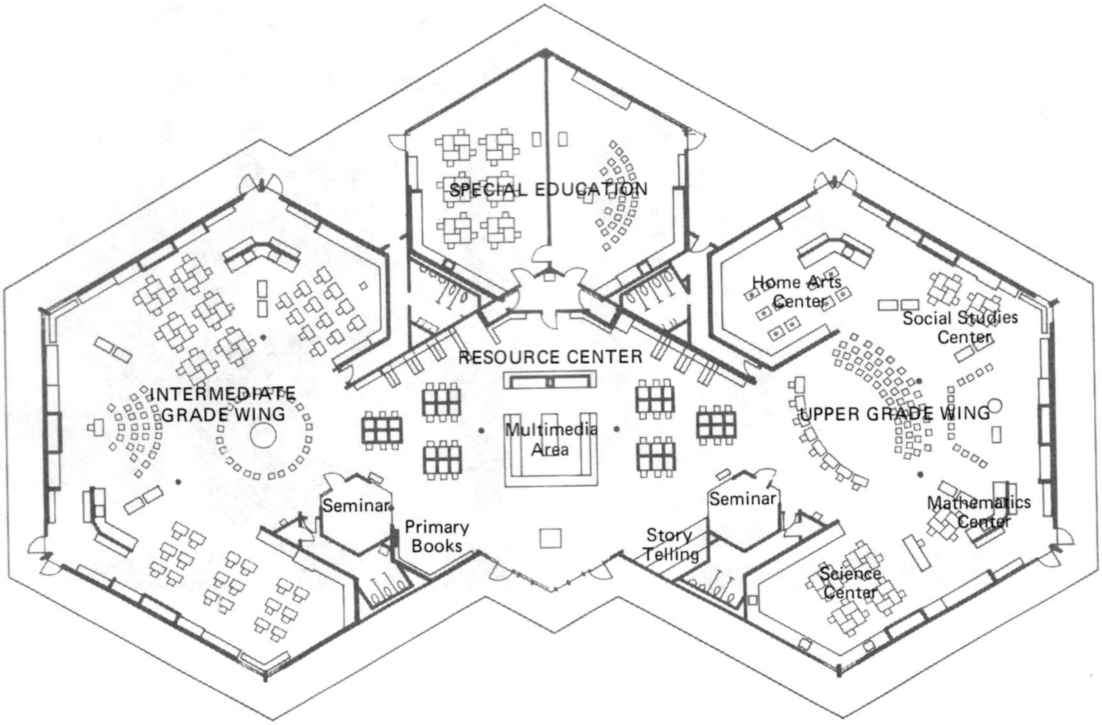

Figure 1.16 In some newer schools, clusters of classroomlike areas surround a learning resource center. Such facilities are the result of cooperative planning by teachers, parents, administrators, media personnel, and community representatives. How do facilities in your school district compare with these?

feeling of accomplishment that encourages further learning.

A teacher who encourages creativity strives to provide a classroom environment replete with materials that capture the imagination—films, filmstrips, models, mockups, videotapes, flat pictures, graphics, and so forth. A rich learning environment must also, of course, include a well-stocked library of books and many opportunities for exchanging ideas and conclusions between pupils and teachers and among pupils.

SYSTEMATIZING THE USE OF LEARNING MEDIA

The responsibility for planning, implementing, and evaluating multimedia instructional strategies rests not only with the teacher but with all those who participate in the planning and execution of teaching programs—on media coordinators, school administrators, school board members, librarians, lay persons, and supervisors. All are linked in a new approach to the improvement of learning referred to as *instructional development*.[5] Instructional development incorporates all that has been said about learning systems to this point into a systematic training program for teams of teachers, administrators, and educational specialists. It is based on the following simple assumptions:

Instructional planning begins with under-

[5] Based on Roger Kaufman, *Instructional Systems Development* (San Diego, Calif.: University Consortium for Instructional Development, United States University, 1975).

standing the nature and needs of learners. Only then can one set objectives related to their problems and bring together the learning media that will be most useful to them. The success of particular teaching strategies and media can be determined from learners' observable responses. Instructional systems should always be open systems. Teaching materials and techniques should be subjected to constant scrutiny and revised or scrapped when they fail to produce a desired response.

IMPLEMENTING AN INSTRUCTIONAL DEVELOPMENT SYSTEM

A systematic approach to instruction is applicable in any kind of teaching situation, in a classroom, in an on-the-job training program, at the first-grade level, or in a class for senior citizens. The instructional development plan outlined here specifically incorporates the selection and use of a wide variety of learning media. A resume of the plan in chart form appears in the Activities section at the end of the chapter.

Step 1. Identify the kinds of learners you will be dealing with, their problems, and their needs. Based on your direct or indirect contact with a given group of students, try to judge what motivates them; what their interests are; what, if any, unique abilities they have; and their sensory capabilities. Pretests will help you determine their threshold levels of information or skills.

Next, review existing curriculum goals, course plans, and work units. Decide approximately where learners fit into the existing instructional plan and what opportunities it provides to motivate them. This will help you to identify target problems, cognitions, skills, and concepts. *Remember that in an open system initial judgments of this kind are subject to change whenever new information or observable learner responses warrant.* Take care also not to confuse problems with symptoms. The fact that children in the fifth grade are unable to spell up to grade level is a *symptom,* probably of a lack of proper learning experiences. This lack is a *problem,* and it can be remedied.

Step 2. State what is to be taught—what the central objective of instruction is and what the supporting or enabling objectives are. Both pupils and teachers should understand what is to be taught, that is, what information is to be imparted and what skills are to be acquired. It is helpful to let students participate in identifying instructional goals. Not only is their participation often enlightening, but it increases their commitment to the learning process.

Step 3. Identify the kind of responses you expect from learners after their interaction with learning media. Unless you know in advance what constitutes progress on the part of your students, it may be very difficult to measure their performance. The cognitions or insights to be achieved, the skills to be learned, the kinds of attitude-revealing behavior hoped for should all be identified early. New data can always be added later.

Step 4. Select specific media to give your students the learning experiences they need. Search for and select media that will help pupils learn particular information and skills and stimulate them to use what they have learned in an innovative way. Investigate school and community sources of materials. Never assume that media are unavailable; check for yourself. Contact those in your school district responsible for audiovisual or other media. Ask them for service publications that list available equipment and materials, catalogs of media resources, and names of local organizations or people to whom you can go for help in planning and originating your own learning media. Also contact local community service organizations, government offices, consulates, embassies, and the district library for information about learning resources that may be suitable for classroom use.

In short, get to know your local school and community resources.

Step 5. Select and decide how you will employ the most appropriate strategies for using learning media. Keeping in mind the learning media you are planning to use and what you have observed about the motivation and learning styles of your students, estimate when you will need to work with large groups, when students and groups of students can work on their own with learning media.

Step 6. Evaluate the effectiveness of the media and instructional strategies you have used by comparing your students' responses to them to the desired responses outlined earlier. If the responses you anticipated do not occur, you must revise your instructional plan.

Step 7. Revise where revision is indicated. No curriculum plan, no instructional procedure, no teaching strategy should ever be fixed. Change is inevitable in an open system, and particularly in a multimedia instructional system like that we have described here.

SUMMARY

Teachers today find themselves in a changing world, playing a changing role. They face challenges stemming from changes in instructional styles and instructional materials.

The twentieth century has seen more developments in the science of communications than any previous era. Teachers particularly are in the midst of a communications revolution, one that has had a tremendous effect on instructional technology.

Virtually all the children in the nation pass through our schools. Inside the classroom they reflect both contemporary progress and contemporary dilemmas, and they pose many dilemmas for teachers. On the other hand, students today are perhaps more ready to respond positively to new communication techniques than any previous generation.

A knowledge of the basic communication process is vital for teachers who want to create a learning environment that includes provisions for the backgrounds, interests, and abilities of students.

Six learning tenets that should be considered in choosing and using media are helpful in overcoming psychological and physiological barriers to communication. An awareness of these principles, together with a systematic integration of new learning media into an overall instructional plan, can bring about a higher level of learning.

Readers can begin immediately to use the media-oriented instructional development plan described in this chapter. Succeeding chapters describe the kinds of media available to make it workable in virtually any teaching situation.

ACTIVITIES

1. Even at this early point in the book, you can begin planning how to incorporate learning media into your own instructional plan. A chart like that on the following pages will help you do this in a systematic fashion. As you read each chapter, make whatever changes you think are necssary in the chart. An instructional plan should always be open to revision.

   You can begin your search for useful learning media by investigating the usual sources of such material in your school and community. Pictures, charts, filmstrips, videocassettes, and the like, are often available from learning resource offices, school media personnel, and community agencies. Material may also be available for the asking from local businesses, foreign consulates, and government agencies. Evaluate items as you

AN INSTRUCTIONAL DEVELOPMENT PLAN

Step 1

Identify the nature of the learners at the onset of instruction.

____

____

State target or problem areas confronting the learners at the onset of instruction.

____

____

Step 2

State the central objective to be achieved by learners as a result of instruction.

____

____

List supporting, or enabling, objectives.

a. ______________________________________

b. ______________________________________

c. ______________________________________

d. ______________________________________

Step 3

Note anticipated, observable learner-performance outcomes.

a. ______________________________________

b. ______________________________________

c. ______________________________________

d. ______________________________________

Step 4

Select specific learning materials to be used.

a. ______________________________________

b. ______________________________________

c. ______________________________________

d. ______________________________________

Step 5

Decide what instructional strategies would be most appropriate.

a. ________________________________

b. ________________________________

c. ________________________________

d. ________________________________

Step 6

Evaluate your teaching materials and strategies by determining the presence or absence of desired outcomes that were noted previously in Step 3.

____

____

Step 7

Make any necessary revisions in your instructional plan.

go along, and keep a written record of what you think will be useful.

REFERENCES

PRINT REFERENCES

Della-Dora, Delmo, and James E. House, eds., *Education for an Open Society* (Washington, D.C.: Assc. for Supervision and Curriculum Development, 1974).

Gwynn, J. Minor, and John B. Chase, Jr., *Curriculum Principles and Social Trends* (New York: Macmillan, 1970).

Klausmeier, Herbert J., and Richard E. Ripple, *Learning and Human Abilities*, 3rd ed. (New York: Harper & Row, 1971).

Kaufman, Roger, *Instructional Systems Development* (San Diego, Calif.: University Consortium for Instructional Development, 1975).

Leeper, Robert R., ed., *Curriculum Concerns in a Revolutionary Era* (Washington, D.C.: Assc. for Supervision and Curriculum Development, 1971).

Macdonald, James B., and Esther Zaret, eds., *Schools in Search of Meaning* (Washington, D.C.: Assc. for Supervision and Curriculum Development, 1975).

Mialaret, G., *The Psychology of the Use of Audio Visual Aids in Primary Education* (Paris: UNESCO, 1966).

Rich, John Martin, *Innovations in Education* (Boston: Allyn & Bacon, 1975).

Rock, Irvin, *An Introduction to Perception* (New York: Macmillan, 1975).

Schramm, Wilbur, *Big Media, Little Media* (Stanford, Calif.: Stanford University Institute for Communication Research, 1976).

Wiman, Raymond V., and Wesley G. Mierhenry, eds., *Educational Media, Theory and Practice* Columbus, Ohio: Merrill, 1969).

MEDIA REFERENCES

Changing Attitudes Through Communication, 16 mm film, sound, color, 23 min. BNA Films.
Communications Primer, 16mm film, sound, color, 22 min. Charles & Ray Eames.
Let Them Learn, 16mm film, sound, color, 27 min. Encyclopaedia Britannica Educational Corp.
Making Sense Visually, filmstrip, sound, color. Eastman Kodak Company.
No Reason To Stay, 16mm film, sound, b/w, 29 min. National Film Board of Canada.
Sixteen in Webster Grove, 16mm film, sound, b/w, 47 min. Carosel Films (CBS distributor)
To Help Them Learn, 16mm film, sound, color, 21 min., Assoc. for Educational Communications and Technology, 1978.
Webster Grove Revisited, 16mm film, sound, b/w, 53 min. Carosel Films (CBS distributor).

Arrangements for the use of the following films may be made through the University Consortium for Instructional Development, United States University, San Diego, Calif.

University Consortium for Instructional Development Film Series:
From Teaching to Learning, 16mm film, sound, color, 14 min.
The Principal, 16mm film, sound, color, 18 min.
Who Is Miss Brett? 16mm film, sound, color, 12 min.
Visual Literacy, 16mm film, sound, color, 18 min.

2 Teaching with Pictures and Graphics

Objectives

To enable you to do the following:

1. Differentiate between visual literacy training and the mere making of pictures, films, or videotapes by students.
2. Design a learning experience that encourages the visual sequencing of ideas.
3. Select from a group of flat pictures and graphics those that are good for teaching purposes.
4. Illustrate two ways in which (a) an impression of depth and (b) an impression of motion can be conveyed in a flat picture.
5. Mount three pictures (or graphics) with different proportions by at least two methods.
6. Evaluate the quality and importance of color in instructional materials.

From the moment we open our eyes in the morning until we fall asleep at night, we are bombarded with thousands upon thousands of sensory stimuli. In one way or another we process these, sifting out most, attending casually to others, and focusing on those that, for whatever reason, interest us.

It is only from stimuli on which we focus that we are likely to learn anything. Teachers, therefore, regularly expend much energy and ingenuity in attempting to focus students' attention on the lesson at hand, on *motivating* them to concentrate. There is much more to learning, of course, than motivation, but little learning is likely to occur without it.

A key problem in motivating students arises from the fact that many of them see little relationship between what they are called on to do in school and the world they see outside school. That world is a highly visual one. Children become accustomed, even before they begin school, to expertly designed visual messages of many kinds. They are graduates of *Sesame Street,* students of *The Electric Company* and *Mister Rogers.* As they grow older, they find the mass media competing ever more insistently for their attention. Powerful visual communications are an inherent part of the out-of-school environment, and young people respond readily and naturally to them. (See Figure 2.1.)

Successful students are able to develop and maintain a kind of perspective that enables them to take their schooling as it is. Others—particularly those from disadvantaged groups—tend to be less successful scholastically from the very beginning, to fall farther behind as time goes on, and eventually to drop out. A common characteristic of many culturally deprived youngsters is difficulty with the language, both oral and written, used in school. The language used in their homes and neighborhoods is apt to be different. Thus they are handicapped at the outset, and unless something other than conventional language-oriented methods and materials is used, their future success in school is, at best, uncertain. By adolescence, they are very likely to have developed a feeling of apathy about ever achieving success in school. Is it any wonder, then, that they get "turned off" and tend to abandon our system of values?

VISUAL LITERACY

Visual literacy training is explicitly designed to motivate students by teaching them to express themselves visually. In early experimental programs, students were given simple cameras and film and taught how to use them to tell picture stories. (See Figure 2.2.) Reports from a number of school systems indicated considerable success, both with average students and with youngsters from economically and culturally deprived environments.

Several years ago, for example, a six-week summer project was conducted with 100 first-, second-, and third-grade children of migrant workers to determine the impact of visual literacy training on language skills. Half of the children were given visual literacy training, and half were given traditional training in language skills. By the end of the summer the experimental group displayed a clear superiority in oral skills. There were some important fringe benefits as well:

Figure 2.1 *Sesame Street* and *The Electric Company* are two children's television programs that bridge the gap between pure entertainment and education. Produced with adequate funds and professional talent, these programs have had marked success in stimulating preschool and middle-grade reading. In this scene from *Sesame Street,* Big Bird, one of the show's featured performers, discusses the letter "M" with one of his human colleagues—one way visual examples help achieve "literacy."

> The excitement implicit in any visual literacy project is difficult to describe to anyone who hasn't seen the wonder on the faces of youngsters when they see their newly processed pictures. The migrant pupils in the experimental classes became so excited that many of them spent time after school discussing their pictures with teachers and the project staff. Such interest in school is highly unusual for such pupils. . . . Even the most silent, recalcitrant pupil will jabber about pictures, but he'll really "go on and on" about his own pictures . . . for they are the most meaningful pictures he can show you.[1]

In another study, visual literacy techniques were used to teach grammar and composition in a college preparatory school. A control group of students was taught by traditional means,

[1] Roger B. Fransecky, "Visual Literacy and Teaching the Disadvantaged," *Audiovisual Instruction* (October 1969), pp. 28–31 ff.

Figure 2.2 Students at both elementary and secondary levels appear to benefit significantly from communicating through pictures. These young photographers are discussing their cameras with their teachers before going out "in the field."

and the experimental group worked primarily with visual materials and cameras. At the end of the experiment the grammar of both groups had improved by about the same amount, but the experimental group's compositions were much better than those of the control group. The traditional group generally turned in the minimum amount of work, whereas the group using films worked long and hard at revising their scripts and generally submitted excellent work. The researcher summed up the results this way:

> *Motivation:* This is the key. While both groups "learned grammar" equally well, the film group enjoyed it and, as a result, was easier to work with. The traditional group dreaded composition and did little or no revision. Revision to them meant "copy it over on good paper." However, the film group wrote compositions that they wanted to write; they used a thesaurus because they wanted "that right word"; they wrote compositions and enjoyed the effort. They found that learning could be relevant and fun.[2]

Recent Developments in Visual Literacy Training

Since the late 1960s, when it first began attracting national attention, interest in visual literacy training (now also being called *visual education*) has spread rather rapidly. In 1975 Lida Cochran of the University of Iowa surveyed representative school systems across the country with organized visual literacy programs.[3] She found considerable variety in types of programs, in the sophistication of programs, in the grades where they are used (K–3 to K–12), and in the number of schools in a system involved. Basically, there are three types of programs:

1. Those designed to develop the students' ability to read and write visually.
2. Those designed to reach subject-matter goals more effectively, particularly reading goals.
3. Those aimed at developing the students' understanding of and skill in using devices that produce visual images and sounds.

For example, Milford, Ohio, has a complete visual communications program of the first type for grades K–12. Perceptual training is also the purpose of PROJECT SEE in Union, New Jersey. The kit developed for this project includes pre- and posttraining tests, worksheets, a perception game, and a teacher's guide. East Setaucket, New York, has a perceptual training program for all K–3 pupils that is integrated with normal classroom work and conducted by

[2] Gerald W. Jaromin, "Teaching Grammar and Composition Using Cameras," in ***Proceedings of the First National Conference on Visual Literacy*** (New York: Copyright © 1970 by Pitman Publishing Corp.), p. 196. Reprinted by permission of Fearon-Pitman Publishers, Inc.

[3] Lida M. Cochran, *Visual Literacy Survey* (Iowa City: University of Iowa College of Education, 1975).

regular teachers. The materials used in this program are available from Science Research Associates.

Some Psychological Reasons for Visual Literacy Training

Several fundamental learning concepts underlie the principles of visual literacy training. These can be summarized in three brief statements.[4]

1. A child's conceptions emanate naturally from a progression of experiences, at first largely physical or kinesthetic in nature, which form a framework for later learning.

Infants, for example, instinctively seek their mothers' breasts and, in the process, experience a total sensory involvement along with the reward of being fed. Thus, through hunger and the expression of it, the impulse to search and find and be rewarded for searching is established and reinforced almost from the beginning of life. This impulse is fundamental to all learning.

2. Children begin early to develop a visual vocabulary that takes on meaning as they interact with and affect things or processes they see.

Long before they learn to talk or to interact selectively with people and objects around them, babies store up visual images that are meaningful to them. When they see their mothers warm their bottles or move their high chairs close to the table, they know that food is coming and respond accordingly. They also learn early how to bring about these desirable events. (See Figure 2.3.) In the process they develop understanding of and skill in what researchers call *visual language*. One element of this visual language is *body language*—physical actions we use, consciously or otherwise, by which we transmit ideas or feelings to others.[5] By the time they are two, babies have become pretty sophisticated at both interpreting and using body language. They have developed an extremely effective visual vocabulary that brings them success and happiness in their own little world. This visual vocabularly becomes the basis for their development of verbal skills later on.

3. Children need a great deal of practice in ordering and sequencing things visually if they are to order and sequence ideas verbally later on.

This ordering takes place naturally in home environments in which infants have opportunities to select and attend to a continuous stream of visual images to which they can react in terms of their needs and their interests at the moment—hunger, curiosity, and so on. Like adults, they must become selective in what they attend to. As they focus on certain things—on their mothers, on their food, on a toy—and ignore others, they learn to make sense, in their own terms, of what they see. Their world comes to have a kind of order.

Deterrents to Visual Sequencing

Preschool children used to get continuous practice in ordering things visually and in choosing what to attend to or ignore. Now, however, they begin at an early age to look at television for long periods of time. Television programs, usually designed for older children or adults, tend to preclude visual selection or ordering. You either look at them or you don't. Furthermore, it is difficult to interact meaningfully with a TV mother, toy, or glass of milk. Children may in fact respond to these things, but nothing they do has any effect on what hap-

[4] See John Debes, "Some Foundations for Visual Literacy," *Audiovisual Instruction* (November 1968), pp. 961–964.

[5] Weldon Kees and Jergen Reusch, *Non-verbal Communications* (University of California Press, 1964), pp. 16–20, 36–41, 189–193.

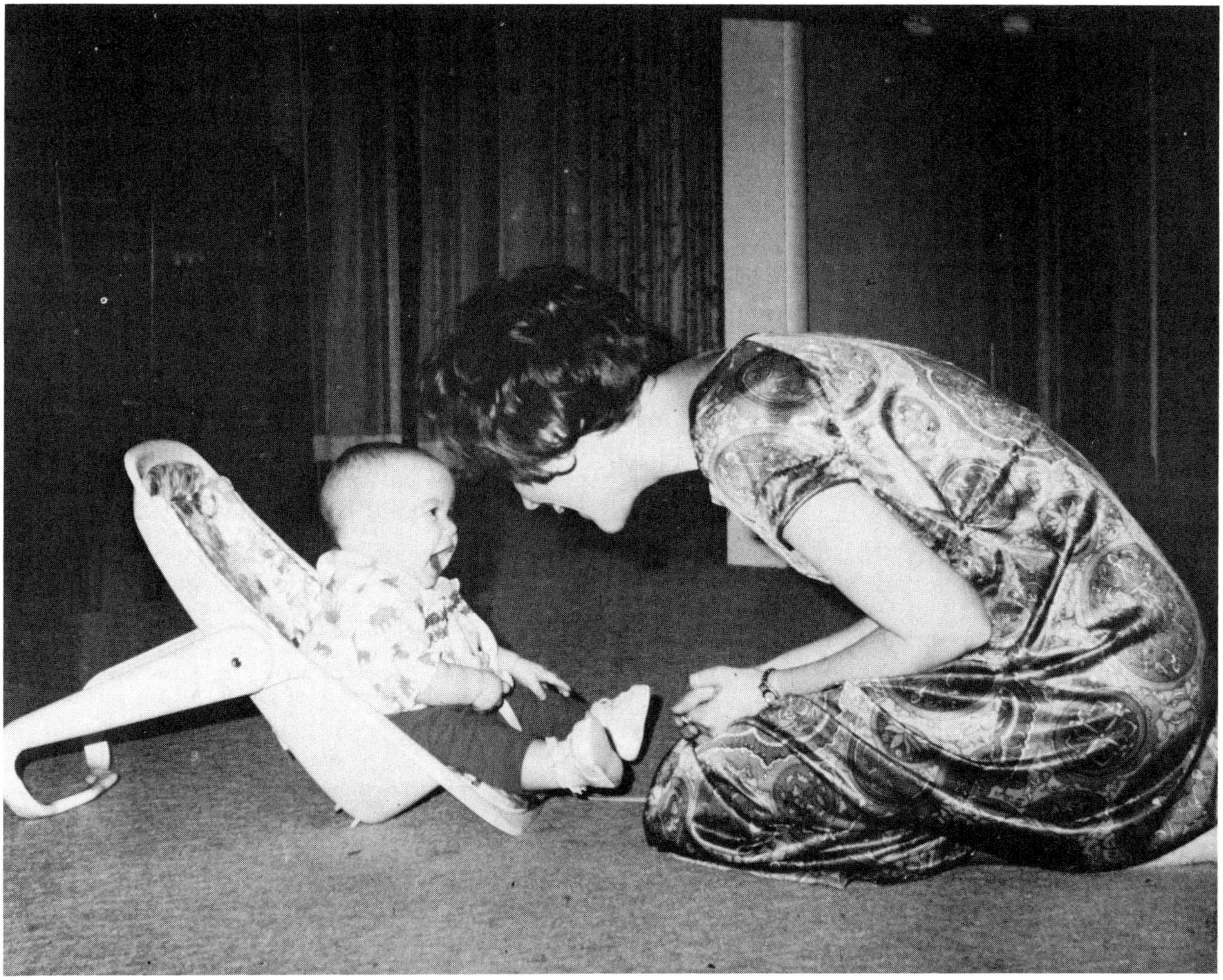

Figure 2.3 Very young children learn to communicate effectively long before they learn a spoken language. Unfortunately, we tend to minimize nonverbal communication skills later on.

pens on the screen. Their role tends to be a passive one. They receive the visual ideas of others, rather than practicing the selection and ordering of their own visual perceptions.

Television, films, and other preprogrammed visual sequences may thus hinder a child's development of verbal skills—particularly in regard to the ordering of ideas. The need for practice in this activity is very real. Specialists who have done considerable work with children with learning disabilities, for example, say that the one factor common to such children is their inability to *order* ideas. Consequently, they recommend that visual sequencing be practiced assiduously.[6]

[6] Marianne Frostig and Phyllis Maslow, "Language Training: A Form of Ability Training," *Journal of Learning Disabilities* (February 1968), pp. 15–24.

Television does not always help the disadvantaged child either. We know that a home environment where there is little conversation or where the language forms are different from those used in school puts a youngster at a disadvantage. Television may make matters worse. As John Debes puts it, "In the nonverbal family, there's not much talk anyway. In the television family, there's even less. Therefore, opportunities to communicate verbally are relatively few; the chances of a child becoming articulate grow dim.[7]

What Is Involved in Visual Literacy Training?

Visual literacy training has six basic goals. They are to teach students

1. To read visuals with skill.
2. To "write" with visuals, expressing one's self effectively.
3. To know the grammar and syntax of visual language and be able to apply them.
4. To be familiar with the tools of visual literacy and their use.
5. To appreciate the masterworks of visual literacy.
6. To be able to translate from visual language to verbal language and vice versa.[8]

Eastman Kodak has produced a series of teachers' guides, filmstrips, and films to help teachers who wish to try the visual literacy route.[9] These materials are designed to help learners "read" pictures skillfully as a basis for creating and "telling" their own picture stories. (See Figure 2.4.)

Although educators still have some questions about visual literacy, it is clear that visual skills give learners an important additional means of interpreting and communicating information

[7] Debes, "Some Foundations for Visual Literacy," p. 963.

[8] John Debes, "The Loom of Visual Literacy," in *Proceedings of the First National Conference on Visual Literacy* (New York: Pitman, 1970), p. 13.

[9] These publications include *A Visual Fable, How Does a Picture Mean? Making Sense Visually,* and *Rhetoric of the Movie,* plus five *Photo Discovery Sets,* pictures students can manipulate to tell a variety of stories. All are now available through the AECT.

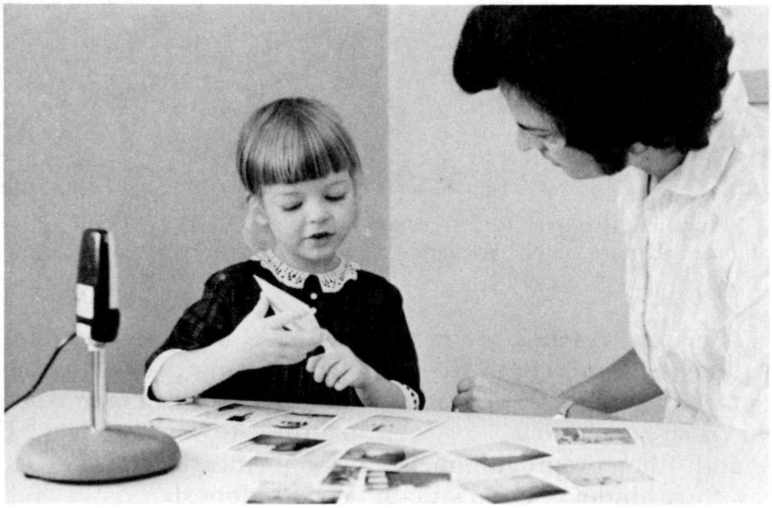

Figure 2.4 Telling a story with pictures is fun. What are three ways that visual literacy training can help pupils achieve traditional school objectives?

about themselves and their environment. Visual literacy appears to have special benefits for those with limited verbal skills. It probably has equal or greater potential for increasing the communication skills of verbally competent and articulate students.

FLAT PICTURES

Although visual literacy training may appear at first to be a unique approach to teaching—and perhaps it is—its uniqueness consists primarily in how media are created and used. Teachers using the visual literacy approach find it necessary to know a good deal more about media—pictures, graphics, slides, films, and so forth—than most of us do. This is because the crux of the visual literacy approach is for students to *communicate* by means of pictures or other visual media. Ultimately, they may translate or interpret those pictures and media with articulate, verbal language. To do this, students must be led to discover the difference between good and bad pictures and how to design and put visuals together so that they tell a story.

We use the term *flat pictures* to describe illustrations in magazines and books, photographs, study prints, and the like—pictures that can be examined without benefit of a projector or viewer. (See Figure 2.5.) *Still pictures* is a broader term for any kind of nonmoving pictures, projected or not. Thus slides, transparencies, and filmstrips, as well as flat pictures, are still pictures.

Actually, the term *still pictures* can be somewhat misleading, because many such pictures clearly show motion, though they themselves do not move. The term *motion pictures* is also, strictly speaking, inaccurate, because the illusion of motion is created both in films and on television by projecting a series of still pictures on a screen or tube in a progression too rapid for the eye to detect. Both terms have the ad-

Figure 2.5 Sets of flat study prints like this are widely available from school supply companies in color and in large sizes.

vantage, however, of being universally understood, and we will continue to use them.

Advantages of Flat Pictures

Like any other instructional material, flat pictures have some unique advantages, as well as limitations.

Low cost and ready availability. Flat pictures are readily available on an almost unlimited range of topics. Literally thousands of good pictures appear each year in magazines, newspapers, and advertising brochures, many of which can be acquired at little or no cost. In addition, modern textbooks normally include large numbers of good illustrations, and there are many excellent sets of study prints schools can purchase.

Ease of use. A second advantage of flat pictures is the ease with which they can be used. Special equipment is unnecessary, though a filing system of some sort is essential. If the pictures are large enough, they can be held up in front of a class. Students, individually or in small groups, can use them for a variety of purposes. They can be mounted to create displays or put together in any order to fashion a visual message.

Ease of making. Teachers and students themselves can draw simple pictures or graphics or take photographs. This, in fact, is an essential element of visual literacy training.

Limitations of Flat Pictures

All teaching materials have advantages for some kinds of tasks and limitations, or disadvantages, for others. Just as teachers should be skilled at selecting suitable reading materials, so they should be competent at choosing appropriate visual materials.

Some limitations of flat pictures are as follows.

Small size. The vast majority of pictures in books, magazines, and newspapers are too small to be used in front of a class. Unless they are enlarged or projected, they cannot be seen well enough by everyone in the class to justify using them in this way. This limitation can be overcome, however, if an opaque projector is available and the room can be darkened. (See Figure 2.6.) Moreover, study prints can be obtained that are large enough to be used in front of a class if attention does not need to be focused on small details in the pictures. Smallness is not necessarily a limitation in pictures used for displays, because if the overall effect of the display is good enough, students will go up to examine it—and the small pictures—at close range.

Lack of depth. When accurate depth perception is essential to learning a concept or skill, a model or a specimen may be preferable to a two-dimensional picture. Stereo pictures are often used in medical schools, along with models, to show the precise relationships of body tissues. Aerial mapping services use flat stereo photographs to provide a basis for contour maps, and technicians' manuals frequently contain complex diagrams of the assembly or disassembly of machines. In all these cases, where depth perception is important, flat pictures are used as supplementary rather than primary sources of information.

What, then, is a teacher to do? The *first* step is to recognize that there is a problem. Few teachers appear to realize that picture reading is a real skill that must be acquired. The development of this skill is one of the important functions of visual literacy training. The selection and use of pictures with good depth and motion cues is a second important step a teacher can take to overcome this problem with flat pictures. Helping students to interpret cues is still another.

There is a *syntax,* or arrangement of elements, in a good picture, just as there is a syntax

Figure 2.6 Small pictures can easily be shown to a whole class if an opaque projector is used.

of grammatical elements in a good sentence. Both the quality of the elements themselves—the depth cues, for example—and how well they are put together are critical to the readability of pictures. In other words, though we tend to assume that pictures communicate more or less automatically, we must remember that this is not the case—pupils need to learn how to read pictures, just as they need to learn how to read words.

There is considerable evidence that beginning learners have particular difficulty in reading three-dimensionality into flat pictures. For some reason, boys seem better than girls at judging depth, though both have normally mastered this skill by the fifth grade.[10]

Familiar scenes provide cues that enable children to sense actual depth relationships rather

[10] Ruth H. Monroe and Robert L. Monroe, "Reading Pictures—A Cross-Cultural Perspective," *Claremont Reading Conference Yearbook* (Claremont, Calif.: Claremont College, 1969), pp. 67–72.

Figure 2.7 The awe-inspiring immensity of the Grand Canyon is apparent in this picture to one who has seen it in person, but much less so to one who has not. Why?

accurately. When scenes contain few familiar elements, however, the accuracy of depth perception may be considerably reduced. The vastness of the Grand Canyon, for example, is extremely difficult to grasp from a picture unless one has actually seen it in person. (See Figure 2.7.)

Lack of motion. Because flat pictures are by definition still pictures, we can readily use them to communicate ideas about essentially motionless subjects and to teach concepts in which motion is not important to understanding. Landscapes, mountains, forests or trees, buildings, objects, animals, or people in still positions are natural subjects for flat pictures.

Flat pictures of moving subjects can also have great value. Stop-motion photographs of hurdlers, for example, help them and others to analyze good points or flaws in their form. *Strobe photography* is a special technique used to produce pictures that are really a series of stop-motion photographs superimposed on one another. They are also very useful in analyzing an athlete's form. (See Figure 2.8.) Still pictures are better than motion pictures for identifying machine parts (though the latter are usually better if the purpose is to explain how a machine operates).

The lack of motion in flat pictures is only

(a)

(b)

Figure 2.8 (*a*) The strobe shot of a badminton player "freezes" his motions in succession. (*b*) Stop-motion photography enables both coach and athlete to analyze a performance in detail.

relative. Still pictures can depict motion very satisfactorily for many purposes. For example, most students have seen television coverage of rocket launchings. Thus they bring to a flat picture of such an event a complete awareness of the motion represented by the outpouring of smoke and flame and by the rocket itself as it moves slowly upward from the launching pad. For them, a picture like Figure 2.9 has a dynamic rather than a static quality.

Many still pictures contain clues to motion. One is a blurring of the image of a moving object, as in Figure 2.10. The blurring is based on the fact that a moving image on the retina produces a blurred impression of an object. Instead of actually blurring an image—or in addition to it—artists frequently use such symbols as the wake behind a boat or clouds of dust behind a stagecoach to suggest motion. Typically, such symbols are exaggerated somewhat to make sure the degree of motion gets across to the viewer. Because these symbols often have no exact counterparts in nature, they must be learned. There is, in fact, a reasonable amount of evidence that children do not normally detect dynamic or active qualities in pictures before the third grade.[11] One significant and still largely unexplained finding in some studies, however, is that, among young children, the use of color substantially facilitates the perception of dynamic clues to motion.

Figure 2.9 Pictures such as this one have become almost routine in our space age but may have even greater value as inherent in today's culture. What concepts might this picture help to teach?

Another clue to motion in still pictures is provided by objects in positions that cannot possibly be maintained. A tree falling, an airplane taking off, a man with both feet off the ground, or an athlete in midair cannot remain stationary, and thus is seen as in motion.

Combinations of motion clues in one or more still pictures of an ongoing process force the viewer to recognize that something has happened, is happening now, and is going to happen. For example, consider a series of scenes showing cows being milked, trucks taking milk to a dairy, milk being bottled, the bottles being delivered by a milkman, and children drinking milk at the breakfast table. Such a series makes it possible for the viewer to relate the various parts of the milk production and distribution process and integrate them into a dynamic whole. Interpreting such a series does, however, require a fairly sophisticated level of perception —the kind of perception necessary to understand flow charts. This is higher than the level of perception needed to interpret, for example, comic strips, which tell a story in a linear fashion. A series of scenes showing how milk

11 Robert M. W. Travers, *A Study of the Advantages and Disadvantages of Using Simplified Visual Presentations in Instructional Materials.* Final Report on USOE Grant No. OEG-1-070144-5235, 1969.

(a) (b)

Figure 2.10 Motion can be shown in various ways in still pictures. In (*a*) motion is shown by blurring the moving object. In (*b*) it is shown by blurring the background.

gets from a cow to breakfast tables is more abstract. Viewers have to fill in gaps to grasp what is going on. Nevertheless, pictures of this type are being successfully used with quite young children in visual literacy projects.

What Makes a Good Picture?

Thus far we have been concerned with the more extrinsic characteristics of flat pictures. These are fundamental. But we also need to be concerned with their qualitative characteristics. As one biology teacher put it:

> I'm a camera fan myself and take a lot of pictures. In the process, I have come to have a great deal of respect for people who can take really *good* pictures. There's a lot of difference between ordinary pictures and good ones, and I try hard to find the good ones to use in my biology classes.

What are good pictures? And why are they better than ordinary pictures for teaching purposes? An art teacher has this to say on the subject:

> What we're really talking about is visual communication, isn't it? . . . I try to instill in my pupils an appreciation for such things as color, line, and composition in good pictures so that they can apply these fundamentals as they make their own sketches and designs. But the same principles apply to any visual material which is intended to communicate. The better a picture is from an art standpoint, the better it is likely to transmit what it has to say to anyone looking at it.

In other words, good art and good visual communication go hand in hand.

Good composition. Good composition, or good overall organization, is fundamental to an effective picture. Usually an effective picture has a clear-cut center of interest. The balance of the picture as a whole, the position and direction of lines, and the use of light, shadow, and color all help to focus our attention on a particular element. This element is rarely in the geometric center of the picture, because another position is usually more pleasing to the eye. To determine if a picture has a good focal point, simply let your eye travel naturally over the picture until it fixes on a key feature. Look away from that feature and see if your eye tends to go back to it. If it does, the picture has a strong center of interest.

Occasionally we see pictures of huge crowds, geometric patterns, or a large number of similar objects that do not have a center of interest in the usual sense. In these pictures an overall effect is the objective. Views of 100,000 people in a public square, row on row of dilapidated houses, or rolling fields of grain may have a powerful effect on the observer. Such subjects are difficult to photograph effectively, however, precisely because they do not have a visible center of interest. (See Figure 2.11.)

A clear message. The principles of good composition apply to all pictures. Those to be used in teaching, however, should also communicate an intended message or idea clearly. One of the most difficult skills for designers of visuals to learn is to define clearly *what* they wish to convey and then control their medium so that the message gets across. A good photographer plans each shot carefully, focusing on a single idea and eliminating all unnecessary details. The resulting pictures are simple, rather than complex, and consist of large, clear images.

Figure 2.11 Although lacking some elements that go to make up a good picture, this scene represents something very "real" in many of our lives. What does it tell you? Is what it says to you partly a result of your own experience with large crowds?

In general, a simple, direct picture, uncluttered with unnecessary details, communicates its message more clearly than a complex picture. In fact, in dealing with complex subjects, it is usually better to use a series of pictures rather than to try to get everything into one picture. This principle of *selective simplicity* applies both in making and in selecting pictures; it applies to other kinds of visual designs, such as displays and graphics, as well. A good rule to follow in deciding whether something should be included in a picture or display is this: Unless it contributes something significant, do not include it. When in doubt, leave it out!

Effective color. Color is a part of our natural environment, and properly used, it adds realism as well as attractiveness to visual media. In pictures selected for use with children, colors should generally be true to life. We seldom see actual primary colors—reds, blues, yellows, and so on—in nature; rather, we see infinite subtle variations of these colors. Visual media should reflect this. As Catherine Williams points out in *Learning from Pictures,*[12] poor quality color "offends the sensitive viewer and prevents the development of good taste by the less sensitive."

Over the years, color film and color reproduction processes have steadily improved, and color pictures of excellent quality are now used extensively as study prints, in texts and reference books, and in mass media.

Black-and-white photography, despite its name, can provide a wide variety of color impressions. (See Figure 2.12.) In fact, many photographers actually prefer working with black-and-white film when color is not essential. In the classroom, good black-and-white photographs are often more effective than mediocre colored ones.

[12] Catherine Williams, *Learning from Pictures,* 2nd ed. (Washington, D.C.: Association for Educational Communications and Technology, 1968.

Good contrast and sharpness. Sometimes in judging a picture's quality we say that it is flat. This may mean several things, one of which is that the important parts of the picture do not stand out enough from the rest. Consequently, the picture as a whole lacks vitality. More skillful lighting, better exposure, and more skillful developing would have produced whiter whites, and a more interesting and effective picture. It is also possible to have too much contrast; this produces a harsh effect. A good photographer or artist strives to achieve just the right amount of contrast.

The clarity and sharpness of a picture are also important in communicating information and ideas. Although softness of focus is effective in portrait work and for portraying certain moods, most educational subjects are better illustrated by pictures that are clear and sharp, because more details of the subject can be seen.

GRAPHICS

Graphics are instructional materials that summarize information and ideas through drawings, words, symbols, and pictures. Most students are initially less familiar with graphics than with flat pictures. Nevertheless, they are a valuable means of communicating certain kinds of information.

Drawings play a role in all kinds of diagrams, graphs, and charts. Symbols, such as those in Figure 2.13, are a form of visual shorthand and are used extensively in diagrams (such as blueprints) and signs, as well as on maps. Words and numbers are used in practically all graphics to clarify the meaning of drawings and visual symbols or to present quantitative information. Pictures are key elements in many charts and posters. Cartoons or comics are special kinds of drawings that convey an idea or tell a story. Thus the term *graphics* includes a variety of

Figure 2.12 The full range of the gray scale is included in this beautiful shot of Mount Hood at sunrise. What advantages can you see for some kinds of study in the many subtle gradations in tone which are possible with black-and-white pictures?

Figure 2.13 Pictorial symbols like these are often used to communicate information and concepts that are fairly complex.

visual forms. Figure 2.14 gives some idea of the variety of charts and graphs in common use.

The instructional value of graphic materials generally lies in their capacity to focus attention and to convey certain types of information in a condensed form. A biology chart on cell division, for example, quickly summarizes the process of mitosis. A diagram of a business organization typically indicates departments, functions, and lines of responsibility. A graph of automobile production shows at a glance whether more or fewer cars are being produced this year than in preceding years. Specific types of graphics are described more fully in the following paragraphs.

Graphs

A graph is a visual representation of numerical data. A table of figures may contain a wealth of information, but a graph presents the gist of it more quickly and effectively. Graphs also reveal important relationships among data, such as trends, and they are inherently more interesting than lists of numbers.

Graphs have all sorts of uses. For example, teachers who want to keep pupils interested in reading books may post a *progress graph* showing the number of books read by each pupil to date. Progress graphs, which can be purchased from school supply houses, have a number of bright red bars that are revealed by removing small sections of a paper overlay. Pupils' names are inserted on the chart, and one section of the overlay is removed each time a project (e.g., a book or a report) is completed.

The major purpose of graphs is to present quantitative information *quickly* and *simply*. (See Figure 2.15.) When a graph is too intricate and difficult to read, it loses its chief advantage. Complex information is more effectively presented, as a rule, in a series of simpler graphs than in a single intricate composite. Even when a composite graph is desirable, it should follow a series of supporting graphs.

(a)

(b)

Figure 2.14 How many of these graphic forms can you identify as specific types of graphics —bar graphs, line graphs, flow charts, and so forth? As you read the following sections on graphs, diagrams, and charts, look back at these examples and see if you can identify them more precisely.

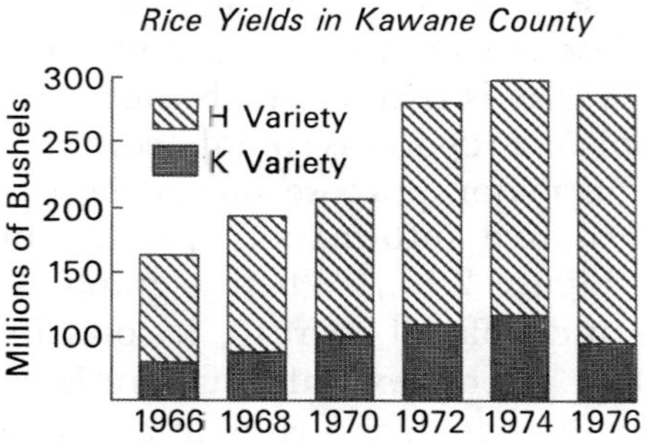

(a)

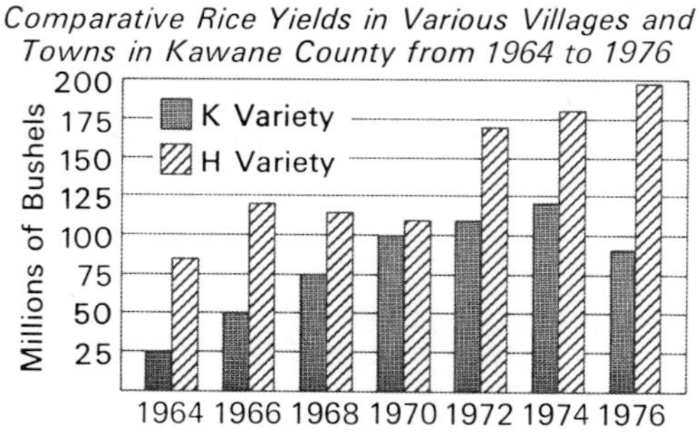

(b)

Figure 2.15 Good graphs are simple, bold, legible, and brief and have adequate margins. Example (*a*) is a good, clear graph whereas (*b*) obviously is a confusing and cluttered one.

Types of Graphs and Their Advantages. There are many kinds of graphs. Among the most common are line, bar, circle (or pie), and pictorial graphs. Each has certain advantages.

Line graphs. Line graphs are potentially the most *precise* of all graphs; they are therefore particularly useful in plotting trends or relationships between two sets of data. A line graph graph should be used (1) when a considerable number of data are to be plotted or (2) when the data form a continuous series that, over a period of time, clearly shows the progress or development taking place. The line graph in Figure 2.16*a* was plotted from continuous data. Numerous variations and combinations of simple line graphs are used, including shaded-surface graphs and silhouette graphs.

Bar graphs. Bar graphs, such as that shown in Figure 2.16*b*, are among the simplest graphs to read. They are also easily constructed. The variables whose values are to be shown are represented by vertical or horizontal bars. The length of the bars depends on the value of the variables; the width of all the bars is the same. Bar graphs are most useful when the number of variables to be compared is small—usually no more than six or eight. Occasionally more bars are used, but then additional elements are needed to make the graphs readable. Bar graphs permit *direct comparisons* of quantitative variables at specified intervals of time.

Circle (or pie) graphs. A circle, or pie, graph is divided into sectors, each of which is used to represent part of a whole. (See Figure 2.16*c*.) Thus circle graphs always show totals, or whole amounts, and their parts or segments show percentages or fractional parts of this whole. When intermediate-grade teachers introduce the subject of fractions, they may begin by cutting an

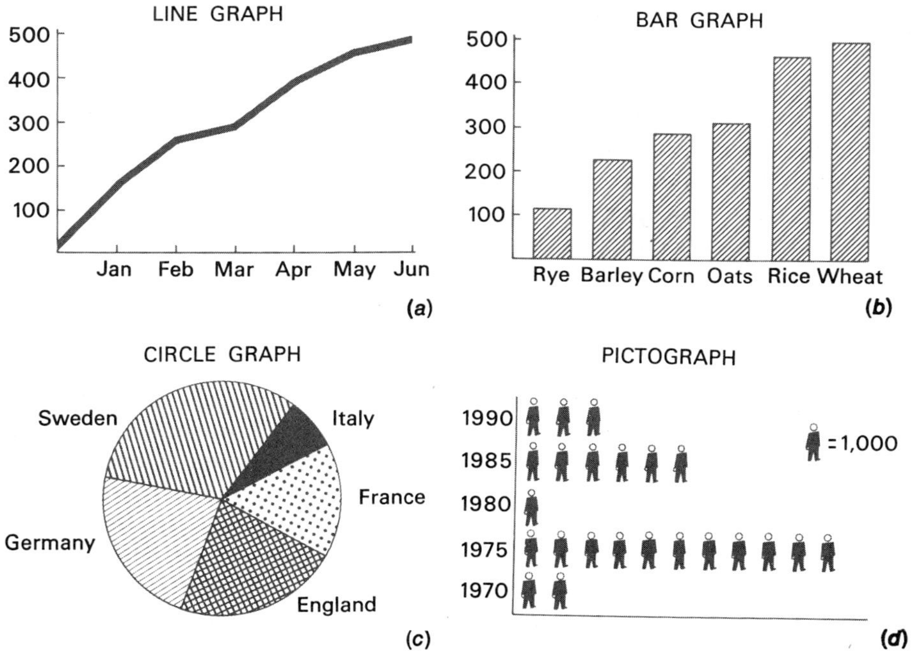

Figure 2.16 These are four of the most common types of graphs.

apple into halves and quarters. Or they may use a felt board, fitting segments of a circle together to form a whole.

Research indicates that circle graphs are the clearest way to compare parts of a whole. For example, if a nation produces 10 million tons of coal per year, 7.5 million of which are bituminous, 2 million of which are anthracite, and 500,000 of which are lignite, this information can be shown on a circle graph by shading 75 percent of the circle to represent bituminous production, letting 20 percent represent anthracite production, and letting the remaining 5 percent of the circle represent lignite production. The resulting "pie" is a natural and easy-to-understand way to present these data. Such information as the sources of budget dollars, the distribution of expenditures of a municipality, or the sources of the world's petroleum supply can also be easily represented by pie graphs.

Pictorial graphs. Pictorial graphs like Figure 2.16*d* have much of the eye-catching appeal of three-dimensional figures. This type of graph is actually an adaptation of the bar graph and generally presents the same kinds of data. It is used widely in magazines and newspapers.

Pictorial statistics were first popularized in Vienna by Otto Neurath, a sociologist seeking a means of conveying statistical information in a way that would be readily understood by people around the world. He developed simplified outline figures of such subjects as men, women, children, cows, ships, and sheaves of grain and used them to represent graphic data. Neurath called his figures *isotypes;* variations of these figures are now used in most countries of the world.

Graphs vs. tables. There have been a number of studies on the relative readability of graphs and tables. The findings include a number of points of interest to teachers:

1. Circle, or pie, graphs are the easiest graphs to read. However, they are useful only for comparing parts of a whole.
2. Horizontal and vertical bar graphs, in that order, are probably the next most readable. A three-dimensional effect (resulting from the way the bars are drawn) does not in itself make bar graphs harder to read.
3. Line graphs are probably best for presenting precise, detailed information or showing significant trends.
4. Comparative-area graphs—squares, circles, rectangles, and so forth—tend to be the least clear.
5. Both bar graphs and short, simple tables are more effective when they are reinforced by verbal explanations.
6. Long tables—even if they are accompanied by explanations—are less effective than other ways of summarizing data visually.
7. Pictorial graphs have essentially the same advantages as similar nonpictorial graphs. Pictorial horizontal bar graphs are easiest to read and, if they are well designed, are probably more interesting to nontechnical readers than other types of graphs.

Diagrams

A diagram is a drawing, consisting primarily of lines and symbols, that shows the outline, interrelationships, or key features of a process, an object, or an area. Diagrams depend almost entirely on lines and symbols to convey information and may be highly abstract. Often special background knowledge and experience are necessary to read them properly. Construction blueprints like those in Figure 2.17 provide a good example of how complex diagrams can be and the difficulties we may face in interpreting them. Yet they are essential to our way of life. There are many simpler types of diagrams, of course, such as those used to show how to thread film into a motion picture projector or how to

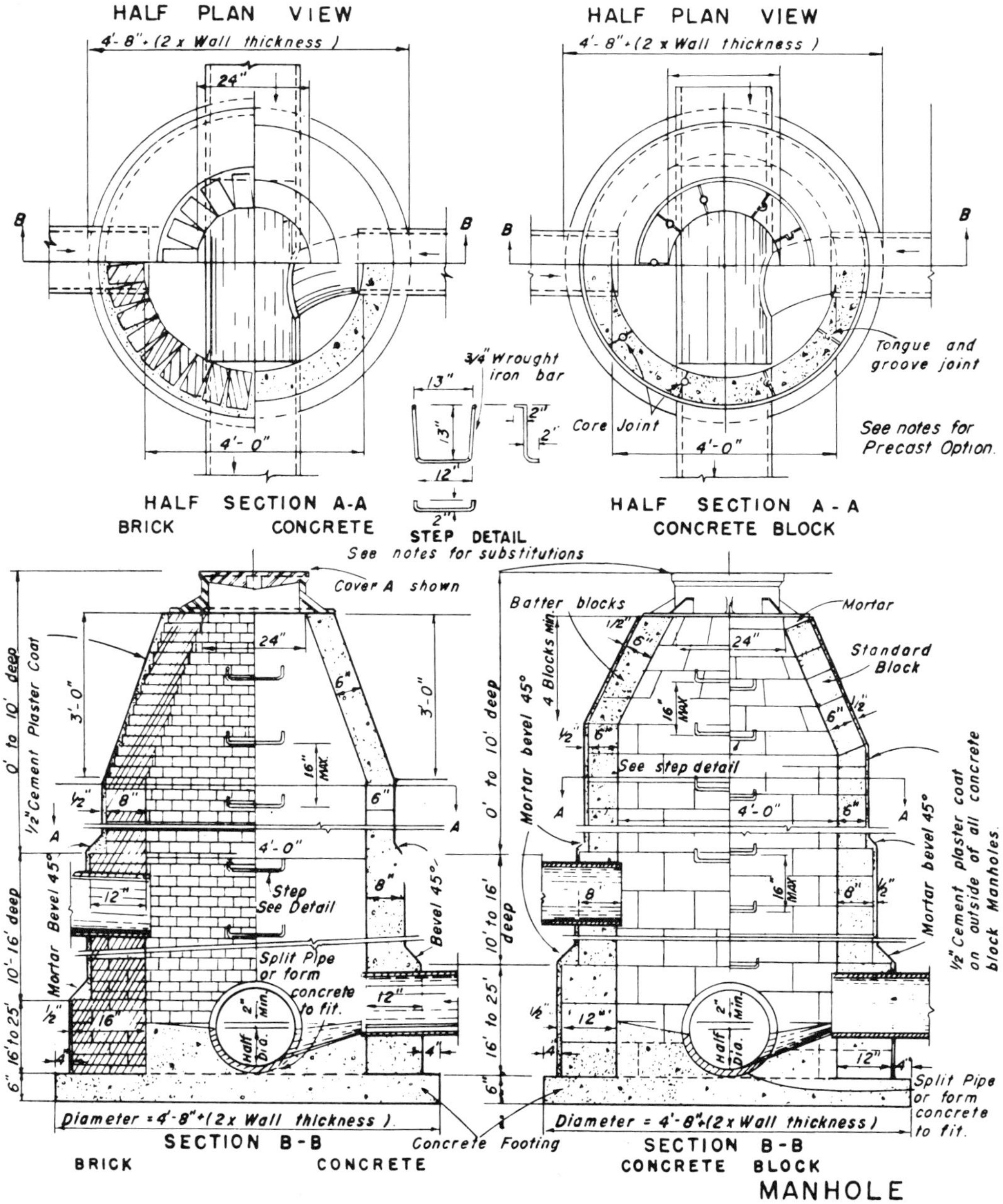

Figure 2.17 Technical fields rely heavily on blueprints to communicate information. Without such diagrams, construction and manufacturing firms could not function.

fit the pieces of a dress pattern together. English teachers for generations have used diagrams to indicate the relationships among subjects, predicates, and other parts of speech. We use process diagrams in social studies to show how a bill becomes a law; cross-section diagrams in science to show how engines, pumps, and hydraulic systems work; and so on.

Charts

Most charts are visual summaries containing a mix of visual and verbal elements. They may summarize data, explain a process, or describe a set of relationships.

The principal steps in the production of steel, the organization of Congress, the parts of a flower, the phases of the moon, parts of speech, or a historical time line can all be clearly indicated by charts. Sets of charts on many subjects are available commercially, but valuable simple charts can also be made by teachers and students. Because of heavy printing costs, commercial producers frequently combine several related charts on one large sheet. In designing your own charts, however, it is easier, and usually more effective, to avoid this. Specific directions for making charts and other graphic forms are described in the *Student Production Guide.*

Types of charts. Charts may consist of almost any combination of visual and verbal elements. Ways of classifying them derive more from their functions than from the kinds of visual or verbal materials they contain. For classroom purposes, we need note only four types of charts: (1) outline and tabular charts; (2) flow, organization, and process charts; (3) tree and stream charts; and (4) time-line charts.

All good charts have the following characteristics:

1. A clear, well-defined purpose. Usually charts describe one main idea, concept, or process.
2. Visual, verbal, or other materials that achieve their purpose.
3. Information in summary form. Good charts typically do not provide large amounts of information. Rather, they summarize key points.
4. Adequate size. Often the principal features of a chart need to be visible across a room.

Outline and tabular charts. Outlines list the key points and subpoints in material. (See Figure 2.18*a*.) Their content may range from simple parts of speech, phonetic words and syllables, and number sets to traffic safety or field trip rules. Tabular charts, as their name implies, present information in columns, as in Figure 2.18*b*. They are commonly used for vocabulary or spelling lists, arithmetic exercises, production or sales figures, and the table of atomic weights in chemistry.

Flow, organization, and process charts. The organization of a student council or a government unit, a manufacturing process, or the steps whereby a bill becomes a law can all be shown clearly by a flow chart (Figure 2.18*c*) or an organizational chart (Figure 2.18*d*). This type of chart is well suited to showing functional relationships and is widely used for this purpose.

Tree and stream charts. As its name suggests, a tree chart has a base composed of various "roots" that lead to a single "trunk." The trunk, in turn, has "branches" that represent developments and relationships. A good example is a genealogical chart like that shown in Figure 2.19*a,* in which two people, a man and a woman, are the "roots" of a family tree. Tree charts are useful in showing developments resulting from a combination of factors—for example, the many byproducts obtainable from coal. They are also effective in showing how iron ore, limestone, coke, and various chemicals may be combined to produce a variety of types of steel. Sometimes

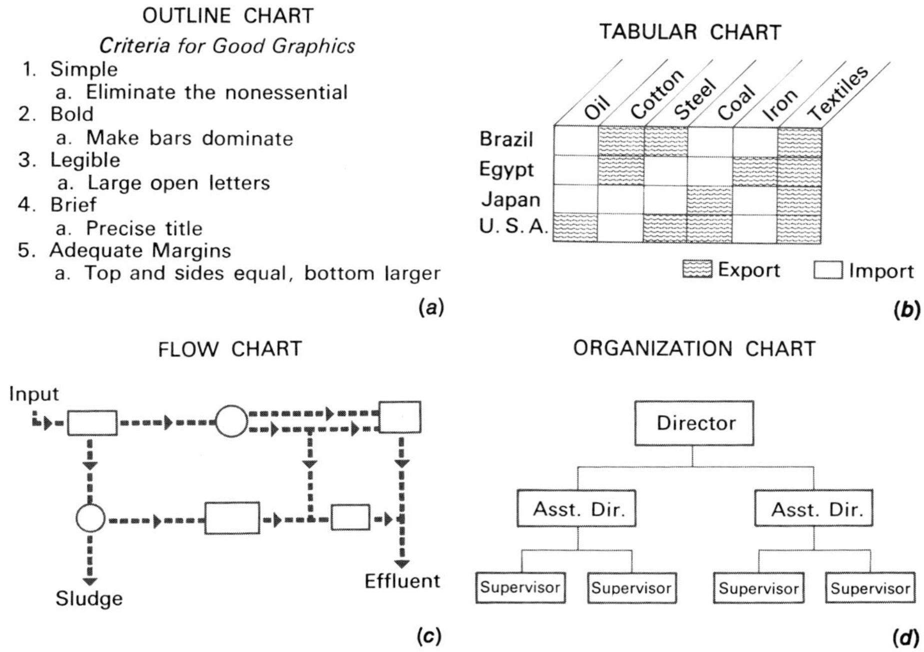

Figure 2.18 These are four of the most common types of charts.

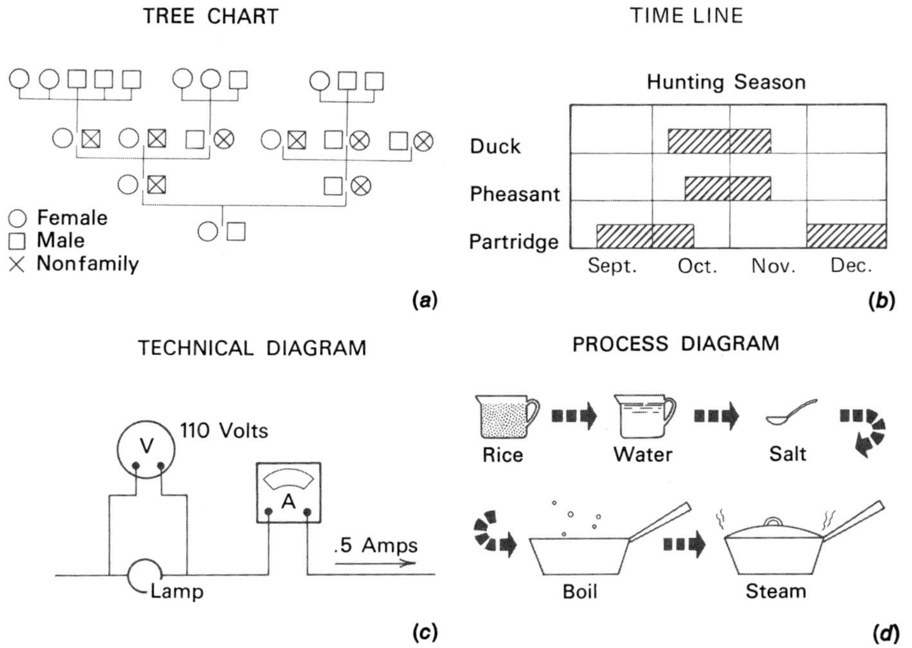

Figure 2.19 These are four of the most common types of charts and diagrams.

a reverse form of the tree chart is useful in showing how a great variety of elements are combined to form one important product. This type of chart, known as a *stream chart,* can be used to illustrate such things as an industrial nation's dependence on other countries for strategic materials.

Time-line charts. Time lines (such as that shown in Figure 2.19*b*) are helpful in summarizing sequences of events or in making chronological comparisons. For example, the wheat production of various nations in a given year might best be shown by a bar graph, but a time line would be better for comparing wheat production in those countries at 10-year intervals from 1910 to 1980.

Technical diagrams. Technical diagrams are used to explain such things as the layout of electric circuits, construction specifications, fuel systems, and the like. In many fields, standard symbols are used that may be unintelligible to laypersons. However, they will be clearly understood by the engineers, contractors, and other specialists for whom the diagram is intended.

Process diagrams. The process diagram in Figure 2.19*d* is a simple one, but such diagrams can be highly complex—for example, when the steps in a complicated manufacturing process are illustrated. A process diagram implies a flow of activity as well as an orderly sequence of separate steps. When the flow, rather than the individual steps, is emphasized, the diagram may be referred to as a *flow chart* or a *flow-process diagram.*

Posters

A poster is a bill or placard meant to be posted in a public place. It generally has a bold design intended to catch and hold the attention of passers-by long enough to implant or reinforce an idea.

Characteristics of Good Posters. Good posters have a dynamic, compelling quality. They are essentially simple and have an immediate impact. They are striking enough to attract attention and convey their message quickly, and they are pleasing to the eye.

The element of dramatic simplicity is well illustrated by the civil rights poster in Figure 2.20. The eye-catcher in that poster is the clenched black fist symbolizing black militancy, which leads the eye to the clasped black and white hands in the background that symbolize the cooperation necessary to solve the civil rights problem. Originally, the poster was used in an advertisement for a filmed history of the civil rights movement, with the clenched fist carrying the eye to the following message, which was printed at the top: "To understand today's black militancy, your students must understand yesterday's civil rights struggle." The design is so strong, simple, and compelling, however, that the poster communicates its basic message without words. This is what makes it an outstanding poster.

Uses for posters in schools. Two types of posters are useful in schools. Posters from such sources as the National Safety Council, the National Dairy Council, the Community Chest, and other agencies are useful to emphasize good safety and health habits, consideration for others, and the like.

Student-made posters, the second type of poster frequently seen in schools, are a valuable tool in visual literacy training. They can be used as a way of expressing something that has been learned or in connection with school and community activities. Campaigns for electing members of the student council, class plays, athletic contests, clean-up campaigns, music festivals, speech contests, hobby shows, and the

Figure 2.20 The attention-holding quality of this poster is based on its stark simplicity and the strength of two contrasting symbols—the clenched fist and clasped hands.

like, are natural occasions for preparing and using posters.

Cartoons and Comics

A cartoon is a satirical drawing designed to influence public opinion or to make a point in a humorous way. A comic is a form of cartooning in which a cast of characters enacts a story in a sequence of closely related drawings. Cartoons are widely used in newspapers and magazines to present a point of view or a position on an important issue or to poke fun at the attitudes, values, and activities of various groups and institutions within our society. (See Figure 2.21.) Both types of cartoons are very much a part of the visual world of students.

Figure 2.21 A succinct idea sharply rendered—usually with a bit of humor—is one of the marks of a good cartoon.

Newspaper comics are ready daily by millions of people, young and old. Charles Schulz's *Peanuts* strip, for example, has a huge adult following because of its whimsical but incisive characterizations. (See Figure 2.22.) Both cartoons and comics can sometimes be used by teachers to make or illustrate a point in a memorable way.

Comic books. Comic books, an extension of comic strips, first achieved widespread popularity in the 1930s. Instructional comics, particularly in the area of popular science, are produced by a number of companies and have achieved some degree of success.

Student- and Teacher-Made Graphics

Designing and making their own graphics gives students an opportunity to express what they have learned in a creative way and, simultaneously, reinforces that learning. It also gives them an insider's view of these visual media. Original graphics can be used in all sorts of ways. For example, English pupils can prepare charts of the story line of a play or novel; science students can use diagrams to explain the operation of retrorockets; and home economics students can construct charts to show the calories in meat cooked by various methods.

Students should understand that graphics are a means of expressing information and ideas. Their decision to use a chart, graph, or poster should be based on a determination to communicate something important and perhaps unique. Accordingly, one circumstance in which it makes sense to construct a graphic is when one is needed and is not otherwise available. Another circumstance in which the construction of graphics is warranted is when the act of preparing them will contribute significantly to the students' understanding of a subject. Preparing a time line, for example, may help pupils to see connections between historical events.

Figure 2.22 Comics vary widely in their appeal to different age levels. A few, such as *Peanuts,* have exceptional appeal to a wide range of readers, both young and old. What accounts for this? (© 1974 United Feature Syndicate, Inc.)

A related consideration is the fact that we learn a good deal about interpreting graphs, diagrams, posters, cartoons, and some charts by making them. There is a close relationship between a student's ability either to make or to interpret graphics and his or her grasp of related concepts. The ability to count and some concept of scale are necessary to construct the simplest bar graphs; a knowledge of percentages and the calculations necessary to convert information to more complex scales is required for most circle or line graphs and for time lines.

It is also important for students to learn how graphics can misrepresent information. As students become alert to distortions, interrupted scales, changes in the size of symbols, and other sources of false impressions on graphs and charts, critical thinking becomes easier. In constructing charts or graphs, students often become more conscious of these pitfalls than they do through exposure to ready-made graphics. Attention to the source of the data (which should always be noted) is another thing students need to learn in order to deal intelligently with the profusion of graphics used in the world around them.

Teachers can construct a wide variety of *achievement* and *progress* charts. *Number* charts can help bring students to the critical realization that numbers are abstract ideas. *Phonetic* charts are enormously helpful in establishing familiarity with common syllables and words and introducing the link between writing and speech. *Work* charts can list series of problems or questions to be answered. They also help develop reading skill and speed.

Specific suggestions about methods and materials for making graphs, diagrams, and charts are given in the *Student Production Guide.*

SELECTING AND USING PICTURES AND GRAPHICS

The abstractness and complexity of illustrations constitute one of the chief factors to be considered in deciding whether to use them with a particular age group. In general, as we have seen, circle graphs, bar graphs, and line graphs are easier to read than other types. As we have also noted, diagrams are often abstract, and special background knowledge may be needed to interpret them. Some graphs and charts are more difficult to read than others. One picture may illustrate a point clearly, whereas another may do it poorly or even be distracting.

In considering visual material, teachers should ask themselves two questions. First, is a visual illustration necessary at all? Second, if it is necessary, how much does the one being considered contribute to understanding the concept or process being taught?

In examining the characteristics of good flat pictures and graphics, we have, in effect, been establishing the criteria for their selection and use. Generally speaking, pictures that communicate well have a strong center of interest, good composition, good color where color is important, and a sufficiently sharp focus to show necessary details.

Graphics, by definition, synthesize information, pulling it together and highlighting its most significant elements. Normally, this kind of material is more useful after students have moved along in a subject than it is at the beginning. Pictures, on the other hand, can be useful at almost any point in a lesson. There are some graphics, however, that are very useful in the motivational or developmental phase of a lesson.

In some cases, teachers may want to have a carefully selected set of pictures available for students to work with. In other cases, they may ask students to seek out pictures from magazines and picture files—or to take their own pictures. Picture taking is particularly valuable for studies involving the local community and as a form of visual literacy training.

MOUNTING FLAT MATERIALS

The very profusion of pictorial, graphic, and related materials creates problems in caring for them when they are not in use. Most new schools have libraries or learning resource centers where files of pictures and similar materials are maintained. However many teachers also develop personal files of their own. Because more flat materials are damaged by poor storage methods than by actual use, some knowledge of mounting and other protective techniques is helpful.

Some pictures and graphics are more valuable for certain purposes than others. Outstanding or unique pictures that may be difficult to replace should be mounted to protect them from damage. Less valuable pictures may be filed unmounted. They can then be temporarily mounted quite easily if necessary for use in class or in study displays.

Some Guidelines for Mounting

1. Use generous margins. Generous margins are not merely a matter of artistic taste; they help attract and hold attention. Any object tends to attract more attention when it is by itself than when it is crowded in with a number of other, similar objects.

Correct proportions for mounting pictures of various shapes are shown in Figure 2.23. Note the width of the margins used. The width of the top and bottom margins is determined by the shape of the picture, as the illustration shows. Note also that the bottom margin is *always* wider than the top one. The side margins are always equal and usually in between the size of the top margin (which is smallest) and the bottom one (which is largest).

2. Use colors that direct attention to the picture and not to the mounting. As a rule, it is best to select for a mounting a color that ap-

(a)

(b)

(c)

Figure 2.23 These mountings show the value of generous margins and proper margin proportions. Note that the bottom margin is always wider than the top and side margins.

pears in the picture in a relatively minor degree. This repetition of color adds a pleasing harmony to the total effect. It is usually not wise to use a color for the mounting that predominates in the picture itself, because of the resulting loss of contrast. A picture of a field of ripe grain will not appear to the best advantage on a yellow mounting, nor will a picture with a broad expanse of blue sky look well on a light blue mounting. In such cases, the picture loses definition because it tends to merge with the mounting.

In general, neutral tones are more satisfactory for mountings than primary or brilliant colors, although there are exceptions. Bright red or green mountings look well with Christmas pictures, orange mountings are fine for Halloween subjects, and gay pastel mountings harmonize with Easter decorations.

3. Use borders and texture effects on occasion. Often a narrow border will help to set off a picture from its mounting. Sometimes an inked line around the picture is effective. A similar effect is obtained by inserting immediately behind the picture, a sheet of mounting paper slightly larger than the picture and of a different color from that used for the mounting itself. Because this sheet extends slightly beyond the edges of the picture, it provides a border in a contrasting color. White is often highly effective for a border of this kind because it brings out the color in the picture.

Although colored drawing paper is inexpensive and probably the most readily available material for mounting, you may occasionally want to use other materials for variety or special effects. Tag ends of wallpaper in subdued allover patterns or with textured surfaces are one good possibility. Others include fabrics of various kinds, dress and suit boxes, and even corrugated cardboard. You can also check with the school's art department for ideas.

Temporary Mountings

There are various relatively simple ways to mount pictures and other flat visuals on a backing. *Rubber cement* has long been used; a few dabs will usually suffice. Because rubber cement tends to soak into more porous materials and can be a bit messy, some convenient substitutes are also widely used. One of these is a *spray adhesive* that comes in an aerosol can. Another is a commercial *waxer*. Some waxers are quite inexpensive and are practical for school use; the wax backing serves as an adhesive. *Gummed tapes* can also be used without difficulty; double-surface masking tape applied to the back of a picture is particularly useful. A synthetic waxlike adhesive called *Bulletin Board Styx* is also used for mountings; this is particularly useful for mounting pictures on solid, rough, or glossy surfaces. Small bits of this adhesive will hold pictures in place for as long as necessary.

When pictures or graphics are to be displayed on cork or some other porous surface, the fastest and simplest method of temporary mounting is to use *straight pins,* as many art teachers do. The pins, which hold both the mounting and the picture in place, cannot be noticed from more than a few feet away; this fact makes pins preferable to thumbtacks, too many of which detract from the effectiveness of a display. Several types of mounting and fastening devices are shown in Figure 2.24.

Permanent Mountings

When flat visual materials are to be used repeatedly or handled regularly by students, some type of permanent mounting is desirable. A fairly stiff backing material should be used for the mounting. Any of several good permanent mounting techniques can be employed. Most schools today have dry-mount presses and Thermofax machines; many, in addition, are ac-

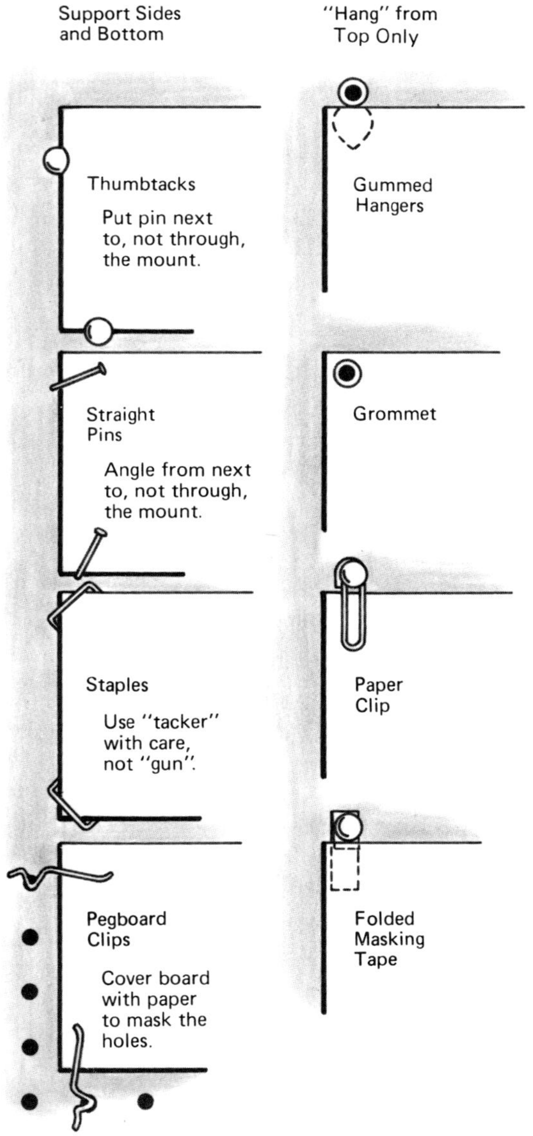

Figure 2.24 Here are some examples of effective methods of fastening pictures on various surfaces.

quiring laminating machines. These are all useful for mounting.

Dry mounting requires a special tissue material that is affixed by means of a dry-mount press or a hot iron. Dry-mount tissue can be obtained in rolls or sheets from photographic supply stores. A piece of the tissue is trimmed to the size of the picture and put on the back of it. The picture and the tissue backing are then placed on the mounting material and covered with a piece of plain white paper. When they are put in a dry-mount press (or when an iron heated to about 300 degrees is used on them), the picture fastens firmly to the mounting. The picture is then sprayed with a clear flat lacquer to protect it.

Lamination seals mounted or unmounted visuals in a clear, nonglossy plastic covering that permanently protects them from dirt, moisture, and tearing. Laminating machines are needed for this kind of mounting, but there are useful substitutes where such machines are not available. One of these is a clear plastic film that can be applied to a picture by putting it through a Thermofax machine. Also available are inexpensive clear vinyl sheets that can be purchased in many household supply stores and applied with a hot iron. School- and art-supply houses carry clear plastic sheets especially designed to protect pictures. Some are applied with heat and pressure; others are self-adhesive and can be applied by hand. Large pictures can be protected readily and inexpensively by spraying them with a coat of clear lacquer.

Sectional Mountings

It often is advantageous to use a series of identical mountings for magazine-fold pictures or murals that are too large for a single mounting. When displayed, the series appears as a unit, for the individual sections are identical in size and coloration. When fitted together, they look

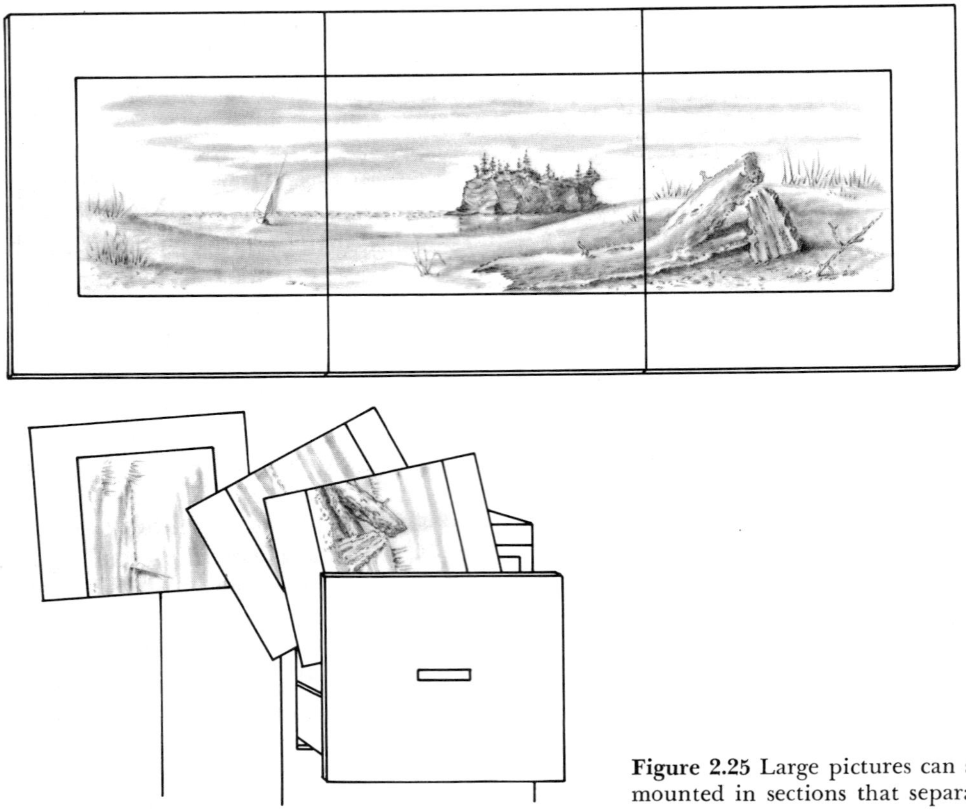

Figure 2.25 Large pictures can sometimes be mounted in sections that separate for filing.

like a panel, but they can be separated for filing and storage. (See Figure 2.25.) Another method of sectional mounting is to fasten lightweight sections together with masking tape or cloth tape and fold them, accordion fashion, when they are not in use. Either method is a practical solution for handling the ever-increasing number of excellent two- and three-fold materials in popular magazines.

The permanent and temporary mounting techniques just described are the most common. However, during the past decade or so, business has addressed itself seriously to the development of better equipment and materials for teachers and learners. Progress in picture-mounting techniques is one result of this, and further improvements may be expected. You should be on the alert for new techniques as you visit convention exhibits and scan the advertisements in professional journals. You should also consult sources listed at the end of the chapter for ideas.

STORING FLAT MATERIALS

Teachers who go to some trouble to find good pictures and graphics know the importance of proper storage and filing of such materials.

Filing Systems

The simplest way to file pictures and related flat materials is to group them according to the teaching units in which they are used or by topic. When large numbers of pictures are involved, subheadings are helpful. For example, pictures on Greece may be filed under the subheadings "Greece—Mountains," "Greece—People," "Greece—Farming," and so forth. Tabbed or color-coded separators should be used, and the pictures in each section should be listed in pencil on the separator. Other indexing systems include notebook lists, with pictures identified by numbers or topics; similar lists in lesson plan folders; and a simple card file, with related groups of pictures listed on each card. Filing and indexing systems should be as simple as possible, but flexible enough to accommodate additional pictures and sections. Furthermore, the system of classification and labeling used needs to be geared to the maturity of the pupils using it.

Visual Files as Learning Experiences

Having students create files of visuals can be a valuable form of visual literacy training. In the process, they can gain valuable experience in the selection of good visuals and in using them to communicate ideas.[13]

To begin with, the teacher can provide a nucleus of pictures, which can be kept loose in envelopes or folders. Students can then select those that fit the particular topic being studied. After some instruction, they can mount the better pictures and graphics and use them in whatever ways appear suitable. At an appropriate point, questions can be raised about how good and suitable the selected pictures are, and students can be encouraged to bring in additional or more appropriate pictures that they themselves have found or taken. In a subsequent evaluation session, the students can select the best of the pictures that have been brought in, then repeat the mounting exercise, perhaps using backing materials they themselves have brought in.

You can make judgments as you go along about how many topics to treat in this way. It is important to keep the proper perspective. Though an exceptional file of pictures and graphics may, of course, be assembled and mounted in this manner, what is significant is what the students learn from the experience. By working with visuals in this way, they may improve their ability to read pictures and to communicate ideas with them. Experience in selecting and evaluating visual materials will help them to discriminate between good and poor pictures and perhaps to appreciate those that are exceptional.

Storage Facilities

In addition to a workable filing system that makes it possible to locate materials readily, storage facilities are essential. These can range from fairly elaborate built-in facilities to simple but workable portable substitutes.

Filing cabinets. Modern classroom facilities usually include built-in drawers and cabinets in which various instructional materials can be stored. Standard, letter-size cabinets are suitable for small mounted pictures in folders; but legal-size files are better, because they accommodate material up to 11 by 14 inches, and vertical filing cabinets are now available in sizes up to 14 by 18 inches. Horizontal flat files with a number of shallow drawers are particularly good for larger materials, up to 40 by 60 inches. When such facilities are not available, various types of cases, cartons, and boxes are often used; particularly useful are the strong and inexpensive plastic and laminated cardboard cartons and cases now available. (See Figure 2.26.)

Portfolios. Portfolios are also an excellent means of protecting pictures when they are not in use or while carrying them; they have been used by artists and art teachers for many years. A portfolio is nothing more than two pieces of heavy cardboard or similar material hinged with

13 Suggested by Professor Wilfred Veenendaal of the Instructional Media Center, Michigan State University.

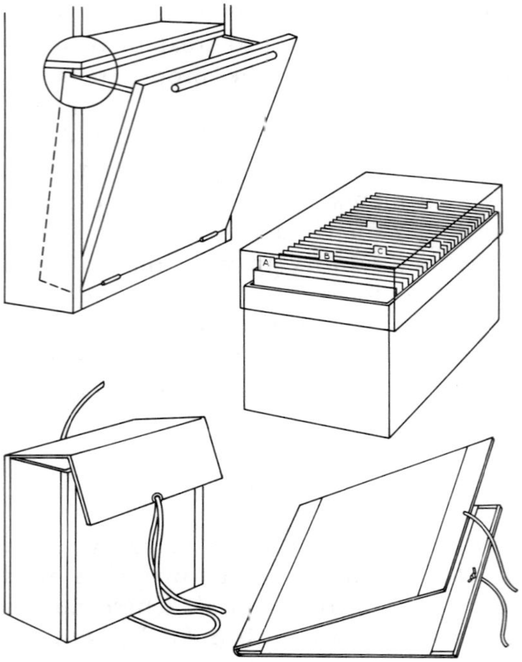

Figure 2.26 Here are a few suggestions for storing pictures. The dimensions of these files and portfolios can be adjusted to suit your needs.

flexible tape on one of its long sides. (See Figure 2.26.) Pictures or graphic materials are laid flat in the open portfolio, the cover is closed and tied, and the pictures are ready to travel. A portfolio can be made up in any size; one 34 by 44 inches will accommodate most pictures and small charts and still will be easy to carry.

COLOR AND LEARNING

Color is an important consideration in selecting, using, and producing many kinds of visual materials. Research on colored media shows them to have little or no advantage over black-and-white materials when purely cognitive effects are measured except where color is inherent in what is to be learned. However, color does appear to help focus attention, to improve retention of details, and to enhance motivation. Further, color appears to have significant impact in the affective areas of learning.

Many decisions on the nature, format, and color of the instructional materials we use have already been made for us by the producers of those materials. Wilbur Schramm suggests, for example, that with practically everything available in color, we have in fact, a whole new "ball game." "Not only must we think twice before presenting environment in monochrome in the classroom when it is typically shown in color in the living room, but we also have practical teaching options of trying all kinds of interesting combinations of monochrome and color in ways such as to improve clarity, focus attention or amplify and reinforce meanings in our visual presentations."[14]

In addition to differences in hue, colors also have various properties (warmth, depth, intensity, and the like) that are important in designing visual messages. A simple color wheel will help you select colors and shades that harmonize to produce a desired effect. Colored paper can be used to test the effect of particular color combinations.

SUMMARY

Visual literacy training is a relatively recent and promising development in media-oriented learning. In brief, its goal is to develop students' abilities to read visual materials and to express themselves through them. Experiments in which students use their own pictures to communicate ideas have been highly successful in motivating students to learn and have had a positive influence on their oral and written language as well.

Flat pictures are so readily available that it

14 Wilbur Schramm, from a note to the authors, July 30, 1975.

is easy to underestimate their importance in teaching and learning. Pictures have a universality and a versatility that no other medium of communication shares. Although somewhat less familiar to students than pictures, graphic materials are a valuable way of summarizing significant information. Like other media, both pictures and graphics have strengths and limitations. And although they can be combined naturally and effectively in a lesson, they have distinct functions. Pictures illustrate or represent actual objects or scenes. Charts, diagrams, and graphs compress and distill information and show relationships and trends. Posters and cartoons can illustrate some fairly complex and abstract ideas.

In general, it is better to use a few carefully selected pictures and graphics than to use too many. Those that are large enough can be used in front of a class; those that are small can be projected using an opaque projector or incorporated in study displays. Both are also valuable in teaching individuals and small groups.

Care in the selection of pictures and graphics is essential for effective learning. And the starting point for selecting the best materials is to define your objectives. The next step is to choose pictures or graphics that are directly pertinent to those objectives. They must also be suited to the maturity of the students and be of good quality. Mounting flat pictures increases their effectiveness and preserves them. Also important is a system of filing and storage that gives ready access to material when it is needed.

ACTIVITIES

As you review the ideas about visual literacy, flat pictures, graphics, and color discussed in this chapter, consider them from two perspectives: (1) in light of the objectives stated at the beginning of this chapter and the activities in this section, which are based on those objectives; and (2) in light of the instructional development plan outlined at the close of Chapter 1. Pin down your understanding of the objectives and test the extent to which you have achieved them through the activities. Then use what you have learned to expand your instructional plan. Select a topic you will probably be teaching, a goal, and supporting objectives. Locate some visual media that will help your students achieve those objectives and decide how you will use them. If you are not sure how to proceed, ask your instructor for help.

1. View the films *Hey, Look at Me* and *The Growing of a Young Filmmaker* (see Media References for sources), and do a critique of them, keeping in mind Objective 1.
2. Find (or take) a set of pictures on a subject suitable for a particular grade level that students can use in an ordered sequence in a legitimate learning experience.
3. From a set of pictures and graphics provided by your instructor (or from magazines or other sources) select (a) two that have good composition, (b) two that have a clear message, (c) two that use color effectively, and (d) two that have a desirable amount of contrast and sharpness. Be ready to justify your selections.
4. Identify a teaching situation in which flat pictures that convey a sense of depth are important. Find pictures that do this in two ways, and be ready to describe how the effect of depth is achieved. Do the same with a set of still pictures that indicate motion by two or more means.
5. From a group of mounted pictures or graphics, select three that are mounted effectively. Be ready to defend your selections before the class.
6. Select five colored media of the type discussed in this chapter. Assess (a) the importance of color for learning purposes in

each one and (b) the quality of the colors and the color harmonies employed. Show the materials to small groups of your classmates and see if they agree with your judgments.

REFERENCES

PRINT REFERENCES

Arnheim, R., *Visual Thinking* (Berkeley: University of California Press, 1969).

Birdwhistell, Ray L., *Kinesics and Context* (Philadelphia: University of Pennsylvania Press, 1970).

Brigham, D. L., *Interdisciplinary Visual Arts in Learning* (Attleboro, Mass.: Attleboro School Department, 1969).

Booth, A., "What Gives a Picture Pupil Appeal?," *Times Educational Supplement* (May 2, 1975), p. 14.

Broughton, G., "The Use of Pictures: Learning Through Experience," *Times Educational Supplement* (March 21, 1975), p. 39.

Brown, Les E., "Another Look at an Old Medium—Using Pictures in Social Studies," *Audiovisual Instruction* (November 1969), pp. 72–73.

Ciemba, John, "Photography: A Key to Learning," *Audiovisual Instruction* (November 1969), pp. 66–67.

Conlan, Kate, *Poster Ideas and Bulletin Board Techniques* (Dobbs Ferry, N.Y.: Oceana, 1965).

Crouse, R. and E. Rinehart, "Creative Drill with Pictures," *Arithmetic Teacher* (April 1973), pp. 300–302.

Debes, J. L., "The Eyeful Power," paper presented at the AECT National Convention, Dallas, Texas, April 15, 1975. Association for Educational Communications and Technology, Washington, D.C., 20036.

Designing Instructional Visuals (Austin: University of Texas Instructional Media Center, 1968).

Dondis, Donis A., *A Primer of Visual Literacy* (Cambridge, Mass.: MIT Press, 1973).

Dwyer, Francis M., "Exploratory Studies in the Effectiveness of Visual Illustrations," *AV Communication Review* (Fall 1970), pp. 235–249.

———, "The Effect of IQ Level on the Instructional Effectiveness of Black-and-White and Color Illustrations," *AV Communications Review* (Spring 1976), pp. 49–62.

Fleming, Malcolm L., *Perceptual Principles for the Design of Instructional Materials.* USOE Final Report, Project No. 9-E-001: Grant No. OEG 5-9-245001-0016 (010), January 1970.

———, "The Picture in Your Mind," *AV Communications Review* (Spring 1977), pp. 43–62.

Formanek, Ruth, and John Swayzi, "Teachers and Technology: Exploring Visual Literacy," *Audiovisual Instruction* (March 1971), pp. 86–87.

Fransecky, R. B., and J. L. Debes, *Visual Literacy, a Way to Learn, a Way to Teach* (Washington, D.C.: Association for Educational Communications and Technology, 1972).

Geschwind, Norman, "Language and the Brain," *Scientific American* (April 1972), pp. 76–83.

Griffin, Paul F., and Ronald L. Chatham, "The Still Picture in Geography Instruction," *Journal of Geography* (May 1967), pp. 222–230.

Haber, Ralph N., "How We Remember What We See," *Scientific American* (May 1970), pp. 104–112.

Holliday, William G., "Teaching Verbal Chains Using Flow Diagrams and Texts," *AV Communications Review* (Spring 1976), pp. 63–78.

Krampen, M., "Signs and Symbols in Graphic Communication," *Design Quarterly, 1962* (Minneapolis: Walker Art Center, 1965).

———, "The Psychology of Visual Communication," *Dot Zero I* (Glens Falls, N.Y.: Finch, Pruyn, 1966), pp. 12–15.

Lasser, Michael L., "A Humanist Looks at Visual Literacy," *Audiovisual Instruction* (September 1975), pp. 31–32.

———, "More than Photography, Less than Panacea," *Audiovisual Instruction* (May 1972), pp. 8–10. (Note: The May 1972 issue of *AVI* is largely devoted to visual literacy.)

Levin, Joel R., Bruce Bender, and Alan Lesgold, "Pictures, Repetition, and Young Children's Oral Prose Learning," *AV Communications Review* (Winter 1976), pp. 367–380.

Macklin, Ronald R., "Fitting Together the Visual Puzzle," *AV Communications* (August 1967), pp. 13, 38–41.

Minor, Ed, and Harvey R. Frye, *Techniques for Producing Visual Instructional Media* (New York: McGraw-Hill, 1970).

Moorhouse, C. E., ed., *Visual Education* (New York: Pitman, 1974).

Oh, C. Y., "Student Preparation of Instructional Materials, *Audiovisual Instruction* (January 1974), supplement, pp. 2–3.

Parker, J. E., "Visual Literacy for Minority Youth," *Audiovisual Instruction* (December 1969), pp. 24–26.

Planning a Photo Essay (Rochester, N.Y.: Eastman Kodak Company, 1966).

Randhawa, B. S., "Intellectual Development and the Ability To Process Visual and Verbal Information," *AV Communications Review* (Fall 1971), p. 298.

Ross, S. B., "Exploring the Concept of Visual Literacy," *The Independent School Bulletin* (October 1969), pp. 44–46.

Williams, Catherine M., *Learning from Pictures*, 2nd ed. (Washington, D.C.: AECT, 1968).

Williams, Clarence M., and J. S. Debes, eds., *Proceedings of the First National Conference on Visual Literacy* (New York: Pitman, 1970).

MEDIA REFERENCES

A Visual Fable, filmstrip sound (record), color, 18 min. AECT, 1969.

Bulletin Boards and Displays, filmstrip. BFA Educational Media, 1966.

Cameras in Education, Educational Media Laboratories Technifax Education Division, 4101 S. Congress Ave., Austin, TX 78745. A series of sound filmstrips, overhead transparencies, and manuals designed to present the camera as a creative teaching tool.

Chalkboards and Flannel Boards, 35mm filmstrips (4), color, 30 frames each. Bailey Films, 1967.

Charts for Creative Learning, 16mm film, sound, color, 10 min. Bailey Films, 1966.

Educational Graphics, Hester & Associates, 11422 Harry Hines Boulevard, Dallas, Texas. A series of ten film loops averaging four minutes in length dealing with such local production skills as lettering, mounting, laminating, and composition.

Effective Visual Presentations, slide/tape, sound. Eastman Kodak Company, 1969.

Flannel Board Use, filmstrip, b/w or color, 30 frames. Bailey Films, 1966.

Graph and Picture Story Skills Kit. Science Research Associates, 1967.

Graphics, series of 17 transparencies from *Instructional Media Transparency Masters*—a series of 147. Keuffel and Esser Company, 1969. *Chalkboards* (4) and *Flat Pictures* (5) are also part of the series.

Hey, Look at Me, 16mm film, sound, color, 12½ min. AECT/Screenscope.

How Does a Picture Mean?, filmstrip. AECT, 1968.

Language of Graphs, 16mm film, sound, b/w, 13 min. Coronet Films, 1948.

Making Sense Visually, filmstrip, sound, color, 77 frames. AECT, 1969.

Mounting Still Pictures, filmstrip, color, 58 frames. Visual Instruction Bureau, University of Texas, 1956.

Photo Discovery Sets, picture sets. AECT, 1967.

Pictures for Teaching, slides, Chandler, San Francisco, 1965.

Posters, 16mm film, sound, color. ACI Productions, 1968.

Story Starters, super-8 cartridged film loops. Ealing Corporation, 1969.

Study Pictures and Learning, filmstrip, color, 63 frames. Teaching Aids Laboratory, Ohio State University, 1960.

Teaching with Still Pictures, filmstrip, color, 53 frames. Basic Skill Films, 1958.

Teaching with Visual Materials, filmstrip series, color, 35–40 frames each. McGraw-Hill, 1964. The Chalkboard, Parts I and II, and Posters for Teaching.

The Growing of a Young Filmmaker, 16mm sound film, b/w, 17 min. Screenscope/AECT.

The Simple Camera, 12 color filmstrips and 5 instructor's manuals. An introductory course in picture taking for students of any age, and for teachers who want to integrate photography in visual literacy training. AECT, 1977.

Using Charts and Graphs in Teaching, 35mm, filmstrip, color, 51 frames. Basic Skill Filmstrips, 1958.

What Is a Graph?, filmstrip, b/w, 26 frames. Visual Education Consultants, 1965.

STUDENT PRODUCTION GUIDE REFERENCES

The *Student Production Guide* is a supplement to this book that provides information on how to make simple audiovisual materials and on the operation of projectors, tape recorders, and videotape equipment. References will be given at the end of most text chapters to the *Student Production Guide* chapters that supplement the text discussion so that readers can easily consult them.

For material on topics in this chapter, see the *Student Production Guide,* Chapter 3, "Graphics Techniques for Instructional Materials Production," particularly the sections on design, color, bulletin boards, chalkboards, and graphs; dry transfer lettering, Wrico lettering; rubber cement mounting; and lamination.

SOURCE REFERENCES

This section lists representative sources of materials and equipment you may wish to know about in developing an instructional plan along the lines suggested in Chapter 1. There are, of course, literally hundreds of suppliers of some types of materials across the country, and it would be impossible to include them all here. We have opted, therefore, (1) to list original sources, such as manufacturers of equipment and long-time producers of films, filmstrips, and the like; (2) to give the names of regular exhibitors at AECT national conventions; and (3) to try for as broad a geographic distribution of sources as possible.

Art Supplies—General

Dick Blick Co., P.O. Box 1267, Galesburg, IL 61401.

Milton Bradley Company (Educational Div.), Springfield, MA 01101.

Arthur Brown and Bros., 2 W. 46th St., New York, NY 10036.

Creative Playthings, A Div. of CBS, Edinburg Rd., Cranburg, NJ 08512.

M. Grumbacher, Inc., 460 W. 34th St., New York, NY 10001.

Macmillan Arts & Crafts, 9520 Baltimore Ave., College Park, MD 20740.

Comics

Children's Television Workshop, 1 Lincoln Plaza, New York, NY 10023.

General Electric Company, Educational Relations, 570 Lexington Ave., New York, NY 10022.

Flat Pictures

American Museum of Natural History, Central Park West at 79th St., New York, NY 10024.

Artex Prints, P.O. Box 70, Westport, CT 06880.

Audio-Visual Enterprises, 911 Laguna Rd., Pasadena, CA 91105.

Creative Educational Society, 123 S. Broad Street, Mankato, MN. 56001.

Demco Educational Corporation, P.O. Box 1488, Madison, WI 53701.

Denoyer-Geppert Company, 5235 Ravenswood Ave., Chicago, IL 60640.

Documentary Photo Aids, P.O. Box 956, Mt. Dora, FL 32757.

The Fideler Company, 31 Ottawa Ave., N.W., Grand Rapids, MI 49501.

Friendship Press, 475 Riverside Dr., New York, NY 10027.

Hammond, Inc., 515 Valley St., Maplewood, NJ 07040.

Hi-Worth Pictures, P.O. Box 6, Altadena, CA 91001.

Instructor Publications, Dansville, NY 14437.

Jam Handy Organization, 2843 E. Grand Blvd., Detroit, MI 48211.

Library Services, 42 Dartmouth St., Malden, MA 02148.

McGraw-Hill Book Company, 1221 Avenue of the Americas, New York, NY 10020.

National Aeronautics and Space Administration (NASA), Washington, D.C. 20546.

New York Graphic Society Ltd., 140 Greenwich

Ave., Greenwich, CT 06830. (Fine arts reproduction.)

A. J. Nystrom & Company, A Div. of Carnation, 3333 Elston Ave., Chicago, IL 60618.

Popular Science Publishing Company, Audio-Visual Div., 355 Lexington Ave., New York, NY 10017.

Rand McNally & Company, Education Div., P.O. Box 7600, Chicago, IL 60680.

Society for Visual Education, 1345 W. Diversey Parkway, Chicago, IL 60614.

United Nations, Public Inquiries Unit, Dept. of Public Information, New York, NY 10017.

Graphic Supplies

Adhesives

Addressograph-Multigraph Corporation, Charles Bruning Div., 1834 Walden Office Square, Schaumburg IL 60172.

Bell and Howell Company, 6800 McCormick Rd., Chicago, IL 60645.

Brandywine Photo Chemical Co., Inc., P.O. Box 298, Avondale, PA 19311.

Brooks Manufacturing Company, 11333 Williamson Rd., P.O. Box 41195, Cincinnati, OH 45241.

Daige Products, 160 Denton Ave., New Hyde Park, NY 11040. (Daige Speedcote wax coaters & adhesive wax.)

Lea AV Service, 182 Audley Dr., Sun Prairie, WI 53590. (Bulletin Board Styx.)

Letro-Stik Company, 3721 Broadway, Chicago, IL 60613 (Letro-Stik).

Charts and graphs

Aero Service, Div. of Western Geophysical Co. of America, 4219 Van Kirk St., Philadelphia, PA 19135.

American Forest Products Industries, 1619 Mass. Ave., N.W., Washington, DC 20036.

American Museum–Hayden Planetarium, 81st St. and Central Park West, New York, NY 10024.

Clay-Adams, 1299 Webro Rd., Parsippany, NJ 07054.

The Conference Board, 845 3rd Ave., New York, NY 10022.

Eye Gate House, 146-01 Archer Ave., Jamaica, NY 11435.

Forest Service, U.S. Dept. of Agriculture, South Bldg., Washington, D.C. 20250.

Graphics Institute, 42 W. 39th St., New York, NY 10018.

Public Relations Staff, General Motors Corporation, General Motors Bldg. 1-101, 3044 West Grand Blvd., Detroit, MI 48202.

National Forum Developmental Guidance Series, c/o American Guidance Service, Inc., Publishers' Bldg, Circle Pines, MI 55014.

Ward's Natural Science Establishment, Inc., 3000 E. Ridge Rd., Rochester, NY 14603.

Coloring and shading materials

Bourges Color Corp., 20 Waterside Plaza, New York, NY 10010.

Cello-Tak Manufacturing, 35 Alabama Ave., Island Park, NY 11558.

Chartpak, One River Rd., Leeds, MA 01053 (Con-tak).

Craftint Manufacturing Company, 18501 Euclid Ave., Cleveland, OH 44112 (Craf-tone).

Mico/Tape Div. of C-Thru Ruler Company, 12032 Vose St., N. Hollywood, CA 91605.

Peerless Color Laboratories, 11-13 Diamond Place, Rochester, NY 14609.

Graphic tapes

Chartpak, One River Rd., Leeds, MA 01053.

Demco Educational Corporation, P.O. Box 1488, Madison, WI 53701.

Graphic Products Corporation, Rolling Meadows, IL 60008 (Flexiline).

Mico/Tape Div. of C-Thru Ruler Company, 12032 Vose St., N. Hollywood, CA 91605.

Laminators

Cam-Lox Media, P.O. Box 366, Redondo Beach, CA 90277.

Laminex, Inc., Matthews, NC 28105.

Mounting materials

Brooks Manufacturing Company, 11333 Williamson Rd., P.O. Box 41195, Cincinnati, OH 45241.

Cam-Lox Media, P.O. Box 366, Redondo Beach, CA 90277.

Demco Educational Corporation, P.O. Box 1488, Madison, WI 53701.
SOS/Photo-Cine-Optics, 315 W. 43rd St., New York, NY 10036.
Union Rubber & Asbestos Company, 232 Allen St., P.O. Box 1040, Trenton, NJ 08606.

Posters

Argus Communications, 7440 Natchez, Niles, IL 60648.
American Dental Association, 211 East Chicago Ave., Chicago, IL 60611.
Cunard Line, 555 Fifth Ave., New York, NY 10017.
Food and Agriculture Organization of the United Nations, Liaison Office for North America, 1776 F Street, NW, Washington, DC 20437.
National Safety Council, 425 N. Michigan Ave., Chicago, IL 60611.
Spenco Medical Corporation, P.O. Box 8113, Waco, TX 76710.

Lettering

Lettering equipment

Dick Blick Company, P.O. Box 1267, Galesburg, IL 61401.
Carter's Ink Company, 239 First St., Cambridge, MA 02142.
Chartpak, One River Rd., Leeds, MA 01053.
E. Dietzgen Corporation, 2425 N. Sheffield Ave., Chicago, IL 60614.
Faber-Castell Corporation, P.O. Box 330, Lewisburg, TN 37091.
Keuffel & Esser Company, 20 Whippany Rd., Hoboken, NJ 07960.
Koh-i-noor Rapidograph, Inc., 100 North St., Bloomsburg, NJ 08804.
Letterguide Company, 4247 O St., Lincoln, NB 68510.
Mark-Tex Corporation, 161 Coolidge Avenue, Englewood, NJ 07631.
Showcard Machine Company, 320 W. Ohio, Chicago, IL 60610.
Varigraph, Inc., P.O. Box 690, Madison, WI 53701.
Wood-Regan Instrument Company, 184 Franklin Ave., Nutley, NJ 07110 (Wrico).

Letters

Arthur Brown & Bros., 2 West 46th St., New York, NY 10036.
Artype, Inc., 345 East Terra Cotta Ave., Crystal Lake, IL 60014.
Cello-Tak Manufacturing, 35 Alabama Ave., Island Park, NY 11558.
Chartpak, Inc., Leeds, MA 01053 (Deca-dry).
Demco Educational Corporation, P.O. Box 1488, Madison, WI 53701.
Demp-Nock Company, 21433 Mound Rd., Warren, MI 48090.
Graphic Arts Center Div., Nax-Dar Company, Inc., 1534 W. 7th St., Los Angeles, CA 90052.
Graphic Products Corporation, 3601 Edison Place, Rolling Meadows, IL 60008.
The Holes-Webway Company, Webway Park, St. Cloud, MN 56301.
Mitten Designer Letters, 85 Fifth Ave., New York, NY 10003.
Redikut Letter Company, 12617 S. Prairie Ave., Hawthorne, CA 90250.
Stik-a-Letter Company, 1787 So. Iris Lane, Escondido, CA 92026.
The Tablet & Ticket Company, 11021 W. Adams St., Chicago, IL 60607.

Photographic Equipment

Lighting

Brewster Corporation, 50 River St., Old Saybrook, CT 06475.
General Electric Company, Lamp Business Div., Nela Park, Cleveland, OH 44112.
Mole-Richardson Company, 937 N. Sycamore Ave., Hollywood, CA 90038.
Smith-Victor Corporation, Griffith, IN 46319.
Westinghouse Electric Corporation, Lamp Div., 1 Westinghouse Plaza, Bloomfield, NJ 07003.

Still cameras

AIC Photo, Inc., 168 Glen Cove Rd., Carle Pl., NY 11514.
Bell & Howell Company, 7100 McCormick Rd., Chicago, IL 60645.
Charles Beseler Company, 8 Fernwood Rd., Florham Park, NJ 07932.

Eastman Kodak Company, 343 State St., Rochester, NY 14650.

Graflex Div., Singer Education Systems, 3750 Monroe Ave., Rochester, NY 14603 (Graflex.)

Karl Heitz, Inc., 979 Third Ave., New York, NY 10022.

Honeywell, Inc., Photographic Div., 5501 S. Broadway, Littleton, CO 80120.

E. Leitz, Inc., Rockleigh, NJ 07647.

Minolta Corporation, 101 Williams Dr., Ramsey, NJ 07446.

Polaroid Corporation, Cambridge, MA 02139.

3 Three-Dimensional Teaching Materials

Objectives

To enable you to do the following:

1. List five advantages of models and specimens as teaching devices.
2. Demonstrate the effective use of three-dimensional materials in a teaching situation.
3. Identify useful sources of 3-D materials for a particular subject and grade.
4. Discriminate between learning situations in which 3-D materials are of significant value and those in which they are not.
5. Plan an effective teaching display using 3-D materials.
6. Identify and explain four unique and significant properties of outdoor learning laboratories.

Things in the real world always have three dimensions. We sense this from infancy. When we look at flat pictures of familiar things our minds add the depth we know is there. When things are unfamiliar, the process of judging depth from pictures becomes more difficult, and three-dimensional teaching materials may be necessary.

We use our physical senses almost constantly in interpreting our surroundings, in refining our understanding of things, and in acquiring new knowledge. Experience is an important factor in determining the amount of sensory information we need about something. For teachers the best course is usually to assume that students' experience is limited and that even fairly sophisticated learners can benefit from "hands on" learning. Much of the weakness of educational approaches based on lectures and reading—particularly where physical phenomena are involved—derives from the frequently erroneous assumption that students have enough experience to visualize things without help. The approach to instructional planning outlined in Chapter 1 avoids this pitfall by first requiring you to identify the stage of development each learner has reached. Only when you have decided what students are presently capable of, can you determine what new goals to set for them, and the most practical means of getting the behavioral response you want. To put it another way, we choose teaching materials because of what they communicate, and how. We put together a team of several types of appropriate materials, and we use it to provide a particular learning experience. When sensory experiences are called for, we try to supply them.

Social studies teachers, for example, need to bring realism to descriptions of far places—mountains, plains, deserts, and jungles; people and customs of long ago; and the trade, industry, agriculture, and government in the many sections of our own country. They can draw on a great wealth of printed materials, and they use them extensively; but to give added meaning to what their pupils read, they use films, maps, field trips, and other devices that make learning experiences more lifelike.

Of course, many things are difficult to understand, even when we observe them firsthand. One can visit a power plant without gaining much understanding of how the generators work. One can watch a diesel locomotive move a train without having any idea of how it operates, and one can observe the moon for a lifetime without understanding its phases. The operation of some things, like a pump, a generator, or an engine, cannot be determined from examining their exterior. We must look inside them to see how they work, and even then they may be baffling. The solar system can be seen to some extent, but it is too vast too comprehend from direct observation alone. Teachers must modify direct experience in such cases to help their pupils learn. One way of doing this is by using three-dimensional teaching materials.

TYPES OF THREE-DIMENSIONAL MATERIALS

Models

A model is a recognizable three-dimensional likeness of a real thing. Models may represent things that are very large, like the earth or the

Figure 3.1 Models can facilitate understanding of a range of concepts from simple to advanced, as here, with a molecular structure model.

solar system, or things that are very small, like an atom. They may represent an inanimate object, such as a mountain, a monument, or a mine shaft, or a living organism such as a paramecium, an elephant, or a man. They may represent something as intricate as a jet engine, a nuclear-powered submarine, or a spacecraft, or something as simple as an elementary counting device. They may be complete in every detail or simplified.

Why models are so effective. Models are effective teaching devices for several reasons:

Models are three-dimensional. As we have already remarked, most objects have three visible dimensions; that is, they have a perceptible thickness as well as height and width. Depth is one of the characteristics of models that contributes significantly to their realism. If the depth or thickness of something is unimportant to comprehension, a model is probably unnecessary. A picture or chart may serve as well and may be easier to get. Models, however, can greatly enhance learning. Working with them makes it easier for students to understand the parts of the eye and other body mechanisms.

Models can reduce or enlarge objects to an observable size. Even from a high-flying jet we can see only a small portion of the earth's surface. Astronauts can see much more, but even they can view only part of the planet at a time. A globe, small though it is, enables us to picture the whole earth without difficulty. Conversely, the greatly enlarged model of an anopheles mosquito in Figure 3.2 enables Indian children to understand the enemy in their country's war against malaria.

Ideally, a model should be large enough to be readily visible to a whole class. Frequently, however, cost and storage problems make it necessary to use somewhat smaller models.

Models can provide interior views of objects. A cutaway model of a human tooth reveals layers of enamel and dentine and a nerve, which otherwise would be difficult to visualize. The rapidly spinning parts of a generator, a steam turbine, or an automobile engine are completely enclosed, but simplified models with removable sides make it possible to see how they work. A model like that in Figure 3.3 helps an industrial arts teacher show details of the construction of a house that are normally not seen.

Models can simplify complex objects. As you lift the hood of an automobile, the impression you receive is apt to be confusing because of the intricate array of wires, belts, hoses, and accessories that confront you, in addition to the engine itself. But such a look may be more revealing if you have studied a simplified model of the engine. Many complex mechanisms can be readily explained with the help of simplified models.

Models can accent important features. Color can be used in models to serve two purposes. The first is to identify important or related parts. The second is to make it clearer how a thing operates. In addition, color often makes models more eye-catching and attractive.

In algebraic models, color enables students to trace what happens when sums are squared and cubed. In anatomy models, colors make it easier to see organs, musculature, circulating systems, and the like. The colors used may be natural (which is desirable in some cases), but more often they are made brighter or otherwise altered for the sake of visibility. For example, in anatomy models arteries are generally bright red and veins bright blue, though actually there is no difference in the color of these blood vessels and very little difference in the color of the blood within them. Parts of a model that

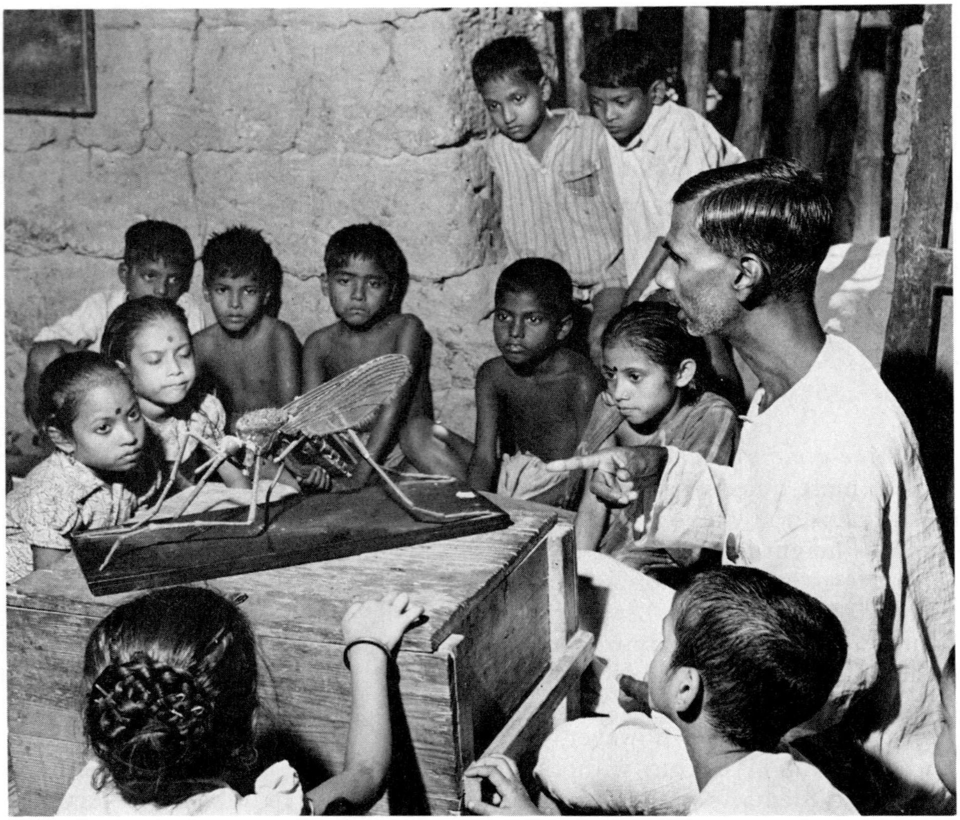

Figure 3.2 Models such as this make it possible for a group to study very small objects or specimens without a microscope.

are not essential to understanding its workings are often shown in muted colors.

Varied surface textures are also used to differentiate parts of a model. The pistons and other moving parts in a cutaway model of an engine may be chrome-plated for better visibility, whereas other areas may be left unplated and unpolished. Rough and smooth textures on relief maps have a special significance. Texture is also important in certain models used in anatomy and biology.

Models can be created in class. It would be wrong to leave you with the impression that, to be useful, models must be complex and expensive. Many useful models can be made rather easily from paper, papier-mâché, wood scraps, wire coathangers, and other common materials. For example, the "home-made" papier-mâché volcano in Figure 3.4 erupts convincingly, using ammonium dichloride crystals as fuel for the volcano. The crystals burn slowly, spitting sparks several inches high, emitting smoke, and spreading dark ashes down the sides of the cone.

Students can make small weather vanes, anemometers, and similar models from scratch. They can also learn from constructing inexpensive commercial models, which are particularly

Figure 3.3 This teacher-made model is used to show key elements in the construction of a frame house. What are the particular benefits of such a model in an industrial arts class?

valuable because with them it is practical for pupils to make models of quite complex organisms and structures, such as molecules, cells, and motors.[1]

Models can often be assembled and disassembled. The value of models in instruction lies not only in their realism, but also in the fact that they can be touched. Particularly in the case of young learners, touching things is often vital to understanding them.[2] The anatomy model in Figure 3.5 can be taken apart so that each part can be examined individually. Moreover, fitting each part back in its proper position gives the student a degree of familiarity with the structure of the human body that is difficult to achieve in any other way.

[1] See the references section, particularly the articles by Carboni, Hyer and Young, Kniskern, Larson, and Scuorzo, for more suggestions on model making.

[2] See Jean Piaget, *The Child's Conception of Physical Causality* (Totowa, N.J.: Littlefield, Adams, 1960), pp. 272–273, 281–287.

Specimens

Speciments are objects that are representative of a group or class of similar objects. There is little point in using a model if the real thing can be brought to the classroom and if it is not too complex to understand. (See Figure 3.6.) You would not, for example, use models of Indian arrowheads, tools, and cooking utensils if you could secure samples instead. Models and specimens should supplement each other.

When objects are removed from their normal setting so that they can be studied, they may appear less real than they do in nature. A mounted hawk in a display case filled with mounted birds loses some of its realism even if it is a good example of taxidermy. Obviously, however, this limitation of classroom specimens is much less important than the advantage of being able to examine them at close range and in detail.

Instructional uses of specimens. There are significant advantages in using actual specimens in the classroom. First, even though they are removed from their normal surroundings, they are real. This tends to make the learning situation more concrete, more authentic, and more interesting. An opportunity to observe chicks hatching firsthand, for example, can provide an unforgettable experience for young students. (See Figure 3.7.) Second, specimens make it possible to study birds, insects, and plants close up without traveling to their natural habitats, which is often impossible or impractical. Finally, a collection of similar objects makes possible comparisons that could not be made if each object had to be seen separately in nature. For instance, imagine how long it would take to accumulate from field observations the essen-

(*b*)

(*a*) (*c*)

Figure 3.4 The specific learning objectives for which models are used vary according to grade levels. Combinations of 3-D and flat displays can often supplement and reinforce one another, as in this case.

tial information about minerals that can be gained from a collection of rocks.

Most children are avid collectors, and teachers can sometimes channel this natural interest into useful learning experiences. The objects and specimens pupils collect can be used to advantage in teaching in many ways. The following list gives only a sampling of such materials.

1. For science classes: cocoons; rock collections; plants and flowers; fish, mice, worms, and other small animals (see Figure 3.8); different kinds of coal, oil, and other fuels; samples of ore; seashells; a telegraph key, radio set, doorbell, or telephone; dry cells and storage batteries.
2. For social studies classes: locally manufactured products; period costumes; relics and souvenirs (as of political campaigns); coins and stamps; fuels; raw materials such as cotton, wool, flax, ores, and grains; early American utensils, toys, tools, furniture, spinning wheels, pictures, and books; folk art materials such as those in Figure 3.9.
3. For English classes: period costumes, clothing and relics, letters and manuscripts, musi-

Figure 3.5 Learning how body parts fit together can be fascinating; 3-D models make it much easier to see what goes where.

cal instruments, fabrics, stage props, tapestries, a speaker's podium and microphone, printing type and layouts.

4. For mathematics classes: slide rules, micrometers, vernier scales, and other measuring instruments; sextants, compasses, timepieces, and navigation charts; bottles and other containers for measuring volumes; coins; drafting tools, such as dividers, T-squares, and triangles; identical familiar objects for instruction in addition, subtraction, division, and multiplication.
5. For home economics classes: fabrics and sewing equipment; foods and utensils; period costumes to show trends in design; raw fibers, such as cotton, wool, flax, and silk; wallpaper sample books; paint and papering tools; table settings.

Mock-ups

A mock-up is generally an operating model of something, usually full scale, that students can work on or with. Mock-ups may or may not be similar in appearance to the real thing. In some mock-ups, some parts may be purposely left out in order to focus attention on others.

Figure 3.6 These children are learning what an ancient urn really looks like.

Instructional uses of mock-ups. Simple mock-ups are frequently used by kindergarten and primary-grade teachers who have pupils build a grocery store, a flower shop, or a railroad train out of blocks or cardboard cartons. (See Figure 3.10.) The purpose of these activities may be to train the children in cooperative activity, develop reading readiness, or introduce elementary number concepts.

A useful mock-up for industrial arts classes has all the elements necessary for the lead-in

Figure 3.7 When the real thing is available, it may provide the best learning experience possible. What do you think these children will learn from watching eggs hatch?

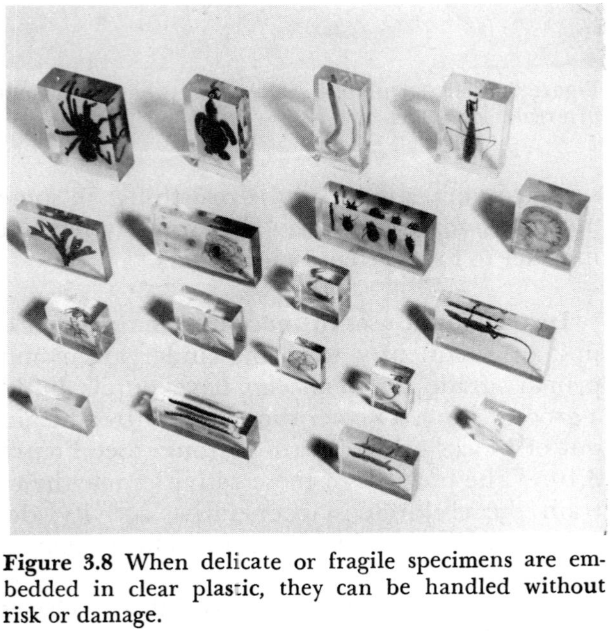

Figure 3.8 When delicate or fragile specimens are embedded in clear plastic, they can be handled without risk or damage.

wiring of a house on one panel. Placing these various elements on one panel makes it possible to show students the complete installation, parts of which are normally separated by a floor and walls. Thus they can see quickly just how the installation should be done.

Mock-ups like those in Figure 3.11 are often used in driver training classes.

Dioramas

Dioramas are three-dimensional scenes, often in miniature, in which models of objects and figures appear in a natural setting. Their universal appeal is well known to everyone who has seen them in museums, in advertising displays, or in classrooms. The diorama is usually set up on a miniature stage with a group of objects and figures in the foreground, blended into a painted, realistic background. (See Fig-

Figure 3.9 Materials from a kit on Japanese folk art circulated in Los Angeles elementary and secondary schools. Such materials add an important dimension to students' understanding of cultures other than their own. (Some 200 kits on various subjects are used in Los Angeles schools.)

ure 3.12.) The objects in a diorama are seldom made to scale. A building, for example, will be made to look smaller at the far end in order to exaggerate the impression of depth. Thus as you look *down* at the diorama, a street may seem too narrow at the far end. This is one of the methods used to achieve *perspective,* which is essential to any representation of depth. Figures of diminishing sizes and exaggerated perspective can produce an effect of considerable depth in a remarkably small space.

Instructional uses of dioramas. Modern museums make extensive use of dioramas to show distant places and historical periods. Teachers in schools in the vicinity of such museums are well aware of the vast educational potential of dioramas. Even where such museums are not available, the advantages of dioramas need not be lost. Good dioramas can be constructed by students from easily available, inexpensive materials. Paper leaves dipped in stained wax are a good way of representing some kinds of tropical foliage, fine sawdust stained green will do for grass, the furrows in a plowed field can be indicated by running a comb over a bed of wet clay, and pieces of green rubber sponges can be used for the foliage of shrubs and trees.[3]

[3] Additional suggestions for constructing dioramas are illustrated in the film *How to Make and Use a Diorama* and the filmstrip *The Diorama as a Teaching Aid.* (See the media references at the end of this chapter.)

Figure 3.10 Precise realism is of little or no importance when young children are building their own house of boxes and boards, but 3-D is important to give their imaginations full sway.

Figure 3.11 Driver-trainer simulators of this type are highly effective for driver education. As students respond to filmed problems, their responses, including their reaction time, are recorded electronically. At what point or points in a training program would such trainers be valuable?

One of the benefits of constructing dioramas is that they provide the teacher with an interesting way to evaluate what pupils have learned. To plan and complete a diorama requires both knowledge and skill. Facts and concepts that might otherwise remain vague must be thought about and drawn on to create a realistic effect. Making a diorama is an excellent source of creative involvement in learning.

Natural Materials in Outdoor Laboratories

An outdoor laboratory is an area on or adjacent to a school site used for studies of aquatic, terrestrial, or geological environments. The importance of "land for learning" is underlined by the following quotation from a 1964 report on conservation:

> Due to the encouragement of far-sighted school board members and superintendents, school sites are becoming larger—increasing from a corner lot just off the village square or an acre in the corner of a cow pasture in a rural neighborhood to 20, 30, or 40 acres and even more in some instances. This space has rich potential for outdoor laboratories in which plant and animal life can be studied. Yet in far too many school districts, these potential laboratories are underdeveloped and unused, while pupils in classrooms a few hundred yards away pore over dry, stale subject matter pertaining to rocks and plants and wind and rain in outdated books or pamphlets.[4]

[4] *Conservation in the Peoples' Hands* (Arlington, Va.: American Association of School Administrators Yearbook, 1964), pp. 294, 296.

Figure 3.12 This diorama of otters in their natural habitat is taken from an actual setting in Michigan. The area represented is over a mile in depth. Note how well it is reproduced here in a space only a few feet deep through techniques that exaggerate the depth of the diorama. Actual materials in the foreground are cleverly blended with painted but highly realistic background.

Under the leadership of Dr. Russell Wilson of the University of Michigan, many Michigan schools have established outdoor learning laboratories. For example, in two districts there are newly built, biologically valuable ponds within walking distance of the high school buildings; the Ann Arbor school system has systematically laid out and planted nature trails; other systems have developed criteria for choosing school sites, that are rich in natural learning resources—trees, shrubs, small mammals, birds, and streams or ponds.[5] (See Figure 3.13.)

In addition to ponds and bogs and woodlots where a variety of biological specimens and phenomena can be studied, Wilson suggests the following very useful outdoor displays:

[5] Russell E. Wilson and June S. Wilson, "School Site Development," unpublished report on the Title III Project, Croton-on-Hudson, N.Y. (August 1968), p. 2.

Figure 3.13 The spark that fires the mind of a future scientist may come from examining a plant; it may come from studying tracks in the snow; it may come from gathering insect specimens in the woods or noting the growth of algae in ponds. Studying the real world firsthand in outdoor laboratories can have significant benefits for both learners and teachers. What are two of these benefits? How might you take advantage of them?

1. Bench marks. A bench mark indicating the latitude, longitude, elevation, township, section, and range of a site can be useful in social studies, mathematics, and science classes.
2. Base lines. A surveyed, straight, north-south or east-west line at least 1000 feet long can be used as a base line for mapping exercises, range finding, pacing, and similar purposes. The line should be divided into marked 100-foot intervals, with one of the end intervals subdivided into 10-foot units.
3. Rock walls. A rock wall, possibly a retaining wall, can be constructed containing a gradational pattern of rocks. (See Figure 3.14.) The specimens should be large, cut and trimmed but unpolished (except in the building stone section, which should contain polished examples obtained from a local monument maker).
4. Boulder scatter fields. Large, native, uncut boulders can be set on gravel or crushed stone.
5. Sundials. Large sundials can be designed to fit the decor of the school.
6. Foucault pendulums. The Foucault pendulum provides visible evidence of the rotation of the earth and needs a support about 52 feet high. Because most schools do not have ceilings this high, such a device, if it is constructed at all, usually must be outdoors. If it is constructed outside, however, it should be sheltered from the wind as much as possible.

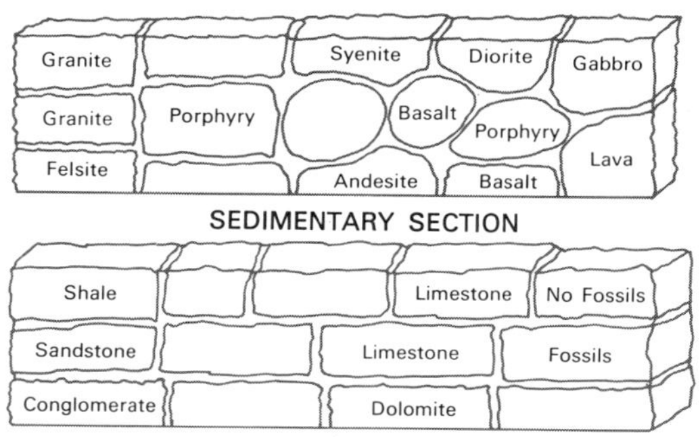

Figure 3.14 To save time and energy, we can sometimes "improve" on nature by bringing examples of her handiwork together in one place, as in a rock wall that contains examples of all the principal rocks of a region. There should usually be separate sections of igneous, sedimentary, and metamorphic rocks, plus a section of polished building stones. In mountainous areas, an additional structure can show ripple marks, joints, faults, folds, geodes, concretion, and other types of mountain formations.

7. Compass roses. A large compass rose can be inset in a school playground or located on a nature trail.
8. Dynamic water basins. Artificial basins 30 feet by 30 inches can be used to study many active geologic processes, such as sedimentation sequences and rates and erosion. Half of such a basin should have a constant 2-foot depth; the other half should be graded from 1 foot to the surface. (See Figure 3.15*a*.) A valve to regulate the water level and a drain are essential.
9. Erosion slopes. An erosion slope can be divided into compartments 3 feet wide and 6 feet long. There should be a collection trough at the base. (See Figure 3.15*b*.) The materials in each compartment (sand, loam, clay, grass, ground covers) can be varied for different experiments. The collection trough allows students to determine

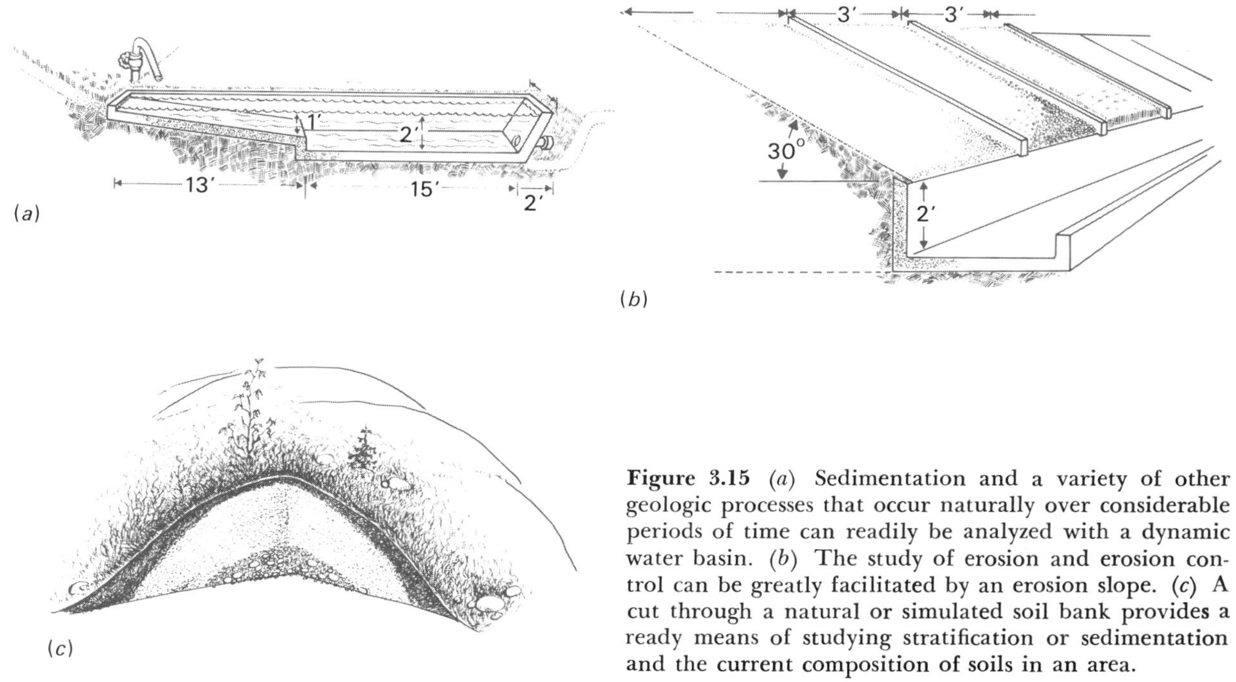

Figure 3.15 (*a*) Sedimentation and a variety of other geologic processes that occur naturally over considerable periods of time can readily be analyzed with a dynamic water basin. (*b*) The study of erosion and erosion control can be greatly facilitated by an erosion slope. (*c*) A cut through a natural or simulated soil bank provides a ready means of studying stratification or sedimentation and the current composition of soils in an area.

the amount of runoff, soil loss, and so forth. Conservation techniques can thus be studied under natural conditions.

10. Soil profiles. Cutting through a section of a hill permits the study of mass-wasting talus slopes and erosion patterns, as well as the soil profile revealed. A 5- or 10- foot bank should be sufficient. (See Figure 3.15*c*.)
11. Footprint areas. Dinosaur tracks in concrete can form part of a science terrace or patio. A collection of tracks of native animals is useful in biology as well as paleontology. The tracks should be varied to show animals walking, running, and leaping.
12. Standard weather stations. A complete weather station can be purchased, or various instruments can be collected and a shelter for them constructed as a class project.

Outdoor displays like these can be of keen interest to both young and old. Like sports facilities and playgrounds, they should be open to the public when schools are not in session. Although it would be more difficult and expensive, urban versions of outdoor laboratories might be created even in the asphalt jungles of large cities.[6]

Museum Exhibits and Materials

Until the late nineteenth century, museums were primarily repositories for indiscriminate and somewhat disorganized collections of many kinds. Since then, however, they have changed radically and have, in fact, become a significant force on the educational scene. Museums today are not only places to see exhibits on a great variety of subjects, but also valuable sources of instructional materials. The Los Angeles County Museum, for instance, sends kits of materials to local schools. The Washington State Museum at the University of Washington performs a similar service. A number of museums, such as the Milwaukee County Museum, not only produce and distribute visual materials and publications, but also present fascinating programs for students. Modern museums try hard to take their programs to the public as well as to attract the public to their exhibits.

There are literally thousands of museums across the United States. Most of these concentrate on some type of art or historical or scientific materials. Some—such as the Museum of Modern Art in New York; the National Gallery of Art in Washington, which specializes in the art of the Western world; the Museum of Science and Industry in Chicago and similar museums that focus on the applied sciences; natural history museums; historical museums; children's museums; folk museums; marine museums; and anthropological museums—are of particular interest to schools. The beautiful Museo Nacional de Antropología in Mexico City (Figure 3.16) is recognized as the outstanding museum of its type in the world. Exceptional display techniques are used, and thousands of people, including many groups of schoolchildren, visit each week.

The modern functions of museums. Early museums, as we have noted, were conceived of primarily as places where collections could be observed and perhaps studied by a select few. The modern museum, however, specifically seeks to "acquire and study objects of historic and aesthetic value which serve to illustrate certain developments and trends, and from these to select objects and exhibit them . . . to inspire or educate the public."[7]

[6] For suggestions for improving and using the city school environment, see "The City: A Laboratory for Learning," *Conservation Education* (Fall 1964), Conservation Foundation, 1250 Connecticut Ave., N.W., Washington, D.C. 20036. The foundation also publishes the monthly *Conservation Foundation Letter*, available on request.

[7] Hans Huth, "Museums and Art Galleries," *Encyclopaedia Britannica*, vol. 15 (1960), p. 991.

(a)

(b)

(c)

Figure 3.16 The Museo Nacional de Antropología in Mexico City (*a*) combines an exceptional exterior design with outstanding displays and exhibits. Note the space and settings accorded the huge round Aztec calendar on the wall (*b*) and the dramatic use of outside display space (*c*).

The important words here are "illustrate certain developments and trends." Most museums work closely with schools, given the opportunity, and try in every way to make their exhibits interesting to the general public. But they recognize that to be of lasting value, museum experiences must *select* and *interpret* exhibits with regard to man's basic interests and needs. Thus we often see displays on such subjects as the conquest of space, pollution, soil erosion, population control, highway safety, and economic development that show humanity's relation to nature as well as to history. The Museum of Science and Industry in Chicago, the Oregon Museum of Science and Industry in Portland, and science museums of various types in Los Angeles, Boston, Philadelphia, and other cities make a determined effort to interpret the applications of science to industry *in terms of* people's physical, social, and cultural needs.

The result of all these activities has been a growing interest in museums and educational exhibits of all kinds. A major impetus to this interest has also come from world's fairs, such as Expo '67 and the New York World's Fair, and from such places as Disneyland. The millions of visitors to these justifiably famous attractions find them a compelling combination of entertainment and education. The Bicentennial Hall of Presidents, Monsanto's 360° theater tour of "America the Beautiful," RCA's Space Mountain, and G. E.'s Carousel of Progress at Disney World are only a few of the exciting and unforgettable learning experiences they provide for people of all ages. (See Figure 3.17.) Not only are these productions imaginative, but they take full advantage of modern media and technology to achieve the optimum sensory, emotional, and intellectual involvement of their audience.

Figure 3.17 "One nation under God" is the inspirational theme of the Walt Disney World "Magic Kingdom" presentation that includes this Hall of Presidents. Replicas of the 36 presidents of the United States appear on stage together, life-sized and lifelike, speaking to the audience through the patented Disney "Audio-Animatronics" process. (© Walt Disney Productions)

TEACHING WITH THREE-DIMENSIONAL MATERIALS

Selecting 3-D Materials

By this time it should be obvious that three-dimensional materials, like other audiovisual materials, should be used when they can make a unique contribution to a lesson. Three-dimensional materials are more real to the student than pictures because they have depth and substance. They can be seen and handled and sometimes smelled or tasted, providing a more complete perceptual experience.

In learning situations where three dimensions are important, a suitable model, specimen, or mock-up should be used. Real things should be used when possible. (See Figure 3.18.)

In all such situations, one question to be answered is whether the time and effort involved in making a model, mock-up, or diorama is justified. The same question applies, of course, to collecting specimens and preparing displays. It cannot be answered categorically or on the basis of content alone, because, as every experienced teacher knows, the value of such activities to pupils is due partly to the experience they gain in cooperative achievement, the satisfaction they get from accomplishment, and the joy of having their accomplishment recognized by others in a group.

Figure 3.18 Children are shown how to use authentic American Indian tools when they visit an exhibit on Connecticut's Indians at the Museum of Art, Science, and Industry in Bridgeport, Connecticut. A "look and touch" show, "Connecticut's Indians" traces local tribes back to their origins 2000 years ago. Visitors can go into a real wigwam, handle Indian artifacts, and study related exhibits. The lecture is accompanied by a series of color slides.

Using 3-D Materials

Like all instructional materials, three-dimensional teaching tools will not be effective—no matter how suitable they are potentially—unless they are used properly as part of a well-thought-out teaching strategy. There are, however, some basic guidelines for their use.

Be sure everyone can see them. All visual materials being used with a group must be visible; this is particularly true of small models and specimens. Ideally, models should be large enough to be seen easily by everyone in a class

Figure 3.19 Teachers should make sure everyone gets a good, close-up view of models and mock-ups. As this illustration shows, they can be fascinating.

at one time. Though this is often impractical, materials should be large enough for all to observe their general features.

Use 3-D materials with other materials. When you use a model of a flower, for example, to explain pollination to a biology class, you may wish to use a large wall chart to show details. You can then go back and forth between the model and the chart to establish the relationship between parts and functions. At an appropriate point, you may also show an animated film of the fertilization process. Flat pictures may be useful to show the flower in its natural surroundings, and closeup slides of blossoms may be helpful in identifying the principal parts of various flowers. In spring or fall, you can probably bring in some real flowers to show the class. If your school has an outdoor laboratory or a nature trail, you can have your students examine flowers in their natural habitats.

In short, to get the most benefit from models or real things, you should make them part of a *team* of materials, each chosen because it does a particular job well.

Practice using materials before class. Though it may seem rather obvious that teachers should practice using materials before class, teachers sometimes find themselves stumbling through a presentation because they have not thought about each point carefully or have not practiced a demonstration using models and related materials. The more complex the material, the more important it is to practice the demonstration.

Make sure students are aware of the correct size of things. One of the dangers in using three-dimensional materials is that the pupils may get distorted ideas of the actual size of things. A curator of the Milwaukee County Museum, for example, tells the story of an intermediate class studying some Polynesian exhibits. The students were particularly interested in a small-scale diorama of a native village. Actual coins used by the natives were included in the exhibit. The people in the diorama were only a few inches tall, and some of the coins were nearly as large. Perplexed, a number of pupils asked how the natives managed to carry their money around with them!

One way of emphasizing the correct size of objects is by making comparisons with familiar objects. For example, a small model of a large turbine engine can be used in conjunction with a picture in which a workman appears.

Let students examine 3-D materials. Unlike pictures, models, mock-ups, and real things can appear different from every angle and hence should be examined from various points. Moreover, letting students handle a model as well as look at it makes a learning experience more concrete and memorable. Models and specimens that are too fragile or too small to be handled can be mounted in clear plastic to protect them from damage.[8]

Anyone who has seen intermediate-grade pupils making their own models or junior and senior high school pupils concentrating on collections of insects will have little doubt of their ability to handle models and specimens with care. Experience with outdoor laboratories and nature trails confirms the fact that the large majority of students will exercise care in handling plant life and specimens provided for their benefit. Encouraging students to help in the selection of models and specimens and in collecting specimens and objects for use in class should strengthen even more their sense of responsibility for such materials. (See Figure 3.20.)

Store materials when they are not in use. Storage problems frequently lead to classrooms that are cluttered with all kinds of objects,

[8] For directions on simple and effective means of plastic mounting, see Herbert E. Scuorzo, "Embedding Realia in Plastic," *Grade Teacher* (January 1963), pp. 10 ff.

Figure 3.20 This high school student on an archaeological research team is beginning a "dig" on an Indian campsite in Oregon. What else do you think she is learning, besides some basic archaeological techniques?

specimens, and models. At the proper time they are hauled down, dusted off, used, and then put back on the shelf for another semester. Too often these collections are in full view of the students at all times, distracting attention and lessening their effectiveness when they are used for instruction.

Although some materials, such as aquariums, terrariums, and globes, lend themselves well to continuing observation and form a natural part of the classroom environment, most teaching materials are unsuited for this purpose. Enterprising teachers see to it that they are stowed away until the right moment arrives for using them. Not only are "newer" materials more interesting to students, but it is easier to focus their attention on one item if unrelated materials are not visible. Some teachers cover the glass in classroom storage cabinets with colored paper; others ask the art department to use this space for simple, decorative designs that are not distracting. When no storage space is available in the classroom, cartons or boxes may be used to store three-dimensional materials.

SCHOOL DISPLAYS AND EXHIBITS

Three-dimensional materials are widely used in educational displays and exhibits—at parents' nights, hobby shows, and so on. Vocational schools and technical high schools make regular use of displays to show the work done by various departments. Most of the newer elementary and secondary school buildings have built-in display cases in the corridors for educational exhibits during the school year. In all of these, three-dimensional materials play a prominent part.

Conditions for Using 3-D Materials in Displays

Study displays are discussed in detail in Chapter 6. Now is a good time, however, to point out that the effective use of three-dimensional materials in learning displays depends on the following things:

Appropriate balance. The first consideration is the relative importance of the three-dimensional material to the display. If a model or mock-up is to play a featured role, it should have a prominent position—but it should not obscure other materials in the display. If several objects and specimens are to be used, they should be arranged in a balanced way.

Design and color. Sound principles of design and color should, of course, be observed in using three-dimensional objects in a school display. These are essentially the same principles discussed in connection with picture quality in Chapter 2—good organization and composition plus an effective choice of colors and the right degree of contrast.

Lighting and motion. Lighting and motion are important features of effective study displays involving three-dimensional materials. Because they are discussed in some detail in a later chapter, we will merely say here that color and lighting go hand in hand in highlighting key features of a display and in attracting attention to it. Moving figures in a diorama or moving parts in a working model can likewise enhance both the attention-getting and interest-holding qualities of displays or exhibits.

Viewer involvement. Any display or exhibit can profit from heightened viewer involvement. Often this can be achieved by having people do something other than merely look at an exhibit. (See Figure 3.21.) Pushing buttons to activate a display or putting on headphones to hear taped explanations are simple actions that involve the viewer in a display. Intricate mechanisms like those sometimes used in large exhibitions, such as World's Fairs, or in museums are not required.

The fact that people learn more from active involvement in an exhibit was vividly demonstrated by people in two suburban Cleveland communities who cooperated to build a model "safety town" in a school playground. They constructed small buildings, laid out streets, bought pedal-type cars and trucks, and even supplied a policeman to help with safety instruction for kindergartners. Some children "drove" around the town while others were

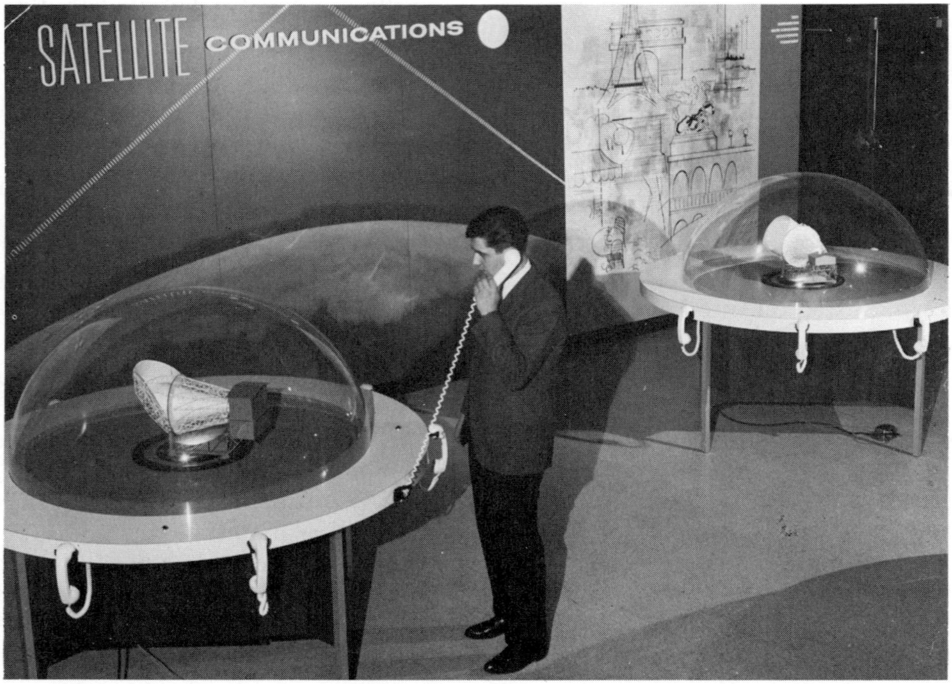

Figure 3.21 Participation is frequently the name of the game in effective professional exhibits. As far as is practical, the principle of viewer involvement should also be used in school exhibits and displays.

taken around as pedestrians by their teachers. Then the groups reversed roles. All learned their safety lessons so well that there was a sharp reduction in the number of traffic accidents involving children.[9]

SUMMARY

Much of the effectiveness of direct, concrete learning experiences comes from the fact that such experiences involve the use of the intellect and the physical senses. Although providing firsthand experience with content is impractical in many teaching situations, important segments of reality can be brought into the classroom by means of models, objects and specimens, mock-ups, and dioramas.

These three-dimensional materials can help to make the learning situation more lifelike and interesting. Furthermore, they are frequently an improvement on reality for teaching purposes. Models of the solar system and of one-celled animals, for example, reduce the vastness of the former and enlarge the microscopic proportions of the latter to a size that can be seen and studied. Cutaway models provide interior views of objects that are not ordinarily possible. Models can also be simplified so that important features stand out clearly, and many have removable parts.

In response to the modern emphasis on ecology and environmental studies, many school systems are providing outdoor laboratories and nature trails where a variety of natural phenomena can be studied firsthand. Museums also provide potentially valuable learning experiences. Their exhibits can bring the past alive, interpret the present, and anticipate the future.

In order for three-dimensional teaching materials to be effective, students must be able to see them clearly and examine them from various angles. Students should also be permitted to handle 3-D materials whenever possible. Teachers must be careful to avoid giving a class a distorted impression of the size of things when models are used, and they should combine a variety of materials to achieve specific instructional objectives. In general, three-dimensional materials should be stored out of sight when they are not being used.

Displays and exhibits for special events offer a good opportunity for students to work with three-dimensional materials and to become creatively involved in the learning process.

ACTIVITIES

1. Get together with four or five other students in your class, and ask your teacher to obtain for you several different models and specimens used for instructional purposes in the local school system. Examine them and discuss their advantages. During the next class session report on the advantages and limitations of each one.
2. Work out a teaching demonstration of up to five minutes involving 3-D materials for a particular subject and grade. Present the demonstration before the class and ask for comments.
3. From the source lists in this chapter and your own research, prepare a list of sources of 3-D materials for a particular subject and grade. Add brief annotations about distinctive items or features.
4. Prepare a list of 10 specific learning objectives for a particular subject and grade, and identify those objectives that 3-D materials would help you to achieve. Be prepared to justify your selections.
5. Working with a small group of other students, select a legitimate topic for a study exhibit involving 3-D materials. Work out

[9] "Teach Tots Safety with a Model Town," *School Management* (August 1962), pp. 42–43.

a design for the exhibit on a large piece of heavy paper and present it in class.

6. Again working with a small group of other students, visit a nearby outdoor laboratory, if one is available, or write or phone for information on unique learning experiences available through outdoor laboratories in various subjects and at various grade levels. Do a brief report on the subject in class.

REFERENCES

PRINT REFERENCES

Carboni, Remo, "Plaster and Burlap—How to Make a Large Landscape Model," *School Arts* (September 1963), pp. 16–17.

David, M., "Great Junk Math Materials," *Instructor* (April 1973), p. 110.

East, Marjorie, *Display for Learning,* 2nd ed. (Washington, D.C.: Association for Educational Communications and Technology, 1968).

Educational Displays and Exhibits (Austin: University of Texas Instructional Media Center, 1965).

Harding, Robert G., "New Dimensions to School-Produced Media," *AV Instruction* (April 1969), p. 65.

Hyer, James E., and Richard G. Young, "Making a Collection of Preserved Animal Specimens," *Grade Teacher* (March 1964), pp. 28–29 ff.

Johnson, D. A., and others, "Using Models as Instructional Aids in the Teaching and Learning of Mathematics," in *National Council of Teachers of Mathematics Yearbook* (1973), pp. 233–296.

Kemp, Jerrold E., *Planning and Producing Audiovisual Materials,* 2d ed. (San Francisco: Chandler, 1968).

Kniskern, Edna Maki, "An Easily Made Cell Model," *American Biology Teacher* (March 1964), pp. 191–192.

Larson, G. Olaf, "Paper Stereomodels," *Journal of Chemical Education* (May 1965), pp. 274–276.

Minor, Ed, and Harvey R. Frye, *Techniques for Producing Visual Instructional Media* (New York: McGraw-Hill, 1970).

Morlan, John E., *Preparation of Inexpensive Teaching Materials* (San Francisco: Chandler, 1963).

Ruby, Doris, *4-D Bulletin Boards That Teach* (Palo Alto, Calif.: Fearon, 1960).

Sanderson, R. T., *Three-Dimensional Teaching of Chemistry* (New York: Van Nostrand Reinhold, 1964).

Scuorzo, Herbert E., "Embedding Realia in Plastic," *Grade Teacher* (January 1963), pp. 10 ff.

Sheppard, D., "A Method for Assessing the Value of Exhibitions," *British Journal of Educational Psychology* (December 1960), pp. 259–265.

Witmeyer, Stanley, "Display Is Visual Communication," *Instructor* (May 1960), pp. 47–50.

MEDIA REFERENCES

Atomic Models, Valence, and the Periodic Table, 16mm film, color, 45 min. University of Iowa, 1962.

The Diorama as a Teaching Aid, 35mm filmstrip, color, 58 frames. Ohio State University, 1957.

How to Make and Use a Diorama, 16mm film, color 20 min. McGraw-Hill, 1956.

How to Make Papier Maché Animals, 16mm film, color, 12 min., BFA Educational Media, 1954.

Models and Realia, series of 8 transparencies from *Instructional Media Transparency Masters—A Series* (of 147), Keuffel and Esser Company, 1969. Exhibits (2 transparencies) are also part of the series.

Museums for School Children, 16mm film, b/w, 21 min. United World Films, 1950.

Relief Models, 16mm film, color, 10 min. David Lipscomb College, 1955.

Simple Exhibit Technique, 35mm filmstrip, color, 40 frames. Ohio State University, 1958.

Successful Exhibit Ideas, 35mm filmstrip, b/w, 81 frames. Pocket Films, 1958.

A Special Set of Models for Introducing Chemistry, 16mm film, color, 45 min. University of Iowa, 1962.

STUDENT PRODUCTION GUIDE REFERENCES

See the *Student Production Guide,* Chapter 3, "Graphics Techniques for Instructional Materials Production," particularly the sections on design and color.

SOURCE REFERENCES

Storage Facilities

Demco Educational Corporation, P.O. Box 1488, Madison, WI 53701.

Plastican Corporation, P.O. Box 157, Butler, NJ 07405.

Plastic Sealing Corporation, 1507 N. Gardner St., Hollywood, CA 90046 (plastic sheet slide holders).

Models

Robert Brunner Div., Cadan Corporation, 635 Madison Ave., New York, NY 10022 (cut-out model of human brain).

Creative Playthings, A Div. of CBS, Edinburg Rd., Cranbury, NJ 08512 (manipulative materials for instructional materials centers and classrooms—grades K–8).

B. F. Goodrich, Koroseal Div., Oak Grove, Marietta, OH 45750 (Koroseal flexible magnetic strips).

Imitation Food Display Company, 197 Waverly Ave., Brooklyn, NY 11205 (models of food).

Louis Paul Jonas Studios, Box 59-A, R.D. 1, Hudson, NY 12534 (miniature animals).

A. J. Nystrom & Company, 3333 Elston Ave., Chicago 18, IL 60618.

Revell, Inc., 4223 Glencoe Ave., Venice, CA 90291.

Silver Burdett Company, 460 So. Northwest Highway, Park Ridge, IL 60068.

Weber-Costello Company, 1900 N. Narragansett Ave., Chicago Heights, IL 60639.

Scientific Materials and Specimens

Central Scientific Company, 2600 S. Kostner Ave., Chicago, IL 60623.

Clay-Adams, 299 Webro Rd., Parsippany, NJ 07054.

Denoyer-Geppert Company, 5235 Ravenswood Ave., Chicago, IL 60640.

Hubbard Scientific Company, P.O. Box 105, Northbrook, IL 60062.

Pacific Bio-Marine Supply Company, P.O. Box 536, Venice, CA 90291.

Sargent-Welch Scientific Company, 7300 N. Linder Ave., Skokie, IL 60076.

Turtox/Cambosco, MacMillan Science Company, 8200 S. Hoyne Ave., Chicago, IL 60620.

United Scientific Company, 216 South Jefferson St., Chicago, IL 60606.

Ward's Natural Science Establishment, 3000 E. Ridge Rd., Rochester, NY 14626.

4 Community Study and Learning

Objectives

To enable you to do the following:

1. Identify the curricular and sociological bases for incorporating community study into the central stream of classroom learning experiences.
2. Identify specific ways in which the six media-related learning tenets described in Chapter 1 are implemented through community study.
3. List and briefly explain six kinds of community study experiences.
4. Select one community study learning experience that relates to your own emerging instructional development plan.
5. Demonstrate your ability to organize this learning experience, using the six-step method described in this chapter.
6. Demonstrate your mastery of the information in this chapter by completing activities 1 and 2 in the activities section.

Among the British Museum's many exhibits is one portraying high points in the lives of modern educators. Among the displays devoted to the work of Comenius, Pestalozzi, Herbart, and Froebel is a quotation that shows the central thread of their beliefs: "The most effective way to help students to become informed about their social and natural environment is to provide for them learning experiences which are real or lifelike, and which are available to them for firsthand scrutiny, questioning, and cognition."

This idea has stood the test of time. During every summer vacation, enormous numbers of young people can be found traveling the world in groups of two, three, or more to see new people, places, and things. Like learners of all ages, they have a natural desire to see for themselves what life is all about.

Although this fundamental fact has long been recognized to varying degrees in the schools, there is a periodic resurgence of interest in its possibilities. During the 1970s there has been a growing interest in providing opportunities for learners to interact directly with elements of the natural and manmade world. This trend has been given impetus by the Elementary Secondary Education Act (old Title III and new Title IV), which encourages school districts to create curriculum plans that foster community study.

School districts have been carrying on many experiments in community study in recent years. Sometimes, faculty members and students have worked together to design courses or projects. For example, at Adlai E. Stevenson High School in Prairie View, Illinois, students were asked what kind of contact with the community they thought would be relevant to their own goals. As a result, invitations were extended to people knowledgeable about space science, banking, the stock market, law, medicine, politics, writing, and the arts to come to the school for rap sessions. (See Figure 4.1.) Field trips were scheduled and some students were given a chance to work as aides or interns. All in all, 3000 students participated in the program.

There was a positive reaction to the program. Parents felt that the regular school program should include a greater use of community resources, work experiences for students, a wider range of electives, and more opportunities for students to choose particular learning experiences. Teachers felt that students developed a greater sense of responsibility, a heightened interest in learning, and wider horizons because of the program. The students enjoyed helping to plan the program. They felt that it gave them freedom, a variety of new experiences, an opportunity to choose for themselves what they would learn, and a sense of community with their teachers.[1]

Though we cannot expect all schools to reorganize immediately to allow students and teachers to plan programs together, to permit flexible scheduling, and to give students the freedom to investigate the community at first hand, some departures from traditional programs must be made if relevancy is to be achieved. With this objective in mind, let us explore briefly the nature and status of some existing community study programs. Commu-

1 "Free-Form Learners," *Nation's Schools* (September 1969), p. 48.

Figure 4.1 These community representatives shown at Adlai E. Stevenson High School in Prairie View, Illinois, are among many who were invited to "come to school" to provide experiences in contemporary living for students. Pupils also left the school to participate in relevant community activities. Do you always consider whether the learning activities you plan are relevant?

nity study is firsthand study of the real world: of manmade things like cities, businesses, and governments; of natural things like rivers, forests, and plains; and of the relations between the two. It provides opportunities for the young to learn by doing, to achieve insight into manmade institutions and natural processes by observing them directly and interacting with them.

COMMUNITY STUDY DEFINED

The terms used to describe the various forms of community study vary widely: It is called environmental education, eco-studies, career education. It includes tours, field trips, excursions, and so on. In many school districts, attempts are being made to transform community study from a casual appendage to the curriculum to that of the central core. Whereas in earlier days a school district might arrange an occasional "Know Your Community" day, during which business and government representatives would come into the school to hold question-and-answer sessions with interested students, this same school district today will be experimenting with community studies at every grade level and in most subject areas.

In this chapter, the term *community study* is used to describe *activities that are integral to a curriculum plan—that part of a formal school program that extends the classroom into the community or brings the community into the classroom to give pupils direct experience with people, places, and events.*

Figure 4.2 Exploring their surroundings is natural to children. This child is learning what is relevant to him.

THE SCOPE OF COMMUNITY STUDY

If teachers and school personnel believe that the central goal of education is to prepare young people to understand the world, is it wise to keep them literally in school until commencement day? When is a child old enough to participate in community activities?

For many years it was accepted that children should learn by sitting quietly at desks arranged in rows while an authority figure—the teacher—gave instructions from the front of the room. This idea has met with some violent challenges in the twentieth century, and for good reason. If we accept what most learning psychologists believe, that firsthand experiences with people and things are a primary source of learning, then we must be willing to reevaluate the learning experiences we provide for young people with this in mind.

Until they enter kindergarten or first grade, children spend most of their time probing, examining, questioning, and experimenting in order to gain some understanding of things in homes, backyards, neighborhoods, and other parts of their environment. They have taken walks and trips with their parents, wandered off with their age-mates, and pulled apart their toys; they have asked endless questions of the grocer, the plumber, or the automobile mechanic. In innumerable ways, they have satisfied their innate curiosity through firsthand observation. (See Figure 4.2.)

Yet when they come to school, these same children, who have spent so much of their lives wiggling, crawling, and exploring, find themselves within the restraining walls of a classroom, confined to chairs, and restricted to those activities prescribed by a teacher. To expect 6-year-olds to conform to the restrictions of a traditional classroom five hours a day, five days a week runs counter to all we know about their mental, emotional, and physical makeup. Older children, too, have a natural need to explore, to be physically and mentally active, and to express themselves through social channels. Yet too often the school—a social setting deliberately provided for children—thwarts rather than fulfills these needs. Such an approach to education is anachronistic, to say the least, when it is followed by those who claim to be students of the nature and needs of children.

Arrangements should be made for pupils to continue their natural exploratory behavior in directed activities. Children should be allowed to pry into every corner of their environment through carefully planned learning experiences. Their schoolroom should include the schoolyard, the town or city in which they live, and the open country beyond. The school day should include talks and visits with postal workers, the police, local merchants, and civil servants and elected officials. Older students should be permitted to range farther afield. Extended stays at school camps, overnight study tours, and visits to nearby governmental agencies, manufacturing plants, and public works projects will help them to understand how society works and the opportunities it provides.

The National Park Service, which has become very concerned about the abuse of the country's parks by campers and other visitors, has put together a program to show young people the causes and effects of pollution and how it can be overcome. The program, which is called National Environment Education Development (NEED), operates in conjunction with traditional courses in science and social studies in the elementary grades and in high school. The basic idea is to present preliminary information on a problem in the schools and follow it up with an actual field trip to a national park. The purpose of the trips is not simply to identify plants and animals; rather, it is to create an attitude—to promote understanding of how we humans use and abuse nature. The program seeks to help young people make value judgments about their environment and show them what impact their own actions can have on it. (See Figure 4.3.)

Figure 4.3 These learners are exploring part of their community "schoolroom." This "aquarium" is more complete than any artificial school aquarium could be, yet specimens from it can be taken indoors for study. To what "subjects" is this kind of activity related? Math? Language arts? Ecology? Are the outcomes cognitive? Affective? How much time should be allowed for it? When?

The traditional concept of the classroom is slowly changing. More and more, it is becoming a base from which occasional forays into the larger world are expected. In the Thomas A. Stewart High School in Peterborough, Ontario, for example, students in grades 11 and 12 can arrange to spend about half their schoolday working in social service agencies in the community—in day-care centers, in city planning departments, in workshops for the handicapped, in schools for exceptional children, and in programs for senior citizens.[2] Plans are under way to expand the program to include studies of the problems of the aging, community uses of cable television, youth employment opportunities, and the like by teams of students supervised by teachers and local professional people. The goal is to give young people an objective view of their community, both the good and the bad, that will lead to constructive action in the present and after graduation.

In some areas, the Girl Scouts' Aide Project provides a preview of vocational and service options for high school girls. Together with their counselor-leaders, participants in the project prepare inventories of their interests and skills and try to identify careers where they would be useful. Next, they conduct a study of community job options. Finally, with the help of school personnel, the girls become volunteer aides in a vocational situation of their choice.

[2] David W. Brison, "Out-of-School Education in the Social Service Sector," *Phi Delta Kappan* (December 1973), p. 237.

For many, the experience is an adventure in self-discovery.[3]

The immediate community often provides opportunities for learning. It is the responsibility of school administrators and teachers to investigate community resources that will give students insight into their world.

THE INQUIRY METHOD AND COMMUNITY STUDY

Education is a search for the truth about natural and man-made things and events. Once learners have decided what it is they wish to know *about*—what their questions are—they learn well through direct observation. In Chapter 1, we talked about the inquiry approach to learning. This is an approach that lends itself well to the kind of participatory education that community study entails.

Community study brings learners to where things are happening. It includes walking trips, automobile or bus trips, hiking or boating trips, stays at school camps or in forests, and, in some cases, extended journeys. All these activities open new vistas for students and encourage them to investigate the world. They develop an enthusiasm for knowledge, for firsthand observation, and for making judgments based on what they see.

Community study can become a valuable lifelong pursuit. Some of the experiences to which you can introduce students of various ages are described in more detail below.

Walking Trips

In the lower grades, it is easy to arrange visits to nearby parks, forests, and zoos and to observe the activities of those in the community who work close by. Walking trips make it possible for pupils to learn about the work of firemen, police, park and arboretum attendants, water supply personnel, zookeepers, and others. Such people often work near a school during the course of their day, and one of them—for example, a telephone lineman or woman—might well arrange to be available for a demonstration of his or her duties and for questioning at a prearranged time.

In the lower grades the buddy system—in which each child is paired off with a dependable fellow student—is one way of getting the members of a class to a place within walking distance of the school. The best position for the teacher is at the rear. Experience will show which children in your own classes can be depended on a lead a column.

Educational sorties into the neighborhood can provide very valuable learning experiences. Frequently, students—and teachers too—are so preoccupied with getting from where they live to school that they entirely overlook the fact that they can learn from the environment through which they pass. It makes much more sense to ask students to study the environment through which they move and to make judgments about it than to read textbook descriptions of a similar environment.

In one junior high school, for example, a group was beginning a unit entitled "Investigating Soil." During a preliminary discussion, the students expressed curiosity about the texture of earth; its chemical composition; the effect of heat, light, and the seasons on soil; and soil fertility. The young people had been thumbing through their books when their teacher asked, "If you could have your choice of ways to find answers to our questions, what would you really like to do?"

There was some talk about going to the library, consulting encyclopedias, and seeing films. Then one student hazarded a daring suggestion: "Maybe we should go out and dig around in the soil—do tests on it." To this

[3] Sarah Ann Bermont, "Options for Senior Girls—What Are the Alternatives?" *Girl Scout Leader* (June 1975), p. 8.

group, the impetus to get out of the schoolroom and into the immediate environment was a natural outgrowth of their questions about a natural thing—the soil.

According to one earth scientist, we should "create instructional tactics and strategies that will enable students to use the resources of their own environment. . . . Instead of asking the student to respond to a textbook abstraction of his environment, [invite] the student to invent the abstractions that describe what he finds around himself."[4] There is a great deal to be learned about soil from books and films, but there is also something to be learned by looking beneath our feet.

It is not always necessary for a class to embark on community research as a group. Students who demonstrate that they are able to assume responsibility can be given opportunities to leave the school grounds alone or in groups of two or three to investigate something of interest, to report what they find, and perhaps to take pictures (Figure 4.4). Needless to say, parental and administrative support for such activities must be secured beforehand.

Figure 4.4 The reasons properties like this are abandoned are found in social studies books. What added insights does actually being there provide for young students as they take visual "notes" on what they see?

Field Study

Field study is the term usually used to describe getting out into the urban or rural neighborhood of the school and observing what goes on there, asking questions or documenting pertinent happenings with audio, video, or photographic equipment.

For example, the Miami, Florida, school district uses the whole of Dade County as a laboratory for students interested in finding out what is happening to the natural environment as a result of man-made "improvements." The Center for Urban Research in Environmental Education (CURES) conducts field trips into the county after students have discussed problems and posed questions.

[4] *Environmental Studies* (September 1, 1970), p. 1.

CURES hopes that raising the consciousness of students about what is happening in their community will result in some constructive action. Junior high school pupils, for example, go to the local airport to measure air pollution and noise levels, they visit housing developments affected by noise and air pollution, and they talk to personnel at the local water purification plant. They even go to a ghost town created by environmental forces. As Georgia Slack points out, "Today's students need to be made aware that as adults they are going to have to grapple with these problems. . . . these are the kinds of problems that don't end with taking the garbage out to the curb or turning on the faucet: they really just begin there."[5]

Another example is the Foxfire Project directed by Eliot Wigginton, a teacher of high school journalism at the Rabun Gap-Nacoochee School in Georgia. The essence of the project is to encourage students to discover their community by interviewing people about things which occurred in the past and are still in evidence today.

Students first carried on word of mouth interviews, but as events unfolded were able to acquire tape recorders and video recorders as well as cameras to document what they saw and heard. (See Figure 4.5.) One of the most widely acclaimed outcomes has been the student written and published, magazine, Foxfire. The title, Foxfire, reflects their appreciation of the American Literature from which the title was selected.

Consider also the cooperative effort by teachers, specialists, and researchers that produced a guide to field trips in and around Nassau County, New York, that observes curriculum lines—language arts, communication arts, social studies, science, fine arts, and the like. It suggests ways to travel to sites, gives the names of local experts, provides useful maps and diagrams, and even has a section on establishing learning objectives.[6] The body of the guide is a virtual directory to the life and activities of those who live and work in and near Nassau County. It covers local industries, government offices and services, parks, forests, museums, beaches, camps, conservation demonstrations, ocean and rail terminals, farms, nurseries, historical sites, restorations, and even skyscrapers in nearby Manhattan. (See Figure 4.6.)

A similar emphasis on incorporating contact with the community into the curriculum is found almost everywhere environmental studies are pursued. The underlying assumption is that the dynamics of this nation are demonstrated by the millions of people whose minds and hands generate our lifestyle.

Figure 4.5 Students and teacher interrupt an interview to allow an "old-timer" to satisfy his curiosity about the video recording system being used. What kinds of attitude changes are apt to occur?

That learners generate great enthusiasm for acquiring information by visiting community resources is evident. Students feel the thrill of discovery when they witness things for themselves, and set out to explore on their own. This kind of opportunity results in direct involvement in learning.

Environmental Studies

Because population growth and accompanying food-supply trends have become a subject to be

[5] Georgia Slack, "Toward Understanding the Faucet," *American Education* (April 1974), pp. 17–23.

[6] *Boces Field Trip Guide,* available from the Research and Development Division, Nassau ESEA Title III Regional Center, 125 Jericho Turnpike, Jericho, N.Y., 1972.

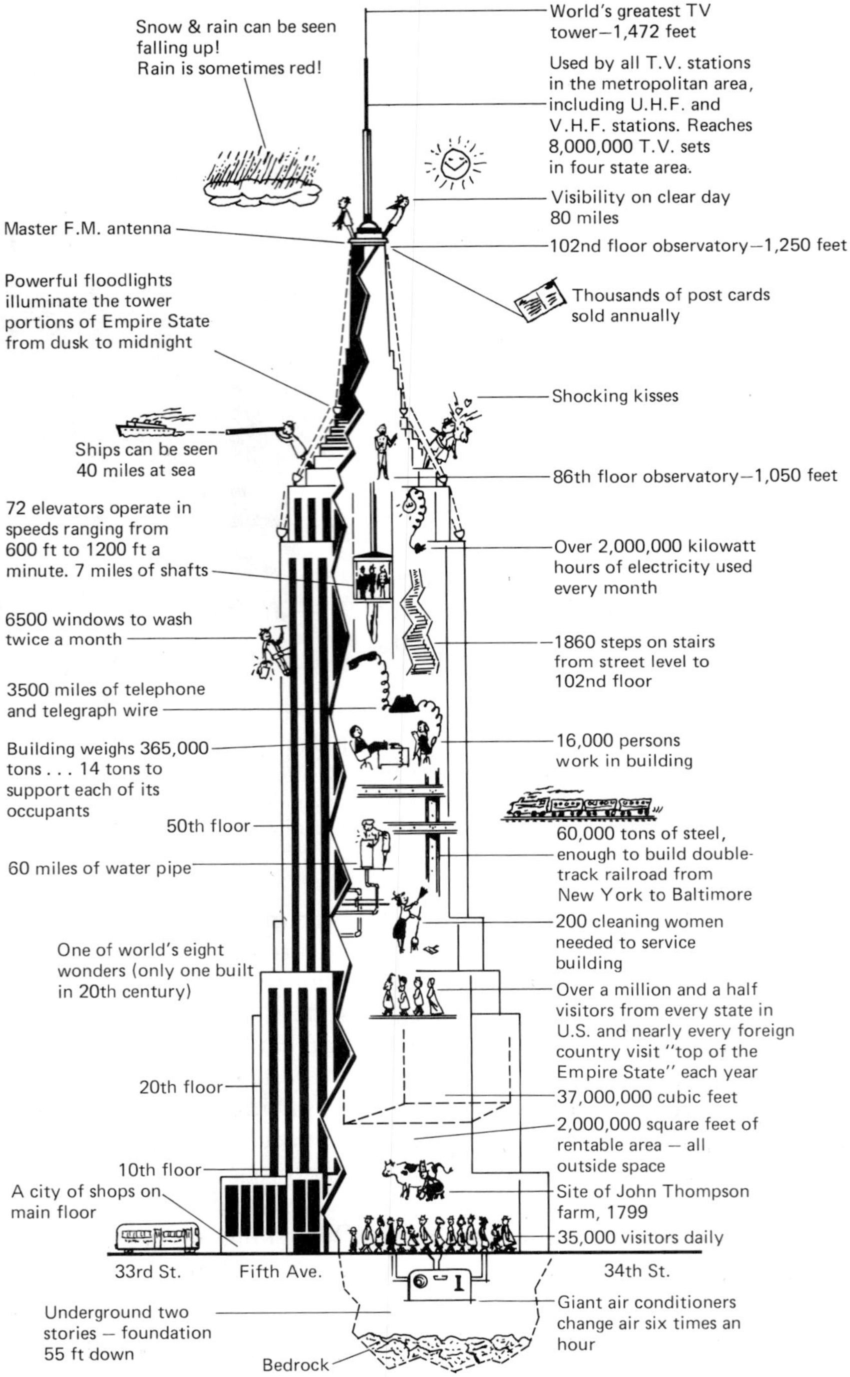

Figure 4.6 Many school districts provide supplementary field study information such as this chart of the Empire State Building. How would you use this kind of material?

studied from grade school through high school, and as concern has grown about our deteriorating natural environment, new provisions to study such topics have been made in curriculums throughout the country. The term for such studies is usually *environmental studies, marine studies,* or *Ecostudies.*

In inland areas students may be taken to school-owned forestland or camps, to shorelines, to swamps, or down rivers. In some school districts in the maritime states students can make ocean voyages that last from a half day to a week. In each case, the goal is to make it possible for students to gather data firsthand, evaluate it, and use it as the basis for some type of activity.

For example, in Hawaii the Blue Water Marine Laboratory (actually a small sailing vessel fitted out with basic oceanographic research tools) is available to teachers and students from intermediate grades to college. Study trips of from half a day to 5 days can be arranged, at cost, for up to 20 students and 4 teachers. While at sea, teachers and students conduct research planned before the voyage. They may use a tow net to collect plankton, other devices to capture open-water specimens, and a bottom trawl to dredge up mud dwellers, coral, and the like.[7] (See Figure 4.7.)

Projects having to do with land and water environments are to be found in every state of the union. A new film from the U.S. Office of Education entitled *Environmental Education, a Beginning* gives a documentary account of various experiments in the schools.[8] Not every type of ecological project can be incorporated into every instruction plan, of course, but you should make note of those that may be feasible in your own area for your own students. (See Figure 4.8.)

You will probably not have to look far for ideas for environmental projects of your own. Sources of air and water pollution, erosion, abandoned and abused land in cities or along highways, decaying buildings, and filthy shorelines are all too prevalent. Once the possibility of doing something real about them is pointed out to students, things will begin to happen.

Extended Community Studies

On occasion, a project that involves extended travel may be feasible. Careful planning is necessary when a student group goes farther abroad and stays longer than usual. One such community study experience was organized by a group of teachers in training in the Leeward School District of Oahu, Hawaii. They began with walking trips along the Waianae shoreline and up into the nearby valleys. As the program evolved, several students suggested that there was a lot of information to be had on the area from local residents, particularly some of the old-timers. Interviews were set up with some of these people, and fascinating information was uncovered about the early history of the locality. As the students' curiosity grew, they asked questions on many subjects. They wanted to know about the irrigation canals under and through the Waianae mountains and whether other people built canals like these. They discovered a Hawaiian *heiau*—an ancient place of worship—and asked whether other people had religious places like these. They discovered abandoned railroad tracks and found that they had conflicting ideas about why the iron horses had disappeared. Was it because of the automobile? A question that naturally followed was, "Do other people change their forms of transportation and communication? If so, why?"

The children found some answers shortly afterward during a study of the civilization of

[7] Douglas Pendleton, *Information Letter,* The Blue Water Marine Laboratory, Sea Grant, 2540 Maile Way, Honolulu, Hawaii 96822, rev. 1976.

[8] *Environmental Education, A Beginning,* 16mm, sound, two versions (15 min. or 30 min.). Available on loan, free, from Dept. EE, the Office of Public Affairs of the USOE, Washington, D.C. 20202.

Figure 4.7 These young people are using real oceanographic tools to discover answers to questions about specimens they identify and then "place" in the food chain. How would such an experience have contributed to your ideas about ocean life? How can such experience affect one's feelings and attitudes?

the Navajo Indians. They became curious about the Navajos' way of life, and the possibility of actually visiting a Navajo reservation in Arizona was batted about. It produced a flood of enthusiastic comments. Caught up in the spirit of things, some of the children made a further suggestion. "Why couldn't some of those mainlanders visit us here in Hawaii?" one asked. Others chimed in, "They must be curious about a lot of things, just as we are." Interest in the idea grew, and eventually teachers and pupils met with local school authorities to gain sanction for just such an adventure. The cost of the trip at first seemed to be an insurmountable barrier, but funds were eventually provided by local business people, parents, other members of the community, and a local newspaper.

Thus in the spring of 1970, several teachers and parents accompanied 20 Hawaiian schoolchildren as they traveled by air to the West Coast to begin a journey of discovery that took them to several cities, the Grand Canyon, and,

(a)

(b)

Figure 4.8 Environmental studies can take many forms. In (*a*) a child engages in creative dramatics to express her ideas about how settlers dressed and lived on the frontier. In (*b*) a high school boy develops leadership skills as he helps younger students discover what he has already learned about the natural world.

ultimately, the largest Navajo Indian reservation in the country. While there, they lived with the families of children of the same age. Two weeks later, 24 Navajo children returned the visit, experiencing life in Hawaii for the first time. (See Figure 4.9.)

Such extended journeys are possible when pupils, teachers, parents, and administrators cooperate in their planning and supervision. The distance traveled need not always be so great, of course. For example, every year in the small city of Madison Heights, Michigan, the members of the fourth grade at the Lessenger Elementary School climax weeks of planning, letter writing, and discussion by traveling by train and bus to visit fourth graders in Three Rivers, Michigan, a rural community about 150 miles southwest of Madison Heights.

Thousands of high school students visit the nation's capital each year. At certain periods, parking areas are jammed with school buses from communities as far as 2000 miles away. Needless to say, such trips are costly; they also present certain risks. They can be accomplished, however, with careful planning and organization.

Some Alternative Community Study Suggestions

Research surveys are a valuable community study activity. Often they include fact-finding interviews with business, government, or community leaders at their places of work. This form of community study is usually engaged in by selected groups or by students who have given evidence of their ability to handle such opportunities. Gifted pupils, in particular, benefit from the opportunity to ask professionals about taxation, law, transportation, com-

(a)

(b)

Figure 4.9 (*a*) When these Hawaiian youngsters "tried out" living in Arizona on a Navajo reservation, they had the unexpected bonus of seeing snow for the first time. (*b*) Two Navajo children arrive in Hawaii. Do you hope to arrange similar adventure in learning as a teacher?

munications, art, literature, housing, and job opportunities.

To get the most from a community survey and interviews, students must prepare carefully. They should discuss what they have read on key topics, formulate well-thought-out questions, and, with the aid of their teacher, list the names of the authorities they feel can answer their questions. Letters should be written well in advance asking each of these people for an interview on a specific day. When they are given ample time to schedule an interview, they are more likely to do so.

Interviewing lawmakers and others is more difficult when they have no local headquarters. The cost of transportation may make visiting them in person impossible. One unique solution to this problem was worked out at Stephens College, Missouri, which conducts speakerphone interviews with experts thousands of miles away. (See Figure 4.10*a*.) Often an entire 40-minute class period is devoted to such in-

(b)

(a)

Figure 4.10 Two-way communication between students and authorities on various subjects can be provided by telelectures. Audio telelectures are very effective and can now be arranged quite economically using portable conference telephones. The sets, which can be plugged into any standard jack, are telephones with loudspeakers built in and two remote microphones added. The telephones are used to contact the speaker; then, by taking turns with the microphones, students can ask questions. The teacher or a student moderator can control the microphones. (*a*) High school students seeking vocational guidance interview a local businessman, who is speaking from his downtown office. (*b*) In a New York State elementary school, telelectures are used successfully to stimulate greater interest in reading. Here a pupil using one of the microphones questions Jay Williams, author of a popular series of books for fourth- and fifth-graders. The author speaks to the children from his home in London. (*c*) When a video telelecture can be arranged, using closed-circuit television, it adds an extra dimension to the exchange of information. How would you use such equipment in your own teaching?

(c)

terviews. Depending on the distance involved, interviews of from 30 to 40 minutes cost from $12.50 intrastate, up to about double this for calls into distant states. This kind of research can be done entirely by letter, of course, but at the expense of the give-and-take of a normal conversation. A long-distance speakerphone interview is much more spontaneous, and informative.

PLANNING COMMUNITY STUDY EXPERIENCES

Planning community study experiences is a task that should be shared by the school board, local school administrators, the teaching staffs, parents, representatives of the community, local professionals, and the pupils themselves. The role of the school board is extremely important. All the examples of community study described in this chapter had the stamp of approval of their local boards. Once approval has been obtained for a general plan, school administrators, the teaching staff, and pupils can work out the details.

Parent groups have a definite responsibility to consider and support community study. In Manhasset, New York, a committee of parents and teachers decided to survey the area's human resources—people with special skills and abilities who could enrich particular learning experiences by their presence. The committee interviewed numbers of professional and business people, gradually building up a catalog of local talent willing to contribute time. It discovered, for example, that a very able lawyer could be available when the social studies class was investigating court procedures. A nurseryman who had developed certain grafting techniques would explain them to general science students. A ceramist was willing to explain and demonstrate glazing techniques to art classes. A music-shop proprietor who was also a skilled cello player was willing to help the members of the cello section of the school orchestra.

The Winnetka, Illinois, public schools have long had a committee of parents available to give advice to student groups that seek information on various careers. The Beloit, Wisconsin, public schools have a schedule of community days during which committees of teachers are invited to visit local service organizations and businesses. Appropriate opportunities for community study are later arranged for students. The Milwaukee public schools annually produce a revised list of community study experiences sanctioned by school authorities.

Know the Resources of the Community

In some areas, a catalog of community study resources may be published periodically. Usually, however, it is the individual teacher who must come up with project ideas. The first step, obviously, in such a situation, is to get to know the learning resources (apart from the usual libraries and museums) available locally.

A good way to begin is to ask members of your classes about learning experiences they have had outside of school. Often their experiences will provide a clue to unrecognized community resources. Your next step might be to consult the checklist of sources of information in the activity section at the end of this chapter. A reference file of useful community study sites can be compiled over the course of a semester as field trips, walking tours, and the like, are organized. Talking to local people can also result in a wealth of suggestions.

Incorporating Community Study into an Instructional Plan

Instructional planning should reflect the thinking of both learners and teachers. The basic question to be answered before committing

(a) (b)

Figure 4.11 For Milwaukee public school students many learning experiences occur outside the classroom. (*a*) Children engage in actual conservation work as they plant seedling trees in a state park. (*b*) Two high school students put information learned in marketing classes to use in a school-sponsored apprenticeship program. What parallel experiences would be valuable for the pupils in your area?

oneself to any project is, *"Will the needs of the learners be well served?"* If the answer is yes, then go ahead. (See Figure 4.11.)

Decide What Your Objectives Are

Pupils and teachers should share this task. The ultimate question here is, "What is worth knowing?" Encourage your students to pose questions they think are worth answering and to suggest conditions they think should be investigated. In short, develop clear and relevant objectives. Only then can you take the next step—deciding, at least tentatively, what end behaviors, or outcomes, you hope to achieve.

Decide What Outcomes You Seek

Although this question should be considered early by both teachers and students, changes in hoped-for outcomes can be made as events unfold. In open-ended planning, change is always possible. Nevertheless, students and teachers who decide in advance what is to be accomplished by the end of a period of instruction have the best chance to succeed. The important question at this point is, "What kinds of creative, innovative responses will learners be apt to make as they internalize and put to use the information gained through community study experiences?"

Among the alternative outcomes that may be specified at the beginning of a community study plan are

1. Written summaries of factual information accumulated during interviews with local authorities.
2. Photographic summaries of conditions documented.
3. A display of graphic materials secured from resource personnel—pictures, brochures, mock-ups, specimens, and so on.
4. Films or videotapes of interviews, demonstrations, or environmental conditions.
5. Dramatic reenactments of encounters with people, environmental conditions, or social situations.

The purpose of thinking through such creative responses is not to fix in advance a definite pattern of outcomes, but to alert learners to the wide range of creative responses that may become feasible during the course of a learning experience.

Consider the Use of Various Learning Media

Continuing thought should be given to the possible use and impact of various media. As a community study plan unfolds, students will profit by considering, as we have just proposed, the creative use of photographs, audio and video recording, and so on, in reporting what they have learned. The value of particular media will depend on the kind of outcomes to which they are likely to lead.

Select the Most Workable Strategies

In deciding the best way to approach community study, some of its unique characteristics should be considered. Teachers did just this in the following cases.

Earlier in the chapter we mentioned an exchange program between fourth-grade students at the Lessenger Elementary School in Madison Heights, a suburb of Detroit, and their country cousins in rural Three Rivers. Let's see how this program came about. The children at Lessenger were studying how the people of Michigan lived and worked as part of the regular curriculum plan for community study. It was, however, up to the students and the teachers to make this study meaningful.

The usual school learning materials were examined and discussed—books, government publications, films on the state's resources and activities, sets of pictures, and so forth. Then one student made a suggestion: "In the summer," he remarked, "my parents take the family up into northern Michigan. We visit friends, take walks through the forest, go fishing in the streams, visit the cranberry farmers, even watch wild rice being gathered. We always see so many things and do so many things. Can't we make arrangements to see more of our state, even though we're in school?" Other children agreed that this was a good idea. Perhaps they could find a rural community where some of them already had acquaintances and arrange a field trip there. If they could actually live in the community, not just overnight, but for a week, they would have time to see what life was like there. After some discussion, it turned out that a number of the children had friends or relatives in Three Rivers. That, it was decided, would be the best place for the class to explore.

Letters were written to fourth-grade students at the Three Rivers school, asking, among other things, how lodging, food, and transportation could be arranged. The children themselves arranged all the details of transportation. They read schedules, collected money, and purchased tickets. The housing problem was solved by exchanging visits with Three Rivers students who wished to come to Madison Heights.

Once the tactical problems had been solved, the students could concentrate on the real purpose of the trip—to discover, by direct observation, the answers to the questions they had previously worked out, questions that were actually their learning objectives. At Three Rivers the children visited small business establishments; they watched and participated in routine farm activities; they learned about dairy herds, domestic animals, rotating crop procedures, harvesting and processing grain; they visited local industries—the cheese plant, the dairy, the lumber mill; they saw forests and recreational areas —streams, lakes, and winter sports facilities.

When the Three River students came for their visit to the metropolitan Detroit area, they toured museums, went through customs on a visit to Canada, toured the airport, saw the assembly line of an automobile plant, and visited other manufacturing plants. (See Figure 4.12.)

During both visits, family groups spent hours discussing what the children had seen, what understandings had been gained, and what use they would make of their new discoveries. Ideas were recorded on tape, photographs were taken, notes were made, and pamphlets, postcards, and other printed materials were collected.

Back in their respective classrooms, the children turned excitedly to projects for reporting their experiences—class exhibits, short stories, a classroom newspaper, a display of pictures taken during the tour and organized into a filmstrip story with text written and, later, recorded by the students. So valuable was the trip and related activities and so great was the enthu-

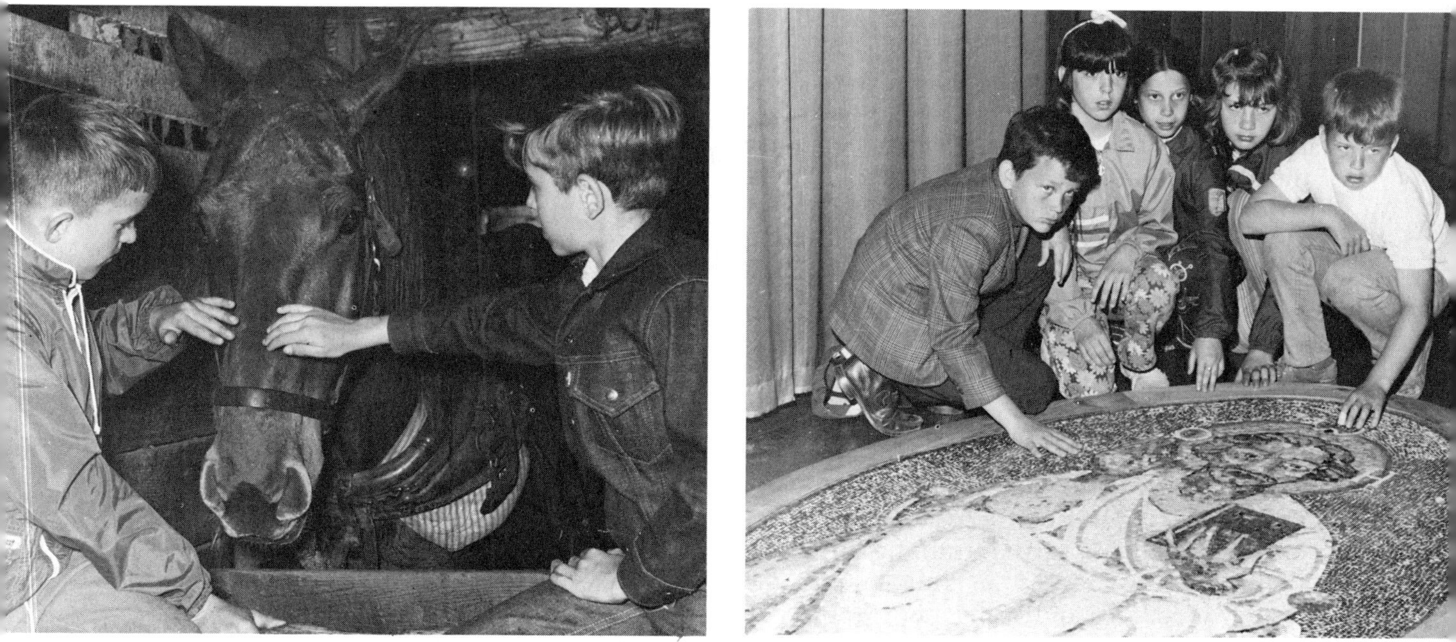

(*a*) (*b*)

Figure 4.12 Pupils from two Michigan communities exchange week-long visits to observe and learn. Touching is essential to full perception, whether (*a*) city dwellers are learning about a horse on a farm or (*b*) rural children are learning about mosaic art in a museum. Is such an exchange an entertainment or an innovative learning experience?

siasm it generated that it soon became an annual institution.

EVALUATING COMMUNITY STUDY IN TERMS OF OBSERVABLE OUTCOMES

As we have already pointed out, the outcomes desired as a result of community study should be worked out during the planning phase, although they may be modified later. These outcomes may include the demonstrable acquisition of information, understandings, and attitudes. The ways sudents show what they have learned can and should vary.

The media they use should include not only the usual discussions, written exercises, and the like, but graphs, charts, pictorial displays, models, mock-ups, audiotapes, videotapes, films, and so on.

Community study can be assumed to have been worthwile if all or most of the outcomes planned at the beginning or during the course of the study occur. If they do not, the learning experiences provided should be reviewed for flaws and restructured or dropped. In evaluating a particular community study experience, ask yourself the following questions:

1. Did it encourage learners to ask questions and make discoveries?
2. Was it related to known curriculum goals?
3. Were school district regulations concerning safety, costs, permission for particular activities, and the like observed?
4. Were participants given training in visual literacy techniques: in making graphs and charts, in taking and using photographs, in making video or audio recordings, and the like?
5. Were participants provided with the supplies and equipment they needed for visual communication?
6. Were participants encouraged to evaluate their own creative efforts (the ultimate outcomes of the community study experience) in terms of the information and skills they involved, the changes in attitudes they reflected, and the satisfaction obtained from them?

LIABILITY DURING COMMUNITY STUDY

How liable are teachers for accidents or injuries to pupils that occur during community study? In answering this question, the following points should be kept in mind:

1. The school board should have a definite policy on community study acknowledging it as a desirable part of the school system's regular program.
2. Principals should make the board's policy known to teachers.
3. The school board should provide liability insurance for teaching staffs. In Wisconsin, for example, and in many other states, school boards are legally authorized to spend public money for this purpose.
4. Teachers and principals should plan community activities that will help to accomplish existing curriculum goals. Such activities should not be confused with festivals, holiday excursions, and other recreational out-of-class activities.
5. The teacher, with the guidance of the principal, should arrange transportation via school buses or other bonded carriers required by law to carry liability insurance.
6. Teachers should never assume responsibility for conducting pupils through an industrial plant themselves, but should arrange to have the management supply a guide. As soon as the tour is ended, the teacher should have the

pupils return to school by a prearranged method of transport.

7. Parents should be informed that community-study experiences that take pupils out of the classroom are an accepted part of the school program, but that they have the option to refuse to allow their children to participate in them. (See, for example, the accompanying sample permission form.) But the granting of parental permission does not absolve the teacher who takes a class out into the community from exercising the same reasonable care expected in the classroom.

The teacher and the school who follow these suggestions will proceed with confidence and enthusiasm toward achieving valuable school and community relationships.

SUMMARY

Community study is the means by which teachers and learners observe and interact firsthand with persons and things in the real world. Whereas community study activities were once thought of as incidental to the curriculum, today they are an integral part of it.

The relationship of community study to the learning tenets described in Chapter 1 is very close, and numerous examples were given in this chapter to show that this is true. The commu-

Dear __________ (parent's name) __________

Because we wish to make your child's experience in ____ (subject or grade) ____ as valuable as possible, we want to give him/her firsthand experience with things we are studying in the community. We are planning to visit __________ (person or place) __________ on ____ (date) ____ as a part of our regular study program.

We encourage only those students who prove themselves trustworthy and responsible to participate in community study activities.

Will you kindly sign below to indicate that you want _____ (pupil's name) _____ to participate, and return this letter to me?

Very truly yours,

__________ (Teacher) __________

We wish to have ____ (pupil's name) ____ take part in the community study experience described above. We will discuss with him/her his/her responsibilities in this connection.

__________ (Parent's signature) __________

nity study projects described included walking trips, environmental projects, ecostudies, field trips, extended tours, and career education. Although in many communities plans for curriculum-related community study are made available to teachers, in many instances they are not. Where they are not, teachers themselves must study the community's human and natural learning resources. It is the responsibility of all teachers today to know the community in which they work and to coordinate in-school learning experiences with related community study opportunities.

This chapter explains the interrelated roles of teachers and pupils in applying inquiry techniques to the planning and accomplishment of community study learning experiences. The relationship of community study to the real world is stressed. Teachers are encouraged to examine two types of community study: that in which members of the community come into the classroom and that in which young people leave the classroom to examine social, natural, or economic phenomena firsthand. They may travel to nearby places during the schoolday or make lengthier excursions to more distant places. In either case the opportunities for involvement with real things can be very great.

Ways of planning community study and some of the responsibilities it entails are also discussed. The chapter provides guidelines for selecting community study experiences and incorporating them into an ongoing instructional plan. It also suggests ways of evaluating community study experiences for future reference.

ACTIVITIES

1. With the help of your teacher, make a systematic survey of the community to determine what sort of community study activities are possible there. Begin by consulting the local chamber of commerce, the local telephone directory, and the local offices of city, county, state, and federal agencies. Also contact your own school supervisers, the school's media specialist, its media librarian, and persons in the community affairs.

   Continue your survey by investigating specific local and regional offices and agencies:

   a. Local, state, and federal agencies responsible for parks, restorations, conservation demonstrations, arboretums, wildlife sanctuaries, reforestation, walking trails, marine reserves, rivers and swamps, and canoe trailways.
   b. Urban public service organizations responsible for health care, crime prevention, youth activity programs, sex information, legal aid, public housing, middle-income housing, and career-internship programs.
   c. Local service associations such as the League of Women Voters; associations of college and professional men and women; Rotary and Kiwanis clubs; local medical, nursing, and dental associations; and local community associations. Persons who hold leadership positions in such organizations are often rich sources of information about a community.
   d. Local, state, and regional business organizations. Often the best course is to address inquiries to persons who hold such titles as educational officer or public service officer.
   e. Local representatives of foreign governments—information services, embassies, consulates, tourist boards, and the like.
   f. Utilities, such as the local electric, telephone, gas, and water companies. Most utilities employ educational consultants who will arrange field trips.
   g. Regional authorities such as harbor, river, or dam control groups. Local representatives of such agencies are known to most local business or civic leaders.

Bring your community study plans to the attention of community leaders. In most instances your efforts will be welcomed with enthusiasm and many suggestions and offers of assistance will be forthcoming.

2. Select at least three community study experiences you would like to incorporate into your emerging multimedia instructional plan. Describe in detail the community resources involved. Outline the objectives of the experiences and the outcomes you hope will occur.

REFERENCES

PRINT REFERENCES

Bermont, Sarah Ann, "Options for Senior Girls—What Are the Alternatives?" *Girl Scout Leader* (June 1975), p. 8.

Blever, T., "Class Trip to Montreal," *Seventeen* (January 1975), p. 36.

BOCES Field Trip Guide, Research and Development Devision, Nassau ESEA Title III Regional Center, 125 Jericho Turnpike, Jericho, N.Y. 1972.

Brinson, David W., "Out-of-School Education in the Social Service Sector," *Phi Delta Kappan* (December 1973), p. 237.

"Free-Form Learners," *Nation's Schools* (September 1969), p. 48.

Kreitlow, Burton, Tuskegee, "Are You on the Line?," *Adult Leadership* (November 1974), p. 23.

Nelson, C. L. and Klavon, "Extending Your School to the Community and University via Conference Phone," *Agricultural Education Magazine* (October 1974), p. 24.

"Free-Form Learners," *Nation's Schools* (September 1969), p. 48.

Pendleton, Douglas, *Information Letter,* The Blue Water Marine Laboratory, Sea Grant, 2540 Maile Way, Honolulu 96822, rev. 1976.

Rubin, Harold, "Telephone Network Courses," *Educational Screen and Audio Visual Guide* (March 1964).

Slack, Georgia, "Toward Understanding the Faucet," *American Education* (April 1974), 17–23.

Van Reekam, C., "School Camp Success," *Camp Magazine* (May 1975), p. 8.

Wagner, J., "Call an Author," *American Education* (May 1976), p. 27.

Wigginton, Eliot, *Foxfire 2* (Garden City, N.Y.: Anchor Press, 1973).

Wigginton, Eliot, *Foxfire 3* (Garden City, N.Y. Anchor Press, 1975).

MEDIA REFERENCES

Community Resources in Teaching, 16mm film, sound, b/w, 17 min. State University of Iowa.

Field Trip, 16mm film, sound, color, 11 min. Virginia State Department of Public Instruction.

Field Trips for Discovery, 16mm film, sound (b/w. McGraw-Hill Films, New York.

Foxfire, 16mm film, sound, color, 21 min. McGraw-Hill Films, New York.

Near Home, 16mm film, sound, b/w, 27 min. New York University Film Library.

Passion for Life, 16mm film, sound, b/w, 85 min. Brandon Films.

World in a Schoolroom, 16mm film, sound, b/w, 17 min. (Produced by U.S. Army National Audio Visual Center.) Universal Education and Visual Arts.

5 Displays for Learning

Objectives

To enable you to do the following:

1. Identify three basic functions of displays.
2. Identify the physical and instructional advantages of six different types of display areas or surfaces.
3. Apply the principles of effective design, color, and lettering in developing a display.
4. Explain and demonstrate the physical characteristics of effective displays.
5. Describe and demonstrate four effective ways of using chalkboards.
6. Describe specific instructional uses of display techniques.

The face and feeling of American schools have changed dramatically in the last decade or two. The rows of boxlike classrooms where knowledge is dispensed in much the same manner to all students are giving way to learning centers where the nature, the needs, and the interests of young people shape the curriculum, the methods, and the organization of school programs. The rate of change varies from place to place, and even from school to school within a district—but it is under way. And you as a teacher can do much to shape and support future developments.

NEW ENVIRONMENTS FOR LEARNING

School designers have lately become much more conscious of the need for an environment that is conducive to learning. The institutionalized appearance of traditional classrooms, libraries, and corridors is giving way to warm, attractive surroundings with learning resource centers as focal points and with a wealth of display spaces. There is extensive display space in classrooms, halls, and the resource center. (Even in older schools, inventive ways are frequently found of using bare wall spaces, ceilings, and free-standing temporary display arrangements. In the newer schools there are lighted display cases in the corridors and in some classrooms. (See Figure 5.1.) In some of the larger, divided classrooms, there are "teaching walls"—sliding panels like those in Figure 5.2 that have multiple uses. Even the ceilings are used for free-form mobiles and models of the solar system. The school grounds include carefully designed geological paths, erosion study slopes, botanical gardens, soil plots, and aquatic areas.

In short, the term *learning displays* now brings to mind much more than bulletin boards. Study displays have become part of a total learning environment designed to involve students, and the walls of classrooms like the one in Figure 5.3 give dramatic evidence of pupil and teacher activities. Colorful displays that communicate information and generate interest and involvement impart personality to a school and its classrooms. They suggest something of the vitality and excitement of what goes on there.

STUDY DISPLAYS

A *study display* is an organized arrangement of visual and verbal learning materials that presents significant information or ideas on a topic or theme. It may be two- or three-dimensional, simple or complex, and located on any available vertical or horizontal surface—a display board, a chalkboard, a table top, or a display case shelf.

An effective study display is a stimulating experience. It may include diagrams, photographs, pictures, graphs, news clippings, tape recordings, mobiles, and three-dimensional objects and specimens. It may be planned and developed by teachers or pupils or both. Today's teachers know that effective displays can help pupils learn, and they are always on the alert for new ideas and materials.

Functions of Study Displays

Good study displays can achieve several purposes. They can be categorized, broadly, by func-

Figure 5.1 To be effective, displays must be seen. Display areas such as these enhance the effectiveness of displays and encourage creativity.

tion, as motivational, developmental, or summary. At the outset of a work unit, a display may be *motivational,* intended to elicit interest and curiosity. A motivational display is usually designed and put up by the teacher or by assistants. As a unit of work proceeds, a *developmental* display can give extra information on a topic and facilitate comprehension. Students should be actively involved in both the planning and the execution of a developmental display. (See Figure 5.4.) At the end of a unit of work, a *summary* display may pull together the key ideas in the unit. A summary display may be produced by the teacher or students or both.

Teachers should be very clear about the functions they wish a particular display to serve. Their objectives in terms of content, ideas, or behavioral outcomes must be clearly defined for the right outcomes to be achieved. Study displays should be part of a *team* of instructional materials selected with specific objectives in view. That is, like any learning media, they should be incorporated in a unit of study on the basis of a systematically developed plan. This plan should take into account not only the content to be covered but the abilities, needs, and interests of the pupils and the learning problems standing in the way of achieving specific objectives.

Characteristics of Study Displays

Because study displays are composed of a variety of materials, they quite naturally share with these materials the advantages and limitations

(a) (b)

Figure 5.2 In modern school buildings, various ways are used to increase display areas. The sliding panels shown folded against the wall and extended to form a partition in these pictures taken at different schools are one example.

Figure 5.3 Large murals provide opportunities for much pupil involvement in creating displays and in learning from them in the process.

Figure 5.4 Some kind of active involvement is necessary if learning is to take place. Helping to plan and develop a display can be an important way of creating this involvement.

described in Chapters 2 and 3. Nevertheless, when different elements are combined in an effective display, the total effect can and should be greater than the sum of its parts.

For example, displays are uniquely suited to motivate students—much more so, as a rule, than the individual pictures and other materials of which they are composed. Developmental displays that are put together by students require a high degree of planning and application. They can provide useful opportunities for visual literacy training too. (See Figure 5.5.)

A good display can attract and appeal to learners who are primarily visual-minded, stimulate the curiosity and imagination of most pupils, and be of particular assistance to slow learners who can absorb information from it at their own pace. It can provide an effective transition from old to new materials, provide opportunities for less verbal students to communicate visually (and perhaps win needed recognition in the process), and provide practice for all students in ordering and sequencing ideas.

On the other hand, displays have certain limitations. Good displays take considerable time and effort to put together. Furthermore, like any other medium or technique, they can be overdone and lose their freshness and appeal. Too many displays can produce a cluttered effect. Finally, classroom displays may compete for attention with learning activities conducted in their presence. Such factors as these must be taken into account in determining when and how to use them.

There are many examples of effective displays in the business world. Selling displays *must* communicate well to be effective. To find many excellent examples of this type of display, merely stroll by some department store windows or walk along the aisles of a supermarket. A successful commercial display must command attention, arouse interest, and involve viewers sufficiently so that then or later they will be moved to take the action desired by the creator of the display—to buy the product.

Many teachers consult advertising displays for ideas on interesting arrangements, attention-getting devices, the use of color, effective titles, and the like. One obvious characteristic of good advertisements and window displays is the simplicity and conciseness of their design. Generally, they reflect a single clear-cut idea. (See Figure 5.6.) Whether one is selling a product or a concept, it is well to keep the principle of simplicity in mind. It is relevant to all forms of effective visual displays.

PROVISIONS FOR DISPLAY AREAS

Before proceeding further into the planning of study displays, let us look briefly at the various kinds of spaces that can be used for them.

Figure 5.5 "Teaching walls" of various types provide expanded amounts of useful display space and are versatile and attractive as well. The use of such space, however, must be well planned to avoid a cluttered effect.

Spaces Normally Available

Display spaces may be flat or three-dimensional; sometimes, as in dioramas, they are both. Flat display areas such as bulletin boards are typically installed on the walls of classrooms, corridors, and instructional resource centers. In newer schools, up to a third of the usable wall space in classrooms, or a minimum of from 15 to 20 linear feet, may be given over to display boards. In some cases, convertible panels are installed so that the same wall space may contain, alternately, a chalkboard, a display, or a projection screen. In addition, a map rail with sliding fittings is usually mounted above chalkboard areas. The fittings have hooks and clips on which maps or charts can be hung. The rail also contains a narrow strip of cork or a similar substance to which flat materials can be attached with thumbtacks or pins.

Three-dimensional displays or exhibits can be placed on tables or shelves or in display cases built into classroom or corridor walls. (See Figure 5.1.) Display cases are frequently located, as well, at strategic points near school entrances so that visitors too may view displays. Display cases, which may have several shelves, should contain built-in lighting. Each case should also have an electrical outlet for extra lighting, for projection equipment that may occasionally be used in a display, and for devices employing small motors to provide motion.

Chalkboards can also be used effectively for displays. Though they are primarily used for material that will quickly be erased (assignments, notes, sketches, student work, and so on), they can also be used for such things as maps of the local area or charts showing progress in reading, math, or group projects. Class schedules, an attractive calendar of the month, and good student papers are found on chalkboards in many elementary classrooms. At upper levels,

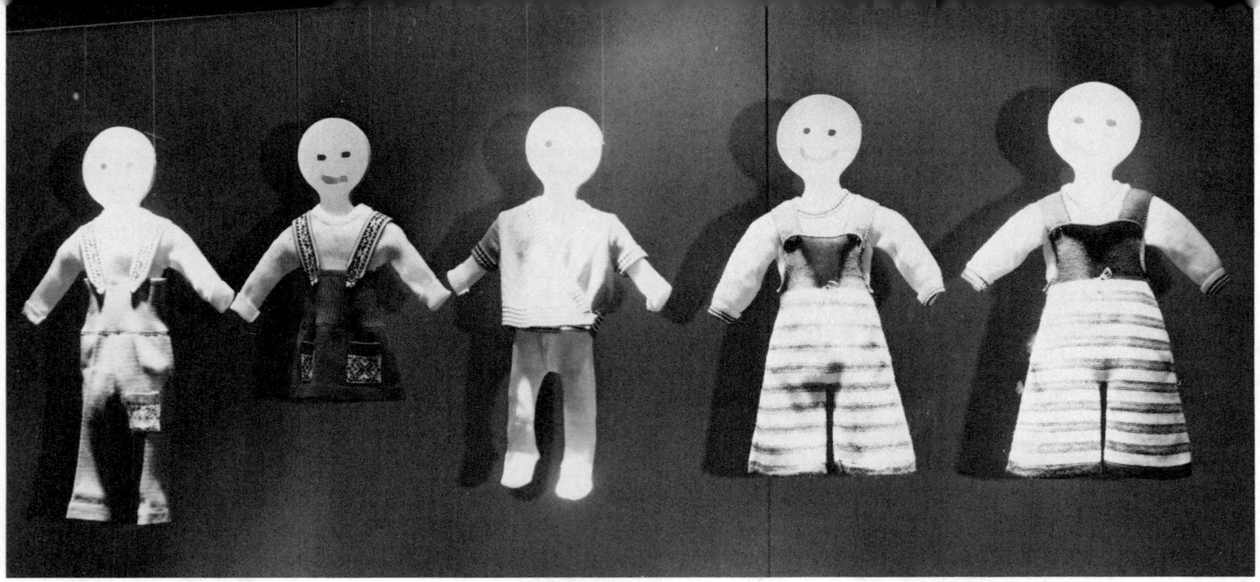

(*a*)

Figure 5.6 We can learn much about effective visual communication from commercial displays. (*a*) Note, for example, the effectiveness of simple, cutout figures against a plain background used in displaying children's clothes. (*b*) The muted earth tones of pieces of slate are used as a background in a display of fine china—along with live plants, for a dress-up effect. Note how the arrangement of clusters and individual pieces invites a closer look and leads the eye across the whole display and back again.

(*b*)

chalkboards with permanent matrices and grids are used in math, highway safety, music, and shop classes.

The ceiling can be used to advantage for suspended displays such as hanging globes; models of the solar system; models of space platforms, spaceships, and airplanes; and mobiles of several types.

Supplemental "Do It Yourself" Display Spaces

Frequently, in older school buildings, official display spaces must be supplemented in one way or another. Simple panels of Celotex or a similar porous material can be set on a chalk rail or on an easel and free-standing or pole-mounted panels and shelves like those in Figure 5.7 can be set up. One or more of the following suggestions may also be applicable in buildings with limited display facilities:

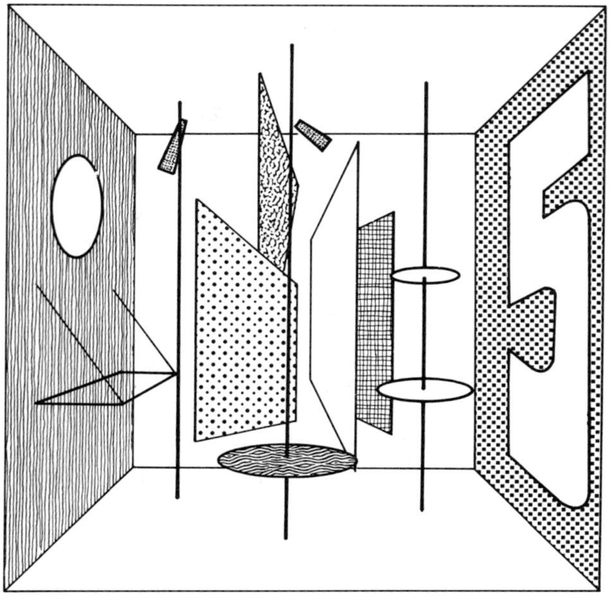

Figure 5.7 Shelving and vertical display areas on extension poles are an inexpensive and interesting way to add flexible spaces for a variety of displays. This composite shows several types from which selections can be made.

1. Unused wall or chalkboard areas can be hung with coarse, loosely woven cloth or heavy paper suspended from a light, strong wire stretched above them. The cloth provides a surface on which flat materials can be pinned. The heavy paper can be used for the same purpose or for murals. Pupils can draw directly on it with crayon or pastel chalk. The paper can be spray-painted with a background water color first if this is desirable. If it is, the corners should be fastened down while the paint dries so they will not curl up.
2. Small areas up to 4 × 6 feet can be converted into display spaces by fitting them with composition board or plywood veneer panels that have been covered with an inexpensive, loosely woven material such as burlap or hopsacking—both of which come in a wide range of colors—or monk's cloth. The material should be slightly larger than the panel so it can be folded over the edges and stapled on the reverse side. Start at the left edge; then staple the top and bottom edges, stretching and smoothing the material as you go along.
3. Free-standing panels of various sizes can be purchased or constructed of inexpensive materials. Lightweight notched panels that fit together at an angle to provide their own support are available commercially, as are lightweight metal extension poles with adjustable fittings to which panels and shelving can be attached. Two panels and three poles provide a free-standing unit; but many arrangements are possible—squares, triangles, and even enclosed areas with walk-through traffic patterns for special occasions such as science fairs or art shows. Free-standing panels or pegboards can also be mounted on pipe stands. (See Figure 5.8.)
4. Clotheslines can be stretched across a little-used corner of a room from hooks mounted in the edges of a chalkboard frame or cabinets.

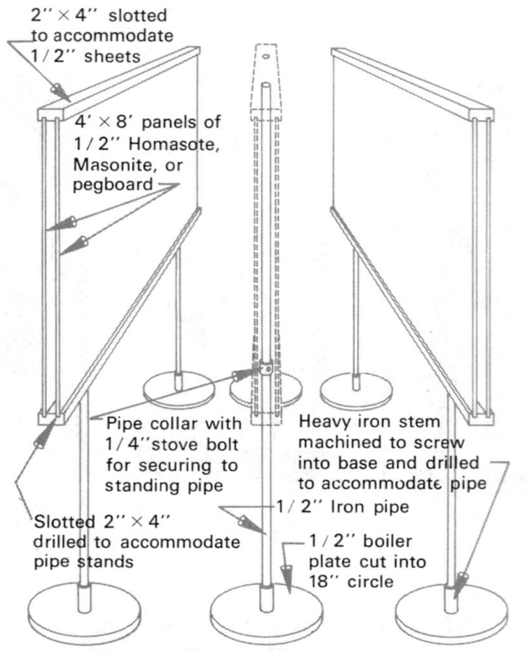

Figure 5.8 This diagram shows how pipestands can be used to form versatile two-sided, free-standing display panels or pegboard panels.

Stretch the lines in a zigzag pattern across the area, then attach large sheets of light but strong cardboard cut from old mattress cartons, large grocery cartons, or card-table containers to them. Use these free-form areas as surfaces on which to display objects, pictures, graphics, or student papers.

5. One of the simplest means of adding display space is to mount materials directly on unused wall spaces in classrooms or corridors. Double-surfaced masking tape or similar adhesives will hold most flat materials. Bulletin Board Styx, a waxlike adhesive of considerable strength, can be used for heavier materials, raised letters, or even three-dimensional objects. The surface must be free of oily film or dust for adhesives to work effectively. Although better suited for some purposes than others, ordinary unused wall space should not be overlooked as a practical supplement to existing display areas. With a little assistance and direction, students in upper grades can readily install most types of supplemental display areas.

SPECIAL DISPLAY SURFACES

In addition to the kinds of display surfaces we have considered, there are several types of specialized display boards, each of which has certain advantages and applications. These include such devices as pegboards, feltboards, hook-and-loop boards, and magnetic boards.

Pegboards

One of the more versatile surfaces for displays is the pegboard. Pegboards, which are made of tempered Masonite, have ⅛-inch holes punched in a regular pattern 1 inch apart over the entire surface.[1] They come in 4- × 8-foot sheets and can be cut to fit any desired space. Special metal hooks, clips, and other fittings, available in any hardware store, can be inserted in any pattern desired; they will support fairly heavy objects. To provide space behind them for insertion of the fittings, pegboards must be mounted ½ inch or so out from the mounting surface.

Pegboards are particularly useful for combining flat and three-dimensional materials. The latter are simply placed on hooks or shelves that can be located anywhere on the surface. The ⅛-inch holes are also the right size for golf tees, which can be used to punctuate or emphasize parts of the visual design or to support maps or charts fitted with grommets. Pegboards make a good backing for display cases as well. The regular pattern of holes is not unattractive as a

[1] Pegboard comes in ⅛-inch and ¼-inch thicknesses, with corresponding hole sizes. The ¼-inch pegboard is used primarily for making grilles and other construction purposes. The lighter ⅛-inch board is preferable for most display purposes.

background, and it can in any event be easily covered with cloth or paper.

Feltboards

Because felt and flannel have a nap or fiber surface, similar materials will adhere to them; this fact makes possible another very useful display surface—the feltboard. Flat, lightweight teaching materials backed with pieces of garnet paper or flannel can readily be used on feltboards. Feltboards can be purchased, or they can be made by stretching inexpensive cotton outing flannel or wool felt over flat panels of plywood, Masonite, or even heavy cardboard. Frequently both sides of such panels are covered to provide additional display space.

This type of display surface is particularly convenient for use with sequential or additive learning materials. In explaining the water cycle, for example, a teacher can begin with a diagram showing evaporation from bodies of water and land, add a second diagram showing cooling and condensation into clouds as warm air rises, and then add a third diagram showing clouds building up and condensing into rain, starting the cycle all over again. In teaching fractions, felt overlays representing halves, thirds, quarters, and so on, can be fitted onto base circles, squares, and rectangles.

Many materials of this type are available inexpensively from school supply houses, but you can also make your own by cutting felt or flannel into desired shapes or pasting small pieces of garnet paper or flannel on the reverse side of pictures, cards, and similar flat materials. Some textured-surface papers like kraft paper have enough nap to stick to feltboards by themselves.

Teachers of very young children can use figures cut from children's magazines or made of kraft paper for a creative story hour. Chemistry teachers can use feltboards in explaining molecular structures, the meaning of valence, or formulas. Physical education teachers or band directors can use feltboards for demonstrating football plays and marching formations. Language arts teachers can use them to show relationships between parts of a sentence, in vocabulary drills, and in similar exercises.

In short, feltboards can be useful in helping students visualize concepts in many subjects and in many grades. They are particularly useful in situations calling for step-by-step development of a topic, but they are valuable as well for discussion or drill periods, for a visual change of pace during the development of a topic, and for involving students in the learning process. Students can easily manipulate feltboard materials, and they enjoy doing so.

Hook-and-Loop Boards

Hook-and-loop boards are similar to feltboards, but they are much stronger, so that relatively heavy three-dimensional objects, as well as pictures and other flat materials can be displayed. The surface of these boards is made of a special nylon fabric that consists of thousands of tiny but very strong loops. An adhesive-backed patch on which comparable numbers of tiny hooks are woven is affixed to the object to be displayed, and the object is then pressed onto the surface of the board. Though the strength of hook-and-loop boards is really quite remarkable, objects affixed to them can be removed very easily. These boards can be used on easels, but it generally makes more sense to fasten them to the wall. (See Figure 5.9.) The two adhesive fabrics, complete boards, and sets of materials for using on them are available from school supply houses. (See the source references at the end of this chapter.)

Hook-and-loop boards can be used exactly like feltboards, with the additional advantage that materials will not shift or fall. Such accessories as precut letters for titles or captions, pads of drawing paper, and even magnetic chalkboards that fit onto the surface—all backed with the

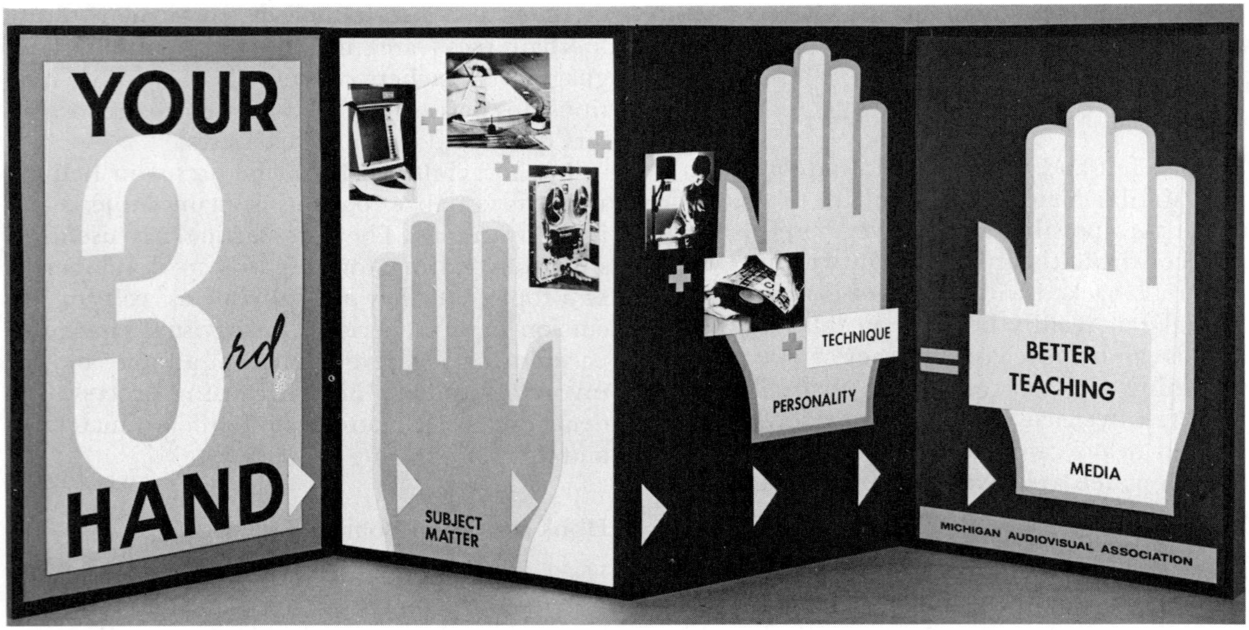

Figure 5.9 Displays require versatility. A hook-and-loop board holds heavy 3-D materials. It is also useful for displaying large flat materials that a feltboard would not hold.

necessary hook-on material—are readily available.

Magnetic Boards and Chalkboards

Magnetic boards are still another type of useful display surface. Magnetic screening is sometimes used behind permanently mounted wall maps to serve as a base for various magnet-mounted symbols or cards showing place names or geographic features. Many schools have installed steel-backed chalkboards that double as magnetic boards. Small magnets to which any appropriate symbols can be affixed will hold wherever they are placed on the surface.

The magnetic chalkboard is a natural for driver education teachers who want to illustrate various driving problems. Small models of cars or people or other objects with magnets attached will hold firmly to the surface but can be moved around easily. Small magnets can also be used to hold papers, pictures, and similar flat materials against the surface of the board.

CHALKBOARDS

Chalkboards are so familiar that they tend to be taken for granted. Many teachers think only of their obvious general usefulness and overlook some of their unique qualities. Thus, although chalkboards have changed considerably over the years, the way they are used has not.

Modern classrooms are generally equipped with nonglare boards in soft green or pastel shades permanently mounted on two sides of the room. The chalk used on them is relatively dustless, and, as we have already pointed out, one or more sections are likely to have a steel backing so that they are magnetic. Let us take a quick look at a few of the uses to which chalkboards are normally put and then go on to a discussion of some of their more unusual possibilities.

The Role of Chalkboards in Instruction

Chalkboards have long been used in the primary grades for stories children tell about their experiences; they dictate and the teacher prints. In the intermediate grades, teachers may introduce a new unit of study by writing questions on the chalkboard. As work on the unit continues, the chalkboard can be used in many ways—for lists of references, for questions and projects, and for summaries of key points.

A combination of chalkboard techniques, including the use of color, is valuable in teaching arithmetic and mathematics at various levels—for example, in explaining the division of whole numbers in the primary grades and algebraic division at the secondary level. *Covered chalkboards* (see Figure 5.10) are valuable for short tests or for drills in arithmetic, spelling, or vocabulary.

The magnetic chalkboard opens up a host of possibilities for visual communication. Lightweight objects can be mounted with adhesive on small magnets for use on steel chalkboards and slid quickly from place to place. Semipermanent diagrams can be drawn with a chalkboard pen and ink and removed later with a solvent. Meanwhile, chalk may be used and erased at will. Magnetic boards enable teachers to explain quickly the theory behind formulas for finding areas, perimeters, and circumferences or the graphing of equations. They have many applications in driver training and in home economics. Athletic coaches may use such a board to lay out game plans and strategies. They can use one set of symbols to represent the players on offense, another for those on defense and can develop offensive and defensive plays. By covering part of the chalkboard with an ordinary window shade or drape, they can also test players' reactions to problems that may arise during a game.

As you learn more about the variety of chalkboard materials available, you can experiment with using them in different ways. Chalkboard illustrations can be used to explain something very complicated, like the workings of an aircraft, or something very simple, like the correct way to sit in a typing class. Using chalkboards really effectively takes considerable thought and a certain amount of creativity. Stick figures are often helpful in explaining the best posture for an activity or the movements required. Sometimes they can be very effective indeed in explaining a point. A teacher in the primary grades, for example, can use them to show pupils what can happen to them if they stand too close to swings or other moving equipment in the playground. Simple sketches can help older students visualize the effect of temperature and time on the growth of bacteria, the osmotic process by which liquids pass through a membrane, or the pattern of winds in the atmosphere. If an opaque projector is available, newspaper or magazine diagrams that illustrate scientific, social, or mathematical principles can be shown using the chalkboard as a screen.

Poor handwriting or an inability to draw should not be made an excuse for not using the chalkboard. There are tools and drawing aids available that enable all but the most inept to make clear chalkboard presentations. Many teachers print rather than write on the chalkboard if they feel their handwriting leaves something to be desired—and find, with a little practice, that they can print rapidly and legibly enough for most purposes. Students should also be encouraged to use the chalkboard—to see it as a medium for two-way communication and as the property of the whole class, not just the teacher. The more aware we become of the chalkboard's many possibilities, the more we will get from using it.

Figure 5.10 Chalkboards are still one of the more versatile and convenient means of visual communication. Here a simple technique enables the teacher to expose items in sequence, revealing them at the most appropriate time for tests or exercises during class.

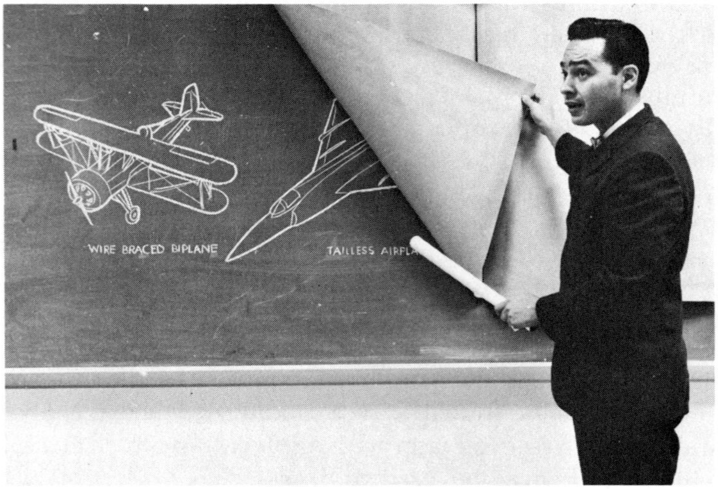

Improving Your Use of the Chalkboard

There are several simple, practical ways of ensuring good results when using a chalkboard, as well as some special tactics that are helpful from time to time. The following simple pointers, though obvious, are frequently ignored.

1. *Use a clean board!* A key element in good visibility is *contrast*. The cleaner the board, the better the visibility of what is written on it. Though a thorough cleaning before each use is not feasible, careful erasing can help considerably.[2]

[2] There are various types of chalkboards, special cleaning procedures for which are recommended by the manufacturers. All boards have an abrasive surface. The ingredients in some cheaper grades of chalk are themselves abrasives, which slowly wear away the surface of the chalkboard. Both good-quality chalk, colored or white, and proper cleaning are important in maintaining a board in good condition.

2. *Make it readable!* Anything on a chalkboard should be readily readable from the back row. Enough pressure should be applied to chalk to produce bold, clear lines and characters. Letters and numbers should be large—at least 2½ to 3 inches high. (See Figure 5.11.) The natural tendency to write small and to crowd as much as possible should be avoided.
3. *Have a plan!* One of the advantages of chalkboards, of course, is that they are always there. They can be used to clarify a point raised during a discussion or to work through a math problem giving students unexpected difficulty. Often, however, the most interesting and effective chalkboard presentations are those planned in advance.

Figure 5.11 A simple but important part of good chalkboard technique is to use large enough letters and numbers and write with enough pressure that material can easily be read from anywhere in the room.

Some Special Chalkboard Techniques

1. Projected drawings. Materials from newspapers or magazines can readily be transferred to the chalkboard by using an opaque projector. The illustrations are merely placed in the projector, which is focused on the chalkboard. A little experimentation in a darkened classroom will show the best position for the projector so that the image will be sharp and the right size. Tracing over the image on the board with chalk is then a simple matter. (See Figure 5.12*a*.) Special outline maps, some of them available on filmstrips, are often used in this way.[3] (See Figure 5.12*b*.)

A variation of this procedure is used by some television weather reporters, who lightly trace in the lines showing frontal systems and pressure areas before they go on the air. Then, during the broadcast, they draw over the barely visible lines quickly and surely.

2. Grid drawings. Grids provide a surprisingly easy way of making enlarged illustrations on a chalkboard when an opaque projector is not available. First, a grid of small squares is lightly drawn over the material to be transferred; then a grid composed of the same number of larger squares is lightly drawn on the chalkboard. The original illustration is duplicated on the chalkboard by copying what is in the corresponding squares, one square at a time, and then erasing the grid. The more detail desired, the greater the number of squares used. With a little practice, almost anyone can become adept at using this technique.

[3] *Basic U.S. Project Maps,* filmstrip series, b/w, Encyclopedia Britannica Films.

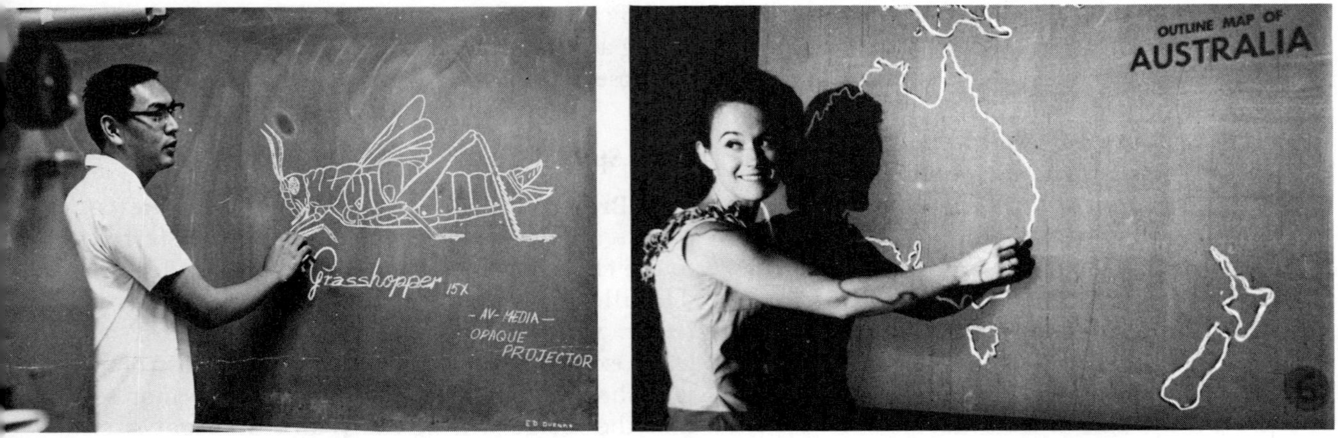

(*a*) (*b*)

Figure 5.12 The diagram of the grasshopper in (*a*) was projected on the chalkboard by an opaque projector and the key lines were sketched in. The map in (*b*) was projected from a filmstrip and used as a guide for tracing. When is the use of a projector to produce chalkboard images more valuable than projecting images directly onto a screen?

3. Patterns. For things that must be drawn frequently, such as state maps for social studies, geometric shapes, and graduated measures for chemistry, patterns or templates can be made from any thin, lightweight material. Sheet metal, thin plywood and Masonite are all good for this purpose. Commercial stencils are also available for such subjects as math and geography. (See Figure 5.13.)

4. Hidden drawings. Putting a series of key points or illustrations on the board in advance, covering them before class, and revealing them one at a time is one way of focusing on various parts of a lesson. The reverse side of a wall map or ordinary wrapping paper can be used to cover material. Wrapping paper can be held up with small pieces of masking tape or thumbtacked to the map rail above.

5. Lines and grids. Many instructors tend to write uphill or downhill. To correct this they draw fine parallel lines or dots as guides and erase them afterward. Either chalkboard T-squares or yardsticks can be used for this purpose.

Inexpensive staff liners are invaluable for teaching music theory. A staff liner can also be used to make parallel lines on the board to guide

Figure 5.13 Templates assure accuracy even in quickly sketched figures. What uses for templates can you think of?

writing or lettering. Permanent or semipermanent grids or matrices are painted on many chalkboards in mathematics and science classrooms to facilitate the drawing of graphs and diagrams.

6. Stick figures. Although few people are good at freehand drawing, with practice anyone can become adept in using stick figures such as those in Figure 5.14. These simplified figures can be very useful in a variety of contexts. They can add touches of humor and interest as well as a change of pace to your use of the chalkboard.

The number and variety of chalkboard uses illustrated above may make it seem that we are encouraging teachers to use chalkboards constantly. However, *too much* reliance on the chalkboard is as undesirable as too little. Communications in the classroom should be varied to make learning experiences interesting, and particular types of equipment should be used because their particular strengths make them the best choice in a specific situation. Some things, such as complicated accounting problems or topics to be studied at length, are better presented by means other than the chalkboard—by printed materials, overhead transparencies, slides, charts, and the like. Often chalkboards can be used along with models, charts, flash cards, and other devices to clarify meanings and relationships.

The approach to selecting instructional media and strategies described in Chapter 1 will help you to avoid overuse or misuse of the chalkboard or any other media. Your own intuitive feeling for the needs of a teaching situation—for the time when a change of pace is necessary, when things need to be done a bit differently—will also help you use the chalkboard effectively.

Figure 5.14 Stick figures are easy to draw, but they are more effective when the proper proportions, shown here, are approximated. Action is emphasized when the lines are slanted.

Choosing and Positioning Chalkboards

As a teacher you may have an opportunity to suggest improvements in the chalkboards in an existing school building or to make recommendations about those chosen for new buildings. If so, bear in mind the following points:

1. Good visibility depends on good contrast between the board and the markings on it. Though the old black slate found in older classrooms provides the most contrast, a soft green (or in some cases another pastel color) board provides adequate contrast and generally makes a room more attractive.
2. The readability of a board also depends on how clean it is. Good boards can be readily erased or cleaned without leaving "ghosts" or smudges, regardless of whether white or colored chalk was used.
3. Yet a third factor in good visibility is the way light falls on a board. Chalkboards should be placed on walls where the amount of glare from windows or artificial lighting is least.
4. The design and placement of the boards should also take into account the average

height of the pupils and teachers who will use them. Both should be able to reach a good portion of the boards without stooping or stretching.

PLANNING AND ORGANIZING DISPLAYS

Because preparing good displays can be a lot of work, it makes sense to plan a few really good displays during a term rather than many. Furthermore, ways should be found to distribute the work involved.

Planning Ahead

You should have a pretty good idea at the beginning of a semester of the units or topics for which displays will be appropriate. It is often best to get things started well ahead of time, to delegate responsibilities early, and to set up a schedule so that, when the time for the display arrives, it can be put together quickly. Not all displays need be worked on in advance, of course; sometimes making a display is an important part of a lesson. Motivational displays and many summary displays, however, often benefit from groundwork done in advance.

Distributing the Work

Students can and should be involved in the preparation of displays. Students can help greatly in the collection and selection of materials, and they can also benefit from helping to design displays. A model display made early in the year can provide a good takeoff point. As the semester progresses, students will learn more about planning visual sequences, layout, design, and composition. Most students acquire considerable facility with visual language before they come to school, and those who are artistically inclined may create some very striking displays.

Although not everyone can or should follow a set plan in developing study displays, certain basic principles must be observed to achieve desired results. There is some order, as well, to the steps involved. For example, it would be a waste of time to start selecting materials before having clearly defined the purpose of a display. The content of a display must be considered in conjunction with the form.

The Content of a Display

Materials selected for a study display must communicate relevant information and be attractive enough to involve the learner.

Content and purpose. In constructing a display, as in any other educational endeavor, you must first know what you wish to accomplish and then plan how it is to be done. A museum exhibit expert gives this sound advice:

> Exhibits are too often made with a minimum of clear thinking and planning. A vague idea is not enough, and even a splendid one needs much detailed work. You would not dare to face a microphone without a script, or film a motion picture without a scenario. Treat your exhibit with equal respect. Put down its purpose in writing: describe the basic idea; be specific about the facts and figures to be used, the technique by which they will be shown.[4]

The goal of a particular display may be to arouse interest, to explain a process, to report facts, to pose a problem, or all these things. In any case, before proceeding further, the primary theme must be known. It is often helpful to include the theme of the display in the title or in an attention-demanding graphic design.

[4] Bruno Gebhard, "How to Make and Use an Exhibit," in *Exhibits: How to Plan and Make Them,* National Publicity Council for Health and Welfare Services, 1946, p. 5.

Gathering materials. Deciding the nature of the materials you want to include is the next step. Usually, a good study display results from a wide search for a variety of materials—newspaper and magazine articles, photographs, charts, graphs, diagrams, and three-dimensional materials, including objects and specimens. Of these, only the best and the most relevant should appear in the final display; that is, only those that are the most *meaningful, graphic,* and *colorful* should be selected. Decisions should also be made about the best headings to be used, what the captions should say, and which pictures or graphics should be mounted.

Selecting provocative material. A good study display entices learners to study it in detail and, ideally, to explore the subject further. This is particularly true of motivational displays that help launch a new unit of study, and it is also true of developmental displays.

A good study display should contain the most provocative information available on a subject and present it in a dramatic fashion that will draw the viewer to examine the less prominent elements of the display as well. These, in turn, should provoke further questions in the viewer's mind. Naturally, teachers cannot rely on displays alone to motivate students, but study displays do have a real potential for arousing interest and imparting information—capacities that should be recognized and used.

The Physical Form of Displays

The materials selected for a display are normally selected because they make a point well or are attractive. However, the individual elements in a display should also be arranged so that they complement one another and enhance rather than detract from the overall effect. The total effect, in other words, should be greater than the sum of its parts. Note, for example, the effective arrangement of elements in the displays in Figure 5.15.

Assembling supplies. The first mechanical step in constructing a display is to gather the raw materials you will use to put it together. These supplies usually include kraft paper; large sheets of heavy paper for backgrounds or paper sculptures; pastel chalk, wax crayons, and show-card colors; lettering stencils and pens; three-dimensional cardboard, plastic, or ceramic letters with which words or phrases can be formed; and masking tape. Mounting supplies must also be assembled: usually wire, tacks, and pins. (See the source lists in the appendix for display materials; also see the media references at the end of this chapter.) Supplies for study displays should be made available to students too.

Planning the layout. The second step after assembling the raw materials for a display is to draw a blueprint. Work out the layout on paper. Show the size of each element, the design to be followed, the color scheme, the lettering, and the placement of materials.

Because a good layout entails imagination and creativity, experiment with different arrangements. Before settling on a final plan, make copies of several parts of the display, lay them out on a table top, and try various combinations until you are satisfied that you have the best one. Cutout paper forms can be moved across a desk top or over the surface of a piece of kraft paper representing the display in miniature.

The layout of a display may have to be modified as students find new pictures, graphics, and three-dimensional materials they would like to use. For example, verbal information may be made more understandable by using diagrams, graphs, or comic drawings. As a rule, however, changes should be tested in the blueprint stage before incorporating them in the final display.

In planning layouts, seven attributes of good

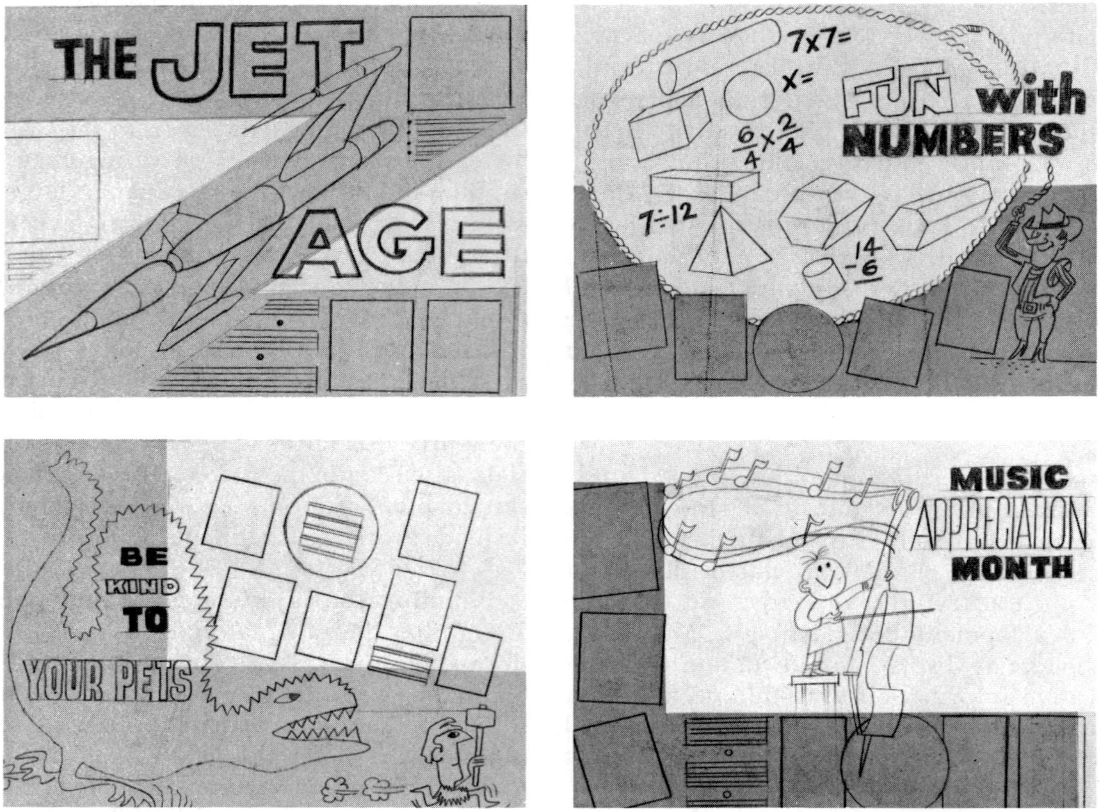

Figure 5.15 The dark-toned areas suggest the eye-movement path of the viewer in each case. What layout ideas can you develop that will lead the viewer to examine all the elements included in your display?

displays should be kept in mind. These are (1) simplicity; (2) the effective use of color; (3) a wise choice of headings and captions; (4) clear, artistic lettering; (5) adequate lighting; (6) motion (when feasible) ; and (7) provision for viewer participation.

1. Keep it simple. In planning a display, it is useful to think of posters. A poster should not be crammed with words and ideas; it should convey one central idea. So it is with displays. If you have more than one crucial idea to communicate, put it in another display.

The *design* of the display should be simple. Basically, designs are merely arrangements of elements that lead the eye where you want it to go and at the same time produce a pleasing overall effect. (See Figure 5.15.) The good and bad arrangements in Figure 5.16 illustrate this point vividly.

An attention-demanding symbol, cutout, or design provides a center of interest for a display. For example, if the subject is the exploration of space, a simplified, abstract representation of a rocket may be used as the key symbol.

2. Use color wisely. Color is an important factor in any display. It can be used to attract atten-

Figure 5.16 Note how the arrangement of elements, lettering, and contrast can make a difference in a display.

tion, emphasize boundaries, indicate categories and groups, and provide an effective background for materials and lettering. Wisely used, it can dramatize or focus attention on key items or relationships. Study displays involving rules, directions, steps in a process, time lines, important dates in history, and so on, will profit from the judicious use of color.

Color also helps you to present visual information accurately. Representations of scenes, costumes, persons, and objects are truer when they are naturally colored.

Color can also heighten interest. Study displays are most likely to attract attention when pleasing combinations of colors are used for backgrounds, for frames for graphics, and so on. Intense colors virtually demand attention, and displays backed by warm complementary colors usually appeal to the learner's esthetic sense. Several suggestions on how to combine colors and use them effectively were given in Chapter 2.

3. Use appropriate headings and captions. Every display should have a central heading that tells people the general theme. Be dramatic. Ask a question; pose a problem; make a direct claim or statement. Headings and captions are extremely important. The headline, or title, of a display is usually one of the means by which it first captures the viewer's attention. The captions used should be as clear, simple, and succinct as possible and carefully planned to hold the viewer's interest as he or she steps closer to examine the display in more detail.

4. Use good lettering. Lettering for displays and exhibits can be done in several ways. Hand lettering by capable students or teachers is distinctive and particularly desirable for large headings. Cutout plywood letters made in manual arts shop are excellent. Three-dimensional letters made of cardboard and plaster are highly effective and can be purchased commercially. Gummed letters in various sizes and colors are also available at low cost. (See the source lists in the appendix.)

Good lettering requires color knowhow. The most important factor in lettering is the difference in brightness between the letters and the background. This difference affects both the distance from which the words can be read and the speed at which they can be read. Research on colors for highway signs is applicable to some extent to study displays. For example, the most attention-commanding background colors for signs are yellow, white, red, blue, and green, in that order.[5] Block lettering with bold, thick lines and open spacing is the most legible.[6] Of course, highway signs must be visible in all kinds of weather, in daylight or darkness, and against all sorts of backgrounds. The conditions in which most educational displays are found can be controlled, but *brightness* and *contrast* are still important. Black lettering on yellow or white, dark green or blue lettering on white, and white lettering on green or blue backgrounds are all effective combinations. Normally, three letter *sizes* will be sufficient: large lettering for the title, intermediate-size lettering to identify key elements, and smaller lettering for captions.

5. Arrange adequate lighting. Lighting is a dominant factor in any display. It not only focuses attention on the display but heightens the effects created with design and color, Artificial light is often better than daylight, which varies in intensity. Furthermore, strong daylight tends to reduce the contrast and thus weaken the character of a display. To see the advantages of artificial light, simply make a mental comparison between a well-designed store window in daylight and its more striking appearance at night.

[5] P. Odescalchi, "Conspicuity of Signs in Rural Surroundings," *Traffic Engineering and Control,* vol. 2, no. 7 (1960), pp. 390–393.

[6] A. W. Christie and K. S. Rutley, "The Relative Effectiveness of Some Letter Types Designed for Use on Road Traffic Signs," *Roads and Road Construction,* vol. 39 (1961), pp. 239–244.

The concentration of light within the window when there is no competing daylight is very important in drawing and holding attention. The same is true of displays.

Intricate and expensive lighting arrangements for study displays and other school exhibits are usually impractical and unnecessary. Spotlights and floodlights that screw into standard light sockets come in various colors and have a pleasing effect. Simple clip-on or self-standing fixtures to hold the bulbs are also quite inexpensive. Whenever a number of fixtures are to be used simultaneously, someone should check with the school electrician or maintenance person to make sure power lines will not be overloaded.

Exhibit cases located in corridors should have concealed fluorescent fixtures to light displays. For special effects, colored gelatin sheets can be placed over the lights. (Because fluorescent light is "cold" light, there is no danger of fire.) Display boards in inside corridors or in dark corners of classrooms need lighting to be effective. A shaded fluorescent fixture at the top of a board is a good way of lighting the display surface evenly. Recessed fixtures in the ceiling over the display area are a decided advantage. Flush fixtures are good for general illumination, and an adjustable "bullet light" is excellent for baby spots. (There should be standard plug-in outlets in all recessed exhibit cases and adjacent to display areas in corridors.)

6. Use motion when it is feasible. Motion can play a very important role in a display, first by attracting attention to it and second by focusing attention on one or more elements within the design. Movement can be provided by small electric motors, a motion picture film, or an automatic slide changer; or it can be simulated by changing light patterns. Changing light patterns can be created using Christmas tree blinker-light fittings, a rotating color wheel in front of a floodlight, or polarized light.

Judgment should be exercised in using movement in displays. Your principal concern should always be to get the message across—to achieve the purpose for which the display was designed. Overemphasizing any one element of the overall design, such as movement, may hinder more than it helps. It is possible, in other words, to enliven a presentation to the point where it is intriguing but confusing. It is much more common, however, for displays to be too dull and, in consequence, to go unnoticed.

7. Involve the viewer. The most effective exhibits frequently require some type of activity on the part of the viewer. Museum exhibits in which the viewer pushes a button or turns a knob to make something happen are extremely popular. So are mock-ups in which the observer operates the controls. Though such exhibits may be too costly or complex for teachers or pupils to contrive, viewer involvement can be achieved in simpler ways. An attractive, arresting heading and good content can result in a very absorbing display. Captions that ask questions or make suggestions are also useful.

EVALUATING LEARNING DISPLAYS

The value of study displays depends on three things: whether they achieve their primary purpose, the effectiveness of their design, and the degree to which they involve students.

What Do They Achieve?

The first question to raise in evaluating a display is, "Does the display have a clear, well-defined purpose, and is it designed for a specific group or audience?" Normally, a display is only one of a series of learning experiences provided during work on any given unit, and it can be difficult to isolate its effect from the effect of other things. Nonetheless, how well it performs the task for which it was designed is fundamental.

As a corollary, the substance of a display should have sufficient merit to warrant the time and effort involved. A display can sometimes be interesting without saying very much. Thus other questions to be asked in evaluating it are, "Does it say or do something important?" "Is the content clearly related to the message?" "Do all the elements fit together?"

How Effective Is the Design?

In considering the design of a display, these questions are important: Does the display have eye appeal? Does it attract attention? Is the lettering effective? Is the overall design simple and unified?

Do Students Become Involved?

The extent to which a display involves students depends somewhat on the type of display it is and how it is used. Nonetheless, the most useful and effective displays are those that actively involve the students, cause them to want to know more, and excite their interest. Students may be involved, first, through helping plan and execute displays. They may also be involved through opportunities to manipulate things or cause things to happen within a display—lighting changes, activation of a taped explanation, or movement of some kind. The question to be asked here is, "Does the display elicit desired reactions from pupils?"

There are many kinds of study displays and they have many functions. No single display can achieve all these functions—nor should it be expected to. But if its purpose is clear, its design appropriate and good, and its subject suitable, it will have the most important elements necessary for success.

SUMMARY

Study displays are a collection of related, self-explanatory pictures, graphics, and three-dimensional objects that *together* convey information and provide visual explanations of processes or situations.

There are three basic types of displays: motivational displays, developmental displays, and summary displays. The design of a display will depend on the purposes it is intended to achieve.

In creating learning displays, the following points should be kept in mind:

1. Study displays are learning experiences.
2. A good display results from good planning.
3. Study displays should be related to the subject being studied and the interests of the learners. The best study displays involve learners and entice them to search further for information on a subject.
4. The best learning displays command attention; communicate concepts, facts, and insights; and develop enthusiasm for the subject being studied.
5. A good learning display has a good physical organization and layout.

Study displays should be a joint effort by teachers and pupils. Often pupils learn more from making displays than from looking at them.

Study displays should be evaluated according to three criteria: whether they achieve their purpose, the effectiveness of their design, and the degree to which they involve students.

ACTIVITIES

1. Write a brief description of the purposes of motivational, developmental, and summary displays. Describe how they are created and who should create them. From illustrations in the chapter, pictures provided by your instructor, or displays in your own school, pick two of each type and briefly explain why they fit a particular category.
2. In two columns labeled "Physical" and "In-

structional," respectively, list the advantages of six types of study displays discussed in this chapter. Check your list with the lists of two or more other students.

3. Select a topic for a study display, and sketch a layout for it. Be ready to justify (a) the display topic in terms of its appropriateness as a display subject and (b) the particular type of display you selected.
4. Using the layout you have already sketched, develop a display that illustrates your grasp of the physical characteristics of effective displays. Bring it or a photograph of it into class so that your instructor and other students can comment on it.
5. With several other students, take 35mm slides of how chalkboards are used in your own school and show them in class. Be ready to demonstrate in class four or more chalkboard techniques you consider effective.
6. Examine at least five displays made by other students, and describe specific instructional uses for them.

REFERENCES

PRINT REFERENCES

Alexander, Larry J., and James A. Farrel, "The Great Once-a-Year Organic Bulletin Board," *Learning Resources* (March 1974), pp. 8–9.

Anyone Can Create a Lively Bulletin Board (Wilkinsburg, Pa.: Hayes, 1968).

Boughner, Howard, *Posters* (New York: Pitman, 1962).

Bowman, William J., *Graphic Communication* (New York: Wiley, 1967).

"Bulletin Boards," *Grade Teacher* (a monthly feature).

Bullough, R. V., "Aesthetics and Instructional Materials: Design of Visual Displays," *Audiovisual Instruction* (February 1974), pp. 69–71.

Comba, John, "Photography: A Key to Learning," *Audiovisual Instruction* (November 1969), pp. 66–67.

Conlan, Kate, *Poster Ideas and Bulletin Board Techniques* (Dobbs Ferry, N.Y.: Oceana, 1965).

East, Marjory, *Display for Learning* (New York: Dryden Press, 1952).

Easy To Make Bulletin Boards (Wilkinsburg, Pa.: Hayes, n.d.).

Educational Displays and Exhibits (Austin: University of Texas Instructional Media Center, n.d.).

Graphic Tips: Advertising Lay-Out Fundamentals (Chicago: NuArt Company, 1967).

Grubola, M. R., "For the Beginning Teacher: Bulletin Boards," *Today's Education* (March 1973), p. 66.

Gumm, Ben, and Jack Blake, "Software," *Audiovisual Instruction* (June-July 1969), pp. 123–124.

Hayett, William, *Display and Exhibit Handbook* (New York: Van Nostrand Reinhold, 1967).

Kelley, Marjorie, *Classroom-Tested Bulletin Boards* (Palo Alto, Calif.: Fearon Publishers, 1961).

Kemp, Jerrold E., *Planning and Producing Audiovisual Materials,* 2d ed. (San Francisco: Chandler, 1968).

Kindergarten and Primary Bulletin Boards (Wilkinsburg, Pa.: Hayes, n.d.).

Laflame, Patricia J., *Exhibits* (East Lansing: Michigan State University Cooperative Extension Service, 1969).

Lockridge, J. Preston, *Better Bulletin Board Displays* (Austin: University of Texas Visual Instruction Bureau, 1963).

Minor, Ed, and Harvey R. Fye, *Techniques for Producing Visual Instructional Media* (New York: McGraw-Hill, 1970).

Phillips, Ward, and John H. O'Laque, *Successful Bulletin Boards* (Dansville, N.Y.: F. A. Owen Publishing Co., 1966).

Randall, Reino, and Edward C. Haines, *Bulletin Boards and Displays* (Worcester, Mass.: Davis Publications, 1971).

Ruby, Doris, *3–D Bulletin Boards That Teach* (Palo Alto, Calif.: Fearon, 1960).

Simmons, G., "Headlines in Visual Design: Charts and Graphs," *Audiovisual Instruction* (February 1973), pp. 59–62.

Wermick, W., "Chalkboard Group Teaching Techniques," *Math Teacher* (May 1975), pp. 426–427.

MEDIA REFERENCES

A Visual Fable, filmstrip, sound (record), color, 18 min. AECT, 1969.

Bulletin Boards and Displays, filmstrip, BFA Educational Media, 1966.

Cameras in Education, Educational Media Laboratories Technifax Education Division, 4101 S. Congress Ave., Austin, TX 78745. A series of sound filmstrips, overhead transparencies, and manuals that present the camera as a creative teaching tool.

Chalkboards and Flannel Boards, 35mm filmstrips (4), color, 30 frames each. Bailey Film Associates, 1967.

Charts for Creative Learning, 16mm film, sound, color, 10 min. Bailey Film Associates, 1966.

Creating Cartoons, 16mm film, sound, color, 11 min. BFA Educational Media, 1956.

Educational Graphics, Hester & Associates, 11422 Harry Hines Boulevard, Dallas, Texas. A series of 10 film loops (averaging 4 min.) dealing with such local production skills as lettering, mounting, laminating, and composition.

Effective Visual Presentations, slide/tape, sound. Eastman Kodak Company, 1969.

Flannel Board Use, filmstrip, b/w or color, 30 frames. Bailey Film Associates, 1966.

Flat Pictures, 16mm film, sound, b/w, 18 min. Pennsylvania State University, 1959.

Graph and Picture Story Skills Kit. Science Research Associates, 1967.

Graphics, series of 17 transparencies from *Instructional Media Transparency Masters*—a series of 147. Keuffel and Esser Co., 1969. *Chalkboards* (4) and *Flat Pictures* (5) are also part of the series.

The Growing of a Young Filmmaker, 16mm film, sound, b/w, 17 min. Screenscope/AECT.

Hey, Look at Me, 16mm film, sound, color 12½ min. AECT/Screenscope.

How Does a Picture Mean? filmstrip. AECT, 1968.

Language of Graphs, 16mm film, sound, b/w, 13 min. Coronet Films, 1948.

Making Sense Visually, filmstrip, sound, color, 77 frames. AECT, 1969.

Mounting Still Pictures, filmstrip, color, 58 frames. Visual Instruction Bureau, University of Texas, 1956.

Photo Discovery Sets, picture sets. Washington, D.C., AECT, 1967.

Pictures for Teaching, slides, San Francisco, Chandler, 1965.

Poster Making: Design and Technique, 16mm film, sound, color, 10 min. Bailey Film Associates, 1958.

Posters, 16mm film, sound, color. ACI Productions, 1968.

Posters for Teaching, filmstrip, color, 40 frames. McGraw-Hill, 1963.

Story Starters, super-8 cartridged film loops, Ealing Corporation, 1969.

Study Pictures and Learning, filmstrip, color, 63 frames. Teaching Aids Laboratory, Ohio State University, 1960.

Teaching with Still Pictures, filmstrip, color, 53 frames. Basic Skill Films, 1958.

Teaching with Visual Materials, filmstrip series, color, 35–40 frames each. McGraw-Hill, 1964. *The Chalkboard, Parts I and II,* and *Posters for Teaching.*

Using Charts and Graphs in Teaching, 35mm, filmstrip, color, 51 frames. Basic Skill Filmstrips, 1958.

What Is a Graph? filmstrip, b/w, 26 frames. Visual Education Consultants, 1965.

STUDENT PRODUCTION GUIDE REFERENCES

See *Student Production Guide,* Chapter 3, "Graphics Techniques for Instructional Materials Production," particularly the sections on design, color, bulletin boards, chalkboards, and graphs; dry transfer lettering; Wrico lettering; rubber cement mounting; and Chapter 4, "Producing Photo and Sound Materials for Instruction," particularly the sections on photo and sound materials. Design and Use, Photographic Slides, and Audiotapes. Pp. 122–178, 237–243 and 280–290.

SOURCE REFERENCES

Art Supplies—General

Creative Playthings, A Div. of CBS, Edinburg Rd., Cranburg, NJ 08521.

M. Grumbacher, Inc., 460 W. 34th St., New York, NY 10001.

Milton Bradley Company, Educational Div., Springfield, MA 01101.

Display Surfaces and Supplies

Bulletin boards and supplies

Advance Products Company, Central at Wabash, Wichita, KS 67214.

Bangor Cork Company, William and D Sts., Pen Argyl, PA 18072.

Bulletin Boards and Directory Products, 724 Broadway, New York, NY 10003.

Eberhard Faber, Inc., Crestwood, Wilkes-Barre, PA 18701.

Koroseal Div., B. F. Goodrich Company, Oak Grove, Marietta, OH 45750.

Lea Audiovisual Service, 182 Audley Dr., Sun Prairie, WI 53590 (Bulletin Board Styx).

Magnet Sales Company, 3935 S. Vermont, Los Angeles, CA 90037.

Masonite Corporation, 29 No. Wacker Dr., Chicago, IL 60606.

Silver Burdett Company, 1900 E. Lake Ave., Glenview, IL 60025.

Chalkboards, magnetic boards, and supplies

Charles Mayer Studios, 140 E. Market St., Akron, OH 44307.

Com-Pak Chemical Corporation, 223 South Holmes St., Shakopee, MN 55379.

Magna Visual, Inc., 1200 N. Rock Hill Rd., St. Louis, MO 63124.

Miami Magnet Company, 7846 West 2nd Court, Hialeah, FL 33014.

Oravisual Company, P.O. Box 11150, St. Petersburg, FL 33733.

Weber-Costello Company, 1900 N. Narragansett Ave., Chicago Heights, IL 60639.

Easels, flannel boards, feltboards, hook-and-loop boards

Arlington Aluminum Company, 19303 W. Davison Ave., Detroit, MI 48223.

Charles Mayer Studios, 776 Commins St., Akron, OH 44307.

Chartpak, One River Road, Leeds, MA 01053.

ESSCO-Educational Supply Company, 2833 Gage Ave., Huntington Park, CA 90255.

Judy Company, 250 James St., Morristown, NJ 07960.

Ohio Flock-Cote Company, Dunham Industrial Park, 14500 Industrial Ave. N., Maple Mts., OH 44137.

Oravisual Company, P.O. Box 11150, St. Petersburg, FL 33733.

Visual Specialties Company, 127 S. Saginaw St., Byron, MI 48418.

Graphics Materials

Adhesives

Addressograph-Multigraph Corporation, Charles Bruning Div., 1834 Walden Office Square, S. Schaumburg, IL 60172.

Brandywine Photo Chemical Company, P.O. Box 298, Avondale, PA 19311.

Cello-Tak Manufacturing, 35 Alabama Avenue, Island Park, NY 11558.

Chemex Industries, 2822 35th St., Tampa, FL 33605 (Base-Tape).

Lea Audiovisual Service, 182 Audley Drive, Sun Prairie, WI 53590 (Bulletin Board Styx).

Letro-Stik Company, 3721 Broadway, Chicago, IL 60613 (Letro-Stik).

Clip art services

Artype, Inc., 345 East Terra Cotta Ave., Crystal Lake, IL 60014.

Multi-Ad Services, Box 806, Peoria, IL 61601.

Technifax Corporation, 195 Appleton St., Holyoke, MA 01040.

Volk Corporation, Pleasantville, NJ 08232.

Graphic tapes

Graphic Products Corporation, 3601 Edison Place, Rolling Meadows, IL 60008.

Mico/Tape Div. of the C-Thru Ruler Company of Calif., 12032 Vose St., N. Hollywood, CA 91605.

Mounting materials

Cam-Lox Products, P.O. Box 366, Redondo Beach, CA 90277.

SOS/Photo-Cine-Optics, 315 West 43rd St., New York, NY 10036.

Union Rubber & Asbestos Company, 232 Allen St., P.O. Box 1040, Trenton, NJ 08606.

Lettering equipment

Carter's Ink Company, 239 First St., Cambridge, MA 02142.

Chartpak, One River Rd., Leeds, MA 01053.

E. Dietzgen Company, 245 N. Sheffield Ave., Chicago, IL 60614.

Feber-Castell Corporation, P.O. Box 330, Lewisburg, TN 37091.

Keuffel and Esser Company, 20 Whippany Rd., Hoboken, NJ 07960.

Koh-i-noor Rapidograph, Inc., 100 North St., Bloomsbury, NJ 08804.

Letterguide Company, 4247 O Street, Lincoln, NB 68510.

Mark-Tex Corporation, 161 Coolidge Ave., Englewood, NJ 07631.

Showcard Machine Company, 320 W. Ohio, Chicago, IL 60610.

Varigraph, P.O. Box 690, Madison, WI 53701.

Wood-Regan Instrument Company, 184 Franklin Ave., Nutley, NJ 07110 (Wrico).

Letters

Artype, Inc., 345 East Terra Cotta Ave., Crystal Lake, IL 60014.

Cello-Tak Manufacturing, 35 Alabama Ave., Island Park, NY 11558.

Chartpak, One River Road, Leeds, MA 01053.

Demp-Nok Company, 21433 Mound Rd., Warren, MI 48090.

Graphic Products Corporation, 3601 Edison Place, Rolling Meadows, IL 60008.

Holes-Webway Company, Webway Park, St. Cloud, MN 56301.

Naz-Dar Company of California, Graphic Arts Center Div., 1534 W. 7th St., Los Angeles, CA 90052.

Redikut Letter Company, 12617 S. Prairie Ave., Hawthorne, CA 90250 (cardboard letters and Plasti-Tak adhesive for mounting on changeable backgrounds).

Stik-a-Letter Company, 1787 So. Iris Lane, Escondido CA 92026.

The Tablet and the Ticket Company, 1021 W. Adams St., Chicago, IL 60607.

6 Audio Learning Materials and Techniques

Objectives

To enable you to do the following:

1. Understand the nature of audio learning materials and their role in helping learners achieve known objectives or outcomes.
2. Identify at least five techniques for recording and playing back sounds.
3. Identify at least five commercial and noncommercial sources of audio learning materials.
4. Describe several self-evaluation techniques associated with audio recording and identify at least three areas in which these techniques can improve specific skills.
5. List the steps in the physiological and psychological processes involved in hearing, listening, and responding and become aware of techniques for improving listening skills.
6. See the relationship between audio learning experiences and techniques and the six learning tenets described in Chapter 1.
7. Become aware of the uses of audio learning activities in working with large and small groups and in individualized instruction.
8. Apply the principles and techniques of pupil- and/or teacher-planned-and-produced audio learning materials and test, where feasible, the effects of such learning experiences during the evaluation phase of your own instructional development plan.

Man is the only creature on earth that talks, and most human communication is via the spoken word. For untold millennia, verbal communication was the only means of passing on knowledge. The American Indians, the Australian aborigines, the Kahunas of the South Pacific, and the storytellers of Africa all learned the lore of their ancestors in this way. Even the philosopher Socrates never wrote down his doctrines. He simply spoke to those who gathered around him in the marketplace and gardens of Athens. Today the bounds of oral communication have been greatly increased.

Our chief concern here, however, is with audio learning exercises in the classroom. Research has established that nearly 50 percent of a typical student's time is spent in listening. The higher the grade level, the more time usually spent in listening. Many college students spend nearly 90 percent of their time listening to lectures and discussions.

So usual is the practice of communication through the spoken word that its inefficiencies, though acknowledged, are accepted as occupational hazards. These hazards include individual variations in the ability to comprehend audio messages and incomprehensiveness or inaccuracies in the messages themselves. Though some listeners understand an audio message immediately, others must listen to it repeatedly before they can fully comprehend it. We shall explore the uses of audio recording and playback devices as a part of an instructional plan here in Chapter 6.

AUDIO LEARNING

The term *audio learning* as it is used in this chapter refers to learning that occurs through exposure to electronically recorded or broadcast explanations, directions, and the like. Instructional material may be recorded on audiotapes, audiocassettes, audiocards, or records. It may also be broadcast on educational radio stations. Audio materials may be played back at normal speaking rates, at slower than normal speeds, or at a rate faster than normal voice speeds, a condition referred to as *compressed speech* because what was originally recorded at, say, 150 words a minute may be played back at speeds of 1000 words a minute or more. Moreover, such changes in speed are possible *without changing the pitch or inflection of the original voice or sounds.*

In this chapter, we shall describe several types of audio recording and playback equipment and commercial audio materials. We shall also discuss the planning, recording, and use of original audio materials. Finally, we shall consider the use of audio learning materials as alternatives in an evolving instructional development plan.

SELECTING AND USING AUDIO EQUIPMENT

Of all the equipment found in schools today, tape recorders and playback mechanisms are among the most numerous; well over 1 million of them are currently in use. Record players,

Figure 6.1 The essence of audio learning is usually found in appropriate listening experiences that *learners* can control.

radio broadcasts, and recorded radio broadcasts are also used to provide audio learning experiences.

Classroom Recorders and Playbacks

Recording equipment is designed to accomplish tasks of varying complexity. A moderately priced medium-fidelity audiorecorder will fill most of the needs of a small class. For most teachers, a knowledge of the intricacies of audiorecording performance as measured by engineers—the frequency response, the output in decibels, and the wave form (fidelity)—are not necessary. What teachers do need to know is why, how, and where equipment is to be used and what learning goals it is expected to accomplish. They can then seek the advice of a media specialist or a local tape-recorder dealer about the best kind of recorder to purchase. In selecting a recorder, simplicity should be the rule. The controls should be simple to operate, and the equipment should be easy to set up and put away. Virtually all classroom recorders use either open reels of 1/4-inch magnetic tape or cassettes (closed plastic containers) that hold either 1/4-inch or 1/8-inch tape.

All tape recorders and playbacks—open-reel or cassette—operate on the same principle: Sound waves are picked up by a microphone and instantaneously converted into a series of electrical impulses. These impulses travel to a small magnet that touches a moving tape coated with a magnetic substance, usually iron oxide. The coating receives and retains magnetic impressions of varying strengths that correspond to the original impulses created by the sound waves. (See Figure 6.2.) The tape can be rewound and played back at once. In this reverse process, the invisible magnetic impressions excite a magnetic head and create electrical impulses that, after being suitably amplified, activate the diaphragm of a loudspeaker to produce sound waves identical to those originally recorded.

Tape recordings can be used again and again. A reel of mylar plastic tape can be run thousands of times without any visible evidence of wear or any decrease in the fidelity of the sound. If, on the other hand, an error has been made or the recording is no longer needed, the magnetic image can be erased in seconds. Erasing makes a tape magnetically neutral and ready for immediate reuse. Many models and types of open-reel and cassette recorders are available, ranging in price from $25 to hundreds of dollars. (See Figure 6.3.)

Open-reel recorders have one significant advantage: The material recorded can easily be edited; that is, it is possible to delete material and rearrange sections of material that are worth saving. Cassette recorders have other advantages: For one thing, they are usually very simple to operate. The tape is permanently enclosed in a plastic container, but the forward or rewind movement is easily controlled by pushing a button or turning a knob. Cassette tapes can be loaded or unloaded in seconds. Prerecorded or blank cassettes drop easily into place and are immediately ready for use. (See Figure 6.4.) By breaking off a small plastic spur on the back of a cassette tape, one can make it impossible to erase the material on the tape or on the instruction track of a multiple-track tape. (See Figure 6.5.)

In examining recording equipment, teachers should ask the following questions:

1. Is the unit equipped with control levers, dials, or knobs that are clearly marked so that even young children can operate it?
2. Is the playback equipment suitable? Will it play back typical classroom communications with fidelity?
3. Is the equipment flexible enough to record radio programs and make copies of existing audiorecordings (a process referred to as *dubbing*) ? Ordinarily, in order to make copies of a tape, a second tape recorder is needed.
4. Is the equipment light, compact, and at the same time rugged enough to be taken on field trips?
5. Is the equipment capable of playing back recorded speech at slower or faster than normal speeds without changes in pitch? This kind of variable-speed capacity has only recently been developed, and machines that

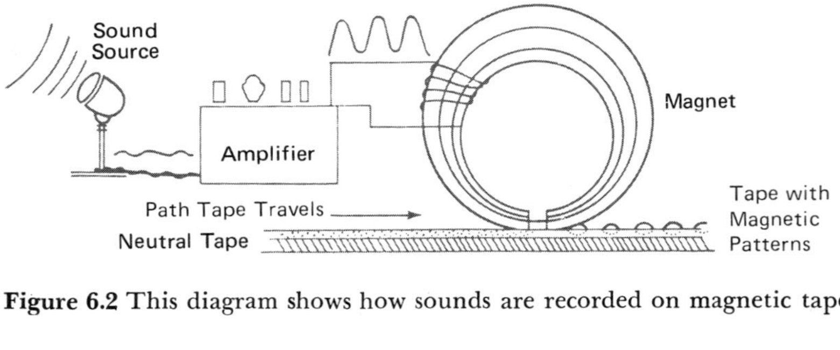

Figure 6.2 This diagram shows how sounds are recorded on magnetic tape.

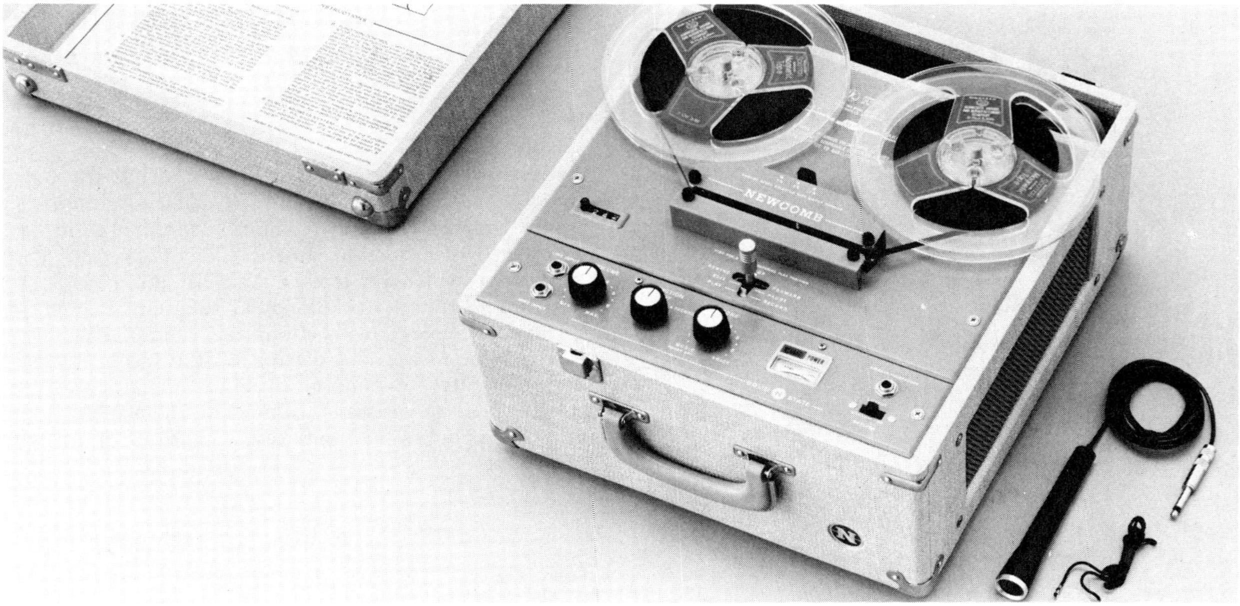

(a)

(b)

(c)

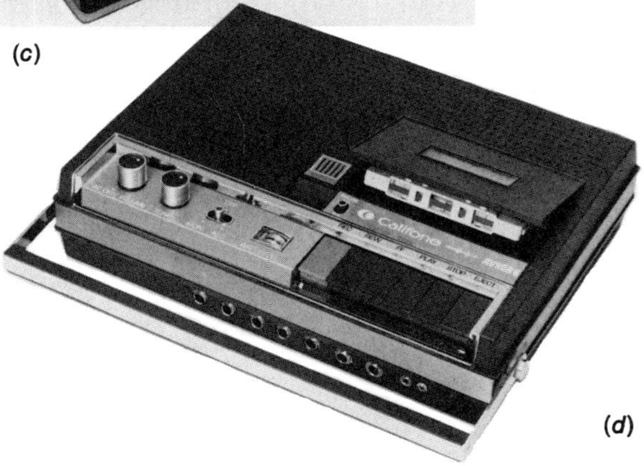

Figure 6.3 These open-reel (*a* and *b*) and cassette (*c* and *d*) tape-recorder–playback machines are but a few of hundreds of models available. In choosing from among such a wide variety of well-made and economical machines, one must first ask, "What kinds of audio experiences do I want learners to have?"

(d)

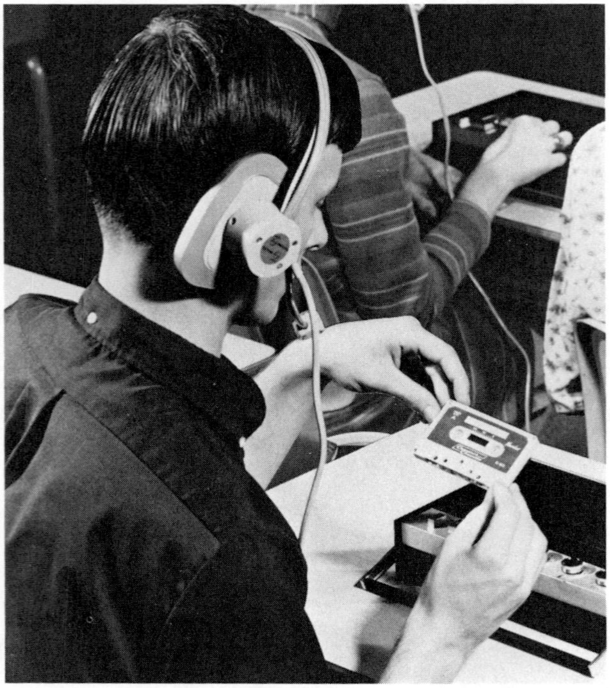

Figure 6.4 This student is about to insert a 1/8-inch tape cassette into a recorder-playback. He may listen, record, move rapidly ahead, or listen again by operating one of four push-button controls. The tape is permanently enclosed in the cassette. What advantages or disadvantages do you associate with such equipment?

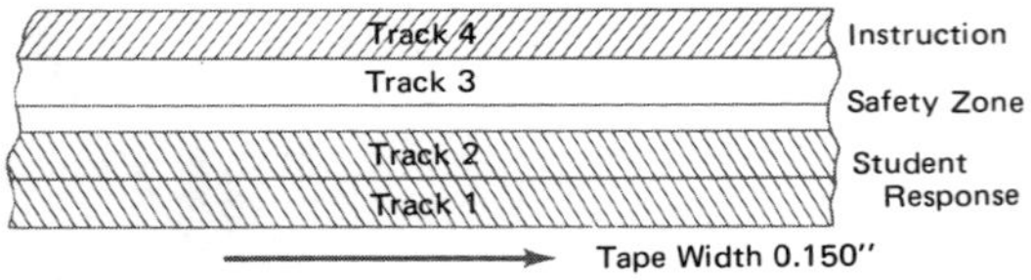

Figure 6.5 This diagram shows how multiple-track tape works. Track 4 contains the teacher's prerecorded "model"; tracks 1 and 2 (combined for monaural use) are used by learners to record their responses. (The *safety zone,* which includes track 3 in this case, is not used for recording; its function is to prevent deterioration of the teacher's instructions and examples while the student is recording and erasing on the response track.) Thus students are able to listen, learn, respond, and evaluate their responses by comparing them immediately with the model. What uses can you think of for such equipment?

have it may be hard to locate. (The advantages of such a machine are described later in the chapter.)

Almost any kind of audiorecording can be made if the right kind of equipment is used.

Recorders for Large Groups

The difference between the audiorecorders just described and those suitable for large groups is often only a matter of degree. Higher-quality microphones and more sensitive recording equipment are usually needed to record large groups in order to capture very low and very high sounds and to reproduce those sounds with enough fidelity at a high enough volume for large audiences to hear comfortably. Equipment of this type is generally larger, heavier, and more costly. Also, more expertise is required of the operator.

As in selecting classroom equipment, one must select recording equipment for large groups only after determining the uses to which it will be put.

Microphones are important. One or all of the three basic types of microphones may be necessary. A *unidirectional* microphone (which picks up sounds from one direction) is best for single students facing an audience. The speaker's voice alone will be picked up, and such audience noises as shuffling feet, whispering, and coughing will be minimized. When two persons or small groups on opposite sides of a microphone speak or perform, a *bidirectional* microphone is needed. *Omnidirectional* microphones (which pick up sounds from all directions) are widely used, but unless they are used carefully they easily become overloaded by excessive sounds and produce annoying squeals called *feedback.* As in the case of other recording equipment, it is a good idea to seek the assistance of a media specialist or a qualified local dealer in selecting microphones. (See Figure 6.6.)

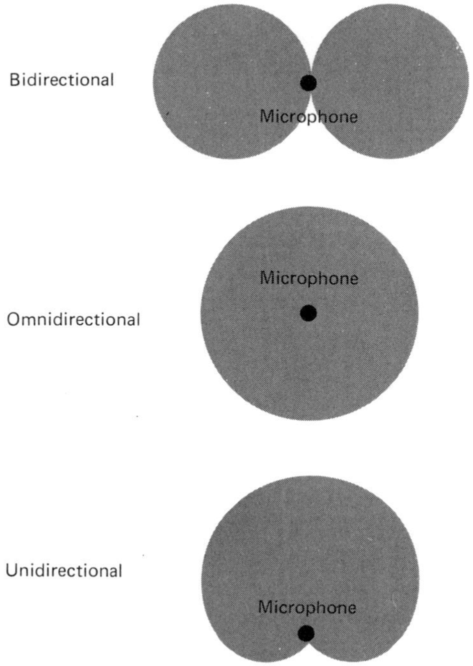

Figure 6.6 This diagram shows the pickup pattern of three types of microphones. Which do you think would be best for a classroom? For use with a large group?

Stereophonic equipment is used in many schools to record, play back, and evaluate choral speaking and dramatic, vocal, and instrumental performances of individuals and groups. In stereophonic recording, two or more microphones are used. The sounds picked up by each are played back separately through two or more speakers or two sides of a headset. The result is lifelike sound. Listeners hear the reproduced sounds as they normally hear sounds from two or more directions at the same time, with an intensity that varies according to their distance and direction.

Listening to stereo recordings is not only a remarkably esthetic experience, but one that enhances audio learning, particularly when the location, and relationship of sounds is important. Using stereo tapes for sound reproduction has the advantage of eliminating both surface noises and the noises due to mechanical sound reproduction techniques. Like tapes generally, stereo tapes do not deteriorate rapidly and hence can be used over a long period of time.

Card-Type Audio Recording and Playback Equipment

In the usual audio learning experiences, students record and listen to material for a few minutes or longer at a time. The use of very short audio messages—three to five seconds long—in conjunction with cards is an exciting new development. Audio flashcard systems have 9- to 15-inch lengths of tape attached permanently to the cards, which are usually $3\frac{1}{2} \times 9$ inches, or 4×15 inches. Words, sentences, questions, symbols, or pictures are written or printed on cards. The strip of recording tape is attached to the lower portion of each card and provides a "sound track" describing the printed material. The student inserts a selected card into a slot on top of a card reader (see Figure 6.7), and the card automatically moves across a magnetic head or vice versa. As this occurs, the user hears his or her own voice or the instructor's voice reading or describing the material printed or pictured on the face of the card.

To reinforce the "seeing" and "hearing" steps in this learning process, students turn a "record" switch and repeat the materials they have just seen and heard. The students' voices may be rerecorded in such a way (on dual-track tape) that they can replay their own responses and those of the "model" for comparison. If the students' performance is faulty, they can erase it and record again as many times as they wish.

Preprinted and precoded card sets on many subjects are now available, as are blank cards. They can be used in teaching vocabulary, math, chemistry, spelling, and grammar and to increase reading comprehension. Teachers can write, draw, or paste pictures on blank cards. By inserting the cards in the card reader, they can then record words or phrases describing the images,

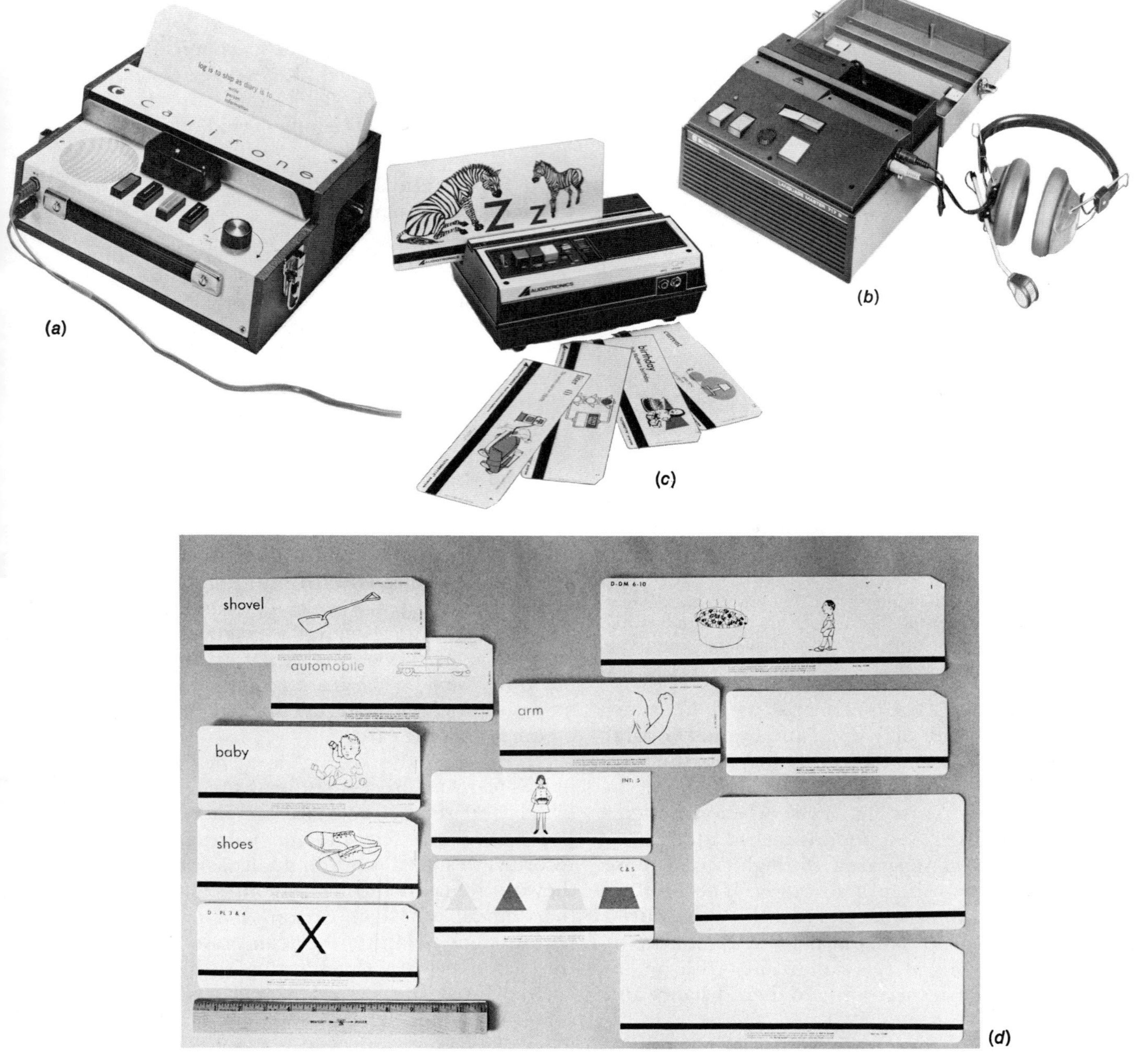

Figure 6.7 Among the most widely used audio card reader models are (*a*) the Califone International card reader, (*b*) the Bell and Howell Language Master unit, and (*c*) the Audiotronics card reader. The sample tape cards shown (*d*) give an idea of the variety of subjects for which cards are available. Can you identify some that would be useful to you? Blank cards allow teachers or pupils to attach cutout pictures of their own, draw on them, or print words or phrases. How would you use blank cards?

(*a*)

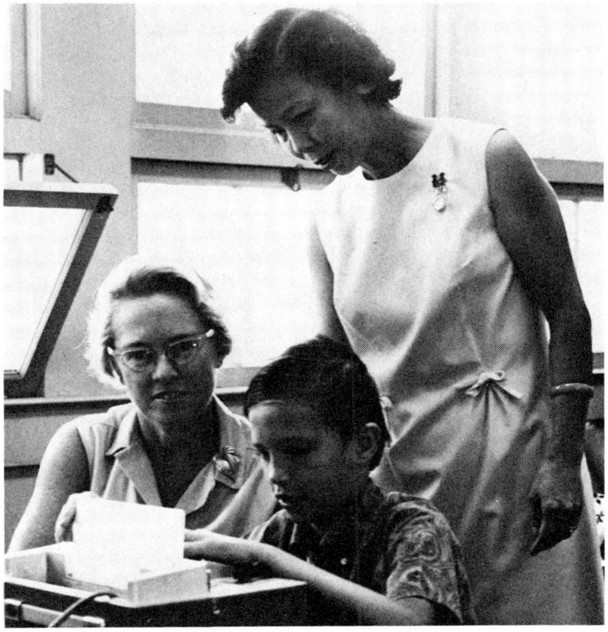

(*b*)

(*c*)

Figure 6.8 Card readers present words, numbers, pictures, and symbols visually and aurally. Learners see the information on the card and simultaneously hear the word, phrase, or sound that relates to it. (*a*) This girl is working on operations with fractions. (*b*) This boy is reporting his progress in vocabulary development. (*c*) These children have cut out pictures, pasted them on cards, and recorded the words that describe the pictures.

symbols, or words. Pupils can use the card to learn at their own pace. (See Figure 6.8.) Card readers are very effective for individualized vocabulary study. They are also valuable for teaching handicapped children (the hard-of-hearing, for example).

Card readers have captured the imagination of teachers, pupils, and manufacturers, and a variety of models are available. In deciding which type of recorder will be the most useful and economical, it is important to remember that good-quality electronic equipment is fairly expensive. A particular model, though it may seem simple to operate, rugged, and attractive, should be purchased only after a classroom tryout has been arranged through a reputable audiovisual dealer. Further, because even the best equipment needs servicing at times, service and repair arrangements should be thoroughly explored before a purchase is made.

Children choose the pace at which they talk, read, and think through a learning experience. Until recently, however, all children, regardless of the differences between them, had to work with audio materials played at a standard speed. Now engineers have found ways to compress speech without changing its pitch and by changing its quality only slightly.

One way of compressing speech is by *speech sampling*. Normal speech contains redundant sounds; that is, it contains more sounds than are needed for words and sentences to be recognizable. In speech sampling, words are segmented electronically into *sound bits*. Up to 50 percent of some sound bits can be removed without seriously interfering with the intelligibility of a word. A second method of compressing speech is to remove the soundless spaces, or pauses, between words. (People who listen to themselves on tape are often amazed at how often they pause.) Still another way of compressing speech is to chop off the ends of vowel sounds.

Audio equipment that does these things has only recently made its appearance, but already alternative systems are available. One system converts prerecorded, normal-speed audio materials into a compressed form for playback at a higher speed. For example, suppose a school library has acquired a set of Dr. Seuss books, each of which is accompanied by an audiotape of the contents. By putting the original recording into a compressor and adjusting the controls, the librarian can rerecord it on a second tape at any speed from 200 words per minute to 500 or more. Listeners can then have the very challenging experience of selecting the higher-speed tape they wish to hear, and they can gradually increase their listening speed. Alternatively, by selecting a piece of equipment such as the Lexicon unit in Figure 6.9, the librarian can play the original recording that accompanies the Dr. Seuss books at faster or slower speeds.

(a)

(b)

Figure 6.9 Newly developed machines make it possible to record and play back material at varying speeds without distorting the pitch. (*a*) This simple-to-operate Lexicon Varispeech machine enables users to record sounds or speech and play them back at from half the original speed, to two and a half times the original rate. (*b*) These children are reading variable-speed materials at up to 450 words per minute. Dr. John Stamper, who developed the materials, looks on.

The effect of variable playback speeds is difficult to describe and should be experienced. One teacher who has experimented with compressed speech reports,

> I am so used to listening at normal speeds [150 words per minute] that I never realized how . . . demanding higher . . . listening speeds can be. The first time I turned up the speed from 150 to 250 words per minute I felt positively threatened. Then, as I continued and forced myself to concentrate, things suddenly got much better. Suddenly, I knew what was going on. The next thing I knew I had turned up the speed to 350 and then 400, and I still could keep up with the information . . . !

Teachers who want to try compressed-speech equipment should seek the advice of a local media specialist or dealer. Also, they should keep in mind the following points:

1. Is the compressed sound normal in pitch and good in quality? Sounds must retain their original pitch and tone for *communication* to be possible at high rates of speed.
2. Is the range of speech speeds appropriate for school use? Students can generally be expected to follow, and find interesting, speeds of from 50 to 500 words a minute.
3. Is the equipment simple to operate, dependable, and easy to service? If possible, a demonstration should be arranged for at which students too can try the equipment.

Record Players and Special Audio Equipment

Record players, which are usually thought of as a traditional means of bringing audio learning experiences into the classroom, are still widely used. Once again, the criteria for purchasing equipment are the fidelity of the reproduced sounds, the ease with which the unit can be operated, cost, and dependability.

Various special-purpose audio learning devices are also available. An audio learning system for typing students in which audio instructions are given directly to individual students has recently been introduced. (See Figure 6.11*a*.) For teachers who wish to record small groups of students doing choral speaking or reading plays, there are recording systems with several high-fidelity microphones. Up to nine speakers can be recorded using equipment like that in Figure 6.11*b*.

AUDIO LEARNING MATERIALS

Audio learning materials for groups and individuals come in a variety of forms. Traditionally, audio messages have been recorded on disks, which come in a variety of sizes (usually 10 or 12 inches in diameter) and spin at various rates. The slower the rate of spin, the more information can be recorded on a given space. *Microgrooving* records further increases the amount of material they can carry. Usually any speed of disk will reproduce speech sounds satisfactorily; however, high-fidelity recordings of music or environmental sounds are usually made on stereo disks that revolve 33⅓ times a minute.

Long-playing records—or LPs, as they are commonly called—are particularly well suited for relatively short educational material, such as poetry, essays or short stories, dramatized historical episodes, or songs. To record such brief pieces on individual tapes would be uneconomical, and to record several such items on a single tape would make it difficult to locate individual selections. LPs that rotate 33⅓ times a minute usually contain from 10 to 15 minutes of recorded information per side, depending on the number and spacing of the microgrooves engraved on them.

Most current audio learning materials are recorded on tape, either open reels or, more often,

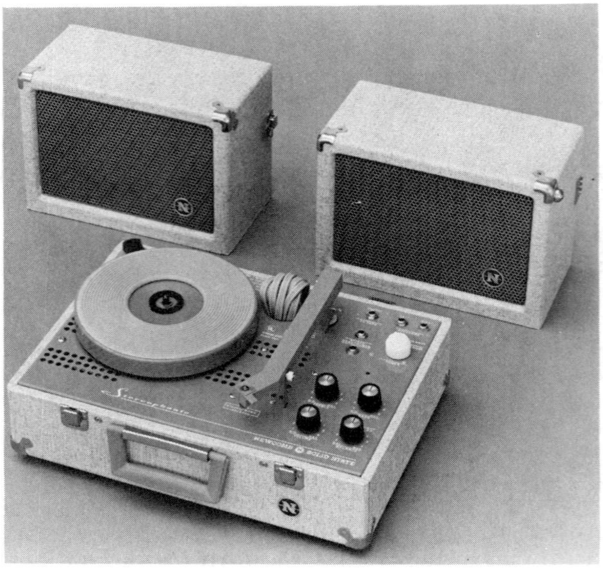

(a)

(b)

cassettes, although they are generally available on records as well.

Taped learning materials have several advantages. They can be played back an indefinite number of times with little or no decrease in the quality of the message. Occasionally a student who is not familiar with open-reel units may accidentally erase information, but proper instruction in using such equipment can prevent this. In the case of cassettes, teachers should make sure the small plastic clip at the rear is removed before the material is used in the classroom. This simple precaution makes it impossible to erase material accidentally.

Cassettes that hold $\frac{1}{8}$-inch-wide tape are very small (only $2\frac{1}{2} \times 4 \times \frac{1}{2}$ inches). They play at a uniform speed of $1\frac{7}{8}$ inches per second and contain from 15 minutes to an hour or more of material. Larger cartridges of $\frac{1}{4}$-inch tape are of somewhat higher quality and are used primarily in language laboratories.

Radio continues to serve as a means of bringing useful audio information into the classroom. In terms of cost effectiveness, it continues to rank high. Innovative uses of radio include the Peace Satellite communication programs of the South Pacific, the correspondence schools of the air that serve the outback regions of Australia (see Figure 6.13), statewide and regional educational broadcasts in the United States.

The variety of uses for audio learning materials is virtually endless. Consider some of the following examples.

In a midwestern elementary school, a music appreciation class assembled within range of a radio receiver two mornings a week to hear a music lesson broadcast by the state university.

In a high school library a student was seated

Figure 6.10 Record players such as the Newcomb solid-state machine (*a*) and the Califone Model 1815K (*b*) are well suited for classroom use, because they can be played at varying speeds. Thus they can play older 78 rpm records as well as 45, $33\frac{1}{3}$, and 16 rpm disks.

(a)

Figure 6.11 Special kinds of playback and recording equipment are available for specific uses. (*a*) This audio keyboard enables each member of a small group to listen to and respond to typing instructions. (*b*) The problem of varying voice levels in group recordings is solved by this device, which picks up, records, and balances as many as nine sound inputs *and levels* simultaneously. What kinds of creative small-group activities does this equipment make possible?

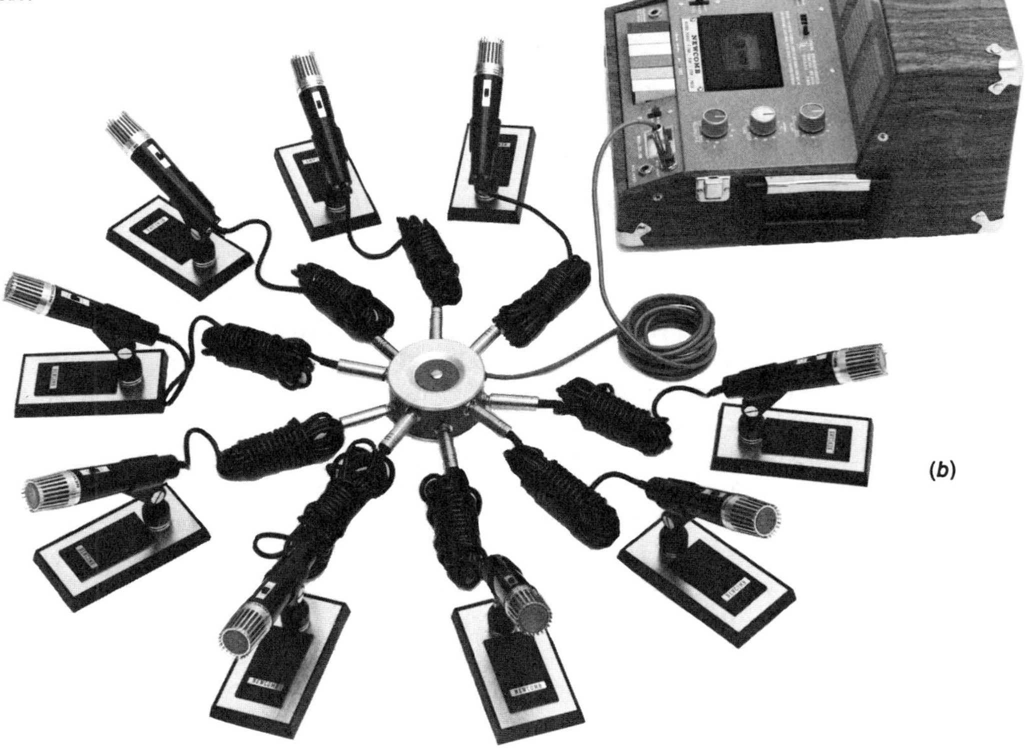

(b)

Figure 6.12 Audio recordings are available in a variety of forms. Shown are (upper left) 1/4-inch tape on 7-inch and 5-inch open reels; (middle left and center) 1/8-inch cassettes; (lower left) 1/4-inch tape cartridges, which are gradually being superseded by cassettes but are still in use; and (upper and lower right) 12-inch and 8-inch records.

before a compressed-speech cassette unit. Moments before, she had taken a standard tape cassette, labeled *Inland Waterways of Central Europe,* from a library shelf. After listening to the opening explanation, she stopped, reversed the tape, and listened to it again. Satisfied that she had understood the information, she increased the playback speed from 150 to 225 words per minute, then slowed it down to 200 words a minute,—a faster-than-normal pace, but one that was still comfortable for her.

In a primary classroom, nearly 60 children aged 5 through 8 were taking part in an exciting individualized instruction program. Even the youngest children were working on their own and at their own pace. Around one table, three children had donned earphones; listening intently, each was following the words of a recorded story in his or her own copy of an illustrated book. "The goal is enjoyment," the teacher commented, but added, "some of the children learn to recognize the relationship between the audio and visual word—and learn to read." At another table two children worked as a team. One checked the other's responses to vocabulary cards that they ran through a card reader. As they listened to the words describing colors or shapes, they learned to associate each audio cue with the correct picture.

During this time three teachers assigned to the 60 pupils monitored the work being done, evaluated the responses of students, helped pupils select and use learning materials, and encouraged them to plan ways to use newfound in-

Figure 6.13 This boy is "attending," via a two-way radio, one of the Australian Schools of the Air. Hundreds of children who live in remote areas get an education by listening to, asking questions of, and getting directions and encouragement from radio teachers. Assignments are regularly submitted by correspondence.

formation—by drawing pictures, writing a sentence or two, or telling other students about some of their discoveries.[1]

Audio learning can be very effective in developing skills. An industrial arts teacher had been concerned about the countless hours he spent repeating directions related to some of the skills needed to do even the most rudimentary woodworking projects. He solved his problem by making a half-dozen audio tapes explaining such things as what basic drawing instruments were like and how to use them, defining various terms used in woodworking, identifying 10 kinds of wood used in cabinetmaking, and so forth. In each case, the audio instructions were related to trays of appropriate objects, tools, and specimens. (See Figure 6.14.)

At another school the audiovisual coordinator solved the fall-of-the-year problem of teachers who had forgotten how to use equipment over the summer by preparing taped instructions on the use of projection devices and copying machines.

SOME ADVANTAGES OF AUDIO LEARNING MATERIALS

Their Suitability for Individualized Instruction

Take any group of 25 young learners and you will find that all 25 differ in the rate at which they comprehend material, all 25 have different attention spans, and all 25 have different interests. Audio learning materials are, by their very nature, a very effective means of taking these inevitable differences into account. Audio learning opportunities can enable any learner, regardless of his or her ability, to become more involved in learning experiences. The fact that learners can choose their own pace in working with audio materials helps overcome the inertia and discouragement that results from moving forward at a pace set by a large group.

Figure 6.15 shows the interaction between a teacher and an actual class of 25 pupils during a 20-minute discussion of a tape on the Panama Canal. What might have happened if pupils 4, 23, and 25 had had the opportunity of using audio learning materials on their own, in addition to participating in the group lesson? What might have happened if pupils 1, 2, and 15 had had such an opportunity? Suppose these three were slow learners who needed more time to listen to and digest information. The right audio learning materials could have allowed them to do this. These children might then have had creative ideas to contribute during the next group discussion. On the other hand, suppose pupils 1, 2, and 15 were so far ahead of their age-mates that they were bored with

[1] *Evaluation Report of the English Skills and Literature Program*, Hawaii Curriculum Center, Honolulu (November 1971).

Figure 6.14 This industrial arts student is being "talked through" the steps in making a molded plastic object. He responds to the taped directions by manipulating tools and identifying chemicals and other equipment used in casting plastic. What advantages do you see in this kind of procedure?

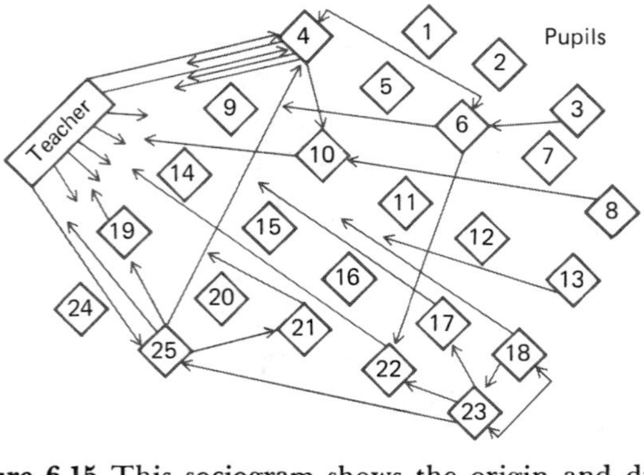

Figure 6.15 This sociogram shows the origin and direction of the responses of 25 members of a fifth-grade class during a 20-minute discussion period that followed their listening, as a group, to a 15-minute tape, *The Building of the Panama Canal.* The discussion centered on questions developed by the pupils and their teacher prior to listening to the tape. The questions had been summarized on the chalkboard. As the diagram shows, 13 pupils entered the discussion. How did the participation of pupils 4, 23, and 25 in the discussion affect the class? What do you think of this group instructional technique? What alternatives are now available?

the pace of the group discussion. The right audio learning materials might have allowed them to search independently for further information, which they could later report to the group.

There are at least 20,000 well-planned audio instructional programs and learning materials available to classroom teachers on open-reel tapes, records, or cassettes, and the majority are useful for individualized instruction. Small groups of pupils should be encouraged to work together in planning activities; selecting audiotapes, records, or cassettes; and using them. Usually it takes some time to build new ways of learning into the habit patterns of students. Those who have spent years actively or passively participating in large-group instruction may find it hard at first to work constructively in the fever atmosphere that individualized instruction produces. It is up to the teacher, then, to guide learners toward profitable learning experiences.

(a)

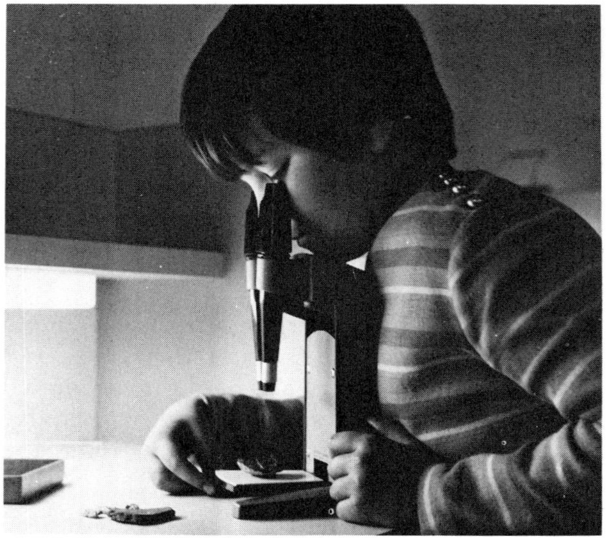

(c)

Figure 6.16 The children in these pictures are seeking information. (*a*) A boy and girl respond to cues given in the tape accompanying a filmstrip. (*b*) Four children follow other audiotutorial suggestions as they evaluate newfound information. (*c*) A girl uses a low-powered microscope in pursuing a learning goal. How do such activities affect your attitudes about teaching responsibilities? What effect do they have on the pupil's involvement in the learning process?

(b)

Their Ability to Repeat Information

In addition to facilitating individualized instruction, audio materials can free teachers from the endless and often repetitious task of "giving information." "How wonderful it is," a teacher reports, "to find that audio . . . instructions and descriptions . . . can be referred to endlessly to [give] the same explanation or describe the same sequence of instructions. . . ." More and more, media are being used to *free the teacher to teach.*

Just as airport traffic controllers can talk down approaching pilots who seek a way in through a fog, so too teachers can explain, on tape, how to determine what information is relevant in an arithmetic problem, how to pronounce new vocabulary, how to use maps and charts to locate rivers, mountain ranges, capitals, principal cities, ports, and so forth.

Their Factual Accuracy and Completeness

Most audio materials currently available from educational or commercial sources are the result of careful planning by professional educators and experts on a given subject. In addition, recorded information is usually accompanied by related learning materials. For example, a taped explanation of the metamorphosis of honey wasps may refer to actual objects and specimens in a learning kit that accompanies the tape—the wings of the honey wasp, a portion of the wasp's nest, the cells within it, and so on.

Initially, audio materials were used simply to give information. Now cues, directions, and suggestions for learners are being incorporated into audio experiences. Audio materials today not only impart information, but refer the learner to related experiences. (See Figure 6.16.)

Their Mechanical Flexibility

Today, thanks to variable-speed tape playbacks, learners can control the speed at which they listen to material. They can slow the playback speed of difficult information or speed up easier material. Observers report that pupils who use controlled-speed playback usually increase their listening speed gradually. They respond in a positive way to the challenge of setting their own listening goals.

SOME SOURCES OF AUDIO LEARNING MATERIALS

The production, distribution, and use of records, open-reel tapes, tape cassettes, and language master playbacks has increased tremendously in recent years. Though this discussion of sources of audio learning materials includes references to the format of materials, the emphasis is on the manner in which they direct the student through *experiences* with interrelated materials such as flat pictures, models, specimens, 8mm films loops, projected stills, workbooks, laboratory manuals, and study sheets.

School Radio Broadcasts

Vast areas of the United States are within reach of the country's 750 educational radio stations, many of which provide systematic instructional programming for school use. Educational radio began in 1919 when the University of Wisconsin's state-owned station WHA began broadcasting. Since then, numerous local, state, and regional educational broadcasting systems have come into existence, among them Empire School Broadcasting Service in New York State, the Wisconsin School of the Air (a network of 12 satellite stations), the Indiana State School of the Air, the Minnesota School Broadcast Service, the Texas School of the Air, and others. In addition, many city school districts use radio to broadcast audio learning programs; Phoenix, Arizona; Los Angeles and San Francisco, California; Carbondale, De Kalb, and Urbana, Illinois; Iowa City, Iowa; Louisville, Richmond, and Lexington, Kentucky; Boston, Massachusetts; Detroit, East Lansing, Grand Rapids, Kalamazoo, and Marquette, Michigan; Portland, Corvallis, and Eugene, Oregon; Philadelphia and Pittsburgh, Pennsylvania; Knoxville, Murfreesboro, and Nashville, Tennessee; Seattle and Pullman, Washington; Provo and Salt Lake City, Utah; among others.

The National Education Radio Network, a division of the National Association of Educational Broadcasters, provides its 200 member stations with a minimum of five hours a week of high-quality instructional programming. The programs are produced by individual network affiliates and made available to association members for rebroadcasting.

Some advantages of school broadcasts. School broadcasts are carefully planned audio learning experiences that use resources beyond those available to the average teacher. They have several advantages:

1. *They are actually team teaching demonstrations.* Educational broadcast series grow out of months of planning and consultation with local classroom teachers and other specialists. They represent the combined efforts of supervisors, teachers, and subject-matter experts who work together to determine what learning experiences are best suited to radio as a medium.

2. *They can document current and historical events.* Live or replayed radio broadcasts of special events can provide audio documentation of historical events, such as the confrontation leading to World War II, the establishment of the United Nations, the lunar landings, and so on.

3. *They can broadcast music for study and appreciation.* Educational broadcasters have arranged for skilled performers to participate in programs with musical themes: the music of other times, the music of other lands, folk music, and so forth. The Civic Orchestra concert sponsored by the New York State Empire Network and *Music Time and Rhythms and Games* and other programs sponsored by the Wisconsin School of the Air are examples.

4. *They are often planned with the active participation of local teachers and pupils in mind.* Radio lesson manuals or handbooks describe the content of programs, outline what pupils are expected to do, and list the materials that should be on hand when the broadcast begins. Such materials are usually prepared for and distributed to teachers well before the broadcast. Preliminary study and discussion of these materials is encouraged. Whenever possible, programs give audio instructions for experiments or activities pupils can participate in during the broadcast or immediately after it.

5. *They are available on tape.* Teachers can obtain "the best of educational radio broadcasts" on tape from the National Center for Audio Tapes.

The National Center for Audio Tapes

The National Center for Audio Tapes (NCAT) is a department of the University of Colorado that selects the best audio learning programs and makes them available through a tape-dubbing service to any school district or educational agency.[2] Many of the programs chosen are educational radio broadcasts, and all can be obtained by individual teachers. Thus a tremendous reservoir of audio learning experiences is accessible to all school districts in the United States, including those outside the reception areas of current educational radio facilities.

Government Sources of Audio Materials

The efficiency of audio materials has been recognized for years by many government agencies that need to distribute information at a low cost to mass audiences. A large number of such informational materials are now available, and many are useful for instructional purposes. For example, the National Aeronautics and Space Administration produces periodic reports about activities at space centers. These reports usually consist of interviews with astronauts, scientists, and the like. Available first as radio broadcast materials, these interviews almost immediately become available on tape for use in schools.

The Department of State produces weekly radio reports that are taped and distributed to schools requesting them. These reports include accounts of current world problems, of the situation in developing countries, and so

[2] Teachers and administrators who are interested in this service should address inquiries to the Director, National Center for Audio Tapes, Stadium Building 348, University of Colorado, Boulder, CO 80302.

on. The departments of the Interior; Agriculture; Health, Education and Welfare; the Bureau of Fisheries; and many other departments and agencies use radio and tapes to disseminate information.

The work of the National Council of Teachers of English in assembling audio materials is well known. Over the years, the council's collection of recorded readings, interpretations, and dramatizations has grown to include the plays of Shakespeare, the prose of American authors, ballads and verses of the American frontier, and many other types of literature. Readings by contemporary English-speaking authors virtually bring them into the classroom to read their own works.[3]

Guides to Audio Learning Resources

Government agencies, businesses, and industries are a source of many useful audio learning materials, and guides and directories to these materials are produced annually. A very timely and comprehensive guide over the years has been the *Educator's Guide to Free Audio and Video Tapes*.[4] This and similar guides to *free* and *accessible* teaching tapes are available for reference in most school libraries.

Audio learning materials in virtually all subjects are now being produced commercially. Newly organized production companies as well as old-line textbook publishers have impressive lists of curriculum-coordinated audio learning materials available in all the standard formats: as tape cassettes, open-reel tapes, and records.

Thousands of audio materials, most of which have been carefully tested in actual teaching-learning situations, are available for learners of all ages. Rather than devote a great deal of space to citing examples here, we have attached a list of tested sources of such materials at the end of this chapter. Requests for information from these sources should specify the grades, the curriculum areas, and the courses for which materials are needed.

Among the materials available are, for example,

1. A complete listening skills set on 12 audiocassettes, a spelling skills set on 12 audiocassettes, a set of oral fluency skills on 12 audiocassettes, and ten other language arts skill sets, each on 12 audiocassettes.[5]
2. A complete anthology of selected books for grades K–8, all recorded on a graded series of 100 tape cassettes.[6]
3. An *Economics Series* including "Rich Nations—Poor Nations," "Gold, Growth, and Greed—The New Global Economy," "The Energy Crisis," "The Age of Scarcity," and other materials, all presented on either cassettes or records with accompanying filmstrips.[7]
4. A *Children's Literature* series of sound-filmstrip sets, each containing either audiocassettes or long-playing records, a filmstrip, and books. The series includes 36 sets of 5 books each.[8]
5. *Mexico, An Overview of the History, Culture and Language,* a series of audiocassettes or open-reel tapes and filmstrips for use in bilingual learning experiences. The entire set includes several hundred graded cassettes or reels.[9]
6. An interrelated series of curriculum-coordi-

[3] See *Resources for the Teaching of English,* National Council of Teachers of English (published annually), 111 Kenyon Road, Urbana, Ill. 61801.

[4] Published annually by the Educator's Progress Service, Randolph, Wisc.

[5] Taylor Teaching Tapes, 737 Third Ave., Chula Vista, Calif. 92010.

[6] *Troll Read-Alongs,* Troll Associates, 320 Rt. 17, Mahwah, N.J.

[7] Westinghouse Learning Corporation, 100 Park Ave., New York, N.Y. 10017.

[8] Weston Woods, Weston, Conn. 06880.

[9] Wible Language Institute, 24 So. 8th St., Allentown, Penn. 18105.

nated audio learning materials with picture sets and filmstrips in such subject areas as Afro-American history, American history, and language arts.[10]

In examining the sources at the end of the chapter, keep in mind your own instructional objectives, and be alert to learning materials that may fit your evolving instructional development plan.

SELECTING AND USING AUDIO LEARNING RESOURCES

Decisions to use audio learning resources should be based on the needs and abilities of learners and what they will find challenging. The materials should be compatible with the recording or playback equipment available, valid in terms of content, and appropriate in relation to the students' known objectives.

Individualizing Instruction via Audiotapes

An elementary school teacher in the upper grades began to individualize the teaching of spelling by using commercial tapes on which words were first pronounced, then spelled. Following this, listeners were invited to spell the words themselves and to listen to their own spelling as a means of reinforcing their mastery of the words.

Because the word lists on the tapes were limited, the teacher recorded additional words nominated by students for taping. Interest in the words the students selected was higher than in the words initially studied. Finally, students selected and recorded still more words. This teacher now depends increasingly on student production of taped word lists each semester as a means of awakening interest in spelling. The students who assume responsibility for the lists develop skill not only in spelling, but in recording techniques as well.

School librarians who keep prerecorded audio materials on the shelves along with books and other learning media report that student use of such materials is increasing. Naturally playback equipment is also kept in the library for students who wish to consult audio references while doing independent research. (See Figure 6.17.)

Librarians also report that when variable-speed playback equipment is available, many students automatically increase the speed at which they listen. It is not uncommon for students who begin listening at normal speech speeds of 140–160 words per minute to end the semester listening to 400–500 words per minute *with no decrease in comprehension.*

Increased listening speeds can lead to increased reading speeds when audio books are used. Talking books, such as the Dr. Seuss series[11] and the *Troll Read-Along,*[12] which are recorded at standard speeds, can be played at a slower or faster rate if variable-speed playback equipment is available.

Research on Compressed Speech

Research on the effects of listening to compressed speech has given rise to the following conclusions:[13]

[10] Encyclopedia Britannica Educational Corporation, 425 North Michigan Avenue, Chicago, Ill.

[11] *Horton Hatches the Egg, Fox in Socks, Bartholomew and the Oobleck,* and other audio-taped books in the Dr. Seuss series are published by Random House.

[12] *Troll Read-Alongs for Grades K-8* (Mahwah, N.J.: Troll Associates, 1975).

[13] Harun Arrasjib, "Listening and Compressed Speech," paper presented at the New York Communications Convocation, Grossinger, N.Y., 1973; James Challis, "The Effect of Fixed and Learner Selected Rates of Compressed Speech in an Audio Visual Learning Environment on the Achievement of College Level Students," thesis, Oklahoma University, 1973, 279 pp., avail. from University Microfilms, 300 No. Zeeb Road, Ann Arbor, Mich. 48106; S. Levine, "Listener Preferences for Rate of Presentation of Recorded Information," Consortium on Auditory Learning Materials for Handicapped, Regional Instructional Materials Center for Handicapped Children and Youth, Michigan State University, East Lansing, Mich. 1974, 96 pp.

Figure 6.17 Audiocassettes are being used increasingly in school libraries. These children tell the school librarian what they need, and she helps them locate useful audio materials. The library stocks thousands of tape cassettes for student use. Information stored on cassettes is economical to update, because the tapes can be erased and reused.

1. Between 90 and 95 percent of the students who have experimented with compressed speech derive satisfaction from the opportunity to change their listening speeds.
2. As materials become more understandable to listeners they usually increase their listening speed. With listening materials appropriate for a grade level, listening speeds can be increased by 50 percent with no loss of comprehension. This, of course, saves a great deal of time for the learner. However, in studying foreign languages, some students tend to slow down material at first. For some this slowing down becomes so comfortable that it becomes a habit and has to be discouraged as the term progresses. Most language students, however, increase their listening and response rates on their own initiative.
3. Most students have the potential to listen to and comprehend information at rates substantially faster than normal speaking speeds.

Using Audio Equipment

Most audiotape recording and playback equipment is so simple to operate that even young pupils soon learn how to use it to record and play back all sorts of material, especially *their own*. Instructions regarding the use of particular units are, of course, provided by the manufacturer. The *Student Production Guide* also gives a number of tested procedures for setting up audio equipment and recording and playing back audio materials.

Microphone Techniques for Teachers and Pupils

Teachers who use original tapes in the classroom soon discover that there is more to making a good recording than merely standing in front of a microphone. *One must know how to use the microphone and its controls.*

A microphone is simply a *means of communication.* Anyone using a microphone should imagine that he or she is conversing with or performing for another human being. It is also helpful to bear in mind the following suggestions:

1. **Be prepared.** Usually the thought of recording information motivates a person to spend a reasonable amount of time preparing a script. This invariably results in a better-organized and more understandable end product than a more casual approach. It is best to use a single-page outline or a series of cards, because the microphone will pick up the sound of shuffling papers. (See Figure 6.18.)

2. **Be comfortable.** After some practice in making recordings, most people are able to relax and actually enjoy the experience. As one teacher put it, "I wouldn't believe the first recording I made. When I played it back I could hear and almost feel the 'uptight' quality. . . . But . . . after working with the students for less than a week, we learned to relax."

Even a little practice in facing a microphone usually results in more assurance in speaking in the same conversational, friendly manner one uses in day-to-day teaching.

3. **Face the microphone.** The most frequent cause of uneven volume in recordings is forgetting where the microphone is. Every time a speaker turns his or her head, the distance to the recording surface is changed. Keep the microphone at a uniform distance from you and in a line between you and the imagined or real audience. Learn to face the microphone constantly by stepping a little to the left if you wish to turn your head right and vice versa.

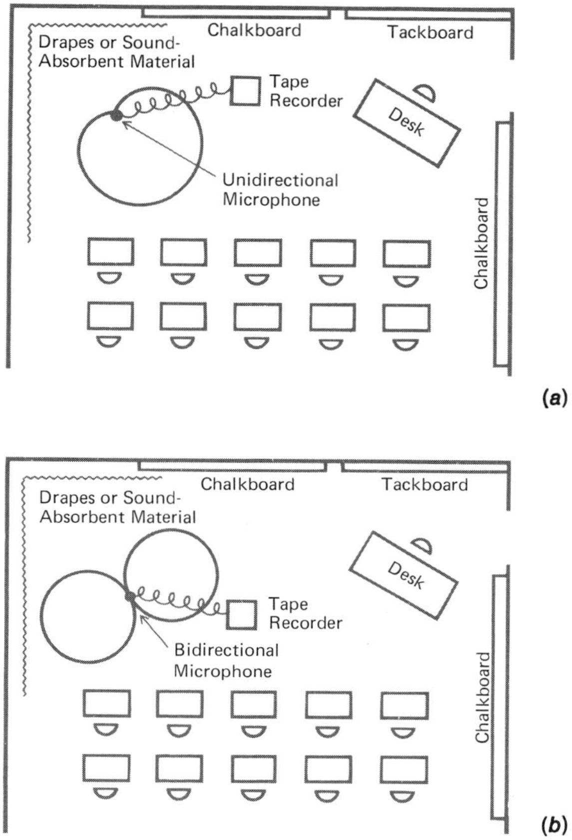

Figure 6.18 These diagrams show two setups for making a classroom recording. (*a*) Pupils position themselves in front of a unidirectional microphone. Those with weaker voices stand within 12 to 15 inches of the mike and those with stronger voices close behind them. (*b*) Pupils position themselves on opposite sides of a bidirectional microphone. Which arrangement is best? Why?

4. **Eliminate human static.** Remember that the microphone records everything it hears. If you are too close to it, it will pick up hissing or sibilants (S-S-S-S-S or Sh-Sh-Sh-Sh-Sh). Weav-

ing forward and backward before the microphone, fussing with it, or brushing against it will produce annoying sounds. Be careful too to avoid superfluous Ah's, throat clearings, U-m-m-m's, and so forth.

5. Let the controls help you. Proper use of a microphone's volume and tone controls will help you achieve a lifelike recording. The higher the volume control is set, the greater the *pickup range* of the microphone. One teacher complained that playground noises outside the building were being recorded along with songs by two children in the classroom. Obviously, the volume control was set too high. Most recording equipment has a visual signal that indicates when the sound level is correct. But the best procedure is to experiment with volume settings until good results are achieved. The rule is, "Record, play back the material, evaluate, then try again."

The tone control determines the degree of treble or bass in a voice, music, or other sounds picked up by the microphone. A little experimentation should reveal when the tone setting is correct.

One of the most frequent causes of poor recording quality is small deposits of magnetic material that brush off the surface of the tape and accumulate on the recording head. To keep this head clean, merely run a cotton swab saturated with any one of a number of special cleaning fluids intended for magnetic heads over it.

Dubbing

Duplicating, copying, or dubbing a tape recording is relatively simple. To be sure you have the most current information, consult your audiovisual supervisor or local dealer. Ordinarily, two machines are used. One plays the recorded tape, and the other duplicates it on blank tape. Special wires with plugs at one end and alligator clips at the other pick up the magnetic sound signals from the machine playing the tape to be copied. The alligator clips go on the speaker posts of the playing recorder, and the other ends of the wires are plugged into the machine with the blank tape. The sounds from the original recording should not be allowed to travel through the air to the microphone of the dubbing recorder, as this lessens the fidelity of the dubbed recording and may result in background noise on the duplicate.

Evaluating Recordings

The proof of a pudding is in the eating, and the proof of a recording is in the playing. In judging the quality and usefulness of a recording, ask yourself the following questions:

1. Is it loud enough for everyone to hear and understand it?
2. Does it have a good tone? That is, do the recorded voices and sounds closely resemble the original voices and sounds?
3. Is it clear and distinct—free of unwanted background noises, interruptions, scratchiness, or other annoying sounds that indicate a poorly placed microphone or wrongly set tone or volume controls?

Pupils who participate in recordings usually profit from an opportunity to evaluate their efforts. (See Figure 6.19.) Often they are more critical of their own efforts than the teacher. For example, fifth-graders in one school decided to make a tape about themselves to send to a group of children in another state. The playback of their first effort, however, came as a shock. "We can't send this!" exclaimed one student. "They'll get a bad impression of us!"

They discussed how to improve the tape, and several groups got together to put on paper the key ideas they wanted to communicate. After three days of writing a script, recording, and rerecording, everyone was satisfied and the tape

Figure 6.19 This photograph captures three pupils' reactions to using a tape recorder to record and play back a short dramatization they have written. What desirable learning outcomes seem to be present?

was mailed. Commenting on the experience, their teacher reported, "The students were very critical of their efforts. They set standards for themselves which they might not have accepted as reasonable had I suggested them."

The use of recordings to encourage self-evaluation is valuable in many subject areas.

The language arts. The opportunity for objective self-criticism provided by tape recordings is apparent even in the primary grades when youngsters attempt to read aloud; when they give "Monday morning reports" on the weather, weekend activities, and events at home; and when they learn how to answer a telephone.

In the upper grades, recordings of panel discussions, book reports, discussions of current events, and student explanations of processes demonstrate the importance of *being able to get up on one's feet and express one's ideas in a clear and well-organized manner.*

Children often become so accustomed to a teacher's admonitions about improving their speech or grammar that such remarks are no longer incentives to improvement. Hearing their own tape-recorded voices, on the other hand, makes errors in grammar and sentence structure and needless repetitions painfully apparent.

"Do I sound like that?" children will ask. "How can I have a better voice?"

"Do I talk that *fast?*" they will say, or "that *slowly?*" or "with all those 'ah's' and 'er's'?"

When the students can hear their own voices, teachers need no longer wear themselves out trying to drill suggestions for improvement into them. Most children will be their own critic, and that of their classmates.

Social studies. A primary goal of social studies teachers is to provide experiences that are so lifelike that they give learners a true understanding of people, places, and things in the world. A tape recorder makes it possible to listen to others as they express ideas and to exchange ideas with others outside the classroom. For example, in one civics class, students were assigned to several committees, each committee being responsible for gathering information on one aspect of government—education, fire and police protection, traffic control, the provision and maintenance of recreation areas, sanitation and public health, and taxation and finance. In their planning sessions, each committee decided which offices and personnel they would visit to gather facts. They set up interviews with various officials, taped them, and later edited the tapes to eliminate secondary information. The end result was, in effect, to bring the officials "into the classroom."

The tape recorder also presents a challenge to those willing to do the research, writing, editing, and rehearsing needed to produce taped reconstructions of historical events, such as the Norman invasion, the Battle of the Coral Sea, or adventures in space. The astronauts' dramatic, "on-the-spot" news accounts with good background effects will hold the attention of most classes, and pupil interest in such projects runs high.

Music. The reality of listening to themselves on tape can be a great incentive to music pupils to improve their performance. Recordings can be made of individual vocal and instrumental performances, as well as quartets and choral singing. Older pupils can record themselves. Many school music departments have tape recorders set up for soloists to record and hear their work. Tape recorders can also be used to help pupils who have difficulty identifying notes and tones accurately.

Business education. Speed tests for typing and shorthand classes and vocabulary and spelling drills can all be recorded on tape. In order to give pupils experience in doing typing and shorthand in actual business situations, one teacher arranged for 15 local businesspeople to dictate on tape three letters of varying length and difficulty selected from their files. The resulting 45 letters were a challenging variation from the regular class routine and gave students a realistic idea of the requirements of business firms. Similar tapes for use in business education have also been commercially recorded. Business education classes also use tapes of business telephone conversations, employer interviews at local firms, and both imaginary and genuine sales talks—the latter given by local sales people.

Dramatics and speech. Unusual examples of speech, debates, reporting, and dramatics are frequently heard on radio or television, and these can be useful in teaching speech or dramatics. Most tape recorders are equipped with a radio or television *takeoff line,* a length of wire with a plug at one end and twin metal clips at the other. By attaching the clips to the voice coils of a radio or television set and then plugging in the tape recorder, teachers can tape an address by the president of the United States, the audio part of a television drama, a panel discussion, or a well-delivered commercial.

Any of these may become teaching materials at the right time and in the right circumstances. Used as models, the tapes can help pupils make judgments about styles of speech, enunciation, phrasing and vocal intonations, vocabulary, and sentence structure.

When a tape recorder is used during any oral presentation—for example, during the rehearsal of a play—the members of the cast can get a vivid idea of their strengths and weaknesses from the playback.

Guidance activities. We are only beginning to realize the many important guidance uses that can be devised for the tape recorder. Suppose that when Johnny (or Jane) comes to kindergarten, a simple conversation with him is recorded. As he goes from grade to grade, his habits of speech, oral reading, and conversations revealing his interests, likes and dislikes, and ambitions, can be captured on tape and filed. On graduation the tapes can be spliced together to make an aural record of his school life and progress. Imagine the interest of his parents, and possibly an employer, in such a document.

For students who plan to start working after high school, the tape recorder is also valuable. After the guidance director has determined what kind of employment offers the best opportunities for a student, both the student and his or her instructor may engage in role playing, with the instructor taking the part of an employer interviewing the student about a job. The taped interview can then be played back and the interviewee's weaknesses worked on.

LANGUAGE LABORATORIES

A language laboratory is a place where students can listen to and study the sounds, pace, words, and word groupings of a language, usually a foreign language, using audio tapes and playback equipment. The classroom is usually the scene of group-learning experiences: listening to the music of a culture, watching films of an area, and carrying on group conversations in the language. But *the language lab is where students do their aural-oral homework.* There each student interacts separately with carefully prepared taped materials. Each pupil listens to and responds to these materials at *his or her own pace.* Tapes can be replayed as often as necessary and, if variable-speed equipment is available, at whatever rate is comfortable.

Usually, language lab materials are recorded on cassette or cartridge tapes. Cartridge tapes are usually superior to cassettes because the fidelity of the sounds is more certain on $\frac{1}{4}$-inch tape than on $\frac{1}{8}$-inch tape. So that students may move ahead at their own pace, multiple copies of lessons are prepared on rapid-duplicating machinery and placed in a "library" in or near the lab. During any of the lab's open hours, students can pick up tapes that relate to a course and work with them. Working with a language tape means listening, responding, listening to the response, evaluating it, correcting oneself, listening again, moving ahead, or going back to review material. (See Figure 6.20.) In some labs students can insert their own tapes into the machines and make a copy of a lesson to take home.

Lab work can be supervised in several ways. A teacher may listen in on one or more machines, sampling individual efforts and offering a word of approval or advice. Or a teacher may ask students to turn in samples of their responses while they are still on the tapes, before the tapes are returned to the shelves.

Many language labs stock not only taped language lessons, but related audiovisual materials as well—films of life in different countries with foreign-language sound tracks that give most learners ample time to understand what is being shown, and series of slides and filmstrips with corresponding tapes. Many teachers use travel posters and pictures of cities, people, and costumes in the country whose language is being studied to provide an appropriate visual environment in language labs. Foreign-language folk songs are often made available, as well as the works of well-known native composers.

The language laboratory, with its audiolingual and related visual materials, should not be thought of as a replacement for the teacher, but as a powerful tool that allows the pupil to hear languages as they are spoken by native speakers and to do carefully controlled and recorded drills. A person learning to speak a language must practice speaking it correctly, and the language laboratory provides some of this practice. In a language lab, the teacher-pupil relationship traditional in language instruction is changed. In traditional language classes, each pupil gets to recite only occasionally. In a language laboratory each pupil is listening about half of the time and "reciting" the other half of the time. Instead of there being 30 children listening to one teacher, there may be one teacher sampling 30 concurrent but individual responses.

A language laboratory is not essential to an audiolingual program, of course. Programs similar to those used in labs but expanded through the addition of related visual media have been developed for use by students who do not have

Figure 6.20 (*a*) This listening laboratory gives students access to hundreds of audiolingual materials. (*b*) The girls shown here are working with records and tapes. Contrast this individualized learning with traditional learning situations where each pupil in a class of 30 or more must wait his or her turn to respond. (*c*) At work in her own carrel, a student listens to an audio lesson, moves ahead rapidly or slowly, "flips back" to relisten occasionally, and records her own responses. What do you think is the worth of such facilities and procedures, not only for language instruction but for individualized instruction in other subjects and skills?

(*a*)

(*b*)

(*c*)

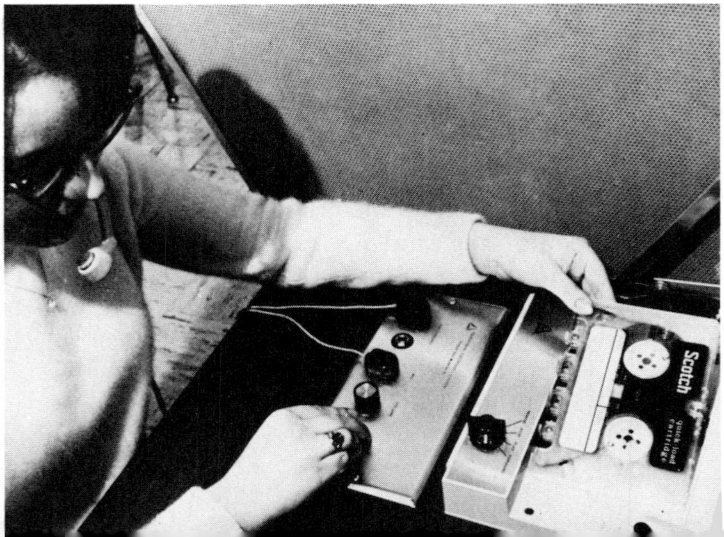

access to language labs but who do have the use of the usual classroom tape recorders, slide projectors, overhead projectors, and the like. (See Figure 6.21.)

TEACHER- AND PUPIL-CREATED AUDIO LEARNING MATERIALS

Many situations arise in which it is profitable for a teacher to create audio learning activities with the help of pupils. For example, in an arithmetic class, the teacher had spent a great deal of time explaining and reexplaining formulas for finding simple areas and volumes. Some pupils understood how the formulas were arrived at, but others did not. Sensing the situation, the teacher called together a trio of students who grasped the concepts. "Why not explain all this on tape," he suggested, "and perhaps refer to some actual cutouts or solid figures?"

Using a tray of small two- and three-dimensional models of squares, rectangles, and triangles, the teacher helped the trio write and correct a tape explaining the relationship between the sides of plane and solid figures and how the sides, or edges, are used in finding areas or volumes. Those who still had difficulty with this kind of problem listened to the tape and examined the tray of models. Some of the slower youngsters needed to hear the tape several times. The pupils who understood the formulas helped those who needed help, in-

Figure 6.21 Children here are using a multimedia audiolingual program in Japanese that includes tapes, charts, pictures, slides, and film loops. Cassette or open-reel playback units are provided by the local schools.

terpreting the taped reference materials and checking answers.

Other examples of audio learning materials[14] created by teachers include an audio learning module on root systems composed of actual mounted specimens of roots and a tape explaining them. At the end of the taped lesson, the listener is asked to identify the various types of roots. If the student's answers do not match the taped answers, relistening is suggested.

In a teacher-created audiotutorial lesson on sharks, learners are instructed to refer to numbered photographs, flat pictures, and diagrams (which are mounted on 7-by-10-inch cards). They hear explanations of each card, learning about the nature, habits, reproductive cycles, and characteristics of several kinds of sharks. Finally, they are given an oral quiz, a chance to evaluate their answers, and suggestions about creative follow-up activities.

In a teacher-created audio lesson on investments, actual investment documents and tape-recorded explanations are used to acquaint students with a variety of investment possibilities.

An audio lesson on Conestoga wagons was an outgrowth of two students' curiosity about the wagons used during the westward expansion of the United States. The tape refers listeners to photographic slides taken from books, wood engravings, and other sources. The range of subjects on which tapes can be made is limitless, and the enthusiasm of students for such projects is generally high.

DEVELOPING AUDIO LEARNING SKILLS

As more and more opportunities arise for learners to use audio learning materials, some formal attention will have to be given to developing listening skills. Learning from auditory experiences is actually more complex than one would think. The mere exposure of pupils to audible words and sounds is no guarantee that they will achieve desired learning goals—or that they will even hear the material presented. Our ears take in sounds from our environment all the time, yet we do not always hear them. The sounds of which we are aware at any given moment are the result of *auditory discrimination*. This discrimination is performed without our knowing it, by autonomic response mechanisms in the brain.

The Audio Learning Sequence

Though audition is too broad a subject to treat comprehensively here, we can describe the basic process fairly briefly. For a pupil to hear an instructional message, the message must be audible to the normal ear. Also, the learner's own hearing mechanism must be capable of responding to vibrations that fall within the normal range of audibility.

Next, the learner must *listen to* the message. It is possible to hear—that is, to be aware of—a sound without *attending* to it. This is particularly true in the case of word sounds, which require attention if the subtle syllabic differences between them are to be distinguished. Only if students attend to audio learning materials will they be able to *respond* to them and demonstrate their grasp of them.

The learner must hear. Basically, hearing may be thought of as a physical response to sound vibrations. Not all learners hear equally well in this sense. It is estimated that 5 percent or more of all children have a hearing problem of some kind.

Obviously, a pupil whose auditory mechanism is impaired cannot be expected to profit completely from audio materials. Thus the teacher's first responsibility is to determine

14 The audio learning materials described here were planned, produced, and evaluated in learning situations at the University of Hawaii by M. Mesaku, W. Yamamoto, N. Harney, A. Yamada, J. Hightower, C. Young, B. Kashiwahara, and A. Allan.

whether the pupils in a class can hear sounds within the normal range. Auditory sensitivity can be measured objectively by periodic audiometer tests administered by speech and hearing specialists. If the behavior or performance of a pupil creates doubt that his or her hearing is physiologically normal, the teacher should refer the child to the proper agency for testing and therapy.

Even when the physiological aspects of hearing are normal, however, some pupils may seem to exhibit a pathological hearing defect for psychological or psychoneurological reasons. Pupils may have become so accustomed to "tuning out" unwanted noise, for example, that they simply do not hear perfectly audible information. Often this turning-out process is so habitual that the pupils themselves are unaware of it. Rather than viewing such pupils negatively, teachers should give some thought to ways to develop their listening skills.

In classrooms where audio techniques are used excessively, fatigue may interfere with the pupils' hearing. Here again, the pupils may tune out material. Fatigue is apt to occur when teachers give endless spoken directions or lectures, during prolonged or tedious class discussions, or when lengthy passages that the students could read individually are read aloud. This kind of thing will exhaust even the most conscientious student. *The alternative, of course, is to develop an instructional plan that includes various audiovisual materials and thus permits multisensory learning.*

Many factors can obstruct pupils' hearing. Extraneous environmental noises, for example, can interfere with the audibility of instructional messages. Noises from out of doors can be very disruptive. Drilling and other building-construction sounds, heavy traffic noises, the noise from school playgrounds, and so forth, can interfere with audio learning. Similarly, sounds generated within the classroom itself—perhaps resulting from poor discipline—can provide highly effective competition to audio instruction. The acoustics of the classroom are also a factor. To overcome these physical barriers to hearing, teachers should see to it that annoying extraneous noises are kept out of the classroom and that a good acoustical environment is provided.

The learner must listen. There are many ways in which teachers can create favorable listening conditions. First, classroom facilities should be arranged in a manner conducive to listening. Next, audio material should be selected that is suited to the age of the learners, their interests, their vocabulary, and *their need for audio experiences.*

It is futile for teachers to enjoin pupils constantly to "be alert," "listen carefully," or "pay attention." Unless the instructional plan encourages pupils to *want* to listen to and to investigate audio learning materials, no amount of telling them to listen will be effective. One way to encourage listening is to arrange audio experiences that answer questions pupils want answers to. It is also important to explain in advance why given audio materials are worthwhile. If possible, pupils should have a voice in the selection of materials. This will give them an opportunity to realize their own responsibilities with respect to audio learning generally, as well as to understand the purpose of specific materials. Also helpful in getting students to listen are positive experiences with audio learning in the past.

The learner must respond. Pupils must not only be able to hear a message and be willing to listen attentively, but be able to demonstrate or apply their newly acquired knowledge. Typically, pupils are asked to demonstrate what they have learned on tests, in reports and essays, or in classroom discussions. They are given little opportunity, however, to use information creatively. As we have stressed earlier, creativity is an important outcome of learning. Producing creative response is the goal of audio learning activities, just as it is of other learning activities. Creative responses that should be encouraged include dramatic improvisations, participating in debates; demonstrating a skill; writing short stories, playlets, or poems; and producing audio, visual, or audiovisual materials. There are many ways in which pupils can express themselves, and they should be encouraged to do so.

Improving Listening Skills

Listening is a skill that can be developed. Students can learn to attend to central ideas, details, inferences, directions, and so on, while studying foreign languages, English, literature, social studies, and many other subjects. The degree to which a teacher can motivate pupils to become better listeners is of great importance. If psychological problems seem to affect a pupil's ability to hear, simply changing the seating arrangements may help.

Skill in listening is usually the result of the pupil's own interest in developing better listening habits and of his or her understanding of effective listening methods. The teacher must begin, then, by awakening the individual's awareness of listening as a skill. Pupils and teachers together can select interesting audio materials for listening practice. Although the materials chosen may relate to the regular curriculum, teachers should bear in mind that the goal of the practice periods is to develop *listening skills,* not to teach a subject. If students are not taking in what they hear in class because of poor listening skills, it may be wise at first to choose listening-training materials that do not seem like work. Later, when the pupils have achieved better coordination of their auditory and mental processes, more substantive material can be introduced.

During listening training sessions, teachers should encourage pupils to record and index—either mentally or in writing—every fact or impression they think is important. It should be made clear to students that they can think faster than a speaker can talk, and thus they have ample time to consider what they hear and draw conclusions about it. Before an actual listening experience begins, teachers may demonstrate how to record useful points of information and provide some guidance about the kinds of information to be listened for. For example, home economics teachers may ask students to list the ingredients of a recipe. English teachers may instruct pupils to jot down the names of key characters in a short story as it is presented on tape and to indicate their relation to one another and to the action. Algebra teachers may read several problems aloud and ask students to record them in symbolic form. Sometimes doodling—sketching symbols, diagrams, and so forth—can help pupils to visualize concepts they hear explained. The sketches and diagrams should be kept simple, however, and the doodling should not be permitted to interfere with listening to the tape or speaker.

Evaluating Skill-Training Sessions

Exercises in developing listening skills should be evaluated in terms of both the quantity and the quality of the information retained. For example, children who record all or most of the names in a story with several characters but who do not properly grasp the roles the characters play or their relation to one another need further training in the *qualitative* aspects of listening. Conversely, children who record accurately the names, roles, and relationships of only one or two characters need further training in listening for *quantities* of information.

It is important to test what students have absorbed immediately after a listening experience and to let them know before the end of the period how they have done. Teachers should explain to each pupil what *kinds* of information he or she failed to notice and what kinds of details should be attended to in future aural experiences.

INCORPORATING AUDIO LEARNING EXPERIENCES INTO AN INSTRUCTIONAL DEVELOPMENT PLAN

Instructional development plans, as we pointed out in Chapter 1, should be flexible and open-ended. Charts like the one at the end of Chapter 1 should be used as a guide or a checklist of things to consider, but they should not be adhered to rigidly. For example, the steps listed need not be taken in the order shown if another order would be preferable, and any part of the plan can be amended at any time. Now might be a good time to reconsider your students' needs in terms of audio learning experiences, to adapt your teaching strategies to include them, and to add to your list of desired behavioral outcomes (learner responses).

Identifying Audio Learning Needs

Learners may need opportunities to listen to audio materials individually or in small groups in order to develop skills, acquire cognitive information, or develop new attitudes about people or cultures. These needs should be noted and incorporated into your instructional plan.

Identifying Central and Supporting Objectives That May Be Achieved by Audio Learning Experiences

Now is a good time to review objectives already decided on to see which ones can be accomplished by the use of good audio learning materials. For example, if increasing your students' reading speed without decreasing the amount of information they retain is one of your objectives, compressed-speech materials might be useful.

Identifying New Learner Responses (Outcomes) Expected at the End of Instruction

We have discussed the benefits of letting students evaluate their own recorded efforts. Would this activity be a useful way of measuring your students' performance? Would any of your students be interested in, or capable of, producing original audio learning materials that demonstrate their mastery of a subject?

Selecting the Best and Most Appropriate Audio Learning Experiences

You have two broad options: to select the best of existing, available audio learning materials or to create your own. Regardless of which alternative you choose, the following checklist may be useful:

	No	Sometimes	Yes
1. Aural explanations are clear and directions are feasible.	____	____	____
2. Presents a dependable message.	____	____	____
3. Manipulative tasks are feasible.	____	____	____
4. Learners can control time and pace of use, and repeat parts at will.	____	____	____
5. Cues are provided for learner responses.	____	____	____
6. Learners have opportunities to evaluate their own efforts.	____	____	____
7. Cues are provided for further work.	____	____	____
8. Learners are encouraged to use information or skills creatively.	____	____	____
9. Material encourages allocation of teacher time to actual teaching.	____	____	____

General comments on specific audio materials can be added at the bottom of a checklist.

Planning Instructional Strategies

Now is the time, too, to add audio learning instructional strategies to your teaching plan. How may compressed-speech equipment be used effectively? Which kinds of individualized audio instruction would your students benefit from? What materials should learners hear in small groups and as a class?

The following questions are helpful in evaluating the effectiveness of teaching strategies and learning experiences:

1. Did the audio materials used provide a learning experience that could not have been provided more simply in another way?
2. Did I make a comprehensive search for the best audio learning resources available, and did I listen to the materials to test their effectiveness before using them in class?
3. Did I help my pupils to get the most out of the audio learning experience by reviewing goals and objectives, encouraging questions and discussion, and relating the pupils' known interests to the audio materials?
4. Did I provide opportunities to ask questions about how new information or skills can be used? Did I encourage the idea that learning is not complete until learners are able to use data or skills in a creative and individual way?

Reviewing the various teaching strategies mentioned in this chapter may help you reach a decision. The facilities available in your school or area must also be considered. In many cases, a few inquiries to school media personnel, department heads, or administrators will help you locate and gain access to audio equipment and facilities.

Evaluating the Effectiveness of Your Audio Learning Plans

As you observe the degree to which the achievement of stated objectives is demonstrated by the occurrence of appropriate behavioral outcomes, you will be able to judge the effectiveness of your use of audio learning materials. At this stage, several audio learning alternatives may appear promising enough to justify substituting them for learning experiences planned earlier. Whether they will be effective in the classroom only time will tell, but the spirit of instructional development is epitomized by a continuing search for the most rewarding learning experiences.

SUMMARY

This chapter introduced readers to audio learning materials. The techniques involved in using tape recorders to evaluate one's own progress were described, and simple but effective techniques for setting up and using microphones were outlined. Various types of audio recording and playback machines were described, including cassette and open-reel equipment and compressed-speech machines.

Two types of compressed-speech equipment were described, one that allows learners to control playback speeds at will and a second that allows specific prerecorded materials to be played at predetermined speeds. Variable-speed playback units are an important breakthrough in the individualization of audio instruction.

Various uses of audio materials were illustrated as vehicles for audiolingual instruction, for self-evaluation in a wide variety of subjects, for acquiring factual information, and for developing skills. Suggestions were made about planning and producing original audio materials, as well as investigating known sources of records and tapes and checking out educational radio broadcasts. Finally, readers were urged to seek audio materials that fit their own instructional plans and to evaluate them in terms of the learner responses they produced.

ACTIVITIES

The following activities are suggested as alternative ways of incorporating audio learning activities into an instructional development plan.

1. Plan and produce three audio learning experiences to achieve specific outcomes. Use audiotapes or audiocards and either regular or variable-speed playback equipment. Blank audiocards can be obtained from dealers. State the objectives of each learning experience, the procedures you plan to use, and the kind of creative responses you expect from students.
2. Bearing in mind the learner needs, instructional objectives, teaching strategies, and expected outcomes outlined in your instructional plan, select at least five radio broadcasts or commercially available audio learning materials that would be useful to your students. Your media librarian or a local media dealer can acquaint you with various sources of material. A list of sources of useful audio learning materials is also included in the following reference section.

REFERENCES

PRINT REFERENCES

Arrasjig, Harun, "Listening and Compressed Speech" (Paper presented at the New York Communications Convocation, Grossinger, N.Y., 1973). ED. 086-250.

Barker, Larry L., *Listening Behavior* (Englewood Cliffs, N.J.: Prentice Hall, 1971). 154 pages.

Challis, James, "The Effects of Fixed and Learner Selected Rates of Compressed Speech in an Audiovisual Learning Environment on the Achievement of College Level Students" (Thesis, 279 pp., Oklahoma University, 1973). Available from University Micro-films, 300 No. Zeeb Road, Ann Arbor, Mich. 48106.

Clark, Milton L., "Teaching to Listen," *Quarterly Review of Australian Education,* vol. 5, no. 4 (1972). 50 pages.

Davidson, Raymond L., *Audiovisual Machines,* 2nd ed. (Scranton, Pa.: International Textbook Co., 1975), pp. 12–21, chap. 2, "The Technology of Recording and Reproducing Sound."

Ernst, Franklin Henry, *Who is Listening?* (Vallejo, Calif.: Addresso-set, 1973). 206 pages.

Morris, Jud, *The Art of Listening* (Boston, Mass.: Industrial Education Institute, 1967). 273 pages.

Plaister, Ted, *Developing Listening Comprehension Among Elementary Students* (Englewood Cliffs, N.J.: Prentice Hall, 1976). 286 pages.

Taylor, Stanford E., *Listening—What Research Says to The Teacher* (Washington, D.C.: National Education Association, 1964). 32 pages.

Skalnik, Robert, "Radio Reading for the Print Handicapped," *Educational Broadcasting* (January–February 1977), p. 23.

Wood, Charles David, *Comprehension of Compressed Speech by Elementary Children* (Bloomington, Ind.: Indiana University, 1965). 178 pages.

Zigmond, Naomi K., *Auditory Learning* (Belmont, Calif.: Fearon Publishers, 1968). 90 pages.

MEDIA REFERENCES

Audiovisual Language Laboratory, 16mm film, sound, 13 min. Purdue University.

Audio-Tutorial System (Postlethwait's), 16mm film, sound, color, 24 min. Purdue University.

Basic Language Laboratory Equipment and Its Use, 16mm film, sound, b/w, 14 min. Pennsylvania Department of Public Instruction, Harrisburg, Pa.

Individualized Instruction: Its Nature and Effects, Materials, and Uses, a series of 6 audio tapes and 6 filmstrips. (See particularly filmstrips 1 and 4.) Association for Educational Communications and Technology.

Microphone Speaking, 16mm film, sound, color, 14 min. Centron, Kansas City.

Planning for the Language Laboratory, 16mm film, sound, b/w, 13 min. Pennsylvania Department of Public Instruction, Harrisburg, Pa.

Speak, Listen, Learn, 16mm film, sound, color, 11 min. Rheem Califone, Los Angeles.

The Tape Recorder, 16mm film, sound, b/w, 6 min. Iowa University.

STUDENT PRODUCTION GUIDE REFERENCES

See Unit 2.7, "The Tape Recorder," and the sections on audiotapes, audio recording and playback equipment, and audio turntables.

SOURCE REFERENCES

Audio Learning Materials on Tapes and Records

American Library Association, 50 E. Huron St., Chicago, IL 60611.

Capitol Records Distributing Corporation, 1750 N. Vine St., Hollywood, CA 90028.

Columbia Records, Educational Div., 51 W. 52nd St., New York, NY 10019.

Encyclopedia Britannica Educational Corporation, 425 No. Michigan Ave., Chicago, Ill.

EMC Corporation, Educational Materials Div., 180 E. 6th St., St. Paul, MN 55101.

Eye Gate House, 146-01 Archer Ave., Jamaica, NY 11435.

Harcourt Brace Jovanovich, 757 Third Ave., New York, NY 10017.

Imperial International Learning Corporation, P.O. Box 548, Kankakee, IL 60901.

London Records, 539 W. 25th St., New York, NY 10001.

Luxor Corporation, 104 Lakeview Ave., Waukegan, IL 60085.

MCA Records, 100 Universal City Plaza, Universal City, CA 90608.

National Council of Teachers of English, 1111 Kenyon Rd., Urbana, IL 61801.

Radio Corporation of America, Audio Visual Marketing Div., Front and Cooper Sts., Camden, NJ 08102.

Random House, 201 E. 50th St., New York, NY 10022.

Scholastic Magazines, 50 W. 44th St., New York, NY 10036.

Schwann Record & Tape Guide, 137 Newbury Street, Boston, MA 02116.

Spoken Arts, Inc., 310 North Ave., New Rochelle, NY 10801.

Taylor Teaching Tapes, 737 Third Avenue, Chula Vista, Calif. Drawer B 92010.

Troll Association, 320 Rt. 17, Mahwah, N.J.

Walt Disney Educational Materials, 800 Sonora Ave., Glendale, CA 91201.

Westinghouse Learning Corp., 100 Park Ave., New York, NY 10017.

Weston Woods, Weston, CN 06880.

Wible Language Institute, 24 So. 8th St., Allentown, PA 18105.

Young People's Records, Children's Record Guild, 225 Park Ave. S., New York, NY 10003.

Audio Learning Materials Indexes

Educators Progress Service, Randolph, WI 53956, *Educators Guide to Free Audio and Video Materials.*

National Audio Tape Catalog, a subject index of more than 14,000 tape recordings for use from nursery school to graduate school. A small fee is charged for duplication. The catalog is available from the AECT, 1201 Sixteenth St., N.W., Washington, DC 20036 or the National Center for Audio Tapes, Educational Media Center, Stadium 348, University of Colorado, Boulder, CO 80302, for $4.50.

Tape Recorders and Record Players (Compressed Speech Units)

Ampex Corporation, Audio-Video Systems Div., 401 Broadway, Redwood City, CA 94063.

Audiotronics Corporation, 7428 Bellaire Ave., No. Hollywood, CA 91605.

Bell and Howell Company, 7100 McCormick Blvd., Chicago, IL 60645.

Bogen Company, Div. of Lear-Siegler, Inc., P.O. Box 500, Paramus, NJ 07652.

Califone International, 5922 Bowcroft St., Los Angeles, CA 90016.

Dukane Corporation, 2900 Dukane Drive, St. Charles, IL 60174.

Lexicon, Inc., 60 Turner St., Waltham, MA 02154.

Newcomb Audio Products Company, 12881 Bradley Ave., Sylmar, CA 91342.
Radio Corporation of America, Audio Visual Marketing Division, Front and Cooper Sts., Camden, NJ 08102.
Radio-Matic of America, 760 Ramsey Ave., Hillside, NJ 07205.
Sony Superscope, 8150 Vineland Ave., Sun Valley, CA 91352.
Tandberg of America, Labriola Center, Armonk, NY 10504.
Telex-Communications, 9600 Aldrich Ave., S., Minneapolis, MN 55420.
3M Company, Mincom Division, 3M Center, Bldg. 223-5E, St. Paul, MN 55101.
V-M Corporation, P.O. Box 1247, 375 West Main St., Benton Harbor, MI 94022.
Webcor Sales Company, 5610 W. Bloomingdale Ave., Chicago, IL 60639.
Zenith Sales Corporation, 1900 N. Austin, Chicago, IL 60639.

Radio Networks

American Broadcasting Company, 1330 Avenue of the Americas, New York, NY 10019.
Columbia Broadcasting System, 51 W. 52nd St., New York, NY 10019.
Mutual Broadcasting System, 135 W. 50th St., New York, NY 10020.

Listening Laboratories

Audiotronics Corporation, 7428 Bellaire Ave., N. Hollywood, CA 91605.
Avedex, Inc., 7328 Niles Center Rd., Skokie, IL 60076.
Educational Developmental Laboratories, Div. of McGraw-Hill Book Co., 1221 Ave. of the Americas, New York, NY 10020.
Hamilton Electronics Corporation, 2003 W. Fulton St., Chicago, IL 60612.
Perma Power Company, Div. of Chamberlain Mfg. Corp., 5740 N. Tripp Ave., Chicago, IL 60646.
Radio Corporation of America, Audio-Visual Marketing Division, Front and Cooper Sts., Camden, NJ 08102.
Tandberg of America, Labriola Center, Armonk, NY 10504.

Tape Manufacturers

Ampex Corporation, 2201 Landmeier Rd., Elk Grove Village, IL 60007.
E. I. DuPont de Nemours & Co., Wilmington, DE 19898.
Memorex Corporation, San Towas at Central Expressway, Santa Clara, CA 95052.
Radio Corporation of America, Audio Visual Marketing Division, Front and Cooper Sts., Camden, NJ 08102.
Reeves Soundcraft Corporation, 15 Great Pastures Rd., Danbury, CN 06810.
Sony Superscope, 8150 Vineland Ave., Sun Valley, CA 91352.
3M Company, Mincom Div., 3M Center Bldg. 223-5E, St. Paul, MN 55101.

7 Still Projection

Objectives

To enable you to do the following:

1. Identify six learning situations in which some form of still projection would be appropriate and design a feasible plan for their use in those situations.
2. Demonstrate one or more unique advantages of each of three types of still projection.
3. Select, from a group of projection stills, the best ones in terms of (a) specified learning objectives and (b) physical quality.
4. Identify, from a collection of catalogs and lists, six or more useful sources of slides, filmstrips or transparencies for the subject and grade you plan to teach.

Since the heyday of the magic lantern, early in the century, the power of the projected image has been widely exploited by the entertainment and advertising industries. Since World War II projected materials have come to be used extensively in education as well. During the past decade, with the advent of increasingly sophisticated instructional systems, such media have acquired a new significance for educators at all levels.

Still projection provides a flexible tool for teachers who want to arrange interesting, effective learning experiences for their pupils. We shall deal individually with several types of still projection in this chapter to clarify their particular characteristics, advantages, and limitations, if any. As you read about these materials, you should be thinking about how each type, by itself or in combination with other types of materials, might be used to meet particular kinds of learning needs. Ask yourself, also, to what extent various types of stills serve the same purpose, in what ways they are unique, and which ones would be of particular value in your own teaching situation.

TYPES OF STILL PROJECTION

Types of still projection vary, from slides, filmstrips, transparencies, and opaque materials to microfilms and holographs. With one principal exception, stills are projected by *passing light through* film or some other transparent material containing images and *transmitting* them onto a screen. The principal exception is opaque materials—pages of books or magazines, say, or a pupil's written work. In this case, a strong light is shone on the material and the *reflected* image is projected on a screen.

Commercial slides, transparencies, filmstrips, and the like are available on practically all subjects. But there are also many ways in which teachers wishing to make their own projection materials can do so. Cameras, copying machines, and other devices for making stills are discussed in detail in the *Student Production Guide.*

2″ × 2″ Slides

The first slides to achieve wide acceptance in teaching were 3¼″ × 4″ glass-mounted slides. Originally called *lantern slides,* they were imprinted with a photographic or handmade image. Early in the century, almost every school owned sets of such slides or could rent them. In fact, many audiovisual centers got their start by circulating sets of lantern slides to schools. However, with advances in photographic techniques, the less expensive and more convenient 2″ × 2″ slide came into general use. Since the development of inexpensive 35mm cameras and color film, 2″ × 2″ slides made from 35mm film have become a popular teaching tool.

One important advantage of 2″ × 2″ slides is that excellent color materials can be obtained at a low cost. Their convenience and wide availability also add to their popularity. (See Figure 7.1.) Commercial slides are usually of excellent quality and are available on subjects as diverse as geography, architecture and the fine arts, the sciences, medicine, agriculture, ecology, nature study, and sports. Teachers can readily make their own slides, because 35mm color film is

Figure 7.1 2″ × 2″ slides can easily be stored in drums and then projected with a drum-type projector such as this. The Ektalite screen shown is a special aluminum-surfaced screen designed for use in lighted rooms.

Figure 7.2 Teachers who use many 2″ × 2″ slides frequently store them in convenient plastic holders that fit in a standard three-ring notebook. Here two students are putting together a special presentation. The slides chosen for the presentation will be loaded in sequence into the drum on the table for projecting.

normally mounted by the processor in 2″ × 2″ cardboard slide mounts, ready for projection. (See Figure 7.2.) In addition, some media centers provide illustrated lists of locally assembled 2″ × 2″ slide sets for distribution.[1]

Slides are readily adaptable to a variety of uses. Slide-tape presentations, for example, can be highly effective for large and small groups as well as for individualized instruction. Although the visual and audio portions of such presentations can be synchronized manually, the process is frequently automated by means of inaudible signals or sync pulses on the tape that activate the advance mechanism of the slide projector. The resulting slide tapes are particularly useful in individualized instruction. Cartridge tapes and simple mechanisms make it unnecessary for an instructor to be present. Computerized, random access systems are currently in use which allow students in individual study carrels to select separate slides, slide tapes, audiotapes, or even motion picture sequences at will.

Animated slides are made of a material that reacts to polarized light in a way that gives an impression of animation. A polarizing spinner is attached to the projector, and the slides are projected through the spinner to the screen. Sets of such slides are becoming available. For example, there is one set called *Science in Motion* designed for grades K–6 that covers such topics as "Exploring the Earth," "Biological Sciences," "The Solar System," and "Exploring Space."[2]

A mechanism that is often used in slide presentations before groups is the *dissolve unit*. This unit is normally used with two projectors. It alternates the images projected with soft fade-in's rather than abrupt switches from one scene to the next. The unit can be operated automatically and set to allow a predetermined number of seconds for each slide, or it can be operated

1 For example, "Italian and Spanish Paintings, Renaissance and Post-Renaissance Periods," *Art History Series*, Department of Education, San Diego County, Calif.

2 American Book Company.

manually. Although dissolve units are not necessary for normal classroom uses of slides, they are good to know about, especially for presentations to the public or auditorium programs. (For slide presentations to large groups, a Xenon high-intensity lamp is usually necessary in the projector.)

Another type of slide that deserves to be mentioned is the double-image slide known as a *stereoslide.* Such slides are prepared in pairs from photographs taken with a stereographic camera. This type of camera takes two pictures simultaneously through two lenses that are a few inches apart, as are human eyes. Each picture is thus taken from a slightly different angle, just as our eyes see from slightly different angles. We have depth perception because of the way the brain combines the images perceived by each eye. When two stereographic photographs are viewed through a *stereoscope,* or stereoviewer, the left eye sees one image and the right eye the other. The brain combines these into one image that has depth, just as it combines actual images. The result is a highly realistic three-dimensional effect.

A convenient way of viewing stereographic slides is with a *stereodisk* that holds seven pairs of 16mm transparencies taken with a stereographic camera. Stereodisks are both compact and inexpensive. (See Figure 7.3.)

Figure 7.3 This is a popular type of stereoviewer containing a disk with seven matched pairs of scenes taken with a stereo camera. Seen through the viewer, the scenes appear strikingly three-dimensional.

Filmstrips

A *filmstrip* is a sequence of related stills imprinted on a strip of transparent 35mm film. A typically commercial filmstrip contains from 20 to 50 frames about ¾″ × 1″ in size. (See Figure 7.4.) A complete filmstrip, usually several feet long, is rolled up to fit into a small container for easy storage. (See Figure 7.5.) Filmstrips are relatively inexpensive ($6 and up), so it is feasible to have sets of them in each classroom for use when they are needed. In addition, filmstrips are simple to use. The projectors are inexpensive, simple to operate, and relatively trouble-free. Good pictures of almost anything can be projected on a screen, since a great many filmstrips are available on a wide variety of topics in most subjects.

The operational advantages of filmstrips help account for their general popularity with teachers, but filmstrips also have some distinctive advantages as learning materials. The sequential order of the frames encourage the treatment of topics in a consistent step-by-step sequence, and there is no way for the pictures to get out of order, as slides occasionally do. On the other hand, since the order of scenes on a filmstrip *is* fixed, it is not convenient to show scenes in another order. For that purpose, slides are better. Nonetheless, when a particular filmstrip fits your teaching purposes, you have a ready-made, efficient, and convenient teaching tool.

Another advantage of filmstrips from a teaching-learning standpoint is that they can be used at any desired pace. This is obviously an ad-

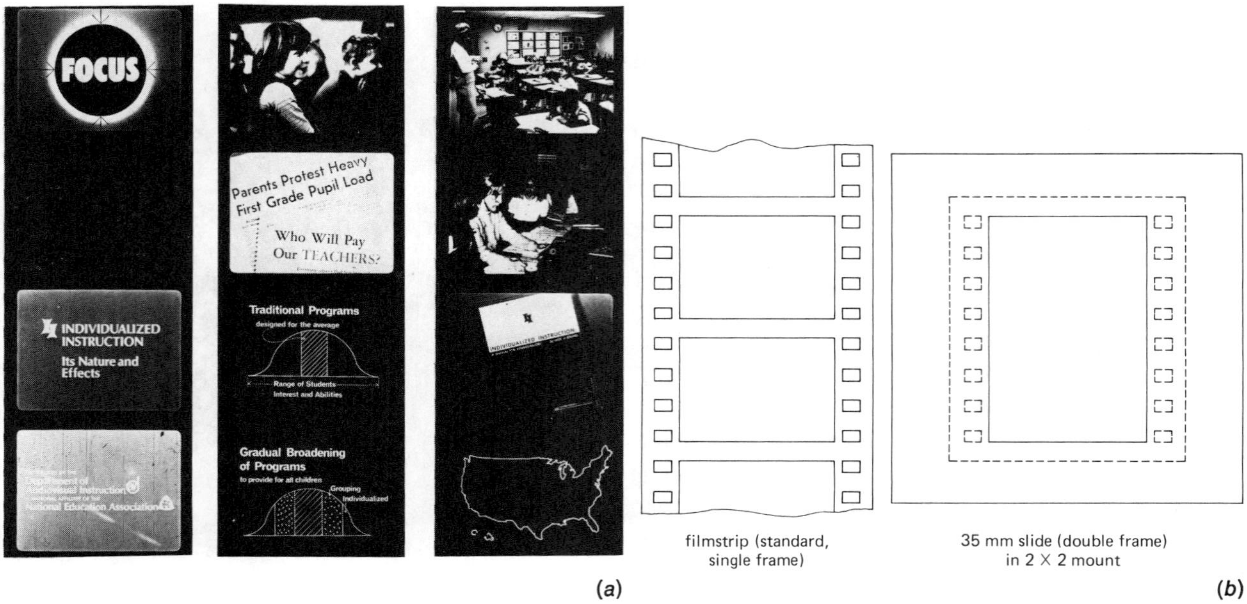

Figure 7.4 (*a*) Almost all commercial filmstrips are single-frame strips like this. (*b*) Double-frame strips have frames that are twice the size of single frames and the same size as 35mm slides. Thus anyone with a 35mm camera can make double-frame strips. (See the *Student Production Guide* for details.)

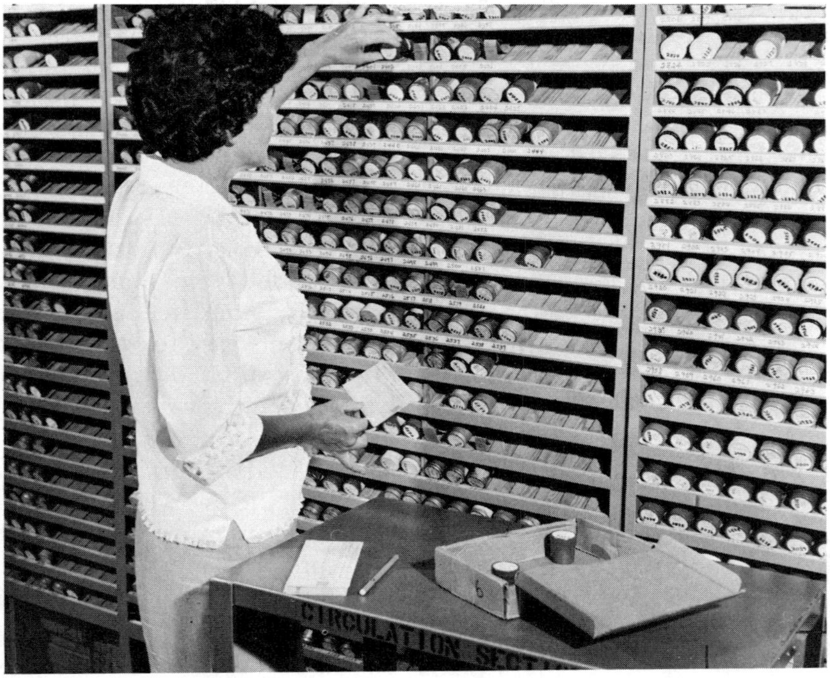

Figure 7.5 The large number of filmstrips used in school systems and their small size makes a rapid, convenient system of storage and retrieval, like this one, important.

vantage in individualized instruction, but it can also be advantageous in working with a group. A teacher can run through a filmstrip quickly to introduce or review a subject. Then, if a detailed analysis is needed later, each frame can be held on the screen as long as necessary.

A third practical advantage of filmstrips is the wide range and number of titles available. Because of their popularity and their relatively low production costs, great numbers of new filmstrips are constantly produced. The range of subjects goes well beyond the elementary school curriculum and includes many topics covered in secondary schools, colleges, and adult education classes. A few examples of the types of filmstrips available are shown in Figure 7.6. This selection would have to be multiplied hundreds of times even to suggest the variety of new filmstrips produced in the United States each year.

The trend toward *packaged materials* for individualized instruction and independent instructional modules is having marked effects on the production of educational filmstrips. This is evident in the large proportion of sound filmstrips being produced now for the school market. Instead of having printed captions, many filmstrips are accompanied by records or audiotapes. (See Figure 7.7.) In many cases, cassettes can be ordered in place of records at a slight additional cost. Projectors are available that not only project the filmstrips but play the record or tape and advance the filmstrip at the proper time by reacting to inaudible recorded pulses. (These machines are similar to the slide-tape projectors discussed earlier.) In addition to verbal information, the tapes and records may contain music or sound effects. *Sound filmstrips* are valuable in a variety of subjects such as music, reading readiness, industrial arts, and social studies. Although they usually cost 50 to 100 percent more than silent filmstrips, their quality, convenience, and adaptability for either group or self-instruction have made them very popular.

When a synchronized recording and filmstrip are used together, the pace of the filmstrip is, of course, fixed by the recording. Although this combination is effective for many teaching purposes, it may be desirable at times to turn off the sound, operate the projector manually, and do the commentary yourself (or have a student do it) at whatever pace is appropriate. This procedure permits a more detailed study of the concepts being shown or a more rapid overview of them.

There is also a combined still and motion picture projection and sound system designed particularly for use in individual study carrels. This consists of an 8mm motion picture projector that can be operated manually or programmed to start and stop and to project individual frames or sequences. (See Figure 7.8.) Like the slide-tape and filmstrip projectors already mentioned, this motion picture projector can be synchronized with a separate audiotape containing verbal information, narration, or directions. Inaudible pulses on the tape vary the speed of the projector from single frames to specified speeds as required. The compactness, convenience, and versatility of the system make it a valuable teaching tool, and it is already being used extensively in military and industrial training. Before schools can put such a system to good use, however, sufficient amounts of relevant, high-quality materials must be made available. In the meantime, material of this kind can be developed by teachers, students, or school media staffs with the relatively inexpensive and foolproof super 8mm cameras now available (see Chapter 8), plus standard tape-recording equipment.

A fourth characteristic of filmstrips that makes them a good medium for instruction is that they lend themselves well to use with *other* media. For example, filmstrips, as a still medium, can imply motion only to viewers with the necessary background of experience; but they are excellent for a detailed study or review of visual information. Thus motion pictures (which show

A
B

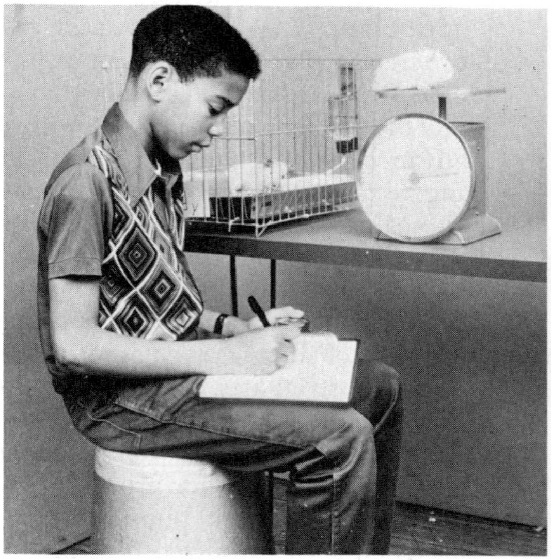

Figure 7.6 These frames selected from nine filmstrips made by three different producers indicate something of the variety of filmstrips available. Except for flat pictures, no other visual materials are so readily available to teachers.

(*a*)

(*b*)

(*c*)

Figure 7.7 Filmstrips are an effective means of teaching small groups and individuals as well as large groups. (*a*) Tapes and headsets facilitate self-instruction and let these children hear explanations of filmstrips without disturbing others in the class. (*b*) This group is using a self-contained projection-tape unit with a rear-vision screen. (*c*) This teacher is recording a narration to accompany a filmstrip.

the motion important to learning certain concepts) and filmstrips (which permit extended analyses of single scenes) often make excellent instructional companions. Filmstrips also work well as an adjunct to textbooks.

A fifth advantage of filmstrips is that teachers and students can make their own. Although single-frame filmstrips are most easily made with special equipment, they can also be made with a regular 35mm camera and a copy stand. (See Figure 7.9.) Double-frame filmstrips can be made with a regular 35mm camera without a copy stand. (See the *Student Production Guide*, pp. 260–267.) Pupils can help in making filmstrips. In fact, class projects that include the making as well as the showing of filmstrips can produce very favorable learning outcomes.

Like any other teaching material, filmstrips

Figure 7.8 This super 8mm motion picture projector can be programmed to show single frames, like a filmstrip projector, as well as motion sequences at standard, slow, or fast speeds.

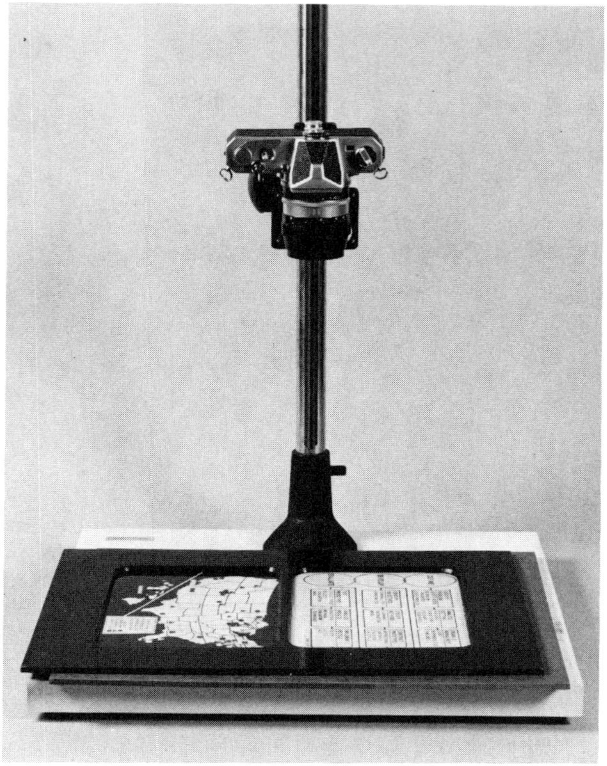

Figure 7.9 A regular 35mm camera takes a picture that is twice the size of a standard (single-frame) filmstrip. (See Figure 7.4.) Thus a mask is used over the material and two frames are photographed at once. (See the *Student Production Guide* for details.)

have limitations as well as advantages. The inherent limitations of nonmoving images in a fixed order have already been mentioned. Filmstrips are also rather easily damaged during projection and need to be handled more carefully than slides or transparencies. Although a filmstrip is resistant to ordinary wear, the sprocket holes tear rather easily if the projector is not properly threaded or adjusted. Properly treated, they will stay in good condition for an indefinite period.

Audioviewer Systems

The trend toward individualized instruction and the increased emphasis on improving industrial and military training programs have led to the development of synchronized sound and viewing units, or *audioviewers,* such as those in Figure 7.10. Although these audioviewers have evolved from the pulse-synchronized audiovisual systems already discussed, they are more self-contained and more integrated in relation to both the materials they use and the way they use them. As of now, most materials for such units (other than cassette sound filmstrips) must still be prepared locally and individually; therefore these audioviewers are being used primarily in community colleges, in the military, and in industry. As the demand for them develops, however, commercial producers may be expected to begin producing synchronized tape-film materials for use in schools.

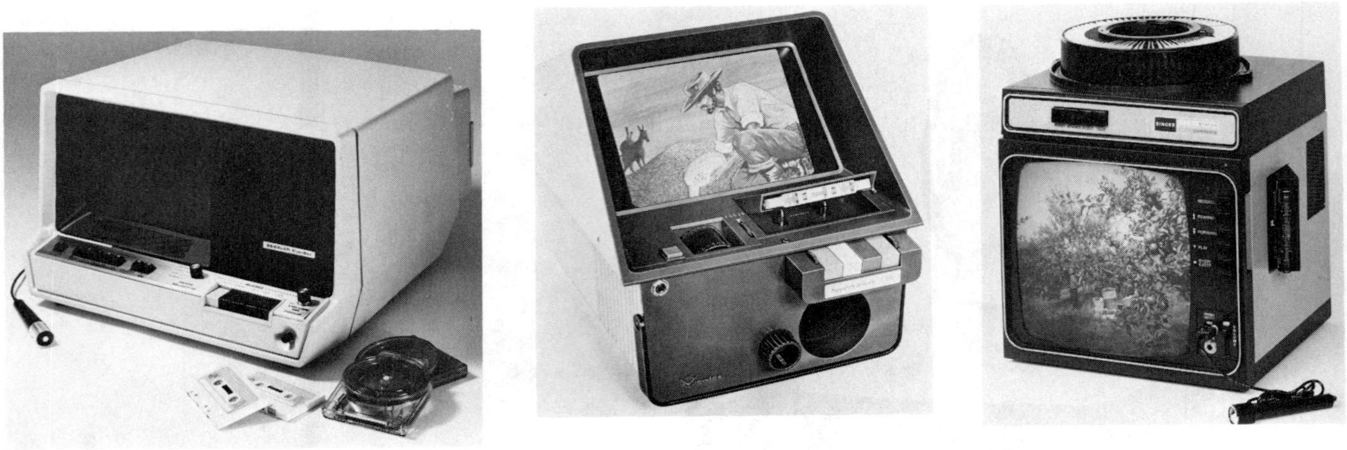

(a) (b) (c)

Figure 7.10 (*a*) A Beseler Cue/See unit. (*b*) A Viewlex Superviewer. (*c*) A Single Graflex Caromate. Self-contained synchronized units such as these, which use super 8 films, slides, or filmstrips for the visual part of the presentation and cassette tapes for sound and pulsing, are an excellent and convenient way to present automated or manually operated self-instruction material. The Cue See unit uses super 8mm film that can be projected at any speed from single frames to 24 frames per second, which produces the effect of natural motion.

Transparencies

Over the years the term *transparency* has come to be accepted as referring to the 10″ × 10″ transparencies used with overhead projectors. (See Figure 7.11.) Overhead projectors are popular for a number of reasons. For one thing, they are operated from the front of the room. Thus teachers can face the class as they use them. They can point to, write, or draw on the transparencies, and whatever they do will show on the screen. Also, the room need not be darkened completely for good visibility. (See Figure 7.12.)

Overhead projectors also have the unique advantage of accommodating overlays that show progressive stages of development or sequences of events. Lettering, mechanical drawing, the various steps in completing a map or assembling a machine, and cumulative additions to a chart or graph, for example, can easily be shown using overlays. (See Figure 7.13.) Typically, the several elements of an overlay are hinged on the sides or corners of the mounting and flipped on or off the basic transparency as they are needed. In some cases, opaque strips are removed one by one to reveal data gradually.

Commercial transparencies, with or without overlays, are available in large numbers in many subjects. Good transparencies can also be made by teachers or students in a variety of ways. (See the *Student Production Guide*, pp. 194–236.)

Research on transparencies has established that letters about $\frac{3}{16}$ inch high are the smallest that can be used if they are to be readable from 20 to 40 feet away and that $\frac{1}{4}$-inch lettering is best.[3] Thus copy prepared with elite or pica typewriters is too small for satisfactory legibility except at very close range. (The subject of let-

[3] Sarah Adams, Robert Rosemier, and Phillip Sleemen, "Readability, Letter Size, and Visibility for Overhead Projection Transparency," *AV Communications Review* (Winter 1965), pp. 412–417.

Figure 7.11 Once an overhead projector has been properly focused and the image aligned on the screen, teachers can keep their attention on their students.

tering is discussed in detail in the *Student Production Guide* in connection with various methods of preparing transparencies.)

Opaque Materials

Opaque materials such as flat pictures, book illustrations, tables, drawings, photographs, students' work, and even certain specimens and objects can be projected on a screen via an opaque projector, which uses reflected light. (See Figure 7.14.) Instructors with access to opaque projectors thus have an almost unlimited amount of illustrative material available at little or no cost. Furthermore, much of this material can be used just as it is, without mounting or other preparation. A theme, a mathematics paper, a sheet of typing, a page or diagram in a book, a picture in a magazine, a culture dish, a watch, coins, stamps, flowers, or leaves—in fact,

nearly anything about 10″ × 10″ in size or less can be projected using an opaque projector. (See Figure 7.15.)

Another distinct advantage of opaque projectors is that illustrative material of various kinds can be enlarged and copied for other uses. Small maps, tables, diagrams, graphs, and similar materials can be projected in enlarged form for discussion purposes; those having more than a transitory value can then be traced on the chalkboard or on a large piece of paper and referred to again.

The principal drawback of opaque projectors is that because they use light reflected by opaque materials, rather than light passing through transparent film, the projected image is not as strong or brilliant as in most other forms of still projection. Thus the room must usually be quite dark to get satisfactory visibility. Nevertheless, teachers at all grade levels find opaque projectors very helpful. For example, they can be used in the elementary grades

1. By language arts teachers for animated word games.
2. By arithmetic teachers for drills in which pull strips are removed to reveal numbers of objects.
3. By science teachers to enlarge pictures to show the true size of things or to show collections of things like shells.
4. By social studies teachers to show maps of the local area.
5. As a means of enlarging figures and diagrams for bulletin boards.

They can be used in the secondary grades

1. In social studies for map projections.
2. In English to show examples of creative writ-

Figure 7.12 The 10″ × 10″ overhead transparency has several distinct advantages. Can you identify three from these illustrations?

Figure 7.13 Large numbers of maps are available on transparencies for overhead projectors. These range from one-color outline maps to full-color general and special-purpose maps with multiple overlays. What advantages are there in presenting maps this way?

ing, corrections on written work, and letter forms.
3. In civics to show current maps and pictures.
4. In art classes to show drawing techniques and illustrations.
5. In science classes to show specimens.

They can be used in college

1. In business education to show business and accounting forms.
2. In journalism to show examples of creative writing and advertising layouts.
3. In home economics to show textiles.
4. In the fine arts to show paintings and drawings.[4]

In short, the uses of opaque projectors are virtually endless.

[4] Ray Denno, *Using the Opaque Projector* (Squibb-Taylor, 1958), pp. 12–25. See also Kenneth L. Bowers, *The Opaque Projector, Bridges for Ideas #10* (Austin: Visual Instruction Bureau, The University of Texas, 1960), pp. 14–25; and the booklet *Digest of Educational Opaque Projection Practices,* published by the Charles Beseler Company, East Orange, N.J. 07018 in 1970, for additional ideas and suggestions.

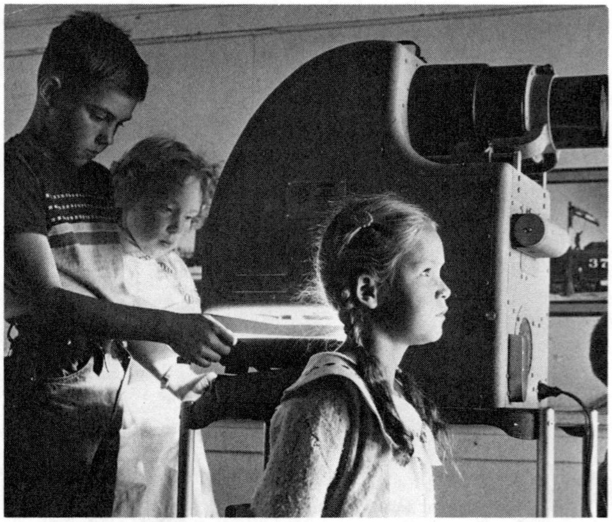

Figure 7.14 Opaque projectors can project virtually any nontransparent material about 10″ × 10″ or less, including students' work.

Microscopic Slides

The terms *microprojection* and *microfilm projection* are sometimes confused. *Microprojection* is the projection of microscope slides, which are discussed in this section. Microfilm projection, which uses film, is described in the next section.

A *microprojector* permits an entire class to see what would be visible to one pupil at a time through a microscope. (See Figure 7.16.) Both wet and dry slides can be projected.

A microprojector not only reduces the need for expensive microscopes, but also assures instructors that their students are seeing precisely what they want them to see. The effective use of microscopes is often difficult to learn, and training in this skill often means taking time away from the subject under study. Even when students have been shown how to use a microscope, the instructor cannot be sure that each pupil has adjusted the lenses properly or is seeing what should be seen.

Figure 7.15 Specimens as well as flat materials can be shown readily using an opaque projector.

Figure 7.16 A microscope slide is projected into a shadowbox screen. A microprojector can be used effectively with an entire class in a darkened room. Three levels of magnification are usually available. For what purposes is a microprojector superior to individual microscopes?

Most microscope slides can be projected with a microprojector, but those requiring high resolution are better examined with a microscope. When live specimens are projected, the light beam must be cool enough not to damage them. It is best to project such materials for only a minute or two at a time. If you want to come back to them, simply turn off the lamp and leave the fan running. Do not expect a very brilliant image on the screen, although the brilliance will vary with the density of the slide and the size of the image projected.

Microprojectors can be used to show a wide variety of phenomena—stresses and strains on fibers, filaments, and surfaces; slides of fingerprints and blood smears; the refraction of light; the properties of crystals and other common compounds, such as minerals, salt, sugar, rubber, and petroleum (by means of white and polarized light); the growth of crystals in various solutions; one-celled animals and plants (on wet slides); cell division; plant and animal tissues; bacteria, mold spores; and the like.[5]

Microfilm and Microfiche

Although their function—information storage—is quite different from the functions of other still projection *microfilm* and *microfiche* (pronounced "microfeesh") are sufficiently important to both students and teachers to be included here. As the volume of human knowledge multiplies, the problem of storing and retrieving printed information becomes increasingly unmanageable. School, college, and public libraries have long since become pressed for storage space for books and periodical files. To ease this pressure, microfilming was introduced and various publications, such as rare books, theses, news-

[5] For additional suggestions, see *Teachers Manual for the Bioscope Microprojectors* (Tulsa, Okla.: Bioscope Manufacturing Co., 1970).

paper files, periodicals, and important documents were photographed on 35mm microfilm. Each frame of the film contained a separate page, greatly reduced. The resulting rolls of film, which look very much like filmstrips, are placed in special projectors called *microfilm readers,* which project each page on a rear-vision screen. (See Figure 7.17.)

As the technology of miniaturization has advanced, microfiche has become another widely used way of reducing information for storage and retrieval.[6] *Microfiche* is a sheet of film carrying many rows of print or other material. The images are much smaller on microfiche than the images on microfilm. Microfiche is usually used in the form of cards of some standard size that can be stored easily.

The technological advances in information storage and retrieval have been rapid, and none have been more striking than those in the area of miniaturization:

> What the transistor is to radio and television, high-reduction photography is to the printed page. By photographing materials at very great reductions onto a small, transparent film card called a microfiche, this process at first was able to transfer a whole book onto a single card. With advanced technology, however, it is now possible to print six books on a single 3″ × 5″ card.[7]

Microfilm remains widely used, for a great deal of material has already been microfilmed, there are a number of well-established microfilming programs, and microfilm readers are widely available in schools, colleges, libraries, and research centers. Recent innovations in information storage and retrieval, however, almost invariably utilize the high-reduction capabilities of microfiche. Among these is what Encyclopaedia Britannica calls a *microbook library,* which it says will cost libraries far less than normal books and which can be stored in a minute fraction of the space. (Some 250 microbook cards fit into a space normally occupied by one regular book.) This process involves *superמicrofiche.* Both a desk reader and a lap reader that can be used at home are already available. These readers automatically center each image on a card and project it clearly on the screen. Furthermore, a reader-printer is under development that will print copies of any desired page.

A similar process, called *ultramicrofiche,* de-

Figure 7.17 The capability of microfilm readers is well illustrated here. A large screen, good definition, and adequate light actually improve the readability of the original front page of *The New York Times.* This unit accommodates 16mm or 35mm microfilm and microfiche cards as well, with an adaptor.

[6] Microfiche should not be confused with *microcards,* which were an intermediate step in miniaturization. A microcard is an opaque, sensitized card on which rows of reduced matter are reproduced photographically. Microcards are rapidly passing out of use as microfiche replaces them.

[7] John Tebbel, *Saturday Review* (January 9, 1971), p. 41.

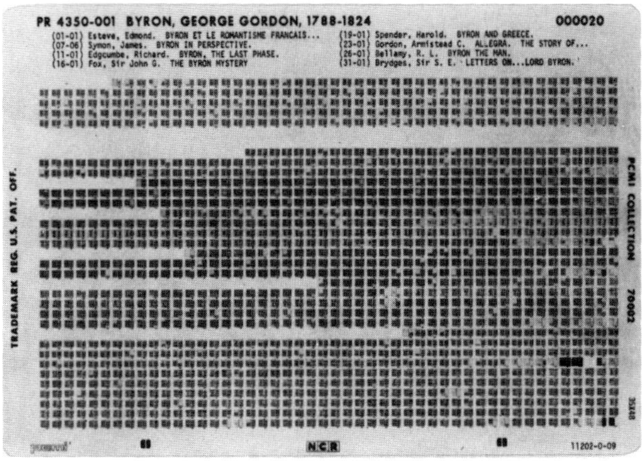

Figure 7.18 The progress of miniaturization is exemplified by this 4″ × 6″ PCMI transparent microfiche card, which can hold 1680 pairs of photographed printed pages—3360 single pages.

veloped by NCR, puts about 3300 book pages on each card. (See Figure 7.18.) These cards are being assembled into a PCMI Library Information System, which will eventually provide whole libraries of information in a manageable space. NCR also markets a PCMI reader that provides an excellent image and a reader-printer. (See Figure 7.19.)

Another significant milestone in information storage and retrieval is the New York Times Information Bank, which began operations in 1972. This is a computerized, fully automated system designed to retrieve general information of the type included in the *Times* as well as material from more than 60 other newspapers and periodicals. Abstracts of the material are stored in computers, and the full texts are carried on microfiche. Initially limited to printed material from periodicals, the system will ultimately be expanded to include printed reference materials and nonprinted materials such as photographs and graphics. National online systems of bibliographic data such as MEDLINE (medical information) and CAIN (science abstracts) are also in the developmental stage.

The educational potential of these and similar developments is enormous. Soon computerized information storage and retrieval systems will be commonplace in thousands of schools and colleges and will be used by millions of students.

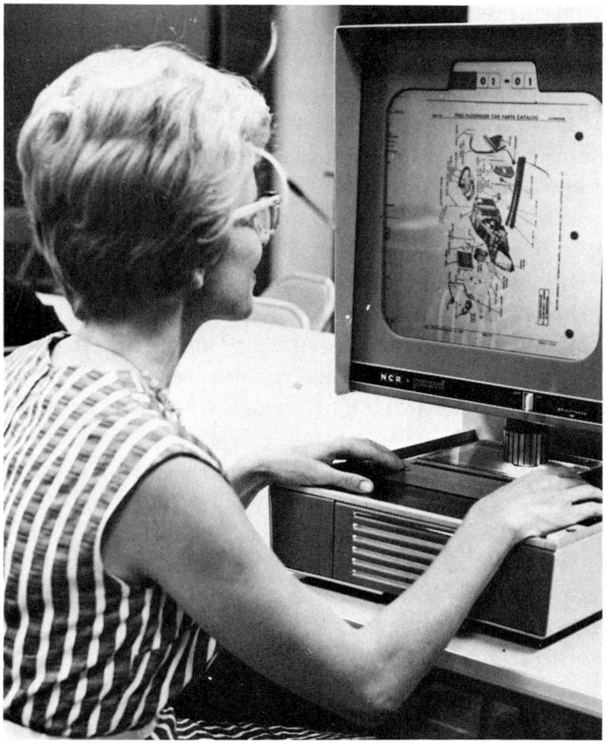

Figure 7.19 This reader quickly locates and focuses on any one of the approximately 3300 pages an NCR microfiche card can accommodate and projects it on a rear-vision screen.

HOLOGRAPHS

There is some question whether a discussion of holography belongs in a chapter on projecting stills. Although successful holographs can be and are being made of still images, holography also has many applications in motion pictures, television, and computers, as well as a great variety of uses in science and industry. But it is, in a sense, a photographic process, like most types of projection. Therefore this seems as good a place as any to describe it.

Holography has been called "the most exciting advance in imagery since photography itself."[8] During the past few years, holography has been successfully achieved in motion pictures in research laboratories, and a holographic video-playback system is being developed for home use. Holograms are beginning to come out of the laboratory to be put to a variety of uses in such varied areas as microscopy, information storage, aerial mapping, nondestructive testing of products, and medical examination of internal organs.[9]

Holography is sometimes called *lensless photography* because images are created on a holographic plate without a camera. Instead, a laser beam is split into two parts, one of which is reflected off the subject onto a photographic plate. The other part of the beam, known as the reference beam, is reflected off a mirror and onto the same photographic plate. (See Figure 7.20.)

Although the scientific explanation of holography is somewhat complex, the basic principles are relatively simple. The first essential is a laser beam, which has two essential properties. First, laser light is very pure, having only one frequency, or wavelength, rather than the many that typically make up colored (or white) light; it is thus *monochromatic*. Second, laser light is *coherent,* which means that the light rays are parallel, appearing to come from a source infinitely distant, as from a star. Ordinary types of light, such as incandescent, fluorescent, or mercury vapor light, have neither of these qualities, because they usually contain a full spectrum of colors and diffuse them in all directions. Only laser light has the precision necessary to set up controlled *wave interference,* a second necessary condition for creating holograms.

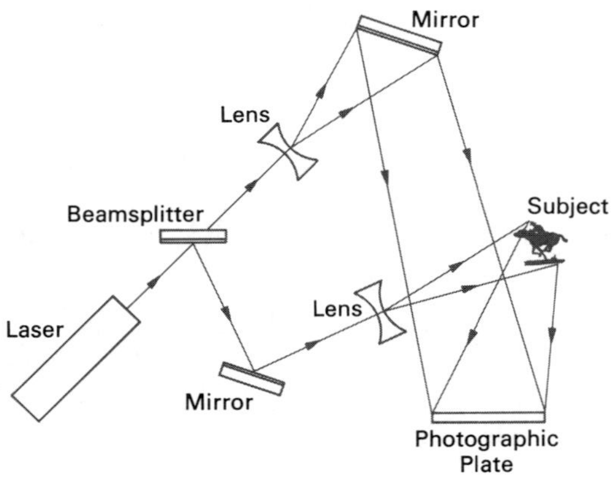

Figure 7.20 A light beam emanating from the laser as a pencil-thin ray is separated into two beams by the beamsplitter. The brighter beam is deflected off a mirror, passes through a diverging lens, and then reaches the subject, from which it is reflected to a photographic plate. The other beam, called the reference beam, passes through the beamsplitter and a diverging lens and is then reflected off a mirror directly onto the photographic plate. The light is reflected off the subject and the reference light combine to set up wavefront interference patterns that are recorded on the plate in the form of a three-dimensional image of the subject—a hologram.

Wave interference can be illustrated by tossing two rocks into a quiet pool. The wave patterns created radiate outward in two sets of concentric circles and, as they meet, interfere with one another. If the waves peak together, they reinforce or amplify one another. If they are out of phase, they tend to minimize or cancel one another. Light waves (and sound waves) from separate sources react in much the same manner, except that they do so in all planes rather than just the horizontal.

These light wave interference patterns completely envelop any object in their path, just as water waves constantly lap on all sides of a boat. There is a difference, however, in the wave action on one side of the boat compared with that on the opposite side—and, of course, at any given instant there are graduated differences in the wave action from point to point around the hull. When wave interference patterns are set up—as

[8] James Forney, "New Wave in Image Making—Holograms Tell It Like It Really Was," *Popular Photography* (January 1967), p. 120.

[9] Richard Straube, "Three-Dimensional Future?" *Industrial Photography* (October 1969), pp. 34 ff.

by the wash from a passing power boat—many of these differences are accentuated, made more visible.

The analogy ends there because waves of light do not have an effect on a physical object comparable to the effect of waves of water. The visual "pond," in other words, remains totally unruffled—flat—until wave interference patterns are set up by split laser beams. What happens then is that the photographic plate records an instant cross section of the wave interference patterns caused by the meeting of the two light beams on the plate. These interference patterns literally produce a three-dimensional image of startling reality. Because the holographic plate simultaneously records in all planes, it records a different image from every angle and combines them, just as the eyes record different images from different angles and combine them.

The plate is then developed by fairly conventional methods. The resulting hologram can be viewed from the front with an almost monochromatic light source such as a sodium vapor lamp; it can also be backlighted or projected with a similar light source. Backlighted scenes in full color are also possible by using one exposure for each of the three primary colors.[10]

The pace of experimentation with holography is steadily increasing; instructional holograms of various sizes can already be purchased for $5 to $10. New developments may be expected to make holographs increasingly practical and functional in education, as well as in many other areas.[11]

SELECTING AND USING STILL PROJECTION

The value of still-projection media in a variety of subjects and grades has been studied here and abroad, primarily with filmstrips and slides,[12] but the principal conclusions are probably applicable to still projection generally. What is learned from such materials has been demonstrated to depend more on the nature and quality of the message than on the medium employed. Effective instructional materials are carefully designed (or selected) to achieve clearly identified and specific objectives—as is done in Instructional Development. Ineffective instructional materials contain little information, have unclear goals, or are of an incidental nature.[13] Within this general frame of reference, research has demonstrated that

1. Still projection is an effective means of communicating factual information and certain skills.
2. Combining still-projection media with other types of teaching materials and methods in terms of a careful analysis of the needs of a learning situation is likely to produce the most efficient learning outcomes.
3. The extent to which still-projection materials embody unique pictorial or graphic content of good quality has a direct bearing on their effectiveness. In other words, like other teaching materials, still-projection materials must

---

10 Those interested in pursuing the technical side of holography will find several articles listed in the references at the end of this chapter. Relevant articles also appear frequently in current issues of *Industrial Photography* and other technical photography journals.

11 The first commercial film to employ holography was *Logan's Run,* completed in 1975 by MGM. In commenting on holography's future in the motion picture industry, the producer stated, "Audiences may soon watch complete movies being shown in midair without the use of screens. It's possible that giant filmed pageants will be created with holograms and projected in the centers of stadiums holding 100,000 spectators." [From a UPI report, "Laser Beam Due to Revolutionize Movie Making," *Sarasota Herald Tribune* (Dec. 6, 1975), p. 10A.]

12 William H. Allen, "Audiovisual Materials," in *Encyclopedia of Educational Research* (New York: Macmillan, 1960), pp. 120–121, provides a very good summary of research on the effectiveness of filmstrips and slides.

13 See Loran Twyford, "Educational Communications Media," in *Encyclopedia of Educational Research* (New York: Macmillan, 1969), p. 371.

be selected and used effectively if they are to provide the maximum benefits.

Selecting Still Projection

The first step in selecting materials is to decide whether a particular material can serve a specific teaching purpose better than another learning device or medium. This decision must be made partly on the basis of what the projected material itself can and cannot do; that is, in terms of its inherent characteristics. Five basic questions to ask are:

1. *Is motion necessary at this point for pupils to understand fully the concept(s) to be learned?* If it is, still-projection media are obviously not the best choice; at best they can only imply motion. On the other hand, projected diagrams, pictures and the like can be effective means of analyzing the *components* of motion in detail if the motion itself is visualized before or after the still projection by a motion picture or a working model.

2. *Are suitable materials available for my particular teaching purpose?* Keeping track of the large number of slide sets, filmstrips, transparencies, and other educational materials put out each year in a given field is a considerable task. Professional journals frequently review new educational materials, and several publications are specifically devoted to providing periodic evaluations of such materials.[14]

3. *Does what I am teaching involve a series of step-by-step developments or a fixed logical progression?* If so, a filmstrip or a series of transparent overlays and an overhead projector may be the best choice. Overlays are particularly appropriate if a teacher wishes to mark up material during a discussion. If overlays are not necessary, a filmstrip may be a more effective way of presenting material. Drum-type slide projectors can be used to show a fixed sequence of slides, but the slides can also be rearranged. In general, slides are most suited to material that does not need to be presented in a particular sequence or that would benefit from changing a sequence to show different aspects of something.

4. *Do I need materials that tell a story primarily through pictures?* Because projection stills are essentially a visual medium, they should be relied on to communicate visual ideas via pictures, graphs, diagrams, and the like. Verbal materials, although useful and often essential for a complete understanding of visual media, should not dominate a presentation (except in remedial reading and arithmetic, where visual images of word and number symbols are used extensively).

Many stills are primarily symbolic. For example, graphics, diagrams, and maps are largely symbolic rather than pictorial. A teacher should decide what kind of material—pictorial, diagrammatic, or whatever—will be the most useful in presenting a concept. It may be best to use a particularly good picture in a recent magazine, projecting it with an opaque projector, or a series of intricate map overlays projected on an overhead projector. Or a combination of several different media and materials may be the best answer.

5. *Is speed or other aspects of timing important to my teaching goal?* Although all still-projection devices permit a detailed analysis of each image by holding it on the viewing screen for as long as necessary, it may occasionally be desirable to show several images in rapid succession to provide an overview or review of material. Furthermore, in such subjects as remedial reading and arithmetic, flash views of single images can be used to advantage. *Tachistoscope* attachments are available for some slide, filmstrip, and overhead projectors, and certain projectors are

[14] The Educator's Progress Service compiles annual revised listings of free films and filmstrips and accompanying instructional materials. The National Information Center for Educational Media (NICEM) at the University of Southern California provides separate catalogs for each kind of medium. The Westinghouse Learning Corporation publishes the *Learning Directory,* a regularly revised index of sources of all types of media. Film evaluation services are available from the Educational Film Library Association and Landers Film Review.

specifically designed for use as tachistoscopes. (See Figure 7.21.) With a tachistoscope, images can be flashed on a screen at speeds of $\frac{1}{100}$ of a second or less. Rapid, brief exposures of this type have been used to increase reading speeds and perceptual spans. However, faster reading speeds must be practiced diligently to become habitual. At first,

> if the student tires, as he must in longer periods, he will have a tendency to revert to a slower and more comfortable rate. After the faster rate becomes habitual, it is no more tiring than a slower rate. Effort requires motivation. [When tachistoscopes are used] the attempt is made to arrange conditions so the student will practice reading in a different way. Mere practice, reading in the accustomed way, will only maintain the status quo. One learns by practice what he practices.[15]

To summarize, teachers must first evaluate the purposes for which learning materials are to be used and then just which types of material and

[15] James B. Stroud, *Psychology in Education,* 2nd ed. (New York: McKay, 1956), pp. 359–369.

Figure 7.21 These students are working with specially designed reading slides mounted on disks and a tachistoscopic projector. The projector, designed for use by individuals or small groups, has a wide range of exposure speeds.

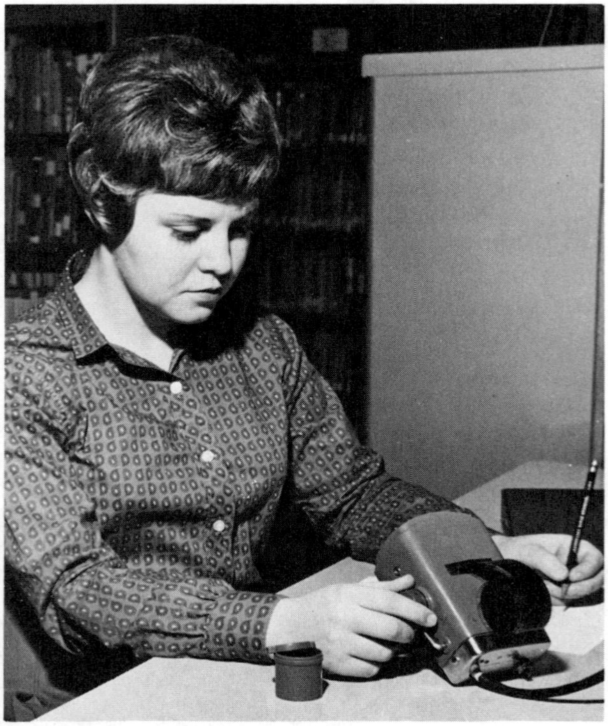

Figure 7.22 Viewing projection materials before they are selected is essential for good results. Simple viewers such as this facilitate the selection process.

means of projection will accomplish these purposes most efficiently. Finally, the visuals they choose must contribute something at once significant and unique to the learning situation. Previewing materials is clearly necessary, not only to judge material, but to plan how to use it—what points to emphasize, what points to clarify, and, unless a filmstrip is being used, what order and sequence in which to present the slides, transparencies, or opaque materials. (See Figure 7.22.)

Using Still Projection

In using still projections and other teaching materials, not only the presentation of the materials, but also the preparation for the experience and follow-up activities should be planned in advance.

Preparing for a presentation. The first step in preparing a presentation is to become fully acquainted with the points to be highlighted or clarified for pupils. In previewing filmstrips, sets of slides, or transparencies, teachers should outline the salient features in order and note any comments or questions they wish to raise in a classroom discussion. It may be desirable to record the presentation or comments on tape. A prerecorded narration not only establishes beforehand the ideas to be covered and the pace at which they will be presented, but also prevents points from getting lost because of pupil questions or spontaneous digressions. The tape—like the projection—can be stopped at any point.

Having planned the overall presentation, teachers must prepare their class to see it. Just how they go about this will depend on the pupils' readiness for and initial interest in the subject. The point to bear in mind is that students should *want* to see the presentation for reasons of their own. Thus, though teachers may feel that they should give an introductory explanation of why the pupils are being shown this particular material at this particular time, the purpose of the experience, and so on, they should at the same time be sure not to overlook the necessity to motivate pupils to become involved in the presentation.

In preparing a class for what they are to see, teachers must be sure that pupils understand clearly what to look for. How teachers use a filmstrip or any other kind of teaching material naturally depends on *why* they are using it—in other words, on their teaching objectives. Should their purpose be to provide a general overview of a subject and to arouse interest in it, they may indicate general rather than specific points to be looked for. On the other hand, if they wish to clarify certain definite concepts, they will wish their students to be alert for the answers to specific questions. For example, in using the filmstrip *The Slide Rule—Multiplication and Division,*[16] a mathematics instructor might well ask the following questions in advance:

1. Which two scales on the slide rule are used for multiplication and division?
2. How should the scales be lined up to multiply? To divide?
3. How and where is the result found?

Teachers should also be alert to new or difficult words, phrases, and symbols and explain them in advance.

Mechanical as well as mental preparation is necessary in using filmstrips, slides, and transparencies effectively. Most teachers quickly realize that it is more convenient, as well as more effective, to have all their teaching materials ready for use at the beginning of a class period. It takes only a few minutes to set up the projector and test it so that at the proper moment a flick of the switch will bring the first picture to the screen. When everything is in readiness, interruptions are held to a minimum. The filmstrip, slide, or other projected medium fits smoothly and naturally into the learning experience. It assumes its proper role in helping to put across ideas without attracting undue and unwanted attention to the mechanics of the operation.

Making a presentation. How projected materials are presented—for example, the pace at which they are presented, the kind of narration or sound effects used, the way captions are handled, and whether other learning media are used in conjunction with the stills—depends on the objectives the teacher hopes to achieve. (See Figure 7.23.) For example, if the initial showing of the material is to provide an introductory overview of a new unit of study, the instructor may wish to show a complete filmstrip at once and save questions, comments, and detailed analyses of particular frames or ideas for later. In this case, the filmstrip may be run through fairly rapidly to emphasize only the highlights. If it is a silent filmstrip, the instructor might read the captions aloud to save time, keep things moving, and assure that everyone is following the story as it unfolds on the screen.

Figure 7.23 This frame from the filmstrip *Teaching with the Filmstrip* suggests several ways in which filmstrips can be used.

When projection stills are to be used as a basis for a class discussion—perhaps a detailed study of materials the students have already seen—there is no reason to hurry, and the entire class period may be devoted to showing just a few frames of a filmstrip or a few slides. In this case, the captions on the filmstrip or slides need not be read aloud, as the concepts verbalized there will undoubtedly be covered in the class discussion. If a sound filmstrip is used, only short segments of the recording may be played, or the sound may be turned off entirely.

Projection stills can also be used spontaneously, to clarify or communicate ideas that have arisen unexpectedly in a class discussion or on

[16] U.S. Office of Education. Available from United World Films.

students' written work. Opaque projectors are particularly good for this purpose.

Finally, filmstrips, slides, or transparencies can be used for a quick review of ideas that have been developed in detail previously. Here, too, the pace of the showing may be fairly rapid, and it may be a good idea to summarize key ideas or concepts. The teacher is the best judge of whether this kind of reinforcement is necessary. If so, perhaps some of the students can do the summarizing. One can tell much about how well pupils understand a subject by the way they summarize or explain the ideas involved. This kind of thing is also a learning activity.

It is now quite common, too, for students, individually or in small groups, to use projection materials by themselves. This is still another way that projection stills can aid learning. (See Figure 7.24.)

A fundamental principle in using media is to provide variety where feasible. For example, several projection techniques and materials can be used together. In geography, for instance, a map of a large area can be projected onto one screen on an overhead projector, and a small section of the map can be projected in enlarged form next to it on another projector. Slides can be used to show what particular areas look like and to help students understand the climatic or cultural effects of geography. Slides, transparencies, or filmstrips can show schematic diagrams of airflows, rainfall, and so forth, or cultural scenes. Likewise, in mathematics, a problem projected on one screen on an overhead projector can be retained while the solution is worked out by using a series of transparent overlays on a second projector or by writing on the surface of a continuous plastic roll on the second projector.

Some learning situations may call for the use of several different media in a single lesson. A few slides, a short film, a section of sound tape, and perhaps a summary of points on an overhead projector may be appropriate.

Figure 7.24 Cassette tapes plus filmstrips provide a valuable information source for individual study.

Follow-up activities. No learning experience is complete without a provision for follow-up activities that permit pupils to evaluate, demonstrate, and apply what they have learned. Such follow-up activities permit teachers to evaluate both their pupils' progress and the relative effectiveness of the media and methods used.

Thus after a filmstrip, slides, or other projection stills have been used, the teacher may wish to give a brief written or oral test on the material covered. Wherever possible, however, teachers should call for a practical demonstration of concepts learned. For example, suppose a filmstrip on how to read a micrometer was shown. The real test of pupil learning in this case is how well each pupil can handle and read a real micrometer. From such evaluative activities, teachers can judge pupils' weak areas and thus the points that need to be reviewed or taught again, individual pupils' difficulties, and the pupils' interest in further learning. Teachers can also judge, from the results of such activities, whether a particular projection medium or method of presenting it has accomplished its purpose. If the class generally exhibits less understanding than was hoped for—if a fairly sizable number of pupils seem to be having difficulty—teachers should review in their own minds the adequacy of the materials and the methods used in presenting them. Perhaps they failed to prepare pupils sufficiently for the learning experience or to interest them in it.

Follow-up activities also give students a chance to apply new learning in areas and ways that interest them. When pupils choose how they will use new knowledge, the new learning is much more likely to become permanent.

Learners normally proceed from concrete observation to an initial understanding of ideas, to application of these ideas in new situations, to generalization drawn from a number of such applications, and finally to assimilation of these generalizations as part of their permanent store of knowledge. Thus viewing or reading materials is only a small part of the learning process.

STILL-PROJECTION EQUIPMENT AND SCREENS

The operation and use of still-projection equipment are discussed in some detail in the *Student Production Guide*. There are a few general aspects of still projection, however, that all teachers should be familiar with, including the various types of equipment and some of their advantages and limitations for particular uses.

Filmstrip and 2″ × 2″ Slide Projectors

A filmstrip projector is essentially a simple mechanism. (See Figure 7.25.) It consists primarily of a lamp, a reflector, a series of lenses, and a smooth channel for the film. Near the base of this channel is a knob that is turned by hand to pull the filmstrip through the projector. The knob turns a sprocket wheel whose teeth fit into sprocket holes on the filmstrip. The projector is easy to set up and operate, inexpensive, and light in weight—all points of practical importance. A filmstrip viewer is similar, except for its self-contained screen.

A slide projector is also a simple mechanism, having essentially the same elements as a filmstrip projector, except for a mechanism to hold individual slides. Some filmstrip projectors can also be used for slides if a slide carriage is inserted. Most 2″ × 2″ slide projectors today, however, use drums or cartridges in which a large number of slides can be loaded in advance. Both types of projectors can usually be operated and even focused by remote controls. An operator is unnecessary because the teacher can change or reverse slides from the front of the room. The convenience and flexibility of drum-type slide projectors have led to their almost universal use. (See Figure 7.26.) Such projectors normally have an automatic device that changes slides at predetermined intervals. This makes them particularly useful for displays. It is also possible to hook up a tape recorder to such a projector and record a narration to fit automatically changed slides. And, as we have already mentioned, an inaudible pulse can be recorded on the tape that changes the slides at varying appropriate intervals. There are many sound-slide and sound-filmstrip projectors available that make such automated presentations practical.

Threading projectors. Most filmstrip projectors are threaded by inserting the film into the film channel from above and pushing it down to engage the sprocket teeth. This method has the advantage of ensuring the correct alignment of the film in the channel and proper engagement with the sprocket teeth. Ease of threading is important because the sprocket holes on filmstrips are easily damaged. Because the damage ordinarily occurs on the leader strip while the

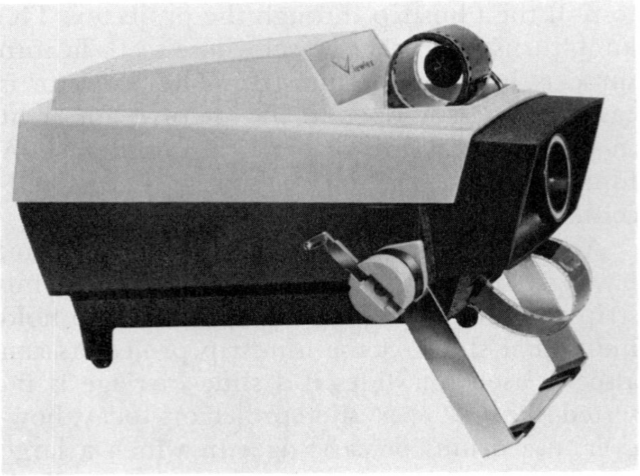

(a)

(b)

(c)

Figure 7.25 These are three of the many models of filmstrip projectors available, some of which also accommodate 2″ × 2″ slides. (*a*) Viewlex, (*b*) Graflex, (*c*) Prima (Hudson).

projector is being threaded, however, it can usually be detected before the picture section is damaged. Rubberized pressure rollers and self-threading cartridge mechanisms are also available, as are filmstrip repair kits. New models of filmstrip projectors also make the threading operation easier and more foolproof.

Overhead Projectors

Overhead projectors transmit a strong beam of light through a transparency and onto a screen behind the instructor, who is generally at the front of the room, facing the class. (See Figures 7.11 and 7.12.) In most overhead projectors, light is reflected through a large plastic lens (a Fresnel lens), which directs it through the transparency into a second reflector above and on out to the screen. (See Figure 7.27.)[17] The light is brilliant enough so that the room need not be darkened much.

The operation of an overhead projector is very simple; little more is involved than placing the transparency on the projector stage. The material is focused by raising or lowering the upper reflector unit by turning a knob. The projection area is usually 10″ × 10″. Most overhead pro-

17 One lightweight portable overhead projector has the light source in the head, directs it downward to a reflector in the base, and then directs it back through the transparency to a reflector in the head and on out to the screen. The principle is the same, though the mechanics are different.

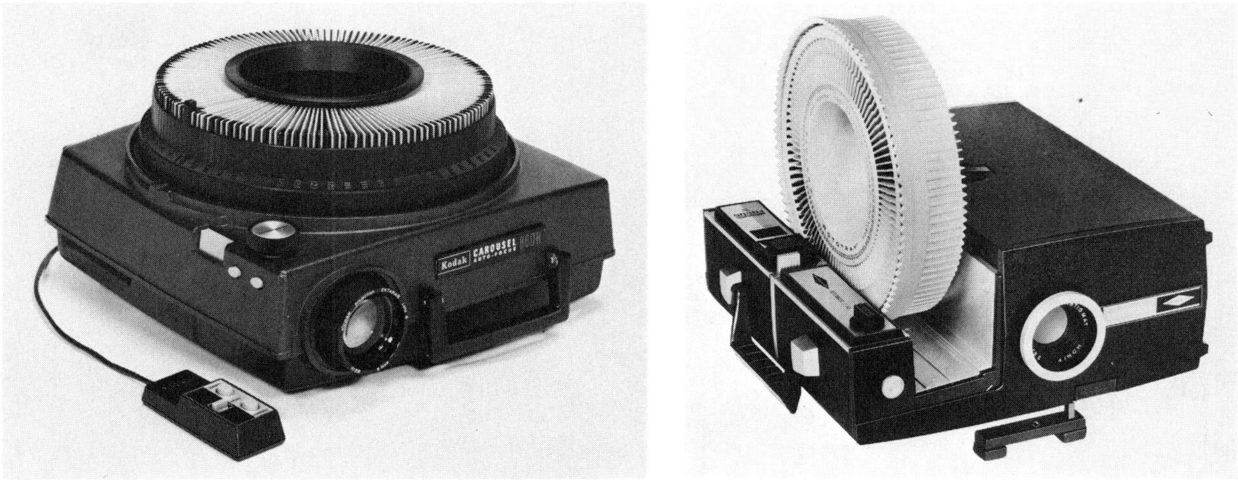

(a) (b)

Figure 7.26 Drum-type 2″ × 2″ slide projectors are more widely used than any other type because they can hold large numbers of slides, usually have remote controls and focusing mechanisms, and are highly reliable. Shown here are *(a)* a Kodak Carousel and *(b)* Sawyer's Rotomatic.

jectors contain a 100-foot strip of clear plastic that passes over the projector stage between two rollers inside the projector. Teachers can write on the plastic as they would on a chalkboard, or they can prepare panels ahead of time and roll them into position by turning a small crank. Diagrams, assignments, tests, and similar material can be presented in this way with a minimum of time and effort.

One useful accessory for overhead projectors has already been mentioned in connection with slides, but it can also be used with transparencies. This mechanism uses polarized light to create the effect of animation on projected transparencies. A motor-driven polarized disk is placed beneath the projector head and polarized strips are placed on the transparencies. The disk revolves, causing the light and color patterns to change rapidly and giving the effect of animation. This device is useful for providing animated diagrams, graphs, lettering, or other display materials.

Another device that can be attached to some overhead projectors, and to some 2″ × 2″ slide projectors, is a tachistoscope. This attachment, as we have noted, enables instructors to flash scenes on a viewing screen at speeds of up to 1/100 of a second. The use of tachistoscopes for improving reading speeds has already been discussed.

Opaque Projectors

Opaque materials are projected by means of *reflected* light. A strong light from the projector lamp is thrown onto a book page or other opaque material and reflected by a tiled mirror through a lens onto a screen. (See Figure 7.28.) Although the image on the screen is less brilliant than in the case of a slide or transparency, highly satisfactory images can be obtained if the room is reasonably dark. Furthermore, the lighting efficiency of the newer projectors has been improved to the point where effective projection is

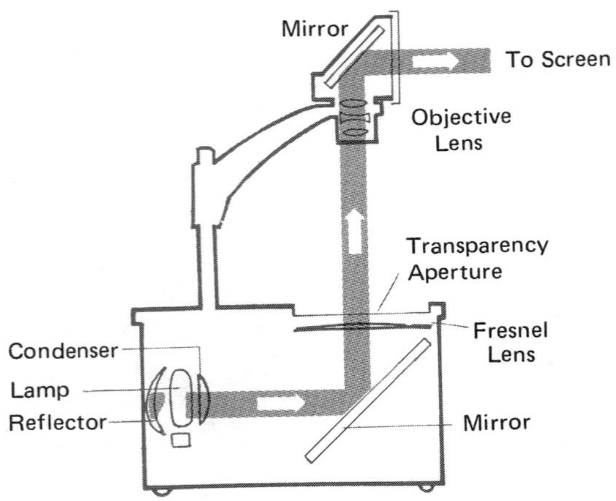

(*a*)

(*b*)

(*c*)

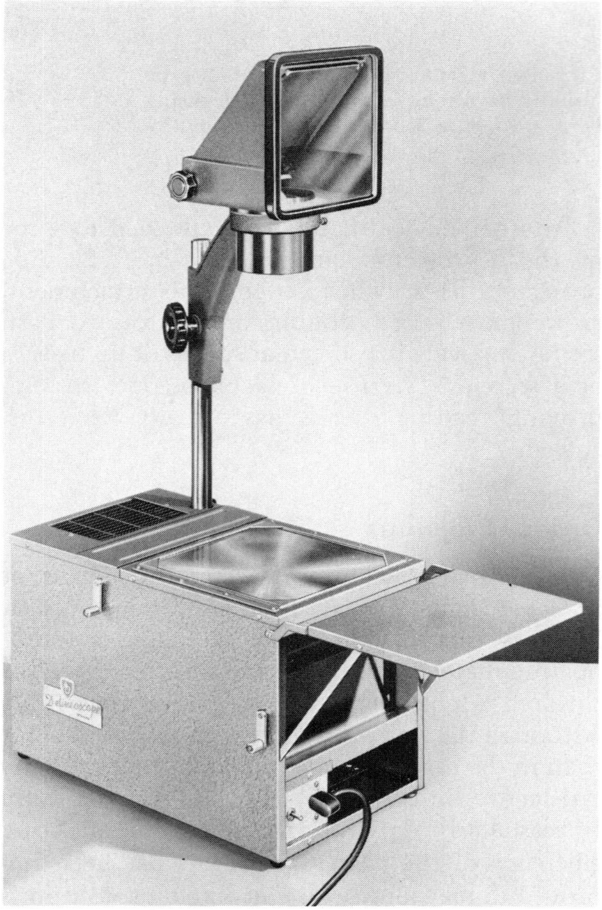

Figure 7.27 (*a*) This diagram shows how an overhead projector works. Two typical overhead projectors are also shown: (*b*) a Beseler and (*c*) an American Optical machine.

possible even in moderately dark rooms. These improved projectors have a 1000-watt lamp, an opening large enough to accommodate 8″ × 10″ materials, and an efficient cooling system. Downdraft ventilation holds loose or unmounted material in place. A loose postage stamp, for example, can be projected without difficulty with this type of machine. When a book page is being projected, a piece of heat-resistant glass holds the page flat so that all parts of it can be focused sharply.

Projection Screens

In all types of projections, the screen affects the quality of the results. Teachers need not be experts on projection equipment to know enough to select from several available screens the best

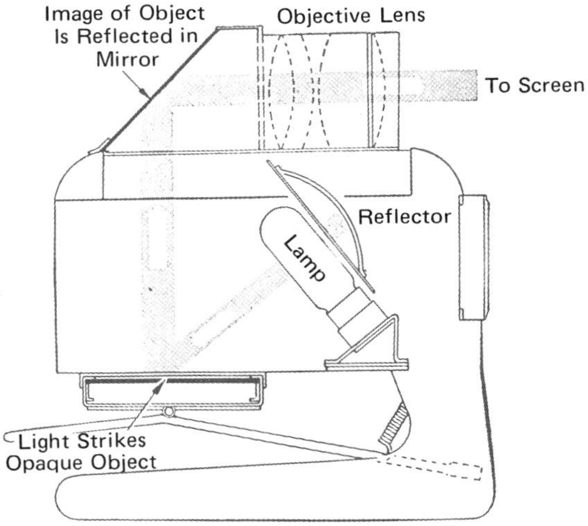

(a)

(b)

(c)

Figure 7.28 (*a*) This diagram shows how an opaque projector works. Two representative 1000-watt projectors are also shown: (*b*) a Beseler and (*c*) a Standard projector with a top loader.

one for them. There are two major considerations: the size of the screen and the type of screen.

The size of the screen. The most useful and versatile screens for classrooms are *square* rather than rectangular. For most purposes, a screen at least 60″ × 60″ is the smallest that should be used. In larger classrooms a 70″ × 70″ screen should be used. A square shape is necessary to accommodate vertical slides, transparencies, or opaque projected materials without cutting down the size of the image. It is readily adaptable, as well, for use with motion pictures.

The type of screen. There are, essentially, four types of projection screens. The most common are (1) beaded screens and (2) matte-surfaced screens. Lenticular screens are especially designed for color projection, as are Ektalite screens. Rear-projection screens, which are translucent, have a variety of special uses. We shall limit the discussion here to the first two types, those commonly found in schools. The other types are described, and additional information on screens is provided, in the *Student Production Guide*.

Beaded screens. Beaded screens are the type most often found in classrooms. These screens provide a very good image on a line directly between the projector and screen and to an angle of approximately 30 degrees on either side. (A new type of chemical coating on some beaded screens may improve the quality of the image and increase the viewing angle.) Beyond that point, the brilliance of the image drops off rapidly; thus beaded screens are best used in long, narrow rooms.

Matte, or flat-surfaced, screens. Matte screens, on the other hand, provide less initial brilliance, but diffuse the available light more evenly than beaded screens and over a wider area. Thus, in rooms that are square or as wide as or wider than they are deep, matte screens are more satisfactory as all-purpose screens.

The placement of screens is a variable teachers can control. Instead of automatically placing a screen in the center of the front wall—theater style—teachers should try for screen positions that reduce the surrounding light on the screen's surface to a minimum; obviously, such positions produce the brightest and most visible projected image. Normally, the best position is in the front corner of the room with the surface of the screen angled away from such light as may be getting in around blinds or shades. (See Figure 7.29.) Often this corner position also provides a better viewing angle for most students. The main thing to remember is that direct light on the screen surface, whether a front- or rear-projection screen is used, drastically reduces the brilliance of the projected image.

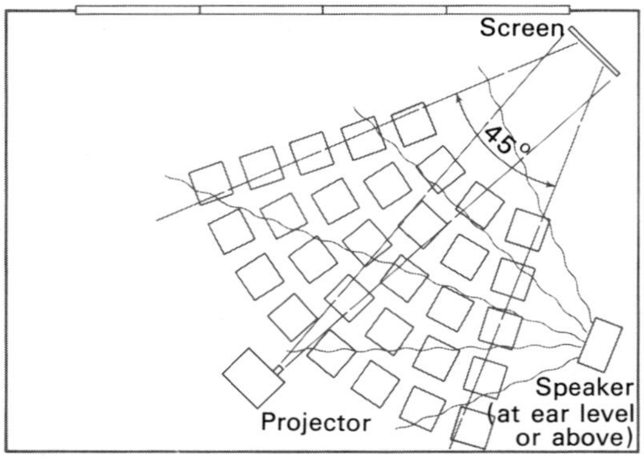

Figure 7.29 For group showing, the best screen position may well be in the front corner of the room next to the windows at an angle that minimizes unwanted light on the screen surface. Another hint: for best sound results, locate the speaker at ear level or above—never on the floor!

SUMMARY

One of the definite advantages of still projection is that individuals or groups can examine the projected images for whatever length of time is necessary. Other advantages include the wide variety of still-projection machines, the ready availability and low cost of materials for projection, and the convenience and ease of operation of most projection equipment.

There are various types of stills, including 2″ × 2″ slides, larger slides, filmstrips, transparencies, opaque materials, microscope slides and microfilm and microfiche. In addition to the general advantages indicated, each of these types of stills has its unique advantages and uses; and, of course, each has certain limitations that must be considered in selecting them. Like the effectiveness of other kinds of instructional media, the effectiveness of projection stills depends to a large extent on *how* they are used. Planning well initially, previewing materials, preparing the class, motivating pupils and telling them what to look for, providing good projection conditions, and ensuring appropriate follow-up activities are all important. Effective methods are flexible rather than rigid and are adapted both to the requirements of the learning situation and the needs of individual learners.

It is important for teachers to know something about still projectors so that they can select the most suitable types for a particular situation and so that they can feel confident about using them. In addition, teachers should be generally familiar with the proper types and sizes of screens to use for various situations and where to place them.

ACTIVITIES

1. (a) Identify six learning situations you might expect to encounter in which one or more forms of projection stills would be a suitable teaching tool. Write a brief explanation of why the medium chosen would be especially suitable in each case.
   (b) Specify objectives in two of these situations that are functionally different from one another.
   (c) Outline a lesson plan for those two situations, indicating the type or types of projection stills you would use and the objectives to which they would contribute. Assume that suitable materials will be available.
2. Demonstrate the unique advantages of three types of projection stills to the class, and answer any questions that may come up.
3. Working with a group of other students with the same or similar career plans, select from a group of slides, filmstrips, and transparencies in various subjects for various grades those that would be appropriate for you. Write a brief evaluation of each.
4. Secure catalogs of representative distributors of still projection materials from a learning resources center or commercial sources. Working with the same group as before, construct a source list for various types of material and have it duplicated for distribution to the class.

REFERENCES

PRINT REFERENCES

Alexander, H., and others, "Color Microfiche as an Aid to Learning." *Journal of Home Economics* (January 1972), pp. 17–19.

Andrews, E. R., "Teaching About Mass Production: Transparency Master." *Industrial Education* (December 1973), pp. 20–21.

Barson, John, and Gerry B. Mendelson, "Holography, a New Dimension for Media," *Audiovisual Instruction* (October 1969), pp. 40–42.

Bellamy, J., "Gaining Another Dimension: Laser Holography," *Times Educational Supplement* (July 4, 1975), p. 39.

Caucutt, A., "Saying It with Slides," *Today's Education* (May 1973), p. 55.

Christensen, Jack, "Sound Filmstrip Programs," *Media and Methods* (February 1974), pp. 14–28.

Gorvine, George, "Using the Overhead to Train Perception," *The Instructor* (January 1970), p. 146.

Greeshaber, Emil W., "Overhead Projection—How to Make the Most of It." *Audiovisual Instruction* (April 1962), pp. 236–237. (Entire issue devoted to overhead projection. Note also articles by Arthur Lalime, Neville Pearson, and Emma Starstream.)

Hall, N., "Adding Impact to 35mm Slides," *AV Instruction* (May 1975), p. 57.

Hartsell, H. C., and Wilfred Veenendaal, *Overhead Projection* (Buffalo, N.Y.: Henry Stewart, 1960).

Hodder, G., "Movie Making with Magazines," *School Arts* (February 1973), pp. 52–53.

Holmes, C. W., "History Is Fragile. . . . Save It! Greeley and Weed County, Colorado," *AV Instruction* (May 1974), p. 85.

———, "Student-Produced Media: A Symposium," *AV Instruction* (October 1974), pp. 4 ff.

Johnson, Roger, "Overhead Projectors: Basic Media for a Community College," *Audiovisual Instruction* (March 1978), pp. 21–22.

Leone, J., "Microfilm Comes into Focus," *Education Digest* (April 1975), pp. 50–52.

Lukas, Terrence, "An Easy and Inexpensive Technique for Group Viewing of Small Biologicals," *Learning Resources* (April 1975), pp. 23–24.

Maddox, H. and R. J. Loughran, "Illustrating the Lecture: Prepared Diagrams vs. Built-up Diagrams," *AV Communications Review* (Spring 1977), pp. 87–90

May, Lola J., "Teaching Tools: How to Use Them in Math," *Grade Teacher* (February 1970), pp. 126–130.

Reinhart, D. H., "Easy-To-Make Casts and Slides," *American Biology Teacher* (November 1972), pp. 475–476.

Richason, Benjamin F., Jr., "Teaching Geography by the Audio-Visual-Tutorial Method," *Audiovisual Instruction* (February 1970), pp. 41–44.

Rocco, John A., "Developing a Transparency File for Elementary Schools," *Audiovisual Instruction* (September 1967), pp. 716–717.

Schubert, W. K., and C. R. Throckmorton, "Making a 360° Hologram," *Physics Teacher* (May 1975), pp. 310–311.

Sheard, B. V., "They Love to Read Aloud from Filmstrips," *Teacher* (May 1973), pp. 66 ff.

Teachers' Manual for the Bioscope Microprojector (Tulsa, Okla.: Bioscope Manufacturing Company, 1970.

Wilson, W. Frederic, "Now Everyone Can Make a 3-D Hologram," *Popular Photography* (November 1970), pp. 82–84.

MEDIA REFERENCES

Children Learn from Filmstrips, 16mm film, b/w and color, 16 min. McGraw-Hill Films, 1963.

Handmade Materials for Projection, 16mm film, b/w and color, 20 min. Indiana University, 1965.

Learning from Projected Slides, 16mm film, b/w, 30 min. Bureau of Audiovisual Instruction, Board of Education of the City of New York, 1964.

Opaque Projector, 35mm filmstrip, color, 46 frames. Ohio State University, Teaching Aids Lab, 1957.

Opaque Projector: Its Purpose and Use, 16mm film, b/w, 6 min. University of Iowa, 1958.

Overhead Projector, 16mm film, b/w, 16 min. Iowa State University of Science and Technology, 1953.

Overhead Projector, 16mm film, b/w, 27 min. 3M Company, 1967.

Photography: Close-up and Copying with 35mm Cameras, 35mm filmstrip/record, color, 55 frames. BFA Educational Enterprises, 1965.

Projecting Ideas on the Overhead Projector, 16mm film, color, 17 min. University of Iowa, 1960.

Projecting Ideas II: Diazo Transparency Production, 16mm film, color, 11 min. University of Iowa, 1964.

Projecting Ideas III: Direct Transparency Production, 16mm film, color, 5 min. University of Iowa, 1966.

Slide Preparation and Presentation, transparencies, b/w. 3M Company, 1965.

Still Projectors, 8mm film cartridges. Chandler Publishing Company, 1965. Series includes:
2 × 2 Inch Slide Projectors, 3 min. 33 sec.
35mm Filmstrip Projector, 3 min. 10 sec.
Opaque Projector, 2 min. 55 sec.
Overhead Projector, 3 min. 33 sec.

Teaching with a Filmstrip, 35mm filmstrip, b/w, 50 frames. Society for Visual Education, Inc., 1953.

Transparency-Making, 8mm film cartridges, color. Chandler Publishing Company, 1965.
Series includes following transparencies:
Adding Color, 3 min. 45 sec.
Diazo Process, 3 min. 45 sec.
Handmake Method, 3 min. 5 sec.
Heat Process, 2 min. 15 sec.
Making Overlays, 3 min. 45 sec.
Mounting and Masking, 3 min. 15 sec.
Picture Transfer 1, 3 min. 10 sec.
Picture Transfer 2, 3 min. 30 sec.
Principle of Diazo Process, 4 min. 40 sec.
Spirit Duplicator, 3 min.

The Filmstrip Projector, 35mm filmstrip, color, 41 frames. National Film Board of Canada, 1962.

Using the Overhead Projector, 35mm filmstrip, color, 43 frames. Educational Media, 1968.

STUDENT PRODUCTION GUIDE REFERENCES

See *Student Production Guide,* Chapter 2, "Equipment Operation," Projection Systems and Techniques, Opaque, Overhead, Slide and

Filmstrip Projector sections; and Chapter 4, "Producing Photo and Sound Materials for Instruction," Transparencies: Design and Use; Thermal Transparencies, Diazo Transparencies, Picture Lift Transparencies, Photographic Slide and Filmstrip Production sections.

SOURCE REFERENCES

Filmstrips

The major source guide for 35mm filmstrips is the *Index to 35mm Educational Filmstrips* published and updated annually by the National Information Center for Education Media (NICEM) at the University of Southern California. 6th Edition, 1977, $86.50.

Basic Skill Films, 1355 Inverness, Pasadena, CA 91103.

BFA—Educational Media, 2211 Michigan Ave., Santa Monica, CA 90404.

Chinese Information Service, 159 Lexington Ave., New York, NY 10016.

Coronet Films, 65 E. South Water St., Chicago, IL 60601.

Cousino Communications, Inc., 1945 Franklin Ave., Toledo, OH 43624.

Demco Educational Corp., P.O. 1488, Madison, WI 53701.

Denoyer-Geppert Audio-Visuals, 5245 Ravenswood Ave., Chicago, IL 60640.

Dukane Corporation, 2900 Dukane Drive, St. Charles, IL 60174.

Educators Guide to Free Filmstrips, Educators Progress Service, Randolph, WI 53956.

EMC Corporation, Educational Materials Div., 180 E. 6th St., St. Paul, MN 55101.

Encyclopedia Britannica Educational Corporation, 425 N. Michigan Ave., Chicago, IL 60611.

Enrichment Materials, Inc., A Div. of Scholastic Magazine, 50 W. 44th St., New York, NY 10036.

Eye Gate House, 146-01 Archer Ave., Jamaica, NY 11435.

The Fideler Company, 31 Ottawa Ave., N.W., Grand Rapids, MI 49501.

Filmstrip House, 6633 W. Howard St., Niles, IL 60648.

Friendship Press, 475 Riverside Dr., New York, NY 10027.

Guidance Associates, 757 Third Ave., New York, NY 10017.

Hubbard Scientific Company, P.O. Box 105, Northbrook, IL 60062.

Jam Handy Organization, 2843 E. Grand Blvd., Detroit, MI 48211.

Learning Resources Company, 202 Lake Miriam Dr., Lakeland, FL 33803.

McGraw-Hill Book Company, 1221 Ave. of the Americas, New York, NY 10020.

Moody Institute of Science, Educational Film Div., 12000 E. Washington Blvd., Whittier, CA 90606.

National Film Board of Canada, 1251 Avenue of the Americas, New York, NY 10020.

Lowell T. Nerge, 11941 Jefferson St. N.E., Minneapolis, MN 55434. (Makes filmstrips from your slides.)

Prima Education Products, Div. of Hudson Photographic Industries, Irvington-on-Hudson, NY 10533.

Sandak, Inc., 180 Harvard Ave., Stamford, CN 06902.

Society for Visual Education, 1345 W. Diversey Pkwy., Chicago, IL 60614.

Teaching Resources Films, 2 Kisco Plaza, Mount Kisco, NY 10549.

Technicolor AV Systems, 299 Kalmus Dr., Costa Mesa, CA 92626.

Time-Life Multimedia, 100 Eisenhower Dr., Paramus, NJ 07652.

Universal Education and Visual Arts, 100 Universal City Plaza, Universal City, CA 91608.

Ward's Natural Science Establishment, 3000 E. Ridge Rd., Rochester, NY 14603.

Weston Woods Studio, Weston, CN 06880.

Slides

Bioscope Mfg. Co., P.O. Box 1492, Tulsa, OK 74101. (Microscope slides.)

Demco Educational Corporation, P.O. Box 1488, Madison, WI 53701.

Denoyer-Geppert Audio-Visuals, 5245 Ravenswood Ave., Chicago, IL 60640.

Clay-Adams, 299 Webro Rd., Parsippany, NJ 07054.

Eastman Kodak Company, Motion Picture and Education Markets Div., 343 State St., Rochester, NY 14650.

Museum of Modern Art, 11 W. 53rd St., New York, NY 10019.

National Audubon Society, Educational Services, 950 Third Ave., New York, NY 10022.

Prothman Assc., 650 Thomas Ave., Baldwin, NY 11510.

Sandak, Inc., 18 Harvard Ave., Stamford, CN 06902.

Society for Visual Education, 1345 W. Diversey Pkwy, Chicago, IL 60614.

United Scientific Company, 216 South Jefferson St., Chicago, IL 60606. (Microscopic slides.)

U.S. Committee for UNICEF, 331 E. 38th St., New York, NY 10016.

Ward's Natural Science Establishment, 3000 E. Ridge Rd., Rochester, NY 14603.

Transparencies

Materials for making transparencies

Arthur Brown and Bros., 2 W. 46th St., New York, NY 10036.

Demco Educational Corporation, P.O. Box 1488, Madison, WI 53701.

Denoyer-Geppert Audio-Visuals, 5245 Ravenswood Ave., Chicago, IL 60640.

Eastman Kodak Company, 343 State St., Rochester, NY 14650.

Eye Gate House, 146-01 Archer Ave., Jamaica, NY 11435.

Holson Company, 111 Danbury Rd., Wilton, CN 06897.

Keuffel and Esser, 20 Whippany Rd., Hoboken, NJ 07960.

Labelon Corporation, 10 Chapin St., Canandaigua, NY 14424.

Ozalid Div., General Aniline and Film Corporation, 140 W. 51st St., New York, NY 10020.

Scott Graphics, 195 Appleton St., Holyoke, MA 01040. (Polarizing materials.)

Seal, Inc., Roosevelt Dr. & B St., Derby, CN 06418.

Ward's Natural Science Establishment, 3000 E. Ridge Rd., Rochester, NY 14603.

Commercially prepared transparencies

There is one reference to commercially prepared transparencies, the *Index to Overhead Transparencies,* which covers over 18,000 transparencies. It is published by the R. R. Bowker Co., 1180 Avenue of the Americas, New York, NY 10036.

A. J. Nystrom & Company, 3333 Elston Ave., Chicago, IL 60618.

Allyn and Bacon, Inc., AV Department, 470 Atlantic Ave., Boston, MA 02210.

John Colburn Assc., 1122 Central Ave., P.O. Box 236, Wilmette, IL 60091.

Creative Visuals Div., Games Industries, P.O. Box 1911, Big Spring, TX 79720.

Encyclopaedia Britannica Educational Corp., 425 N. Michigan Ave., Chicago, IL 60611.

Hammond, Inc., 515 Valley St., Maplewood, NJ 07040.

Keuffel and Esser, 20 Whippany Rd., Hoboken, NJ 07960.

Lansford Publishing Co., P.O. Box 8711, San Jose, CA 95155.

McGraw-Hill Book Company, Text-Film Division, 1221 Avenue of the Americas, New York, NY 10036.

Ozalid Div., General Aniline and Film Corp., 140 W. 51st St., New York, NY 10020.

Rand McNally & Co., P.O. Box 7600, Chicago, IL 60680.

Scott Graphics, 195 Appleton St., Holyoke, MA 01040.

3M Company, Visual Products Div., 3M Center, St. Paul, MN 55119.

United Transparencies, Inc., P.O. Box 688, Binghamton, NY 13902.

Visualcraft, Inc., 12842 S. Western Ave., Blue Island, IL 60406.

Microfilm and microfiche

Dennison Manufacturing Company, Framington, MA 01701.

Eastman Kodak Company, 343 State St., Rochester, NY 14650.

Microcard Editions, 5500 S. Valentia Way, P.O. Box 1154, Denver, CO 80110.

National Cash Register Company, 3100 Valleywood Dr., Dayton, OH 45429.

Zerox University Microfilms, 300 N. Zeeb Rd., Ann Arbor, MI 48106. (Microfilms.)

Photographic Equipment

Still cameras

AIC Photo, Inc., 168 Glen Cove Rd., Carle Place, NY 11514.

E. Leitz, Inc., Rockleigh, NJ 07647.

GAF, 140 W. 51st St., New York, NY 10020.

Karl Heitz, Inc., 979 Third Avenue, New York, NY 10022.

Honeywell, Inc., Photographic Div., 5501 S. Broadway, Littleton, CO 80120.

Minolta Corporation, 101 Williams Dr., Ramsey, NJ 07446.

Nikon, Ehrenreich Photo Optical Industries (EPOI), 623 Stewart Ave., Garden City, NY 11530.

Polaroid Corporation, Cambridge, MA 02139. (Polaroid Land Camera.)

Lighting

Brewster Corporation, 50 River St., Old Saybrook City, CN 06475.

General Electric Company, Lamp Business Div., Nela Park, Cleveland, OH 44112.

Mole-Richardson, 937 N. Sycamore Ave., Hollywood, CA 90038.

Smith-Victor Corporation, Griffith, IN 46319.

Westinghouse Electric Corporation, Lamp Div., 1 Westinghouse Plaza, Bloomfield, NJ 07003.

Slide copiers

Bogen Photo Corporation, 100 S. Van Brunt St., Englewood, NJ 07631. (Bowens Illumitran.)

Honeywell, Inc., Photographic Div., 5501 S. Broadway, Littleton, CO 80120.

Projection Screens

Da-Lite Screen Company., Inc., P.O. Box 629, Warsaw, IN 46580. (Front and rear projection screens.)

Eastman Kodak Company, 343 State St., Rochester, NY 14650. (Ektalite screens.)

Hudson Photographic Industries, 2 S. Buckhout St., Irvington-on-Hudson, NY 10533.

Knox Manufacturing Company, 111 Spruce St., Wood Dale, IL 60191. (Front projection screens.)

Scott Graphics, 195 Appleton St., Holyoke, MA 01040.

3M Visual Production Div., Industrial Optics, P.O. Box 33235L, St. Paul, MN 55101.

TransLux News Sign Corporation, 625 Madison Ave., New York, NY 10022.

Furniture and Facilities

Accoustical materials

Johns-Manville, Greenwood Plaza, Denver, CO 80217.

Room-darkening equipment

Alcan Building Products, Div. of Alcan Aluminum Corporation, Jacobus Ave., Suite 51, So. Kearney, NJ 07032.

Beckley-Cardy Company, 1900 N. Narragansett St., Chicago, IL 60639.

Clopay Corporation, Clopay Square, Cincinnati, OH 45214.

Draper Shade Company, 411 S. Pearl St., Spiceland, IN 47385. (Drapes.)

E. I. DuPont de Nemours & Company, Wilmington, DE 19898.

Duracote Corporation, Ravenna, OH 44266. (Drapery and window shade materials.)

Forse Manufacturing Company, 2347 Sullivan Ave., St. Louis, MO 63107.

Luxout Plastic Products, P.O. Box 1118, Richmond, VA 23208. (Room-darkening and light-control draperies.)

Storage facilities

Demco Educational Corporation, P.O. Box 1488, Madison, WI 53701.

Electronics Div. of Fleetwood Furniture Company, P.O. Box 58, Zeeland, MI 49464.

Joshua Meier Div., W. R. Grace & Company, 7401 Westside Ave., North Bergen, NJ 07047. (Filing and retrieval system.)

Projector Sources	Filmstrip	2″ × 2″ Slide	3¼″ × 4″ Slide	Overhead	Opaque	Microprojector	16mm Sound	8mm and Super 8
American Museum of Natural History Central Park West at 79th St. New York, NY 10024		x						
American Optical Company Eggert Road Buffalo, NY 13215			x	x	x			
Audio-Master Corporation 121 W. 45th St. New York, NY 10036	x							
Audiscan Products Corporation P.O. Box 1456 Bellevue, WA 98009							x	
Bausch & Lomb, Inc. 1400 N. Goodman St. Rochester, NY 14602			x			x		
Bell & Howell Company 7100 McCormick Rd. Chicago, IL 60645	x	x		x			x	x
Charles Beseler Company 8 Fernwood Rd. Florham Park, NJ 07932	x		x	x	x			
Bioscope Manufacturing Company P.O. Box 1492 Tulsa, OK 74101						x		
Buhl Optical Company 1009 Beech Ave. Pittsburgh, PA 15233				x	x			
Demco Educational Corporation P.O. Box 1488 Madison, WI 53701	x	x						
Dukane Corporation 2900 Dukane Dr. St. Charles, IL 60174	x							
Eastman Kodak Company 343 State St. Rochester, NY 14650	x	x					x	x

Projector Sources (*Continued*)	Filmstrip	2″ × 2″ Slide	$3\frac{1}{4}$″ × 4″ Slide	Overhead	Opaque	Microprojector	16mm Sound	8mm and Super 8
Fairchild Industrial Products 75 Mall Dr. Commack, NY 11725								x
GAF Corporation 140 West 51 St. New York, NY 10020		x		x			x	x
Karl Heitz, Inc. 979 Third Ave. New York, NY 10022				x		x		
Hudson-Photo Industries Ozalid Div. General Aniline and Film Corporation 140 W. 51st St. New York, NY 10020				x				
Kalart Victor Corporation Henius St. Plainville, CN 06062	x	x					x	
Keystone View Company 2215 E. 12th St. Davenport, IA 52803		x	x	x	x			
LaBelle Industries 510 S. Worthington St. Oconomowoc, WI 53066	x							
E. Leitz, Inc. Rockleigh, NJ 07647	x	x						
Luminos Photo Corp. 25 Wolffe St. Yonkers, NY 10705					x			
Meston's Travels, Inc. 3801 N. Piedras El Paso, TX 79930		x						
Metropolitan Museum of Art Fifth Avenue at 82nd St. New York, NY 10028		x						
Paillard, Inc. 1900 Lower Rd. Linden, NJ 07036							x	x

Projector Sources (*Continued*)	Filmstrip	2″ × 2″ Slide	$3\frac{1}{4}$″ × 4″ Slide	Overhead	Opaque	Microprojector	16mm Sound	8mm and Super 8
Prima Education Products Div. of Hudson Photographic Industries Irvington-on-Hudson, NY 10533	x	x	x	x	x	x		
Projection Optics Company 271 Eleventh Ave. East Orange, NJ 07018				x	x			
RCA Victor Div., Radio Corporation of America Audiovisual Marketing Div. Front and Cooper Sts. Camden, NJ 08102							x	
Scott Graphics, Inc. 195 Appleton St. Holyoke, MA 01040				x	x			
Singer Educational Systems 3750 Monroe Ave. Rochester, NY 14603	x	x		x			x	
Spindler and Sauppe 13034 Saticoy St. N. Hollywood, CA 91625		x						
Squibb-Taylor, Inc. P.O. Box 20158 10807 Harry Hines Blvd. Dallas, TX 75220					x			
Standard Projector & Equipment Company 3070 Lake Terrace Glenview, IL 60025	x	x			x		x	
Technicolor AV Systems 299 Kalmus Dr. Costa Mesa, CA 92626							x	x
3M Company 3M Center St. Paul, MN 55101	x			x			x	
Viewlex AV, Inc. Broadway Ave. Holbrook, NY 11471	x	x						
Visualcraft, Inc. 12832 S. Western Ave. Blue Island, IL 60406				x				

8 Motion Pictures and Learning

Objectives

To enable you to do the following:

1. Identify at least five characteristics of motion pictures that make them interesting, efficient, and unique learning experiences.
2. Learn of local, state, regional, and national sources of educational films from which you can request materials on subjects you will be teaching.
3. Identify criteria for selecting films and apply them to material obtained from commercial and noncommercial sources.
4. Identify at least three basic pupil and teacher responsibilities in studying films.
5. Identify three teaching strategies that are reasonably certain to produce effective learner involvement in, and responses to, educational films.
6. Describe the best physical conditions for learning from films.
7. Identify ways in which the production of 8mm films can help your students achieve particular learning goals.

When we want to make an exact, lifelike record of people, things, or events, we use motion picture cameras or, as we shall see in the next chapter, videotapes. Although the two are similar from the learner's point of view, they are technologically different. In this chapter, we shall consider the unique characteristics and uses of motion pictures as learning experiences.

The invention of motion pictures brought a new dimension to the communication of information. Films are equally effective for education and entertainment. Their impact has been heightened by television, which shows thousands of films each year. Many film studios devote their entire time to producing films for television.

The governments of the world also produce countless motion pictures, for a variety of purposes. They use them to describe their art, music, and cultural accomplishments and their economic and social lifestyles, as well as to educate their people about technological innovations. American businesses and industries annually produce hundreds of motion pictures describing their manufacturing techniques and their products or services, not only to their own staff members and sales personnel, but to students and the general public. The armed forces use instructional films as an ongoing and important part of training programs.

There are well over 1 million 16mm sound motion picture projectors in use in the United States. Over half of these are used in schools, but a great many are also owned by business and industry, government agencies, and churches and synagogues.[1] Sales of 8mm silent and sound projectors have also grown almost unbelievably during the last decade. Many of these machines are used in sales work and self-tutorial learning.

The availability of innumerable high-quality instructional films has caused fundamental changes in classroom practices. Films are now widely accepted as integral rather than supplemental materials for learning. More than a thousand producers of motion picture films produce thousands of films each year, and most of these are instructional films. Among the most well-known producers of teaching films are the Encyclopaedia Britannica Educational Corporation; Coronet Films; McGraw-Hill's Film Division; Films Incorporated; Universal Education and Visual Arts; the International Film Bureau; and the film-producing divisions of many of the American colleges and universities, including Indiana University, Brigham Young University, and the University of California.

One of the best summaries of educational films is produced periodically by the National Information Center for Educational Media. The current index for 16mm films lists over 70,000 titles. A companion index identifies films in 8mm and super 8mm cartridges. More than 25,000 such films are listed in a current volume, or some 90 percent of all such films. These indexes and others can be found in most school and community libraries.[2]

[1] Hope Reports, Inc., 919 South Winton Road, Rochester, N.Y. 14618.

[2] *Index to 16mm Educational Films,* and *Index to 8mm Motion Cartridges,* National Information Center for Educational Media (NICEM), Univ. of Southern California, University Park, Los Angeles, Calif.

(a)

(b)

(c)

(d)

Figure 8.1 Government agencies often use motion pictures (film) to report their activities and accomplishments. (*a*) This still is from a film about efforts to move sea otters from an ocean area with a depleted food supply to an area with a rich food supply. (*b*) In the film *Project Salt* the Atomic Energy Commission shows how a specially designed transporter carries radioactive wastes to mined-out underground storage areas. Frames from the National Aeronautics and Space Administration film *The Eagle Has Landed* document for a worldwide audience (*c*) Neil Armstrong's planting of the U.S. flag on the surface of the moon, and (*d*) the vehicle in which the astronauts made the journey, and (*e*) first recorded "earthrise."

(e)

(a)

(b)

(c)

(d)

(e)

(f)

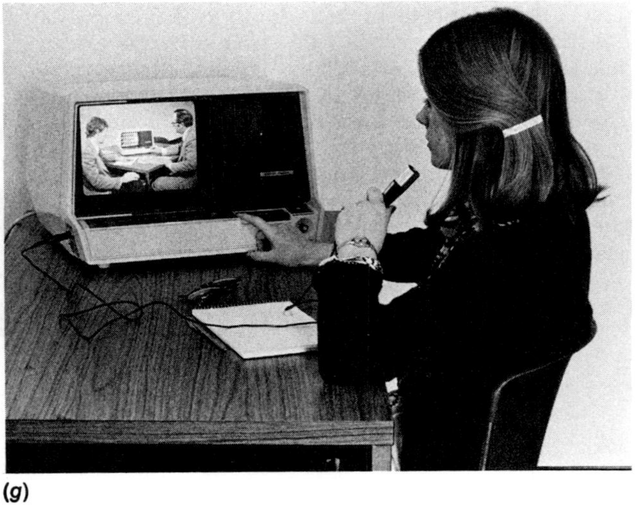

(g)

The planning and production of original films by students has become increasingly popular in recent years. Shooting, editing, and narrating such films now constitute an important part of many language-arts programs. Film making is not only a valuable learning experience in its own right, but also a strong stimulus to a more precise and effective use of language.

Sound films are available in many subjects and for many grades. Carefully selected and wisely used, they can help your students achieve a wide variety of learning goals.

A BRIEF HISTORY OF MOTION PICTURES

A motion picture film is simply a long strip of film containing a sequence of still photographs, each of which is called a *frame*. Nothing moves on a motion picture film except the film as it runs through the projector. (The mechanics of this process are explained in the *Student Production Guide,* pp. 68–87.)

The first films were on flammable film 35 millimeters wide and were, of course, silent. They moved through a primitive projector at a rate of 16 frames per second. Crude and short though they were, they quickly caught the imagination of educators who saw them.

In the early 1920s two devolpments made educational films practical. George Eastman evolved a nonexplosive "safety" film 16mm wide that could be used with smaller (and simpler) cameras and projectors. At the same time, he designed and developed the 16mm silent projector, which was necessary for the new size film. This 16mm machine became the standard size machine for educational use with large groups, supplemented later by the 8mm size, which is now widely used for working with small groups and individuals. (Film 35mm wide is still used for theatrical motion pictures, in addition to 70mm film.)

Soon afterward, in 1922, Yale University began to produce *The Chronicles of America Photoplays,* a series of fifteen 16mm silent films with explanatory titles. Historians and teachers supervised every step in the writing of the scripts and the production of the films. Great care was taken to re-create costumes and properties accurately, and historic sites were actually rebuilt. The release of these films, beginning in 1924, led to the first controlled research on the worth of films in the classroom. The results were positive,[3] as were the results of a second research experiment, involving several films in science and social studies. This second series of films was produced by the Eastman Kodak Company in collaboration with the National Education Association.[4]

These early experiments heightened the interest of educators in film as a means of providing learning experiences. The addition of sound to motion pictures in 1929 and 1930 brought in the era of the educational sound motion picture film. Since that time educational sound films have increased steadily in quality and quantity.

The most recent innovation in motion pictures is 8mm film, which is available not only in the familiar open reels, but also in car-

Figure 8.2 Over a million 16mm and 8mm motion picture projectors are in use in U.S. schools. Most 16mm sound projectors can be manually or automatically threaded. Shown here are (*a*) a Viewlex, (*b*) an Eiki, and (*c*) a Bell and Howell unit. A cross section of 8mm projectors would have to include (*d*) a Viewlex Superviewer, which coordinates silent film cartridges and sound-on-cassette, (*e*) a Fairchild unit, which projects longer sound and motion films, and (*f* and *g*) the Beseler Cue/See, which not only coordinates the showing of short 8mm cartridges with sound on accompanying cassettes but allows students to add their own sound to 8mm film cartridges. Consult the *Student Production Guide* for details about these units and instructions for using them.

3 D. C. Knowlton and J. W. Tilton, *Motion Pictures in History Teaching* (New Haven, Conn.: Yale University Press, 1929).

4 Ben D. Wood and Frank N. Freeman, *Motion Pictures in the Classroom* (Boston: Houghton Mifflin, 1929).

tridges. Most 8mm films are silent, but an increasing number now have sound tracks. An 8mm film is, of course, half the width of a 16mm film, and an 8mm frame is about one-quarter the size of a 16mm frame. For this reason, 8mm film is usually projected onto a smaller screen or onto a rear-view screen in order to produce a well-defined image.

Super 8 film, introduced by Eastman Kodak in 1966, produces a better image by using a considerably larger percentage of the film area for each frame than standard 8mm films. Super 8 films have rapidly overtaken standard 8mm for educational uses; in fact, the use of super 8 is now so general in schools that when the term *8mm* is used in this chapter it can usually be assumed to mean super 8. Because of the difference in the size of the frames and other differences, only super 8 cameras and projectors can be used with super 8 film.

Most 8mm silent films are 3 to 4 minutes long and mounted in continuous-loop cartridges that can be pushed into the projector, shown, and removed for reuse or storage very easily. Sound 8mm films 10 to 20 minutes long are becoming increasingly available, both in standard reels and in larger continuous-loop cartridges. In most cases, the sound is carried by a thin strip of magnetic material on the surface of the film.

The subjects of 8mm films parallel those available on 16mm film. Silent film cartridges, or *single-concept films,* are available in physical education, oceanography, vocational arts, social studies, and many other subjects. Entire series of 8mm sound films are available for teaching foreign languages. Because most 8mm films are silent, they can be used all over the world without costly dubbing of sound-track translations. In fact, these 8mm films are a dramatic force in bringing "American know-how" to schools in the rest of the world. Film makers in Europe, Africa, South America, Asia, and even Iceland are also producing 8mm cartridge films for their own use and for export.

With the exception of the cassette tape recorder, the 8mm silent loop cartridge projector is the piece of audiovisual equipment most frequently added to a school's stock of equipment. Furthermore, 8mm continuous-loop silent film materials are being acquired more rapidly and in greater numbers than any other item of instructional software. These new learning materials have encouraged new ways of organizing learning experiences. Some of these new teaching-learning strategies are described later in the chapter, in the section on teaching and learning through films.

Setting up and using 8mm equipment is so simple that pupils as young as 4 years of age can do it. (See Figure 8.3.) Newly developed 8mm projection equipment permits the use of sound with single-concept film loops as well as short lengths of pupil-produced film. (See Figure 8.2 *e, g,* and *h.*) This subject is explored in more detail later in the chapter, in the section on student-made motion pictures. Simple, lightweight 8mm projection units hold up exceedingly well when subjected to daily use throughout the school year, and the cost per pupil of the equipment is reasonable.

COMMUNICATION THROUGH FILMS

There are four basic techniques used in making films: (1) direct photography, (2) changed-speed photography, (3) photomicrography, and

Figure 8.3 No one has told these children they cannot teach themselves a skill. Nor has anyone told them they are too young to manipulate an automatic 8mm silent film-loop projector. (*a*) A 5-year-old practices writing groups of letters she has taught herself to understand and form. (*b*) A classmate patiently waits while she sponges off her work, readying the materials for him. (*c*) Setting about his own work, he selects an 8mm silent film loop on the letter *m*. (*d*) He easily places it in the projector and turns the unit on. (*e*) Another student works on the letter *l*. The teacher is always present to help with evaluation and encouragement. What are you reactions to this kind of learning?

(a)

(b)

(c)

(d)

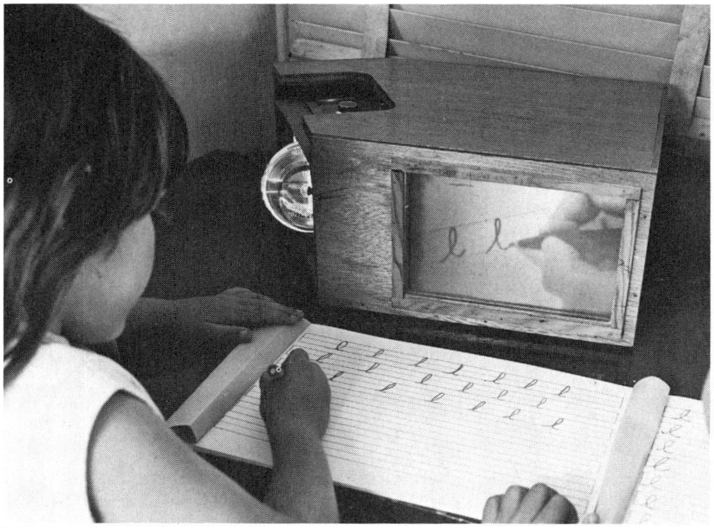

(e)

(4) animation. *Direct photography* is used, for example, in filming historical episodes. When they are part of current history, they are often shot and recorded as they happen. Obviously, historical episodes that occurred before the twentieth century are reenacted. Various natural processes are so slow or so rapid as to be incomprehensible, but *changed-speed photography* can overcome such obstacles. For example, the growth of a plant can be "speeded up," and the flight of a hummingbird can be "slowed down." Through the use of *photomicrography,* things that are too small for the naked eye to see can be filmed and projected in enlarged form on a screen. Things that are staggeringly large, hypothetical, theoretical, or very complex can be visualized by means of *animation*—diagrams, models, or mock-ups that move.

Direct Photography

Direct, or documentary, photography entails basically setting up the camera, opening the lens, and recording what occurs. In this way, "documentation" of an experience, a process, or an event is secured for later viewing. Direct photography is used to capture events at a political convention, life in the wild, landings on the moon, and the life cycles of plants and animals in their natural habitats. (See Figure 8.4.)

Direct photography is often used to "replay history." Castles are restored or duplicated; museums supply authentic costumes, utensils, and other paraphernalia required for historical episodes. When, in addition, historically accurate patterns of speech and pronunciation are used by those who do the sound track, a close approximation of actual historical events can be produced.

Such films as *Westward Movement—The Gold Rush,*[5] *Kentucky Pioneers,*[6] *Down Through the Years,* and *The Romance of Transportation*[7] are typical of those that focus on historical episodes. Other films trace the lives and accomplishments of such persons as Thomas Jefferson, Benjamin Franklin, George Washington, Andrew Jackson, Abraham Lincoln, Eli Whitney, and Andrew Carnegie.[8]

The production of contemporary social studies films is an international pursuit. In Germany, the Institut für Film und Bild (Institute for Films and Pictures), which receives government financial support for curriculum research and film production, turns out three to five sound motion pictures per month. These films are interesting, understandable reports on economic and political problems and social progress. They include, for example, *Tokyo Industrial Worker, New Life for a Spanish Farmer, Miners of Bolivia, Bedouins of Arabia,* and *River Journey on the Upper Nile,*[9] which show how man seeks to improve his life through constructive activity. (Sound tracks in several languages, including English, are prepared and recorded at the time the films are produced. When prints are made of a film for a particular market,

5 16mm film, b/w, min. Encyclopaedia Britannica Films.

6 16mm film, color, 26 min., 2nd ed., Encyclopaedia Britannica Films.

7 16mm films, sound, color, 10 min., National Film Board of Canada.

8 16mm films, sound, color and b/w, 18–23 min., Encyclopaedia Britannica Educational Corp.

9 16mm films, sound, color, 18 min., Institut für Film und Bild (U.S. distributor: Films Incorporated).

Figure 8.4 Anything that reflects light, provides information, and can be communicated through motion pictures is a possible subject for direct photography. Direct photography brings the world of the past, the present, and sometimes the future into the classroom. (*a*) This frame is from the film *First Year in the New World* and reconstructs the past. (*b*) *The World in Transition,* the film series from which this frame is taken, documents all sorts of contemporary innovations. (*c*) The film *South America Today* takes the viewer into the heart of the Amazon jungle to watch new cities being built. (*d*) *Another Man's Family* allows the viewer to survive a fire unscathed while learning a lesson on fire prevention and safety. (*e*) This frame from *Africans All* is one of many used to show the astounding contrasts amid which most modern Africans live.

(*a*)

(*b*)

(*c*)

(*d*)

(*e*)

the sound track in the appropriate language is put onto them. The U.S. Department of State and many other organizations and agencies produce films with sound tracks in a choice of languages.

Direct photography is also used by film makers who wish to reenact episodes from literature. Examples are such films as *Hamlet, Macbeth, Much Ado About Nothing, The Tempest,* and other works of William Shakespeare.[10] Another set of films, *The Humanities Series,* presents excerpts from major literary works such as *The Cherry Orchard, The Doll's House, Dr. Heidegger's Experiment, The Lottery, Great Expectations,* and *Huckleberry Finn.*[11] Narrative comments help viewers understand nuances that might otherwise escape them.

Direct photography of natural phenomena is invaluable in nature study and biological science. (See Figure 8.5.) Direct photography and high-fidelity sound recordings are used to produce such films as *Birds of the Woodlands,*[12] *The African Lion and His Realm,*[13] and *Miss Goodall and the Wild Chimpanzees.*[14] The last film allows viewers to witness Jane Goodall's life and adventures over a five-year period as she befriends and makes unbelievable discoveries about chimpanzees. Direct photographic records make fascinating learning experiences for large groups and are even more significant in leading individuals and small groups to make new discoveries.

Changed-Speed Photography

Cameras can take pictures at a rapid pace or at a very leisurely pace, so that when the result is

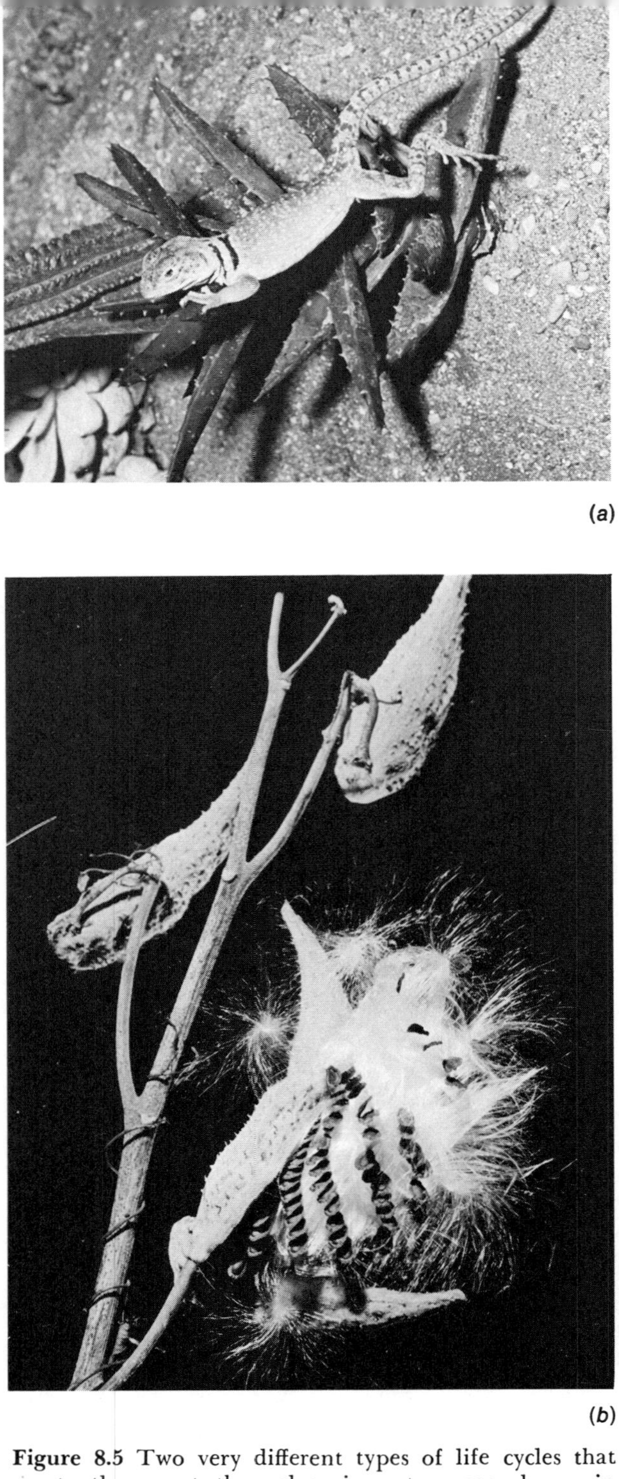

(*a*)

(*b*)

Figure 8.5 Two very different types of life cycles that constantly repeat themselves in nature are shown in (*a*) *Animals Hatched from Eggs* and (*b*) *Seed Dispersal.* What value do you think there is in studying films such as these?

[10] 16mm films, sound, color, 11–13 min., International Film Bureau.

[11] 16mm films, sound, color and b/w, 21–33 min., Encyclopaedia Britannica Educational Corp.

[12] 16mm films, sound, color, 11 min., 2d ed., Coronet Films.

[13] 16mm films, sound, color, 19 min., Walt Disney Productions.

[14] 16mm films, sound, color, 25 min., National Geographic Society.

projected on a screen, motion is either slowed down or speeded up. Many of the things we study, particularly in the sciences, occur either too rapidly for the eye to follow or very slowly. In *slow-motion photography,* high-speed cameras that take as many as 4000 frames per second are used; the actual motion of the human larynx, for instance, is photographed at this high speed. When the pictures are projected, at a normal rate of 24 frames per second, the motion is greatly slowed down and we can see what happened.[15]

In the reverse process, the camera eye is opened at intervals (of 1 second or 1 minute or 1 hour or 1 week—whatever is appropriate) to observe the leisurely blossoming of a flower, the winding tendrils of the pea vine, the metamorphosis of a pupa into an adult insect, and so forth.[16] Through such *time-lapse photography,* developments that take hours, days, weeks, or months to occur can be viewed in a very short time via pictures projected at normal rate of 24 frames per second. (See Figure 8.6.)

Not too long ago, only occasional films used changed-speed photography. Today, hundreds of these films are available, all with sound tracks. One example is *Dr. Heidegger's Experiment,*[17] a film that allows viewers to witness the changes undergone by four aged characters who drink water allegedly from the Fountain of Youth; their bodies change, their wrinkles disappear, and so forth. Another is *Egg into Animal,*[18] which shows, step by step, the actual life cycle from egg to adult of the roundel skate, a

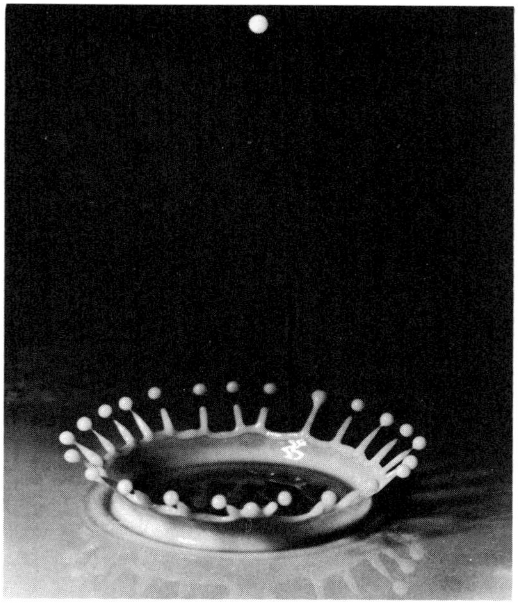

(*a*)

(*b*)

Figure 8.6 Changed-speed photography works in two ways. (*a*) Slow motion photography "stops" actions that are too rapid for the human eye to follow, as are the splashes made by drops of milk falling into shallow water. The still is from *Fluid Mechanics.* (*b*) Time-lapse photography can summarize the life cycle of a bee, from egg to adult, in ten minutes. This still, showing a bee bringing pollen to its hive on its hind legs, is from *Biography of a Bee.* Why should changed-speed photography be explained carefully to young learners before they see such films?

15 *Your Voice,* 16mm film, b/w, 11 min., Encyclopaedia Britannica Educational Corporation.

16 See *The Honeybee,* 2d ed., 16mm film, sound, color, 10 min., Encyclopaedia Britannica Educational Corporation: *Flowers and Bees: A Springtime Story,* 16mm film, sound, color, 11 min., Encyclopaedia Britannica Educational Corporation.

17 16mm film, sound, color, 22 min., Encyclopaedia Britannica Educational Corporation.

18 16mm film, sound, color, 13 min., Sterling Communications.

sea creature. Still another is *Wood Bending: A New Twist*,[19] a film that uses time-lapse photography to show viewers exactly what occurs as wood is bent and twisted during industrial processes.

A noted educator, the late Glenn Frank, vividly described his reactions to *Plant Growth*, a pioneering film of this type:

> Yesterday within the space of 10 minutes, I saw a plant grow to full maturity, bear fruit, and die. As a child I often . . . wondered what it would be like to see the actual processes of growth . . . . I had to wait 40 years, but yesterday, the thing I wondered about as a child happened. I saw the processes of growth as clearly and as plainly as this morning I saw cars streaming by in the street below my hotel window.[20]

Photomicrography

Photomicrography, or microphotography, permits viewers to enter the immense world that is too *small* to be seen with the naked eye. The camera simply "looks through" the eye of the microscope and records what it sees. Films that introduce viewers to the minute worlds of molds, spores, and cell life all use microphotography. Examples include *Molds and How They Grow*,[21] *Cells of Plants and Animals*,[22] *How Green Plants Make Food*,[23] and *The Roots of Plants*.[24] (See Figure 8.7.)

Extremely powerful *electron microscopes* expand our visual field still further. By photographing what the electron microscope sees, we can analyze such things as the contruction of the fibers, fibrils, and filaments of muscles and the regular arrangement of molecules of miocin and actin within individual fibers.[25]

A variation of the same photographic technique, X-ray photography lets us witness the internal mechanisms of the human body in action. For example, a person can be shown eating, swallowing, and actually digesting food.[26] Through these techniques, we can see and understand an endless variety of fascinating life forms and processes.

Animation

Animation is a convenient method of simulating on film processes that are difficult or impossible to photograph as they occur. In most cases, a sequence of drawings is used that shows the things that are changing or being changed at successive times. In some cases, photographs of a model are used rather than drawings. The parts of the model are moved slightly between photographs, and when the pictures are projected rapidly the model appears to move. Teachers often use animated films to explain intangible things—theories, hypothetical situations, and so forth.

Animation is also extremely useful in demonstrating such things as the motion of molecules, chemical reactions, and long-term processes such as the formation of mountains[27] and the creation of fossils.[28] Animation can be used to demonstrate the problems of traveling and

19 16mm film, sound, color, 13 min., International Film Bureau.

20 From an original reaction sheet submitted by Glenn Frank, then president of the University of Wisconsin, 1937, to the University of Wisconsin Bureau of Audio Visual Instruction.

21 16mm film, sound, color, 11 min., Coronet Films.

22 16mm film, sound, color, 11 min., Coronet Films.

23 16mm film, color, 13½ min., Universal Education and Visual Arts.

24 16mm film, b/w, 11 min., Encyclopaedia Britannica Films.

25 *Muscle: The Dynamics of Contraction* and *Muscle: The Chemistry of Contraction*, 16mm films, sound, color, 21 min., Encyclopaedia Britannica Corporation.

26 *The Human Body*, 16mm film, sound, color, 16 min., Coronet Films.

27 *Diastrophism: What Moved the Mountains? What Shaped the Seas?* 16mm film, sound, color, 19½ min., Universal Education and Visual Arts.

28 *Energy and Man*, 16mm film, sound, color, 10 min., McGraw-Hill.

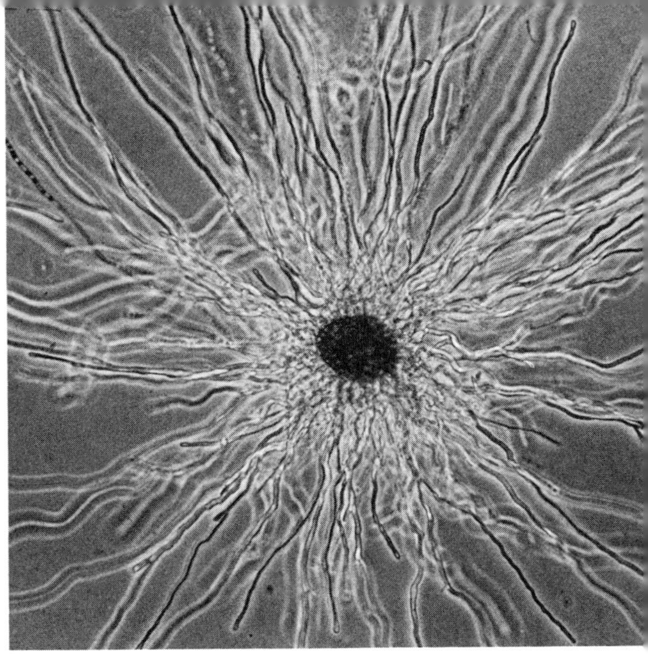

(a) (b)

Figure 8.7 Photomicrography allows an entire group or an individual to see what is beyond the limits of human vision. Through this technique, one may witness microscopic life in all its vividness. (*a*) A colony of volvox as shown in *Microscopic Life: The World of the Invisible*. (*b*) In *Molds and How They Grow,* the development and growth of these minute organisms are shown through a combination of micrography and changed-speed photography. (*c*) The same two techniques are used to permit viewers to witness the actual physical changes that occur as crystallization takes place.

(c)

communicating in space,[29] how water is desalinated,[30] and how television signals are transmitted and received.[31]

Animation is being increasingly used to explain difficult scientific concepts—the action of DNA, the logistics of space probes, and reproductive processes—in a forthright, simple, and understandable manner. Animated films can explain virtually anything the mind can envision. So many animation techniques are available that there are few areas of human experience that cannot be taught by using them.

Some Special Motion Picture Techniques

Nonnarrative films. Recent experiments in the language arts have demonstrated that films without a narration can be very successful in eliciting a response from learners. For example, visuals alone have been used to show effectively the life cycle of the carp,[32] the phenomenon of snow,[33] and the history of the wheel.[34]

An entire series of imaginative nonnarrative films, *Magic Moments,* has been developed by the Encyclopaedia Britannica Corporation, working with Dr. Roach Van Allen.[35] The series is designed to stimulate viewers to respond verbally to the films in a creative way. Learners who see them are invariably moved to express their own reactions.

Third-person case histories. Third-person films have been highly successful in introducing controversial subjects into classroom discussions. The actions of the protagonists in various situations can be weighed and discussed with relative objectivity by students and teachers, and more open and unemotional value judgments can be made. Ideas can be accepted or rejected without damaging anyone's ego or reputation. For example, the *Unfinished Story Series* presents episodes in which students may behave in a questionable way. In one film, a student discovers that she has damaged a record she is about to return to the library.[36] A friend suggests that, because the librarian can't possibly trace the damage, she might just as well forget it and use the money she would spend paying the fine to buy something she wants. Viewers are left to answer the question of what should be done. Other *case films* deal in a forthright way with social problems of students of high school age—for example, the personal penalties likely to result from sexual promiscuity,[37] the circumstances that may lead to drug abuse and its consequences,[38] and the dangers of marrying too early.[39] (See Figure 8.8.)

Iconographic techniques. Iconographic techniques are sometimes used to make printed picture stories come alive for young children:

> Only the camera . . . moves in iconographic photography. Hovering over the enlarged projection of the page . . . the camera probes for

29 *Interplanetary Space,* 16mm film, sound, color, 23 min., McGraw-Hill.

30 *Problems of Conservation: Water,* 16mm film, sound, color, 16 min., Encyclopaedia Britannica Educational Corporation.

31 *Television Line-by-Line,* 16mm film, sound, color, 11 min., International Film Bureau.

32 *Carp in a Marsh,* 16mm film, sound, color, 7 min., Institut für Film und Bild (U.S. distributor: Films Incorporated).

33 *Snow,* 16mm film, sound, color, 8 min., King Screens Productions.

34 *Wheels, Wheels, Wheels,* 16mm film, sound, color, 11 min., King Screen Productions.

35 Titles include *What's Happening?, What If?, Whose Shoes?, Toes Tell Fantasy of Feet, Follow Me,* and others. All are 16mm films, sound, color, 3–5 min., Encyclopaedia Britannica Educational Corp.

36 *Unfinished Story Series, What Will Ramona Do?* 16mm film, sound, color, 7 min., Doubleday.

37 *VD—Name Your Contacts,* 16mm film, sound, color, 15 min., Coronet Films.

38 *The High: Drugs and You,* 16mm film, sound, color, 15 min., Coronet Films.

39 *Anatomy of a Teen-Age Engagement,* 16mm film, sound, color, 15 min., Coronet Films.

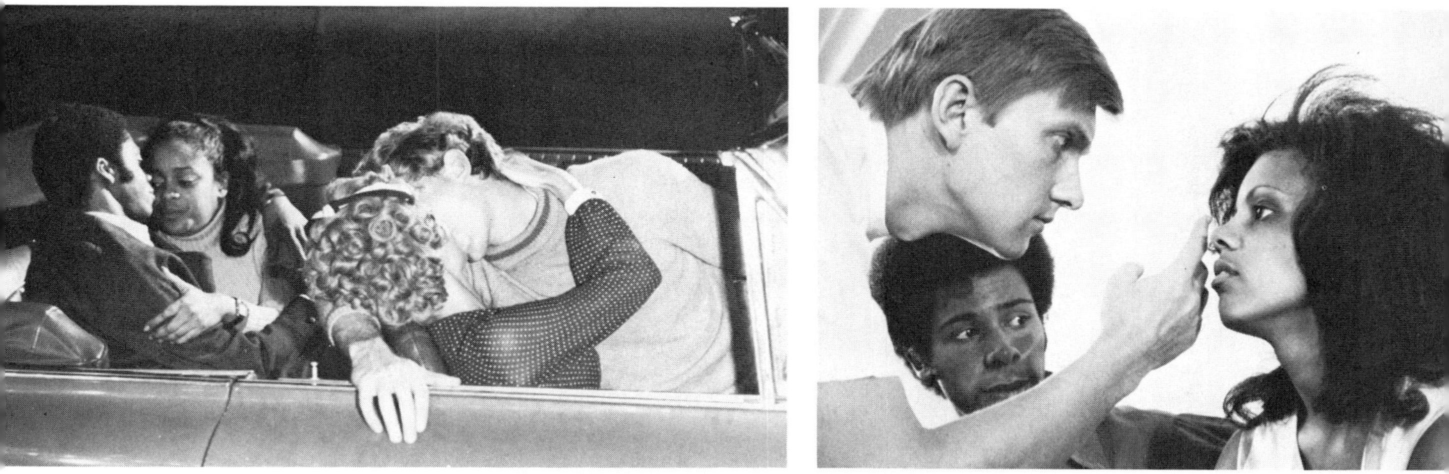

(a) (b)

Figure 8.8 Case study films enable teachers and students to view the actions of other people and to discuss them objectively, without the consequences of direct involvement. What unique advantages do these films have for high school students? (*a*) *VD—Name Your Contacts.* (*b*) *The High: Drugs and You.* What behavioral problems might be suitably studied with such films?

> the essence . . . of each picture. By varying light intensity and perspective, by emphasizing one detail and then another by moving in a deliberate direction at a controlled speed, the camera is made to release the mood and action that the illustrator captured in the pages of his book.[40]

A sound track is then recorded containing the story, a musical score, and sound effects. Two films that use this technique are *Over in the Meadow*[41] and *The Fox Went Out on a Chilly Night*.[42] (See Figure 8.9.)

To sum up, the four basic film techniques and the special techniques just described make it possible to bring an unprecedented degree of realism to today's instructional environment.

[40] Morton Schindel, "The Picture Book Projected," *School Library Journal* (February 1968).

[41] 16mm film, sound, color, 10 min., Weston Woods Studios.

[42] 16mm film, sound, color, 9 min., Weston Woods Studios.

Through such techniques motion pictures bring into the classroom:

1. Things that exist in understandable but inaccessible forms.
2. Things that happen too rapidly or too slowly for the human eye to see.
3. Things that are too small for the naked eye to see.
4. Things that are too abstract, too large, too hidden, or too theoretical to demonstrate visually in other ways.
5. Things that it is better not to experience directly because of their harsh consequences.

FILM SOURCES

16mm Films

As we have already pointed out, the first step in locating worthwhile teaching materials is to get

(a)

(b)

Figure 8.9 Iconographic photography is sometimes used to bring trade books for children "to life." What advantages do you see in the use of such films? (a) *Over in the Meadow.* (b) *The Fox Went Out on a Chilly Night.*

to *know your community resources.* The chances are that within your own community, useful films are already available in the school or community film library, the school or regional learning resources center, through the nearest college or university film library, or for the asking from local or regional government offices. In addition, great numbers of films are available from local businesses and industries and, of course, from commercial film makers, who are the primary source of 16mm (and 8mm) materials.

Commercial sources. There are many highly reputable and experienced producers of teaching films, such as the Encyclopaedia Britannica Educational Corporation, Coronet Films, the McGraw-Hill Film Division, the International Film Foundation, and the International Film Bureau. These and other sources of quality educational films are listed at the end of the chapter.

U.S. government sources. Almost all U.S. government agencies rely heavily on films to disseminate information. The Department of Agriculture, the Army, the Food and Drug Administration, the Marine Corps, the Bureau of Mines, and many other federal agencies have produced nearly 5000 currently available films on a wide variety of topics. All are listed and described in *Catalog of United States Government Produced Audiovisual Materials,* available from the National Archives and Records Service.

Foreign government sources. Most foreign governments also use films for reports on a wide variety of subjects. (See Figure 8.10.) An excellent source of information on these films is the *Educator's Guide to Free 16mm Films,* available from the Educator's Progress Service in Randolph, Wisconsin.

State university sources. Almost all state colleges and universities produce original films and purchase rental films for use by local schools and community groups. So important has this kind of service become that a national Consortium of University Film Centers has been formed. Schools in all parts of the country are within the service area of one or more members of the consortium.

State and local government sources. Like national governments, state and local government agencies rely on films to spread information on many of their programs and accomplishments. Readers should contact local or state government offices in their area for information on film lists and catalogs.

Business sources. The use in the classroom of films sponsored by businesses and industries is increasing, as is the number of titles produced that are acceptable for instructional use. Twenty-five years ago less than 2000 free or sponsored films of this type were available. Over 15,000 titles are described in the current *Educator's Guide to Free Films.*

Whereas years ago the typical sponsored film often contained a strong sales pitch, today the focus is largely on describing skills or services provided to a national audience. In selecting sponsored films, teachers should look for those that will constitute valuable learning experiences.

Now that high-quality and low-cost videotape duplicates can be made of 16mm films, many producers of sponsored films will make titles available either on traditional film reels or in ½-inch or ¾-inch videocassettes. The cost of the videotape versions is substantially less. A few producers of educational films (e.g., Weston

(a)

Figure 8.10 Foreign governments produce many films that show aspects of their environment and culture. These stills from Australian films are examples of the kind of material available. (*a*) *Marsupials—Naturally, the Numbat* features this little-known, small termite eater found only in Australia. Here a baby clings to his mother's back. (*b*) In *Desert People,* an aborigine, watched by his son, cuts out a new spear thrower. What might social studies classes learn from such films? What role might students play in securing, and evaluating, and using such films?

(b)

Woods) also provide videotape versions of titles on request.

Super 8mm Films

Since 1972 the film footage used in the production of super 8mm films for industrial and educational use has outstripped that used for the production of 16mm films. This is attributable in part to the lower cost of super 8 films and in part to their flexibility.

The first comprehensive directory of 8mm films was published in 1964 by the National Information Center for Educational Media (NICEM) at the University of Southern California in Los Angeles. It contained 1000 titles. Since that time, enough 8mm films have been produced each year to warrant the publication of an annual summary of new releases. The organization of this NICEM summary is very convenient for teachers, because films for particular grades and subjects can easily be located.

SELECTING FILM LEARNING EXPERIENCES

Teachers who want to use films usually find that the most readily available ones are those that have already been purchased by the school media staff or media librarian. These are films that have already been judged to have some value as learning experiences. Educational film makers also put considerable effort into creating viable film materials. Still, conscientious teachers will want to carry on a long-range search for the best film materials themselves. The usual procedure is for the teacher or students or both to identify teaching-learning objectives and to look for films that achieve these objectives more effectively than other learning materials. Teachers may seek films to use with large groups, whereas students may seek films that will help them work on their own or with small groups of other students. As good materials are found and used, a record should be made of them. A file of "tested" film resources can be very valuable to future students.

A sample evaluation sheet for films is shown here. Before going on, let us take a closer look at each item, beginning with those items on the top half of the sheet.

Item 1. Films have a variety of formats. Usually, 16mm films are more comprehensive and 8mm silent loops are shorter and explain single concepts. However, many longer 8mm films with magnetic or optical sound tracks are now available.

Item 2. The reputation of the producer is important in selecting films. Those films from such experienced and successful firms as the Encyclopaedia Britannica Educational Corporation, Coronet Films, McGraw-Hill, and others mentioned in the text are almost invariably worthwhile. The date of a film is also important. The production dates of more recent films are given after the title or in the catalog description.

Teachers should be on the alert for *second editions* (revised versions) of films. The fact that a second edition has been produced is usually a signal that a film is a popular one and has been thoroughly worked over to improve its already tested effectiveness as a teaching tool.

The cost of securing films is also important. In most school districts, teachers are told in advance approximately what they can spend. (Rental allowances per teacher vary from $10 to $50 per school year.) However, many free films are available, all or part of which are useful for instructional purposes. Often the task of writing away for and evaluating free films can be undertaken by interested students.

Item 3. The target curriculum—the subject for which a film is intended—is also important. Films produced after a careful analysis of learners' needs in various areas can make unique contributions. Social studies films take learners to areas of the world they cannot ordinarily visit. Science films reenact costly and

FILM EVALUATION SHEET

1. Title of film ____________ 16mm ____ 8mm ____ Sd ____ Silent ____
   Color ______ B/W ______________
2. Producer ____________________ Date produced ____________
   Length ______ Minutes ________ Rental cost ______ Postage ______
3. Target curriculum: Social studies ____ Science ____ Language arts ____
   Other areas of suitability ____________________
4. Target age ____________________
5. What is the film about (major concepts) ____________________
   ____
   ____
   ____

Format

1. Film techniques used (changed speed, animation, etc.) ____________
   ____
2. Sound: Narration quality ________ Environmental sound __________
   No narration ____________ Music ________________
3. Use of color ______________________________________
4. Pace and organization ______________________________
5. Photographic quality ______________________________
6. Recommended for future use: Yes ______ No ______ If yes, how and by whom? ______________________________

Suggested uses

____
____
____

Large groups ______ Small groups ______

Individuals ______ Mastery of skill ______

difficult experiments. Nonnarrative films stimulate students in language arts classes to express themselves.

Item 4. The age level at which a film is directed also is important. Teachers must know how many students in a class are likely to find a film intelligible. A film aimed at the center of the age group will be a useful learning experience for the whole group, whereas a film that contains more sophisticated concepts and vocabularly may be worthwhile only for the more advanced students.

Item 5. A brief description of the content of a film in a teacher's or a student's own words will be a valuable cue in making future decisions about using the film. The central concept of a continuous film loop, the series of central concepts on a more comprehensive 16mm film, or the concepts in one of the new 8mm continuous film loops with sound should be briefly described so that a quick perusal of the evaluation sheet gives whoever sees it a reasonable idea of what the film is about.

Format Item 1. The effectiveness of a film often depends on the techniques used. Changed-speed photography, animation, photomicrography, and other special photographic techniques can sometimes add dramatically to the impact of a film.

Format Item 2. Though most films use sound to reinforce the visual presentation, many films dispense with a narration (though they may use music or sound effects). This fact should be noted. Though a narration is useful in explaining the visual portion of a film, environmental sounds alone are sometimes more effective.

Format Item 3. Color films should be selected when the use of color gives viewers a more accurate understanding of what is being shown. Many subjects—animals, mechanisms, objects in nature—are identified by their color; thus films on those subjects will be far more valuable as learning experiences if they are in color. Teachers should not, however, be carried away with enthusiasm for a film merely because it *is* a color film. In assessing educational films, what matters is whether the color contributes to learning.

In nature, color often plays a vital role. It attracts an animal to its mate or camouflages it from predators. Thus a film that shows, for example, how the color of a desert animal helps it to survive must be in color. Color is equally important in showing what plants, birds, and animals look like. And certain works of art and styles of decoration can be appreciated fully only in color.

When color is used, it should be as realistic as possible. Color film that is heavily overcast with bluish or greenish hues is not desirable because it does not portray things as they really are. Poor color, in fact, is often worse than no color at all.

Although learners can sometimes "read" color into black-and-white pictures, this is not usually the case. When situations are too far removed from their own experiences, they have no accurate basis for estimating the true color of things. In evaluating a color film, ask yourself these questions:

1. What specific additional information was supplied through the color alone?
2. What relationships depended solely on color for meaning?
3. What esthetic feelings did you get from viewing the color film that you would not have gotten from a black-and-white version of the film?

Format Item 4. The pace of a film (the quickness with which it moves frome one scene to another and the speed of the narration) and its organization affect both the quality of the film and the age groups for which it is suitable. In a well-organized film, the learner is hardly aware that one scene has given way to another because the transition is so smooth and logically done. Many films are "punctuated" by *fades* (the slow disappearance of one scene before the next one appears), quick *cuts* (abrupt shifts from one scene to another), and *dissolves* (the merging of the end of one scene into the beginning of the next). A film that is jerky, meanders, or has confusing sequences is unlikely to be an effective teaching tool.

Format Item 5. The quality of the photography in an instructional film should be as nearly perfect as possible, and the camera angles should be carefully chosen to give the viewer the best perspective on what is being shown.

The final items on the evaluation sheet deal with whether a film should be used again, how, and by whom. If the students who viewed the film demonstrated through their responses that they understood it and learned from it, this fact should be noted and the record of the film placed in the "use again" file. A record should also be made of those films that were not successes. Nothing is as frustrating as reordering a film, after some time has elapsed, only to find that it was one students had disliked or been bored by.

Understandably, teachers often run into difficulties in getting films. Often the demand for them is too great to be met by local, school, or regional film libraries. The only solution may be to *investigate community resources.* Unknown numbers of useful films often lie relatively unused in the offices of local government agencies, the files of local businesses, and the headquarters of civic and service organizations. If a teacher is willing to make the effort to locate such films and encourages students to make a similar effort, the results can be a surprising amount of rewarding film learning experiences.

TEACHING AND LEARNING FROM MOTION PICTURES

The ultimate effectiveness of film learning depends on how the teacher arranges for students to become involved in film study. A 16mm film may contain a "package" of information, demonstrate skills, or give students experience with another culture or point of view. A shorter, 8mm film loop will usually present a single episode or concept. The procedures in studying either of these are very similar to those used in studying more traditional materials—reference books, encyclopedias, and periodicals. The key to such study is *to know what is to be learned, to see and hear clearly the film learning experience,* and *to respond to it constructively.*

Knowing What Is To Be Learned

Students exposed to film learning experiences should know at the outset what they are expected to see, hear, and do. Unless careful plans for film study are made in advance, learners are likely to miss the greater part of a film's message. Partly because of their high production costs, films often contain highly concentrated doses of information that follow one another rapidly. Students should be prepared, therefore, to handle a series of rapidly moving, interrelated sound and visual experiences.

Students who study continuous film loops have the advantage of being able to review what they miss the first time simply by going through the loop again and again. When films are used with large groups, individual needs are not quite so easily met. Nevertheless, films should be kept available for reference and review whenever possible.

Research shows that large groups get the most from a film if the teachers discusses the film before showing it and reviews it afterward.[43] (See Figure 8.11.) Children can be prepared to see a film by such activities as

1. Reading a brief description of the film.
2. Studying difficult words or phrases on the sound track.

[43] W. A. Wittich and John Guy Fowles, *Audiovisual Paths to Learning* (New York: Harper & Row, 1946).

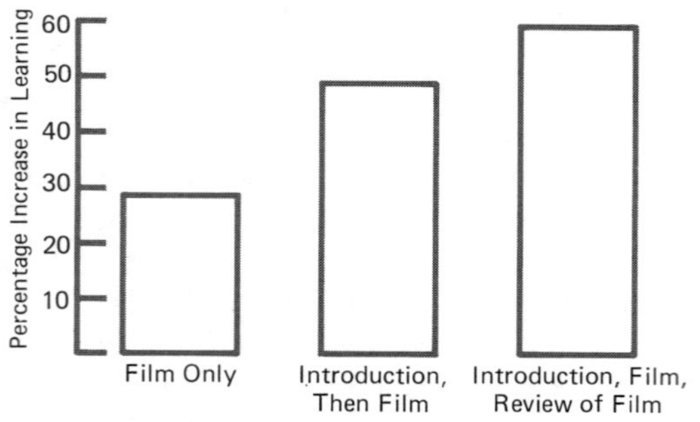

Figure 8.11 This graph shows the effects of three types of film instruction on information learned by elementary pupils in a study done some years ago. Similar findings have been verified by more recent research.

3. Studying questions about the information in the film in advance.[44]

Instructional films are also likely to result in greater learning when

1. Students know how the content of the films is related to the subjects they are studying and thus why they should study them.
2. Students know the specific reason they are being shown the films.
3. Students know what, exactly, they are expected to learn from the films.
4. Students understand that the films are learning experiences and are not being shown merely to provide a break from ordinary classroom activities.[45]

Creating Good Viewing Conditions

Because pupils work on day-to-day projects in the classroom, it is there that teaching films should be shown to and studied by groups. Classrooms should be arranged and equipped so that every pupil can see and hear films clearly without straining. (See Figure 8.12.) When viewing experiences are planned for small groups, areas free from distraction in which optimum viewing and listening conditions are approximated should be set aside. In recent years, of course, special projectors for individual viewing have become available, and many learning resource centers and school libraries now have such equipment. When a film is to be shown, the projection equipment should be set up in advance and the film placed in the projector. Apertures and lenses should be checked to make sure they are free from smudges or dirt. Nothing is so distracting as a large blob on the screen caused by dirt lodged in a corner of an aperture. Projectors and their operation are described in detail in the *Student Production Guide*. The room should be properly ventilated, the acoustical arrangements should be checked, if necessary, and, if the film is to be shown to a large group, there should be some means of darkening the room. The distance from the projector to the screen and the power of the light source in the projector determine whether more or less light should be kept out of the room. Shades, drapes, louvers, or blinds should be standard equipment in every classroom in which projected materials are used with large groups.

Encouraging Creative Responses to Films

Instruction is not complete until students can use information in some tangible way. The traditional ways of demonstrating that material has been learned (class discussions, written response, etc.) should certainly not be overlooked. However, in this era of developing visual literacy, a host of fascinating alternatives are available.

Using Films for Individualized Instruction

In one test program, children learn to write by watching 8mm silent single-concept film loops.

[44] Ibid.
[45] *Instructional Film Research Reports,* vol. 2, United States Naval Training Device Center, Port Washington, N.Y., 1957; C. L. McTavish, Instructional Film Research Program, Pennsylvania State University, 1958.

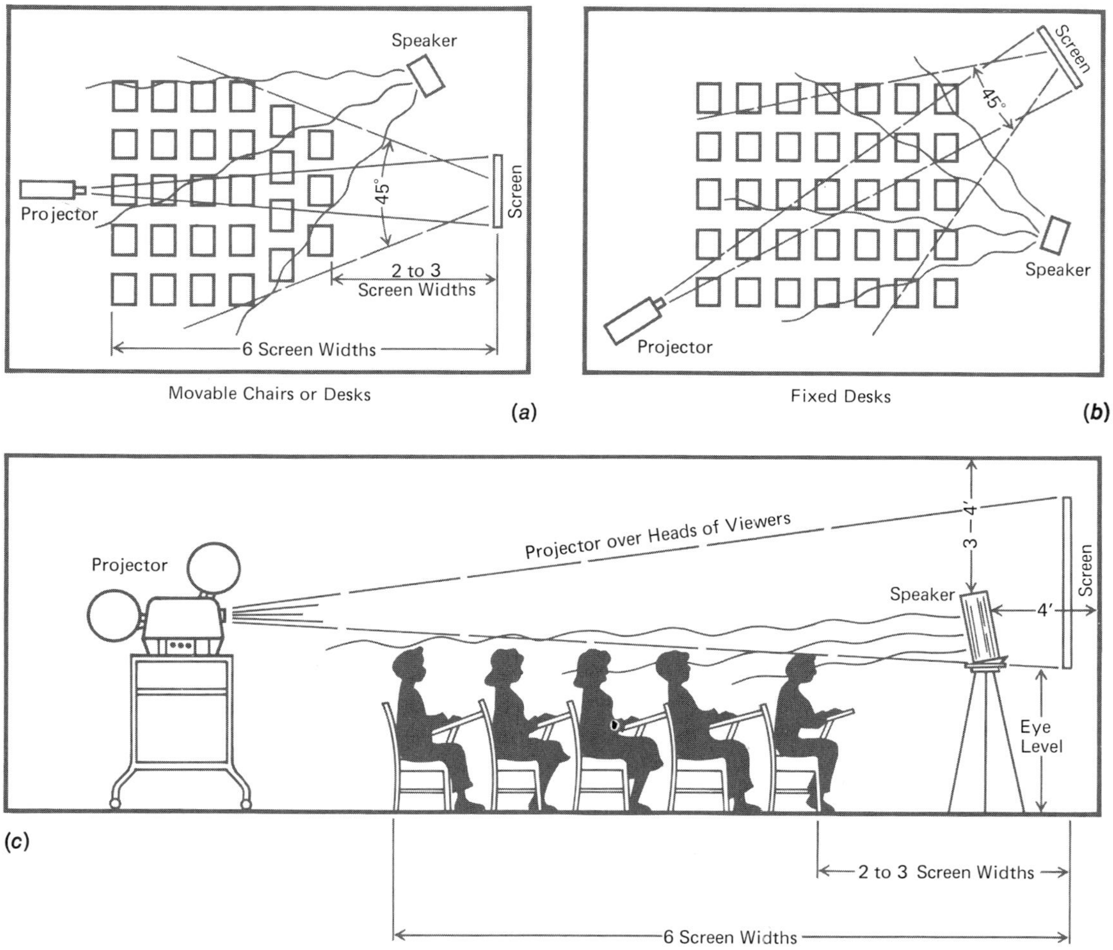

Figure 8.12 The arrangement of projector, screen, and speakers in a classroom is very important. Two possible alternatives are shown in (*a*) and (*b*). The space directly between the screen and projector is the most efficient viewing area. When students sit at a wide angle from the screen, they may see very poorly. How might you arrange a classroom to provide spaces for large or small groups to study films? Consider the possibility of using earphones for small groups. The placement principles illustrated here also apply to film showings for small groups.

When the children come in in the fall, a teacher shows them a shelf of film cartridges, explains how to insert them in a projector, and shows them how to turn it on and focus it.

Most children take quickly to this kind of activity. They begin by selecting a letter to work on. Each cartridge contains a 3-minute silent description of how a letter is formed—how each stroke is done, how high or how low the strokes go, and so on. (See Figure 8.3.)

Each film loop has a companion cue card. The children shove the film in place, turn on the projector, watch the moving hand on the screen as it forms the letter, and imitate it, writing on the plastic-coated washable cue cards.

They show their work to one another and the teacher, who supervises them and gives them whatever help they need.

In general, continuous-loop film learning is most effective when one concept at a time is presented. A student watches the film as many times as necessary. Usually, the teacher evaluates the outcome by observing the child's responses. Students who have used single-concept film loops about finger placement on the clarinet show what they have learned. Pupils who have used film loops of basic woodworking demonstrate the skills they acquire by actually using hacksaws, coping saws, miter joints, drills, braces, and so forth. Series of single-concept film loops are available that teach skills as varied as running the 100-yard dash, spinning flax into thread, and performing arithmetic operations.

But there are many wider uses for 8mm film than teaching skills. A student teacher being introduced to the inventory of 8mm film loops in an instructional materials center selected one of the film loops that struck her fancy, put it into the projector, turned it on, and focused it.

"Why, I've never dreamed such things existed," she exclaimed, as she watched an octopus hatch out of its egg and make its first primitive movements along the ocean floor. She saw the octopus progress through various stages of development and, as it approached adulthood, hunt, capture, and enfold for nutriment lesser creatures that lurked on the ocean floor. As the loop ended, she remarked, "It's so clear—yet so simply done—I can see why learners would love it." (See Figure 8.13.)

When self-tutorial 8mm materials are accessible in learning resource centers, students have at their fingertips film learning resources that are rich, varied, and easy to understand. (See Figure 8.14.) Learning resource centers with inventories of 16mm and 8mm motion pictures and projectors make film learning activities for small groups feasible. This type of learning has some very special advantages.

STUDENT-MADE FILMS

Two factors have influenced the development of student-made motion picture films: enthusiasm of learners to explore the world of motion picture writing, photography and editing, current technological changes in the form of simplified and efficient 8mm motion picture cameras, and editing equipment and projectors. The words of the makers are quite true: "What you can see thru the view finder you get on the finished film." Filmmaking promises to become a most engaging pupil-response to instruction: filmed re-enactments of historical episodes, documentations of class accomplishments, how to do it explanations, using sound on 8mm film, and recording of important interviews or school events.

Pupil Planning for Filmmaking

Storyboarding is the process of thinking visually, recording ideas as simple sketches. "Cues," that is, short word descriptions that develop further the meaning of the sketches of the things to be visualized, may be added. During this process, the students decide where the camera is to be placed, at what angle, and how close. When all these sketches and notations are organized in logical order, the series of sequential "pictures" is the storyboard (see Figure 8.15).

Since the storyboard ideas are expressed as simple sketches on cards, these can be arranged as often as desired to get the best effect. The camera should not be started until the stream of ideas—storyboard ideas—becomes a meaningful sequence.

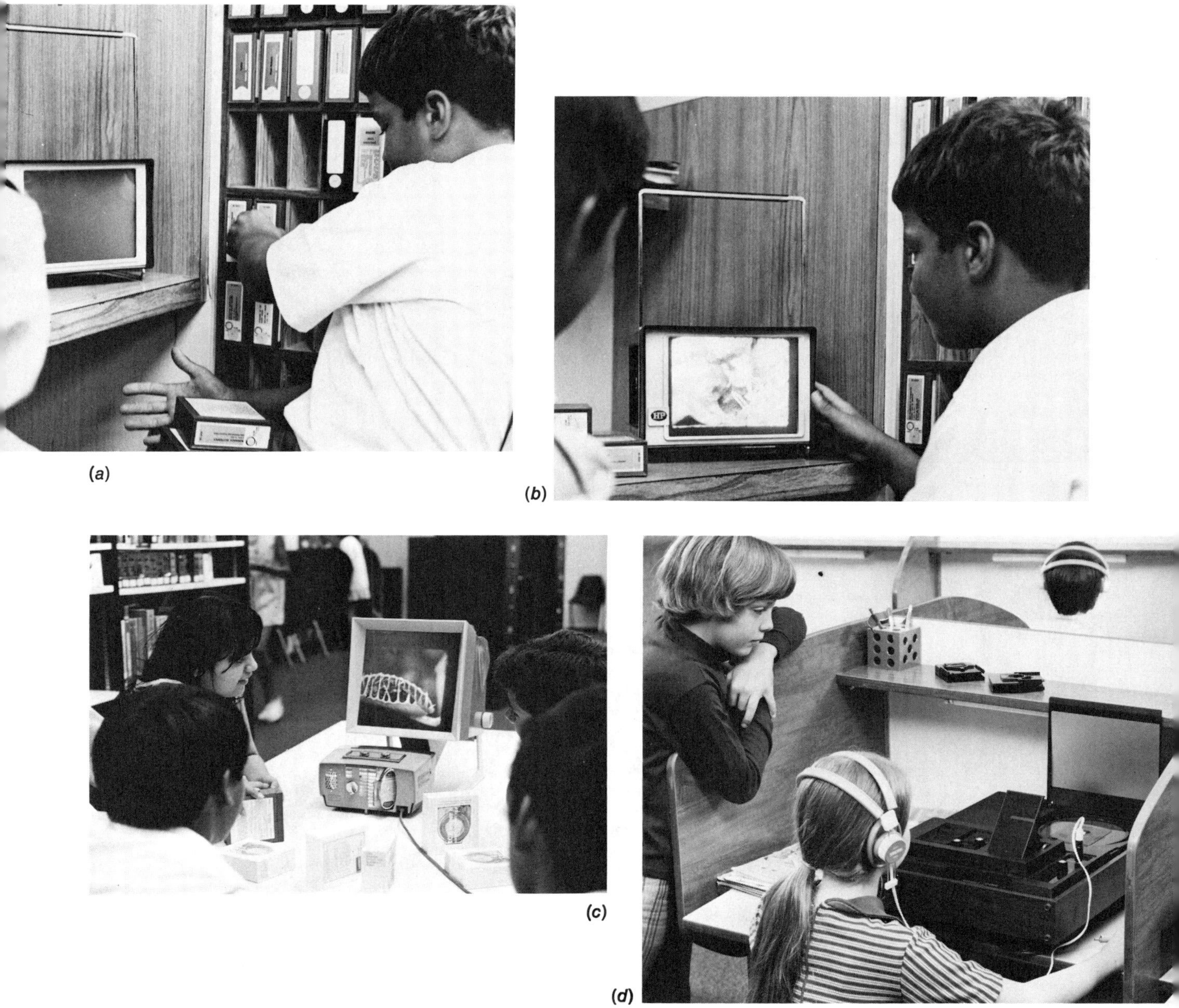

Figure 8.13 More and more, learning resource centers shelve film and other learning materials with books. Fortunately, film loops can be viewed by individuals or small groups in normal light when the right equipment is used. (*a*) A student selects a loop from the library shelf. (*b*) An interested classmate joins in viewing a film projected on a rear-screen viewer. (*c*) Nearby, children study a film projected on a "day-lite" projection device that ensures a sharp, clear image. (*d*) Using still another type of viewer, learners interact with a sound and motion 8mm film experience. What are your reactions to these kinds of learning experiences? Can you think of applications for them that you would like to try out?

(a) (b) (c) (d)

Figure 8.14 These Oxhey School students show what invariably happens when film learning resources are easily accessible to students and the organization of a class is open, or flexible. (*a*) Projection arrangements are do-it-yourself affairs. (*b*) A film is studied. Then, because of differences of opinion, it is run again. (*c*) Plans are made to use newfound information in creative ways. (*d*) The teacher enters the experience by invitation. Her role is to guide, evaluate, encourage, and help. What are your reactions to this kind of learning arrangement? Would you be willing to give it a try?

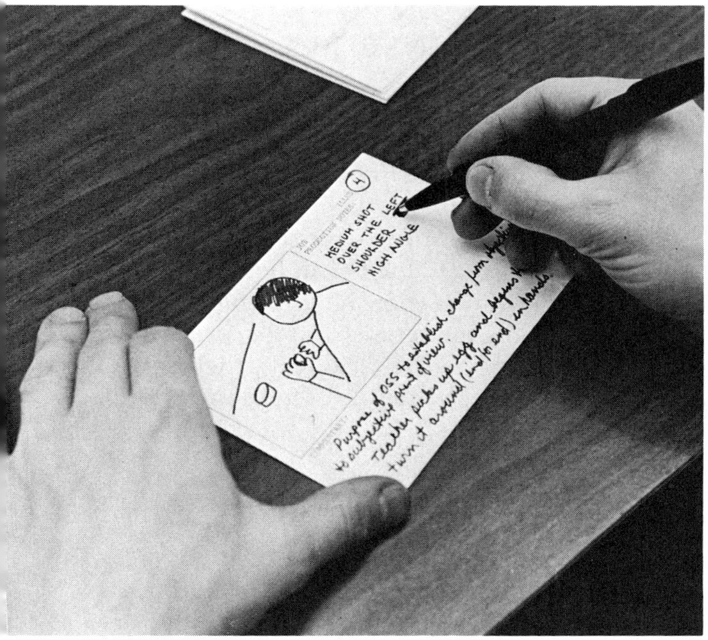

(*a*)

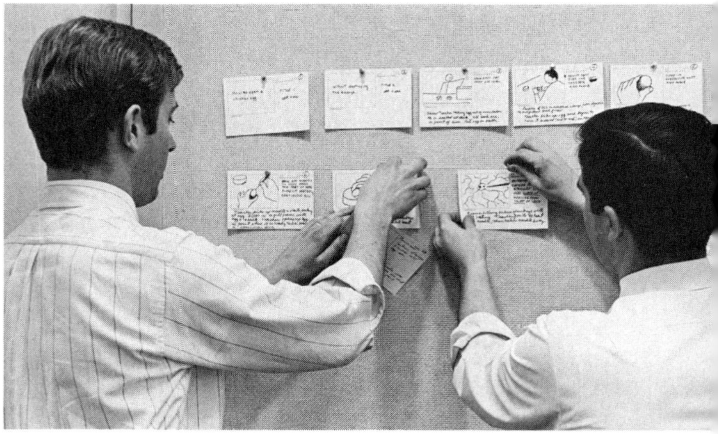

(*b*)

Figure 8.15 Story boarding is the process of visualizing in advance the nature and sequence of ideas to become a film. (*a*) This lad sketches his ideas in advance of actual shooting. Of what advantage is this? (*b*) The elements of the film can be visually arranged in advance, changed, discarded, and added to before the camera used. How does this effect the activity?

Photographing—Shooting the Picture

The basic skills involved in operating an automatic camera are simple and can be learned by studying the diagrammatic instructions in the accompanying manual (see the *Student Production Guide,* pp. 268–279).

Students may wish first to think through the ideas presented in the storyboard, then to practice mentally, looking through the lens as a variety of alternatives for each sequence before selecting the one they wish to record when starting the camera. Allowance must be made for trial and error. Only by exposing a reasonable amount of footage will there be enough variations in camera angles and in types of shots—long, medium, and close—to permit the selection of the very best.

At the point that young filmmakers discuss creative alternative ways for expressing ideas, someone is sure to mention animation—the process of visualizing ideas through the use of drawings, diagrams, or pictures that "move." The search for animation ideas and techniques is a fine questing experience in and of itself. Since television depends heavily on animation, students will enjoy studying what they see on TV. They can discover for themselves how animated movements occur, what parts of a "thing," creature, or person actually move and thus create the illusion of motion. They will discover that speed of motion is but an arithmetic problem having to do with how fast the action will be in terms of how many, and what actual movement changes will need to be photographed each second of *film* time.[46]

[46] See the following current articles about film animation by students: Susan Learner, *Elementary School Pupils Make Animated Movies,* Audio Visual Notes from Kodak, T-91-3-2, 1973; Elizabeth Scwartz, *Film Making and the Curriculum,* School District of the City of Ladue, 9703 Conway Road, St. Louis, Mo., 1973; *Film Making as a Performing Art in the Elementary School,* New York State Education Dept., Albany, N.Y., Bur. of Elem. Curr. Devel., 1973.

Editing—Selecting the Best

The final selection of "shots" may be identified in relation to their counterpart storyboard cards. Once this is done, the entire sequence may be spliced or glued together. The "moment of truth" comes when the result is run through the projector and the final effect is seen for the first time!

Adding Sound

A reasonably detailed description of several ways of adding sound to 8mm films is included in the *Student Production Guide*. However, the teacher who wishes some guidance on this should know that the current preference is for magnetic sound. (See Figure 8.2 where the Cue-See 8mm sound adding mechanism is explained.)

Yet another device which permits good synchronization and which is described more completely in the *Student Production Guide* (pp. 273–276) is the camera that records picture and available sounds simultaneously. The changes that occur in all the equipment are quite rapid; a media specialist and/or local dealer will be able to provide information about new equipment.

Viewing the Film

The finished film may be arranged for viewing in several ways. If it is 3 or 4 minutes long, it may be loaded into a cartridge by a laboratory and projected on 8mm cartridge projectors. An alternative is to use open-reel projection equipment, which also is simple and allows for longer lengths of film to be projected. (Other alternatives are available; they are discussed in the *Student Production Guide*.)

The "proof" is the response of fellow students to a film made by themselves (Figure 8.16).

FITTING FILMS INTO AN INSTRUCTIONAL PLAN

Film-learning experiences should be fitted into your instructional development plan *if they promise to be more effective in a given learning situation than any other kind of learning experience,* and, of course, if the necessary equipment and materials are available or can be acquired. A teacher's goal should not be to lengthen the chain of teaching materials, but to strengthen the chain of experiences through which learners develop intellectually and emotionally and reach learning goals.

SUMMARY

Instructional films are no longer a debatable alternative for educators, but a universally accepted teaching resource. Research has shown that wisely selected and carefully used film materials can motivate learners, teach skills and cognitive information, and encourage socially acceptable behavior.

Educational films have been relatively slow maturers. From primitive beginnings, they have evolved into dramatic visual experiences. They are available in both 16mm and 8mm formats, cassettes have replaced open reels for many purposes, and sound can be added even to 8mm films planned and produced by pupils. Almost every old-line publisher of books for schools has established a motion picture production division or subsidiary.

Readers should keep abreast of new developments in film learning materials, particularly those that may fit their own instructional plan. Films can teach skills or facts, and they can give students insight into the life styles and values of other ethnic and cultural groups. They can give solutions to problems, or they can be open-ended, leaving viewers to draw conclusions about what they see.

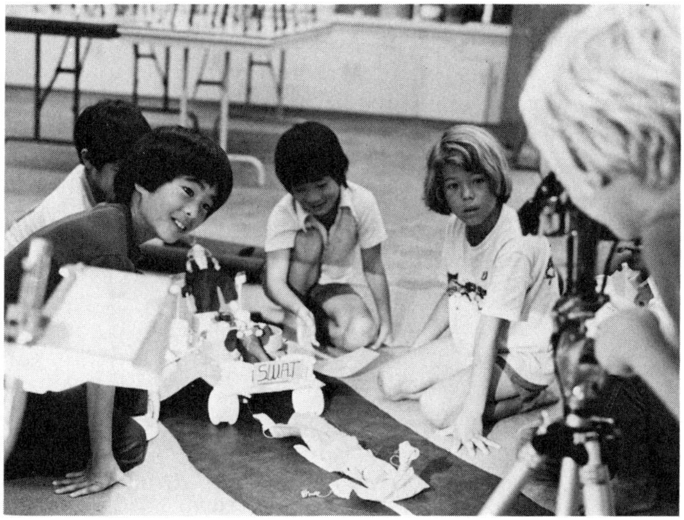

(a)

(b)

(c)

(d)

Figure 8.16 This committee (*a*) planned and constructed the models and (*b*) shot sequences. (*c*) Editing provides the opportunity for self-evaluation as does (*d*) showing the film to the class. What learning and skill outcomes would you anticipate?

Useful films are often available, free, from local businesses and civic groups and from national, state, and local government agencies. Indexes and catalogs of commercial and noncommercial films can be very helpful. Teachers should look systematically for films suitable for their students and keep a record of those used.

Students will learn more from films when difficult concepts or vocabulary are explained beforehand. A discussion session should also follow the use of a film.

Information learned from films should be put to use in original ways. Only by analyzing pupil responses to films can they be evaluated as educational materials. In the case of 8mm continuous-loop films that teach specific skills, the obvious desired result is mastery of the skills. In the case of films dealing with more general areas of cognitive knowledge, many types of responses may be observed: spontaneous quests for additional knowledge, the creation of stories and artwork based on information from films, and so forth.

Film materials are no longer used only with large groups. Often they are used as research tools by small groups or individuals. They should be easily available to students who wish to study them on their own.

ACTIVITIES

1. In order to decide whether there are learning materials that will provide worthwhile instructional alternatives, you must first know how to locate potentially useful films. Investigate the sources of films in your own community. Consult local media specialists and media librarians, visit school film libraries, and investigate materials offered by local businesses, community organizations, or governmental agencies. Also, write to some of the regional or national sources of instructional films listed in the reference section for brochures or catalogs. Make a list of all these sources of films for future reference.
2. Review your emerging instructional plan to see how films from the sources you have listed can be used to achieve learning objectives. Consider too what the production of an original film by students could do to help them achieve particular goals.

REFERENCES

PRINT REFERENCES

Anderson, Yvonne, *Make Your Own Animated Movies* (Boston: Little, Brown, 1970).

Brown, Roland G., *A Bookless Curriculum* (Dayton, Ohio: Pflaum/Standard, 1972). 135 pp.

Eastman Kodak Company, *Movies with a Purpose: A Teacher's Guide to Planning and Producing 8mm Movies for Classroom Use.* Available from most dealers.

Kennedy, Keith, *Film Making in Creative Teaching* (New York: Watson Guptill, 1972). 128 pp.

Kinsey, A., *How to Make Animated Movies* (New York: Viking Press, 1970).

Knight, Roy, *Film in English Teaching* (London, England: The British Film Institute, 1972). 248 pp.

Lacy, Richard A., *Seeing With Feeling: Film in The Classroom* (Philadelphia, Pa.: Saunders, 1972). 118 pp.

Lidstone, John, and Don McIntosh, *Children as Film Makers* (New York: Van Nostrand Reinhold, 1970).

Lowndres, Douglas, *Film Making in Schools* (New York: Watson/Guptill, 1972).

Maynard, Richard A., *The Celluloid Curriculum* (New York: Hayden Book Co., 1971). 276 pp.

Mierhenry, Wesley, *Enriching the Curriculum Through Motion Pictures* (Lincoln: University of Nebraska Press, 1962).

Newren, Edward F., "Trigger Films for Media Specialists," *Audiovisual Instruction* (June/July 1975), pp. 54–57.

Rynew, Arden, *Film Making for Children* (New York: Cebco Pflaum 1971).
Schindell, Morton, "The Picture Book Projected," *School Library Journal* (February 1968), pp. 836–837.
Sohn, David A., *Film, the Creative Eye* (Dayton, Ohio: Pflaum, 1970). 176 pp.
Tapp, Richard L., "A Systematic Approach to Film Making," *Audiovisual Instruction* (September 1975), pp. 44–46.

MEDIA REFERENCES

Children Make Movies, 16mm film, sound, b/w, 10 min. McGraw-Hill.
The 8mm Film in Education, 16mm, sound, color, U.S. Office of Educ., Bureau of Research.
The 8mm Film: Its Emergency Role in Education, 16mm film, sound, color, 28 min. Du-Art Film Laboratories.
Facts About Film, 2d ed., 16mm film, color, 16½ min. International Film Bureau.
Facts About Projection, 2d ed., 16mm film, color, 16¼ min. International Film Bureau.
Film, Art of the Impossible, 16mm film, sound, color, 27 min., Learning Corporation of America.
Film Research and Learning, 16mm film, sound, b/w, 16 min. International Film Bureau.
Let's Make a Film (Yellow Ball Workshop) 16 mm film, sound, color, 13 min., Van Nostrand Reinhold.
Making Films That Teach, 16mm film, b/w, 20 min., Encyclopaedia Britannica Educational Corporation.
Project Discovery, A Demonstration in Education, 16mm film, sound, color, 27 min., Encyclopaedia Britannica Educational Corporation.
Super 8, a Unique Communication System, slides, tape, color, 30 min., Eastman Kodak Company.
Understanding Movies, 16mm film, sound, color, 13 min., Van Prang Productions.
Worth How Many Words, 16mm film, sound, color, 11 min., Eastman Kodak Company.
Young Film Makers, 16mm film, sound, b/w, 31 min., Brandon Films.

STUDENT PRODUCTION GUIDE REFERENCES

See Chapter 2, the section on motion picture projectors; Chapter 4, the section on 8mm motion pictures.

SOURCE REFERENCES

Film Sources

Academy Films, P.O. Box 38753, Hollywood, CA 90038.
Association-Sterling Films, 866 Third Ave., New York, NY 10022.
Athletic Institute, 705 Merchandise Mart, Chicago, IL 60654. (Physical education films.)
AV Explorations, Inc., 505 Delaware Ave., Buffalo, NY 14202.
Avis Films, 2408 W. Olive Ave., Burbank, CA 91506.
Barr Films, P.O. Box 7-C, Pasadena, CA 91104.
BFA Educational Media, 2211 Michigan Ave., P.O. Box 1795, Santa Monica, CA 90406.
Campus Film Distributors Corporation, 20 E. 46th St., New York, NY 10017.
Carousel Films, 1501 Broadway, New York, NY 10036.
Churchill Films, 662 North Robertson Blvd., Los Angeles, CA 90069.
Contemporary Films/McGraw-Hill, Leo R. Dratfield, President, 330 W. 42nd St., New York, NY 10036.
Coronet Instructional Media, 65 East South Water St., Chicago, IL 60601.
Cousino Communications, 1945 Franklin Ave., Toledo, OH 43624.
Film Australia, P.R. Box 46 Lindfield, NSW 2070, Australia.
Walt Disney Films, 800 Sonora, Glendale, CA 91201.
EDCOM Div./ESB Inc., Yardley, PA 19067.
Encyclopaedia Britannica Educational Corporation, 425 N. Michigan Ave., Chicago, IL 60611.
Environmental Films, 8228 Sulphur Mt. Rd., Ojai, CA 93203.
Eye Gate House, 146-01 Archer Ave., Wilmette, IL 60091.

Film Communicators, 11136 Weddington, N. Hollywood, CA 91601.

Films, Inc., 1144 Wilmette Ave., Wilmette, IL 60091.

Guidance Associates, 757 Third Avenue, New York, NY 10017.

Heidenkamp Nature Pictures, 538 Glen Arden Dr., Pittsburgh, PA 15208.

Hubbard Scientific Co., P.O. Box 105, Northbrook, IL 60062.

Paul Hoefler Productions, P.O. Box 1313, La Jolla, CA 92037.

Ideal Pictures, Inc., 15924 Grand River Ave., Detroit, MI 48227.

Indiana University Film Center, Bloomington, IN 47401.

International Film Foundation, 475 Fifth Ave., New York, NY 10017.

International Film Bureau, 332 So. Michigan Ave., Chicago, IL 60604.

Journal Films, 909 W. Diversey Pkwy., Chicago, IL 60614.

Learning Corporation of America, 1350 Ave. of the Americas, New York, NY 10019.

McGraw-Hill Book Company, Text-Film Division, 1221 Ave. of the Americas New York, NY 10020.

Modern Media Services, 45 Rockefeller Plaza, New York, NY 10020.

Moody Institute of Science, Educational Film Div., 13000 E. Washington, Whittier, CA 90606.

Motovational Media, 8271 Melrose Ave., Los Angeles, CA 90046.

National Film Board of Canada, 1251 Ave. of the Americas, New York, NY 10020; P.O. Box 6100, Montreal, Canada, H3c3H5.

National Geographic Society, Film Div., Washington, D.C.

National Education Media, 15250 Ventura Blvd., Sherman Oaks, CA 91403.

Scott Education Division, 104 Lower Westfield Rd., Holyoke, MA 01040.

Society for Visual Education, 1345 Diversey Pkwy., Chicago, IL 60614.

Sterling Educational Films, 241 E. 34th St., New York, NY 10016.

Teaching Film Custodians, Inc., dist. by University of Indiana A.V. Center, Bloomington, IN 47401.

Technicolor, Inc., AV Systems, 299 Kalmus Dr., Mesa, CA 92627.

Universal Education and Visual Arts, 100 Universal City Plaza, Universal City, CA 91608.

Weston Woods Studios, Weston, CN 06880.

Wexler Film Productions, 801 N. Seward St., Los Angeles, CA 90038.

Catalogs, Indexes, and Film Reviews

The Consortium of University Film Centers, established in 1971 by Tom Boardman of the University of Illinois, represents about 50 universities and colleges that have film rental services. The aims of this organization are to make the best film resources more accessible, to foster cooperative planning for their effective use, and to recommend and implement optimal standards of service and distribution.

The name of the consortium member nearest you may be obtained by writing the national headquarters, CUFC, c/o University of Illinois Visual Aids Service, 1325 South Oak St., Champaign, IL 61820.

A Catalog of U.S. Government-Produced Audiovisual Materials, available from the National Audiovisual Center, Washington, DC 20409, The National Audiovisual Center was established in 1969 to provide government agencies and the public with a central information, loan, sales, and rental service for government audiovisual materials such as motion cartridges, films, audiodiscs, audiotapes, slide sets and filmstrips.

Educator's Guide to Free Films (Randolph, Wis.: Educator's Progress Service, rev. annually).

Index of 8mm Motion Cartridges (Los Angeles: University of Southern California, pub. annually).

Index to 16mm Educational Films (Los Angeles: National Information Center for Educational Media).

Modern Talking Picture Service Index to Free Films, 1212 Ave. of the Americas, New York, NY 10036.

Reviews

Efla Evaluations, Educational File Library Association, 17 West 60th St., New York, NY 10023. 1946–1965, 528 pp.

Landers Film Reviews, P.O. Box 69760, Los Angeles, CA 90069.

Motion Picture Projectors—16mm and 8mm. See Student Production Guide.

8mm Motion Picture Cameras, Projectors, and Related Equipment

Bell and Howell Company, 7100 McCormick Road, Chicago, IL 60645.

Eastman Kodak Company, 343 State St., Rochester, NY 14650.

Fairchild Industrial Products, 75 Mall Drive, Commack, NY 11725.

GAF Corporation, 140 West 51 Street, New York, NY 10020.

Minolta Corporation, 101 Williams Drive, Ramsey, NJ 07446.

Paillard Incorporated, 1900 Lower Road, Linden, NJ 07036.

Charles Beseler Company, 8 Fernwood Road, Florham Park, NJ 07932.

Viewlex Corporation, 1 Broadway Avenue, Holbrook, NY 11741.

16mm Sound Motion Picture Projection Equipment

A.V.E. Corporation, 250 W. 54th Street, New York, NY 10019.

Allied Impex Corporation, 168 Glen Cove Rd., Carle Place, NY 11514.

Bell and Howell Company, Audio Visual Div., 7100 McCormick Rd., Chicago, IL 60645.

Eastman Kodak Company, 343 State St., Rochester, NY 14650.

Eiki International, Inc., 27882 Camino Capistrano, Laguna Niguel, CA 92677.

Honeywell Photographic Products Division, 5501 S. Broadway, Littleton, CO 80120.

International Audio Visual, Inc., 119 Blanchard St., Seattle, WA 98121.

Kalart Victor Corporation, P.O. Box 112, Hultenius St., Plainville, CN 06062.

L. W. International, 6416 Variel Ave., Woodland Hills, CA 91364.

Singer Company, Graflex Div., 3750 Monroe Ave., Rochester NY 14603.

Viewlex, Inc., 1 Broadway Ave., Holbrook, NY 11741.

9 Instructional Television

Objectives

To enable you to do the following:

1. Identify at least four characteristics of instructional television that make it an effective learning medium.
2. Identify at least four avenues through which ITV learning experiences can be brought into the classroom.
3. Identify and apply at least four criteria for evaluating ITV learning materials.
4. Identify a teacher's responsibilities in using ITV.
5. Explain and, if possible, demonstrate how creative responses to instructional television can be encouraged.
6. Identify the role changes that occur as learners alternate between watching ITV and using television as a means of self-expression.
7. Explain and, if possible, demonstrate how ITV episodes can prepare learners for real life.

Television channels are so important as a means of communication that their use has, from the beginning, been controlled by the federal government. In 1952 the Federal Communication Commission reserved about 12 percent of all television channels for educational broadcasts. During the 1960s many school districts set up closed-circuit networks of cables to distribute television programs to classrooms. Many of these systems are still used, although open broadcasts by educational stations now bring television learning experiences to 15 million school children.

NATIONAL INSTRUCTIONAL TELEVISION

Instructional television related to ongoing courses and curriculums is made available to schools through the Corporation for Public Broadcasting, the Agency for Instructional Television, and regional and state broadcasting and production organizations. There are over 275 Public Broadcasting Service stations on the air, providing educational programs for everyone from preschoolers to senior citizens. A most recent innovation is the fixed orbiting satellite *Westar,* which provides instantaneous video programming to all PBS member stations.

The Corporation for Public Broadcasting

The Corporation for Public Broadcasting was created by Congress in 1967 to encourage educational broadcasting. Corporation funding makes possible a nationwide communications network of over 275 stations broadcasting both general and instructional TV and radio programs. It also helps stations get the money they need for high-quality educational programming. Educational broadcasters are paid licensees of a corollary organization called the *Public Broadcasting Service,* and also members of a related organization, the *Station Program Cooperative.* Each year the SPC polls its members to learn where money is needed, and for what.

Many private business and almost all professional organizations in the nation contribute ideas, recommendations, money, or talent to educational television. With their help, the CPB and its satellites have created many programs for school use.

Perhaps the most well-known program for young children is *Sesame Street,* which is produced by the Children's Television Workshop. *Sesame Street* is for preschoolers and those just beginning school. It has an estimated daily audience of from 15 to 20 million viewers. Its objective is to teach children the ABC's and numbers before they start school. It is often included in ITV broadcast schedules also.

A logical next step for educational broadcasters, once *Sesame Street* was launched, was a program for the large number of children in the nation's elementary and secondary schools with reading problems. *The Electric Company* is designed to catch the interest of children from 7 to 11 years of age and to improve their reading skills. Two months after the series was first broadcast, over 23 percent of the nation's elementary schools (and 70 percent of those with complete television facilities) were using it regularly. *The Electric Company,* like *Sesame Street,*

Figure 9.1 A volunteer mother, assisted by several neighbors, uses the facilities of her home to give youngsters the opportunity to see *Sesame Street*. Viewing and follow-up suggestions for use by such volunteers are provided by the Children's Television Workshop, which produces the program.

is produced by the Children's Television Workshop. It receives production support from the CPB and the U.S. Office of Education.

A current contender for the attention of school children across the nation is *Essential Learning Skills*, a series of sixty 15-minute programs produced and distributed nationally by the Agency for Instructional Television.

Television's role as a here and now medium of communication is illustrated by *ZOOM*, a program about children's problems in today's society. (See Figure 9.2.) For example, a third of all U.S. parents are divorced. One of the things *ZOOM* has focused on is children who have born the brunt of divorce. In the words of the director of *ZOOM*, Austin Hoyt,

> We're trying to provide positive models. We show kids who have been through traumatic situations and have overcome their difficulties. We never show children who have been defeated. I would rather run the risk of . . . holding out some hope, than . . . be too brutally realistic and negative.[1]

Some adults have criticized *ZOOM* as being too like a soap opera. However, much of the content of the programs is based on letters received from viewers—of whom there are nearly a quarter of a million.

Another program, *Villa Alegre,* is a response to the nation's mounting social and cultural pluralism. Children of all backgrounds can identify with the members of the cast, though the program places special emphasis on the needs of Spanish-speaking youngsters. The goal of the series is to show the many ethnic strains in the country's population and to identify the contribution each makes to the nation's cultural and social life. The cost of such programs, $8–10 million, has been met by the U.S. Office of Education, Ford Motor Company, the Exxon Corporation, and the CPB and its broadcasting agencies, the PBS and the SPC.

Each year the Station Program Service, along with cooperating agencies, also produces 35 to 50 television series or specials aimed at large adult audiences: *Black Journal, Women of the Century, Women in Sports, Wall Street Week, Hometown America, The Indian Way, Sex and You, Political Profiles, Wings of Youth,* and others still in the planning stage.

The Agency for Instructional Television

The nation's central production agency for day-in and day-out classroom and curriculum-centered television is the Agency for Instructional Television. It acts as a kind of general manager and coordinator for the production and distribution of elementary and secondary tele-

[1] *ZOOM Program Guide* (December 1974).

(a) (b)

Figure 9.2 (*a*) These four "kids" are part of the *ZOOM* cast—Cate, Carmen, Tishy, and Red. They act out social situations in which children of today may find themselves. Many program ideas are drawn from the sacks full of viewer letters that arrive daily. (*b*) These youngsters are sampling some of the goodies from their friend the street vender's cart. They play out the impact of ethnic groups on the social scene in a way children of similar ages can understand. How can such programs help you meet learners' needs? Can such TV experiences become a welcome "third party" in the classroom?

vision learning materials. Its function is to bring into focus and respond to the programming needs of the thousands of school districts in Canada and the United States. For example, the series *Inside-out* (see Figure 9.3), which shows ways of coping with social, emotional, and physical problems that trouble 8- to 11-year-olds, was the result of a study by the National Association of Health Educators and a group of learning specialists.

AIT staff members, working with educators, set a tentative production budget of well over $500,000. Because the job was a big one, a consortium of interested producers and school districts shared the production work and the cost. Because of their initial underwriting of the series, it may be broadcast "free of further expense" by the consortium members or leased by other school districts that wish to use the programs. Lessons are available in cassette form or on open-reel videotape.

Other creative and valuable ITV programs produced by AIT-sponsored consortiums are the following:

(*a*)

(*b*)

(*c*)

(*d*)

(*e*)

Cover-Cover, a series of encounters with good books, each of which is read and illustrated with a series of drawings.

Ripples, a series on the child in a changing world and how to live happily with others.

Bread and Butterflies, a series of child-centered explorations of work and career attitudes and options.

Measuremetrics, a series that helps viewers understand the metric system.

Two Cents' Worth—experiences in confronting energy and ecological problems, with an emphasis on what happens as man reconciles his needs and the limits of the world's resources.

Great Plains National and Other Regional Organizations

Another creator and distributor of exemplary video learning materials is the Great Plains National Instructional Television Library, now a part of the Nebraska Educational Telecommunications Center in Lincoln, Nebraska.

Since its beginning in the 1960s, Great Plains has produced, caused to be produced, or acquired more than 150 ITV courses and related materials. In 1972 it pioneered the transfer of original filmed and open-reel vediotaped materials to U-Matic videocassettes. Most school districts now use the U-Matic format in the classroom and 2-inch videotape for broadcast or closed-circuit networks.[2]

Smaller but similar organizations have assumed responsibility for coordinating the creation and distribution of ITV learning resources in other regions. Along the Eastern seaboard, effective leadership is provided by the Eastern Educational Television Network. In an annual bulletin, the member stations of this group announce such timely programs as *Games of Chance,* a description of the principles of matematical probability, and *Tomorrow Starts Today,* an environmental education program primarily for those who live in small cities rather than large urban areas.[3] Teachers who want information on these and other organizations can contact the program officers of their local school district or public television station.

Figure 9.3 The Agency for Instructional Television, a nonprofit organization, was created in 1973 to develop ITV programs for U.S. and Canadian schools. It also acquires, adapts, and distributes a wide variety of television, audiovisual, and printed materials (study guides, for example) . These pictures show scenes from AIT programs: (*a*) "Just Joking," a program in the series *Inside-Out,* examines David, a boy who gets his kicks from playing jokes on others, (*b*) In "Strong Feelings," also from the series *Inside-Out,* Edgar discovers how his emotions—love, fright, embarrassment, and so on—can affect his body. (*c*) A young Navajo boy learns about prejudice in "My Friend," one of the episodes in the TV series *Self Incorporated.* (*d*) In another *Self Incorporated* episode, Alex escapes to forbidden territory as he hides out from his family. (*e*) The series *Bread and Butterflies* raises questions about careers. This scene is from the program "Success Story," which raises questions about different kinds of success. What are the advantages of programs such as these?

The Emergency School Aid Act Children's Television Series

The Emergency School Aid Act series of television programs helps learners cope with the problems of everyday living. The programs are funded by the Department of Health, Education and Welfare and are made available to local broadcasters who will use them for at least a 13-week period. School districts can apply for materials for nonbroadcast use by providing tape for dubbing and paying dubbing charges. Materials for broadcast use are on 2-inch tape, and those for classroom use are in ½- or ¾-inch formats. Schools are invited to dub broadcast programs off the air, because they are in the public domain.

2 *Recorded Visual Instruction,* Great Plains National, Box 806669, Lincoln, NB 68501, 1976.

3 *Instructional Television Programs,* The Eastern Educational Television Network, 1300 Soldiers Field Rd., Boston, MA 02135, 1976.

Two typical programs are:

1. *Gettin' Over,* a series of 52 half-hour programs for adolescents, stressing information they will need to cope with adult responsibilities. Each show concentrates on a single topic, such as homes, autos, consumer skills, prenatal and child care, job hunting, legal rights, and preventive health care; and
2. *Infinity Factory,* a series of 95 half-hour programs for 7- to 12-year-olds that explain the mathematics needed in day-to-day living.

New sources of television programming are appearing constantly. Many industrial groups and service organizations create and distribute informational materials that may be of use in the classroom. Previously filmed information is currently being transferred to ½- or ¾-inch videotape and distributed to schools. Moreover, the cost of doing this is often less than the cost of distributing the original filmed programs.[4]

Local school districts have been at work since the beginning of instructional television, planning and producing ITV materials that reflect local needs. No central production agency can anticipate all local needs, and there will always be a few very worthwhile curriculum areas best served by the creative efforts of local school district TV production centers. Teachers should make it a point to learn what these local groups are doing or planning. Once again, the answer to instructional needs may be to *know your community resources.*

GETTING INSTRUCTIONAL TELEVISION INTO THE CLASSROOM

Unlike most of the other media we have discussed, ITV can be brought into the classroom by several means. In most school districts teachers are informed about local ITV facilities and programs through monthly or semester bulletins that describe the programs and give the time of day at which they can be viewed.

Closed- and Open-Circuit Television

Television programs can be distributed through open or closed circuits. Closed-circuit broadcasts use a network of coaxial cables or wires that carry television signals from a source to reception points, usually classrooms. (See Figure 9.4.) One advantage of closed-circuit systems is the high-quality reception than can be achieved. Open-circuit television, on the other hand, broadcasts signals into the air to be retrieved by antennas.

A third broadcasting technique, a 2500-megahertz microwave system, is a broadcast system, but limited to an area of 5 to 20 miles.

Videocassette Materials

Television programs can be electronically recorded on ½-inch or ¾-inch magnetic tape in much the same way that sound can be recorded on audiotape. In recent years ¾-inch U-matic videocassettes have become widely used. For example, Project Watch-a-Book, begun in 1974 as a means of bringing the best public television programs into school libraries and classrooms has over 1000 programs on U-matic cassettes that may be rented by local schools.[5] (See Figure 9.5.)

Today, open television broadcasts can be recorded for later use simply by connecting a video recorder to the classroom television set. Almost all AIT and PBS programs are in the public domain and may legally be recorded in this way. Two new highly successful ½-inch video tape recording and playback devices were

4 *Educator's Guide to Free Records, Audio and Video Tapes,* Randolph, Wis. Published annually.

5 The Public Television Service, Watch-a-Book Video Program Service, 475 L'Enfant Plaza West, W.S., Washington, D.C. 20024.

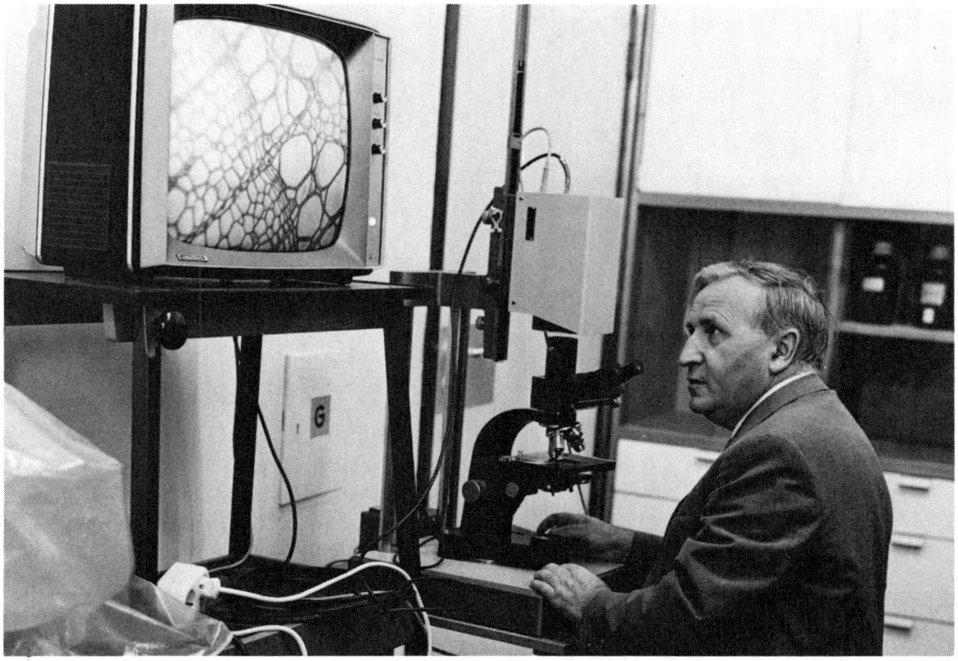

Figure 9.4 This teacher is using a microscope and a television camera to enable students in three classrooms to view the cell section he is describing. What are the advantages of such a procedure?

introduced into school use in 1978: the Betamax (Sony) and Omnivision (Panasonic). These two machines are so successful that American electronics companies are currently purchasing either one or the other, attaching their own trade names and marketing them competitively for use in homes and schools. School models make possible off-the-air recording, live recording, play-back through conventional TV sets, play-back from video cassettes, and the recording of live color provided a color camera is used. (See Figure 9.6.)

Still being perfected is a *videodisk system* for bringing TV learning materials into the classroom. Signals recorded on videodisks, which will be somewhat like thick phonograph records, will be replayed on the screen of a television set using a laser beam.[6]

[6] Bernard Fradin, "Videodisc, State of the Art," *Audiovisual Instruction* (June/July 1975).

SELECTING AND USING ITV PROGRAMS

When television is available to teachers and learners, it enlarges the pool of potential instructional experiences tremendously. It is far beyond the energies or capacity of any one or a few teachers to match the literally hundreds of hours of work and planning that go into good television programs.

The advantages of ITV must be evaluated realistically, however. This means balancing

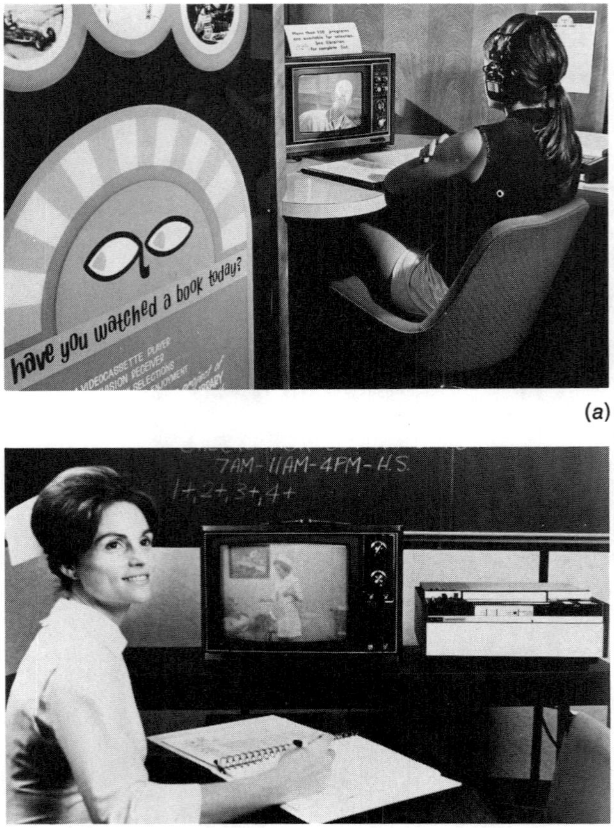

Figure 9.5 (*a*) A student watches one of many public television programs available on videocassettes as part of the Watch-a-Book program. (*b*) A student nurse views one of a series of training experiences available on videocassettes.

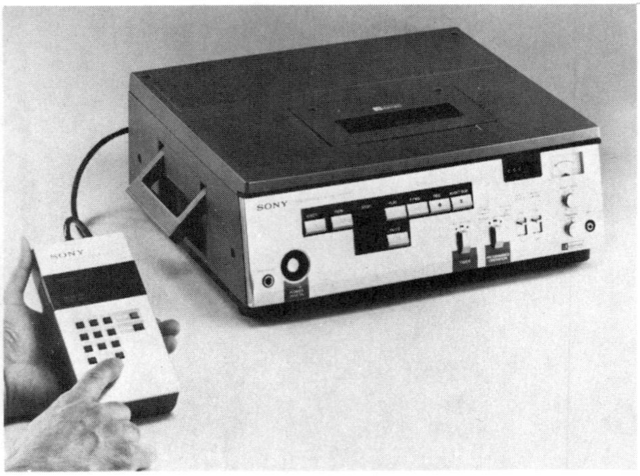

Figure 9.6 This is the Betamax ½-inch videocassette tape recorder-playback machine. Using it allows teachers and students to record live or broadcast TV experiences and play them back immediately or at a time of their own choosing. It is simple to operate and relatively inexpensive. The counterpart of this is Panasonic's Omnivision (not shown).

them against its limitations, among which are the predetermined pace of instruction, the inability of studio teachers or producers to see the kind of reactions the programs get from pupils, and the fact that class scheduling is upset by fixed broadcast schedules, unless current off-the-air, cassette recording is done.

Like all learning media, instructional television entails responsibilities for teachers. However, unlike other learning media, it can seldom be previewed. To offset this drawback at least partially, those who produce instructional television usually prepare lesson plans and descriptions that are given to individual classroom teachers early in the semester. These preliminary announcements and lesson plans usually describe the content and learning objectives of the programs. On the basis of these materials, teachers may decide in advance whether specific ITV lessons will meet the needs of their students.

SELECTING USEFUL ITV PROGRAMS

In selecting ITV programs, the following points should be kept in mind:

1. A good television program gives the student valuable emotional experiences and food for thought, that is, something to work with. It stimulates students, gets them started working together, and is open ended enough to en-

courage creative thinking and creative learner responses.

2. A good television program speaks in a language students can understand and has an element of humor. Viewers should smile once in a while.
3. A good television program makes use of the unique characteristics of television; that is, it tries to expose students to subject matter they would not otherwise be exposed to and to present it in ways the average teacher could not.
4. A good television program often says the same thing twice in different ways to reinforce key points.[7]

A 1972 seminar on the content of instructional television evolved this description of good instructional programming:

> Good ITV programs hold the child's attention while leaving room for thinking; [they] make use of proper repetition, variation, and sequence [they] bring out the creative potentialities and fun involved in learning; and [they] lead the child toward some activity after the program. . . . Good ITV is . . . part of a learning-teaching system.[8]

USING INSTRUCTIONAL TELEVISION EFFECTIVELY

In general, the responsibilities of teachers in regard to ITV are very similar to their responsibilities in using films, pictures, audio instructional materials, and the like. However, because of the strong likelihood that the first time a teacher sees a program will be at the same time the students see it, the suggestions that are now made anticipate the use of videocassette recording of materials off the air during actual use in the classroom. Using any of the newly available $\frac{1}{2}$-inch video recording and playback models described above, the teacher can record a television program while the students are watching it on the classroom TV set screen. A $17.00 one- or two-hour blank cassette is needed. The result will be available for instant or delayed playback, a duplicate of this program witnessed: what advantages would this create? The reader is urged to discuss such possibilities with the school district media or television personnel.

Prebroadcast Activities

Often teachers can determine what kinds of prebroadcast activities will be helpful from studying program descriptions. When the focus of a program is on cognitive information, study guides often outline the key concepts to be developed and any special vocabulary that will be used. A prebroadcast discussion of these things will always be helpful. If the goal of a program is to examine human relationships, it may be wiser not to anticipate their content, but rather to encourage students to respond after the broadcast is over. Ordinarily, however, unless students know in advance what they are expected to gain from an ITV lesson, they may not benefit fully from it.

Ensuring Effective Viewing Conditions

Well before the actual television viewing time, sun curtains should be drawn, pupils and teachers should check to be sure that glare does not impair viewing conditions, and sets to be used should be properly tuned, focused, and adjusted. Students in the upper grades often do this on their own, while the teacher moves around the classroom to make sure that everyone can hear and see well.

Because television screens are relatively small,

[7] Schramm Wilbur, *Quality Instructional Television* (Honolulu: University of Hawaii Press, 1972), pp. 14–22.

[8] *Intrachange* (newsletter), East-West Center, Jefferson Hall, Honolulu (February 4, 1972), pp. 3–4.

it may sometimes be necessary to use two or three receivers so that everyone can see a program well. The best viewing area for a 27-inch (diagonally measured) receiver is shown in Figure 9.7. Students should be no closer than 8 feet and no further than 22 feet from a receiver, with a horizontal viewing angle of no more than 30 degrees.[9] They should not have to crane their necks or bend back uncomfortably to see television receivers mounted too high above them. A receiver placed on a table may be viewed comfortably by small children. For older students, a receiver can be placed 4 or 5 feet above floor level.

During televiewing, light levels should be high enough so that the teacher can see the facial expressions of the group. Facial or physical reactions often show that there are questions or that enthusiasm for a program is high or low.

If television viewing conditions are poor, teachers should not hesitate to report the matter and ask for help.

Ensuring Learner Involvement and Response

In any teaching situation, it is the teachers' responsibility to create opportunities for learners to become *involved* in the learning experience and *respond* to it by using newfound information in constructive, creative ways. This is particularly true in regard to televised learning experiences.

ITV lessons often contain helpful suggestions, although it is the teacher who must decide which of them to adopt.

In Denver, various ways of using television and related media to teach Spanish to elementary school children were tested, with interesting results.[10] ITV programs were used in combination with records, tapes, and a special programmed instruction text in Spanish to which learners could refer. The television programs were used throughout a semester in four different ways with four groups of fifth-graders. All four groups used the same additional learning devices and materials.

The first group viewed the television programs once.

The second group viewed the television programs twice, once when they were broadcast and immediately afterward on videotape.

The third group viewed the television programs once in school and once again in the early evenings at home over open-circuit television. Parents were encouraged to join their children in watching the repeat viewings.

The fourth group viewed the television programs once and then practiced what they had learned orally for 15 minutes under the direction of their teacher.

The test scores achieved by the four groups are summarized in Figure 9.8. As in the case of films, filmstrips, slides, and other visual materials, repeated viewing increases learning. Having parents view the programs also had a positive effect.

The greatest gains were made by those who had a chance to practice orally after each lesson, helped by their classroom teacher.

One of the main conclusions to be drawn from the Denver experience is that the success of the programs was due to the *effective context* created for the televised lessons by the combination of repetition, parent participation at home, teacher participation and guidance, student participation in the programs themselves, and the use of related learning materials. Thus the lessons were not something "done to" the students and teachers; rather, they became part of the learning resources of the schools. They were combined with other techniques to form a new and more potent instructional package.

[9] *Design for ETV: Planning for Schools with Television* (rev. ed.), Educational Facilities Laboratories, 1968, pp. 32–33.

[10] Denver Public Schools, *The Context of Instructional Television, a Summary Report of Research Findings* (Denver Board of Education, 1964).

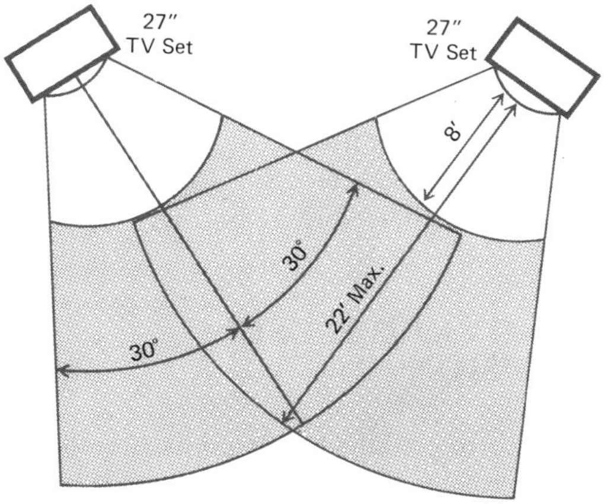

(a)

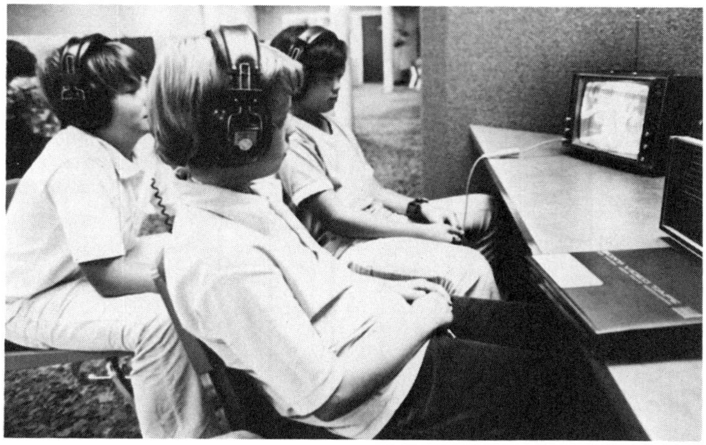

(b)

(c)

Figure 9.7 (*a*) This diagram shows the area in which two standard 27-inch classroom television receivers can be comfortably viewed. At what height should TV receivers be placed? (*b*) What factors apparent in this small-group viewing situation do you approve of? (*c*) What is your evaluation of this group-viewing situation?

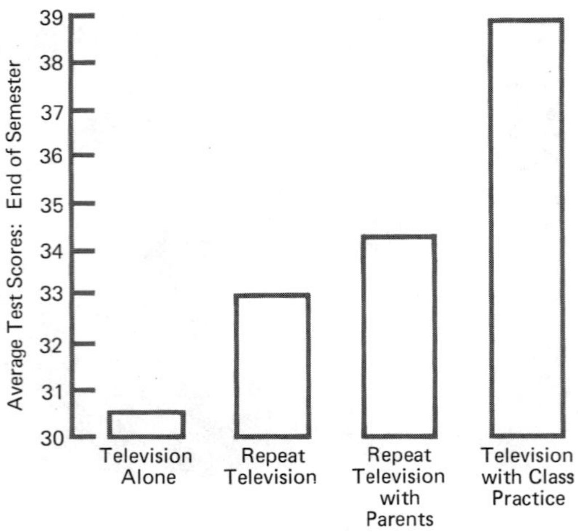

Figure 9.8 The effects of four approaches to learner involvement in television Spanish lessons for fifth-graders.

Evaluating Instructional Television

The most effective means of evaluating instructional television is by observing pupil reactions. These may range all the way from a clearly observable increase in their ability to discuss a subject to a desire to locate and study additional learning materials and plan and create exhibits and displays.

Both those who *plan* and those who *use* instructional television must methodically evaluate its results. The producers and supervisors of instructional television must communicate constantly with classroom teachers to secure reactions to program content, the quality of study guides, and the educational media used to learn how instructional television affects pupil performance. Classroom teachers are obligated, in turn, to report their students' reactions to programs to the proper supervisory authorities. Unless local programming authorities get this kind of feedback, few constructive changes can be expected. Classroom teachers should seek to participate actively in the planning of ITV but also in the evaluation and constructive revision of programs. Only through continual and objective evaluation can higher-quality ITV and better multimedia programming be achieved.

A sample evaluation sheet for ITV programs and related materials is shown below.

SOME INNOVATIVE USES OF TELEVISION

Often what engineers and technicians invent for one purpose creative teachers can use in all kinds of unforeseen ways. So it is with television cameras and the new, lightweight, easy-to-operate videotape equipment—equipment that records sound as well as visual images.

Using Videotapes

In Chapter 6 we discussed using audio equipment to record and play back immediately one's own voice. It is also possible to record a voice or other sounds *and* visual images on tape and play back the result immediately. Instant replays of this kind are familiar to anyone who has watched the Olympics or other sporting events on television. Because they give students, as well as athletes, an unmercifully accurate picture of their own performance, they can be a very effective teaching tool. For example, videotape replays are frequently used to enable student teachers to see and hear themselves. (See Figure 9.9.) They have also been used in teaching deaf children to speak,[11] in drama classes, and to record demonstrations of many kinds of skills. (See Figure 9.10.) Whereas a teacher's corrections may go unheeded, students in this electronic age are well aware that a videotape record does not lie.

[11] Ralph S. White, "Teaching Speech with Television," *Educational Television* (December 1970), p. 40.

AN EVALUATION SHEET FOR ITV PROGRAMS AND RELATED MATERIALS

Program Materials

1. Were a study guide and materials for suggested activities provided well in advance of telecasts?

   Yes ______ No ______ Comments ______________________
2. Does the study guide clearly state the nature of the telecasts and their objectives?

   Yes ______ No ______ Comments ______________________
3. Does the program description contain enough information so that teachers can discuss key points, explain key vocabulary, and outline viewing goals in advance?

   Yes ______ No ______ Comments ______________________
4. Does the study guide include suggestions for involving learners—activities, games, simulations, discussion questions, and so on?

   Yes ______ No ______ Comments ______________________
5. Does the study guide include references to related learning materials—books, films, picture sets, filmstrips, specimens, and so on?

   Yes ______ No ______ Comments ______________________

Program Organization and Content

1. Is the content of the program suitable to the age level and interests of the pupils for whom it is intended?

   Yes ______ No ______ Comments ______________________
2. Are the most effective materials used to present information (demonstrations, models, mock-ups, films, charts, etc.)?

   Yes ______ No ______ Comments ______________________
3. Does the program's organization and content clearly fit announced learning objectives?

   Yes ______ No ______ Comments ______________________
4. Can desirable changes in learner behavior be attributed to the program?

   Yes ______ No ______ Comments ______________________

(a)

(b)

Figure 9.9 (*a*) This student teacher is being videotaped as she works. (*b*) Immediately afterward, she watches the visual and audio record of her actions as the class's regular teacher and another student teacher look on. How does this procedure impress you? Can you think of ways to use such techniques with pupils?

Figure 9.10 A deaf pupil is about to observe her own videotaped efforts to speak correctly. The teacher can stop the tape and repeat useful sections immediately, then resume recording. What applications would there be of this kind of thing for your own work?

Using Videotapes for Individualized Study

Videotape has been proved to be an effective means of demonstrating and explaining ideas. And videotaped lessons can be used anytime and anywhere by groups or individuals.

In the Coatesville Area School District in Pennsylvania, students can retrieve the stored videotaped lessons by going to a library carrel and dialing a selected code number. (See Figure 9.11.) Arrangements can also be made to view materials in a laboratory or shop. Thus industrial arts students can follow videotaped instructions as they stand before welding equipment they are learning to operate, and students learning how to operate a duplicating machine can retrieve videotaped instructions next to the machine. For students studying English, special individualized videotaped lessons are available. Many students who have used the videotaped materials in journalism, English, social studies, and mathematics report that they learned more, progressed more rapidly, and developed more positive relationships with their teachers. Most would like to continue this kind of individualized instruction.[12]

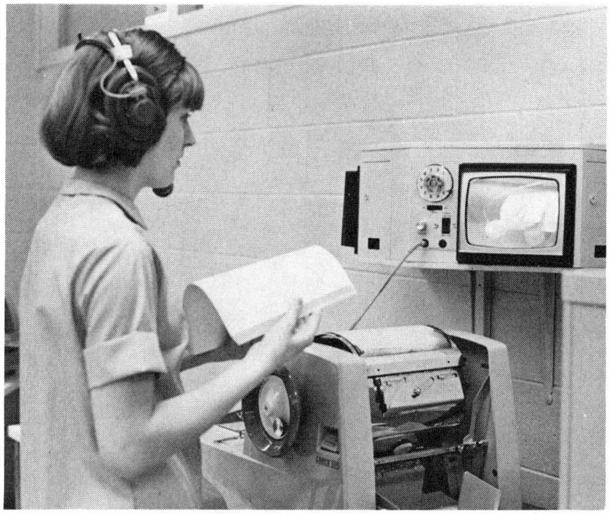

Figure 9.11 This student has dialed a videotaped demonstration of the operation of a duplicating machine. How can individualized video instruction like this affect a learner's progress?

TELEVISION BY AND FOR LEARNERS—AN ALTERNATIVE CREATIVE RESPONSE

Television has for too long been thought of as a medium for experts, something that can only be produced in an elaborately equipped studio complete with technicians, soundproof booths, thousands of watts of light, and so forth. Now, thanks to easily operated, transistorized, classroom versions of "studio" equipment, more teachers and students are realizing that it is a channel of communication they can use themselves. More and more teachers are finding that ITV is a stimulating way of developing *visual literacy* skills and an exciting change from traditional ways of expressing ideas. (See Figure 9.12.)

Like films and audiotapes, videotapes can be used to put students in different parts of the country in touch with one another. They can also be used by students to find out things about their own community. In school, students investigated changes in food supplies and prices. They began by examining the local newspaper, and then went on to interview parents of class members and the local supermarket manager. They recorded their interviews on videotape so that they could be replayed and studied in the classroom.

In many communities, cable television companies will let their studios and equipment be used by serious school groups for creative productions, newscasts about school events, and the like. Such activities not only familiarize students with community cable or open-broadcast facili-

[12] H. Eugene Hollick, "Dial Access Retrieval: The Future —Now!" *Educational Television* (June 1970), p. 11.

(*a*)

(*b*)

(*c*)

Figure 9.12 (*a*) Teachers like Kathleen U. Busick report that many upper-elementary-grade students like these take less than one class period to learn how to use portable TV recording and playback equipment. (*b*) Students work out who will do what in a student-produced program. (*c*) A written plan is used as a blueprint for action. When things don't work out, students quickly discover alternatives. (*d*) The final product is evaluated by the whole class. Students are invariably very critical of their own efforts and put much time and effort into reworking and improving them until they are "good enough to send to friends."

(*d*)

ties, but show the usefulness of traditional communication skills.

Self-tutorial modules on how to operate video port-a-pac equipment can familiarize students with equipment in a very short time. (See Figure 9.13.) The introduction of videotape recording (VTR) equipment into a classroom can open up a whole new creative world for children. Planning and videotaping original lessons and ideas can involve them in the kind of communication procedures in use in the world around them.

(a)

(b)

Figure 9.13 Given the opportunity, learners quickly master new ways to communicate. Using simple classroom television equipment, these pupils created their own mathematics lessons. They planned and designed visual explanations that were recorded by a television camera and evaluated. (*a*) When the children were satisfied with their efforts, the lesson was videotaped and (*b*) played back by other pupils "across the hall." What learning principles are at work here? Why is pupil involvement so intense?

INCORPORATING ITV INTO AN INSTRUCTIONAL SYSTEM

Television can be used in a variety of ways by teachers. In deciding whether to make it part of your instructional arsenal, consider whether it will help you accomplish something *that needs to be accomplished.* The primary considerations should be the interests and learning styles of your students and the superiority of television to other instructional tools for a particular purpose. TV learning experiences should not simply be piled on other learning experiences. This may lead to an information overload. Examine your instructional alternatives and either add ITV (or television by and for learners) to the list, use it to replace some previously selected learning resource, or postpone any attempt to fit it into your instructional plan until a suitable opportunity arises.

SUMMARY

Television is an efficient way of bringing carefully planned multimedia learning experiences to a wide group of learners. Its effectiveness is recognized not only in the United States, but in countries as disparate as Britain, Japan, Niger, and Iran. Many educational programs, like those produced by the Children's Television Workshop, can be seen both in school and at home. Ideas and funding for programs are provided by the Public Broadcasting Corporation, the Public Broadcasting Service, the Agency for Instructional Television, the U.S. Office of Education, and regional and state TV production agencies such as the Eastern Educational Television Network and the Great Plains National Instructional Television Library.

Television programs can be distributed through open broadcasts, closed-circuit, cables and open-reel or cassette videotapes. Research on ITV has been both extensive and intensive. The results indicate that ITV can accomplish the tasks assigned to it very well. To get the most out of ITV, teachers should prepare students to view programs by going over key concepts and vocabulary in advance, encouraging discussions of programs, and supporting creative follow-up activities. Often the study guide provided for a program will contain helpful suggestions in this regard. Through the use of recently perfected off-the-air video recorder-playback equipment, the former inflexible scheduling limitation of broadcast television can now be overcome by the classroom teacher.

Lightweight, easy-to-operate cameras and VTR equipment enable pupils and teachers to use TV much as they would use 8mm motion picture cameras, overhead projectors, or slide projectors to demonstrate skills and report information. They can use videotapes to evaluate their own performance and plan and produce television lessons of their own. In short, ITV has become a relevant, useful, and interesting way for students to learn and respond to learning.

ACTIVITIES

1. Contact your local media and/or local school district instructional television personnel to secure teachers guides or descriptions of current programs. If possible, arrange to preview programs that may be on hand in open-reel tapes or U-matic cassettes.
2. Contact and request program information from national, regional, or state television offices such as those whose addresses are listed in the source references. On the basis of this material, select three or four series that might fit into your own instructional plan.

REFERENCES

PRINT REFERENCES

Chu, Godwin, and Wilbur Schramm, *Learning from Television; What the Research Says* (Stanford, Calif.: Stanford University Institute for Communication Research, 1967). Also ERIC–ED 014900, *Research in Education* (May 1968).

Corporation for Public Broadcasting, *Public Broadcasting and Education* (Washington, D.C.: United Council of National Organizations, 1975).

Dirr, Peter J., "A National Report on the Use of Instructional Television," *Audiovisual Instruction,* January 1978, pp. 11–13.

Eller, Lind M., "Individualized Learning Utilizing TV," *Educational Broadcasting* (July/August 1975).

Gordon, George N., *Classroom Television: New Frontiers in TV* (New York: Hastings House, 1970).

LeBaron, John, "Television: Production for K–12," *Learning Resources,* a supplement to *Audiovisual Instruction* (January 1974).

Schramm, Wilbur, *Big Media, Little Media* (Stanford, Calif.: Stanford University Institute for Communication Research, 1973).

———, *Quality Instructional Television* (Honolulu: University of Hawaii Press, 1972).

Seen but Also Heard, Staff Training Department papers, Swedish Broadcasting Corporation, Stockholm, 1974).

Technological Boundaries of Television, vol. 2 (Washington, D.C.: Federal Communication Commission, 1974).

Tindall, Kevin; Reid, David; and Goodwin, Neville, "Television: 20th Century Cyclops," *Audiovisual Research 2* (Sydney, Australia: Sydney Teachers College Audiovisual Center, 1977).

MEDIA REFERENCES

Instructional TV Series

A Case Study in the Elementary School, 16mm film, b/w, 30 min. National Association of Educational Broadcasters.

Examples in the Secondary School, 16mm film, b/w, 30 min. National Association of Educational Broadcasters.

Preparing the Television Lesson, 16mm film, b/w, 30 min. National Association of Educational Broadcasters.

Promising Practices, 16mm film, b/w, 30 min. National Association of Educational Broadcasters.

The Role of the Classroom Teacher, 16mm film, b/w, 30 min. National Association of Educational Broadcasters.

Television, Line by Line, 16mm film, sound, color, 11 min. International Film Bureau, 1969.

What Television Brings to the Classroom, 16mm film, b/w, 30 min. National Association of Educational Broadcasters.

16mm Films About TV

Learning from Television, 16mm, sound, color, 30 minutes, McGraw-Hill.

Television Techniques for Teachers, 16mm, sound, b/w, 24 min. San Diego Instructional Television Authority.

Video Tape Cassettes

Non-commercial Educational Television, audio cassette, 30 min. Educational Technical Publications, 140 Sylvan Ave., Englewood Cliffs, NJ.

The Potential of the Video-Cassette in Continuing Education, audio cassette, 30 min. Educational Technical Publications, 140 Sylvan Ave., Englewood Cliffs, NJ.

TV for Learning, A bibliography of currently assembled case examples of exemplary ITV programs currently in use across the United States. Programs are available in whatever format is needed locally. Program examples are updated periodically. Apply for currently available programs from TV for Learning, Public Broadcasting Service, 475 L'Enfant Plaza, S.W., Washington, D.C. 20024.

Video Cassettes in Education, audio cassette, 30 min. Educational Technical Publications, 140 Sylvan Ave., Englewood Cliffs, NJ.

STUDENT PRODUCTION GUIDE REFERENCES

See the *Student Production Guide,* ch. 2, "Equipment Operation," pp. 102–119; ch. 4, "Producing Photo and Sound Materials for Instruction," pp. 291–300.

SOURCE REFERENCES

National and Regional Instructional Television Programs

Agency for Instructional Television, Box A, Bloomington, IN 47401. (Formerly National Instructional Television Center.)

Bicultural Children's Television, Inc., 2150, Valdez St., Oakland, CA 94612.

Children's Television Workshop, 1 Lincoln Plaza, New York, NY 10023.

Great Plains National Instructional Television Library, Box 80669 Lincoln, NB 68501.

Instructional Television Cooperative, Skyline Center, Suite 1207, 5205 Leesburg Pike, Falls Church, VA 22041.

National Association of Educational Broadcasters, 1346 Connecticut Ave., N.W., Washington, DC 20036.

Public Broadcasting Corporation, 475 L'Enfant Plaza West, S.W., Washington, DC 20024.

Public Broadcasting Service, 475 L'Enfant Plaza West, S.W., Washington, DC 20024.

Public Television Library, att. Watch-a-Book, 475 L'Enfant Plaza West, S.W., Washington, DC 20024.

University of Mid-America, P.O. Box 82006, Lincoln, NB 68501.

Children's television series

The following children's television series have been or are being produced under the Emergency

School Aid Act. In all, over 500 TV programs have been produced that can be useful in helping meet the problems of minority group children and young people. School systems in areas where a series is being broadcast by a public or commercial station are free to copy them for subsequent use. All ESAA-TV programs are available for school use without a usage fee. All general inquiries should be addressed to the Special Projects Branch, Equal Educational Opportunity, Bureau of School Systems, U.S. Office of Education, Washington, DC 20202. The number for telephone inquiries is (202) 245-2465 or 245-0931

Inquiries about specific programs should be addressed to the producers. Addresses for some popular series are given below:

Villa Allgre. A Spanish-English series of 95 shows intended for Anglo and Latino children 3 through 9. The shows concentrate on one of five themes: food and nutrition, energy, the environment, interpersonal relations, or man-made things. Produced by BC/TV, Inc., Suite 2350, 2150 Valdez, Oakland, CA 94612.

Gettin'Over. Each of the 52 half-hour shows concentrates on a single topic such as the home, autos, credit and related consumer skills, prenatal and child care, job hunting and upgrading, civil and legal rights, preventive health care, and medical services. Produced by the Northern Virginia Educational Telecommunications Association, Inc., Box 1444, North Springfield, VA 22151.

Infinity Factory. This series of 95 half-hour programs will stress how mathematics can help the individual in day-to-day life, exploring its applications in art, science, technology, and nature. Produced by Project One Group, Education Development Center, Inc., 55 Chapel Street, Newton, MA 02160.

Rebop. A series of 26 half-hour programs on such topics as family relationships; friends; school; leisure and play; fantasies, hopes, and frustrations. Produced by WGBH-TV, 125 Western Ave., Boston, MA 02134.

Tension and Conflict Reduction in Schools and Community. A series of 13 one-hour programs on the tensions and conflicts that arise in desegregating schools and in the community at large. Produced by WTTW (TV), 5400 N. St. Louis Ave., Chicago, IL 60625.

South by Northwest. Five half-hour programs about black cowboys and pioneers for 7- to 15-year-olds. Produced by KWSU-TV, Washington State University, Pullman, WA 99163.

The Real People. A series of 10 half-hour programs for children 7 through 12 that focus on the life, life styles, traditions and lore of the plateau tribes of western Washington, the Idaho Panhandle, and western Montana. Produced by KSPS, South 3911 Regal, Spokane, WA 99203.

La Bonne Aventure. A series of 20 15-minute programs intended mainly for children 4 through 8 from French-Canadian backgrounds in the upper Northeastern part of the United States. Produced by the Maine Public Broadcasting Network, Alumni Hall, the University of Maine, Orono, ME 04473.

Vegetable Soup. A series of 39 half-hour or 78 15-minute programs for children 7 through 12 intended to bridge the gap between different racial and ethnic groups. Produced by the New York State Department of Education, Albany, New York.

TV network sources

The following addresses of TV networks are included as sources of special school- or education-oriented broadcasts. Many of these "specials" are excellent.

American Broadcasting Company, 1330 Ave. of the Americas, New York, NY 10019.

Columbia Broadcasting System. 51 W. 52nd St., New York, NY 10019.

National Broadcasting Company, 30 Rockefeller Plaza, New York, NY 10020.

Systems and Equipment

The following table gives information on sources of videotape recording and playback equipment and equipment used for viewing television programs individually in small groups, or in very large groups.

Television Sources	TV Systems, CCTV and 2500 MHz	Tape Equipment	Receivers/Monitors	Projectors
Admiral Group Rockwell International 1701 E. Woodfield Rd. Schaumburg IL 60172			x	
Ampex 2201 Landmeier Rd. Elk Grove Village, IL 60007		x		
Buhl Optical Company 1009 Teech Ave. Pittsburgh, PA 15233	x			
Concord Communications Systems 40 Smith Street Farmingdale, NY 11735		x		
Cousino Communications Inc. 1945 Franklin Ave. Toledo, OH 43624		x		
Doran Precision Hillcrest Binghamton, NY 13902			x	
Eastman Kodak Company Business Systems Markets Division 343 State Street Rochester, NY 14650				x
Electrohome Limited 809 Wellington Street, N. Kitchener, Ontario, Canada			x	
General Electric Company Television Business Department College Blvd, College Park Portsmouth, VA 23705			x	
Hitachi Shibaden Corporation of America 58-25 Brooklyn-Queens Expressway Woodside, NY 11377		x		

Television Sources (*Continued*)	TV Systems, CCTV and 2500 MHz	Tape Equipment	Receivers/Monitors	Projectors
JVC Industries, Inc. 50-35 56th Road Maspeth, NY 11378	x	x	x	
Lafayette Instrument Company P.O. Box 1279 Lafayette, IN 47902				x
Magnavox Video Systems 1700 Magnavox Way Ft. Wayne, IN 46804	x		x	
Neumade Industries 720 White Plains Rd. Scarsdale, NY 10583		x		
Panasonic 1 Panasonic Way Secaucus, NJ 07094	x	x	x	
Peerless Sales Company 4200 West Chicago Ave. Chicago, IL 60651	x			
RCA Broadcast Systems Front and Cooper Streets Camden, NJ 08101	x			
RCA Service Company A Division of RCA Corporation Building 203-3, Dept. 1614 Camden, NJ 08101			x	
Sanyo Electric Company 1200 West Artesia Blvd. Compton, CA 90220	x	x	x	
SC Electronics 530 Fifth Ave., N.W. New Brighton, MN 55112			x	

Television Sources (*Continued*)	TV Systems, CCTV and 2500 MHz	Tape Equipment	Receivers/Monitors	Projectors
Singer Education Systems 3750 Monroe Ave. Rochester, NY 14603				x
Sony Corporation of America 9 West 57th St. New York, NY 10019	x	x	x	x
Spindler & Sauppe, Inc. 13034 Saticoy St. North Hollywood, CA 91605				x

10 Computers, Simulations, and Games

Objectives

To enable you to do the following:

1. Identify and discriminate among three or more distinctive uses of computers in instruction.
2. Assess the relative advantages and limitations of computerized instruction.
3. Identify ten administrative benefits of computer services in education.
4. Assess the probable role of computers in schools and colleges in the near future.
5. Identify, from a list of learning activities, those appropriate to computerized instruction, to simulations and games, and to neither.
6. Describe and differentiate among several types of educational simulations and games.

Although educators have long supported the principles of individualized instruction, they have, in general, done relatively little to implement them. Most teachers try to compensate for a classroom situation in which most students are involved in the same activities at the same time by giving special attention to children who seem to need it. Naturally this kind of attention can be given to relatively few children and perhaps only at the expense of neglecting others. It is impossible for one or two teachers to give each student the amount of attention that individualized instruction implies or to keep track of the many details involved in relating each child's performance to a series of specific performance objectives. This problem is in no sense new, and efforts to resolve it have been legion; but only since the advent of new instructional technology has there been any hope of a real solution. In addition to its other benefits the computer may yet make it possible to truly individualize instruction.

COMPUTERS

Most efforts at individualizing instruction have concentrated on allowing students to work at their own pace. Instituting even this change requires individualized scheduling and extensive record keeping. When we try to go beyond this into letting some students select their own instructional objectives and the learning resources needed to achieve them, the record-keeping and scheduling problems become immense. Now, however, educators are taking a serious look at computers as a practical solution to these problems.

Wayne Holtzman, a psychologist and the dean of the College of Education at the University of Texas, predicts that

> computers will take over most of the drudgery of scheduling, allocating learning resources to individuals and groups, maintaining progress records . . . , compiling and scoring tests, providing . . . access to . . . information . . . and a host of other management activities. For major segments of the curriculum, the computer will also provide direct interaction between the student and the subject matter to be learned. . . .[1]

Many problems remain to be solved before such a complete use of computers in education can become a reality, including the primary ones of cost and the creation of enough tested software. Nevertheless, computers are already being used in education, and the implications of these uses for the future are tremendous.

In this chapter, we shall deal with a number of computer applications in education. Most of them are still experimental, but some, such as those related to administration, are already widespread. As you read about them, consider the implications they may have for your own school and your own role as a teacher in the days ahead.

What Is a Computer?

A computer is a power-driven machine, equipped with keyboards, electronic circuits,

[1] Wayne H. Holtzman, ed., *Computer-Assisted Instruction, Testing, and Guidance* (New York: Harper & Row, 1970), p. 3.

storage compartments, and recording devices, that performs mathematical operations at a high speed. To an extent, a computer is simply a glorified calculator that can store, or "memorize," large amounts of information and produce, or retrieve, it on demand.

The way a computer stores information is similar in principle to the way information is stored on audiotapes. However, a computer stores and processes information on punch cards (this is called *batch processing*) or data fed into it through terminals at other, perhaps distant, locations. Because even one moderate-sized computer can serve numerous users simultaneously or in a very short time, most terminal hook-ups are *time-sharing* operations. The cost of time-sharing is reckoned in terms of tiny fractions of seconds of use. It is more expensive than batch processing because (1) the response is immediate and (2) time-sharing requires a computer, a communications link such as a telephone line, and one or more terminals at the user's location —wherever that may be. It is also important to note that there are two kinds of terminals: (1) those with *teletype* output units, which are slower and noisier, but cheaper and provide written (hard) copy, and (2) those with video CRT (cathode ray tube) screens. Video printouts are faster and quieter than teletype printouts, but they are more expensive and provide, as yet, no hard copy.

Figure 10.1 The use of computers for drill and practice is one of their simplest instructional applications. If this were the only way of using computers in a school, would their purchase be justified?

Computer terminology. In discussing computerized instruction we shall avoid technical terms, because they are unnecessary for our purpose, which is to describe the present and possible applications of computers in education. (See Figure 10.1.) The most common label for instruction in which computers play a role is CAI, or *computer-assisted instruction.* Other labels include CBI (computer-based instruction), CBE (computer-based education), CMI (computer-managed instruction), and CAL (computer-assisted learning). Any single term can mean different things to different people.[2]

2 For those who wish to become familiar with some of the more technical terms, a particularly useful glossary is given in Karl Zinn, *An Evaluative Review of Uses of Computers in Instruction* (Ann Arbor: University of Michigan Press, 1970), Appendix E. Another helpful book is Jeff Maynard's *Dictionary of Data Processing* (1976), available from Newnes-Butterworth, Borough Green, Sevenoaks, Kent, in the United Kingdom, for approximately $10. It contains concise definitions of more than 4000 terms. Short glossaries are available from most computer manufacturers and some professional associations.

How computers function. One of the most obvious advantages of computers is their speed and accuracy in solving mathematical problems, no matter how complex. Let us digress for a moment and explore this capacity a bit further, using as an example a very practical problem—assigning classes to teachers.

Computers are especially helpful in solving problems that involve getting the most out of limited resources. For example, consider a science department chairperson faced with the problem of assigning five teachers to teach classes in five subjects—general science, biology, chemistry, physics, and earth sciences. All five teachers can teach all five subjects, but each one knows more about some subjects than others. Table 10.1 shows their relative expertise in teaching each of the five subjects.

The chairperson's problem is to assign one teacher to each subject so as to make the best overall use of all five. Obviously, the chairperson cannot assign each teacher to his or her best subject because teachers A and C are both best (with a rating of 6) at teaching earth sciences. There are no real options with regard to teacher D, who is "good" (has a rating of 4) in only one subject; but there are quite a lot with teacher C, who is "good" or better than good at every subject. Thus there must be some sort of compromise in order to distribute the five teachers among the five courses in the best possible way. By using some fairly elementary arithmetic and what mathematicians call a *5 × 5 matrix,* it is possible to come up with the solution indicated in Table 10.2 (where the course each teacher should teach is indicated by parentheses) in 5 or 10 minutes using a pencil and paper. Note that three teachers are assigned to their second-best courses and two to their best courses. However, every class has a teacher who is at least "good" (has a rating of 4) in the subject.

The problem we have just described is a relatively simple one. For more complex problems, a computer is indispensable. For example, the five-teacher problem involves only 120 possible combinations. If there were 10 teachers involved

Table 10.1

	General science	Biology	Chemistry	Physics	Earth sciences
Teacher A	1	3	2	3	6
Teacher B	2	4	3	1	5
Teacher C	5	6	3	4	6
Teacher D	3	1	4	2	2
Teacher E	1	5	6	5	4

SOURCE: John Pfeiffer, *A New Look at Educational Systems Analysis in Our Schools and Colleges* (Racine, Wis.: Western Publishing Co., 1968), p. 35.
Note: Rating scale: 6 = excellent; 1 = poor.

Table 10.2

	General science	Biology	Chemistry	Physics	Earth sciences
Teacher A	1	3	2	3	(6)
Teacher B	2	(4)	3	1	5
Teacher C	(5)	6	3	4	6
Teacher D	3	1	(4)	2	2
Teacher E	1	5	6	(5)	4

SOURCE: Pfeiffer, ibid., p. 35.

and the task was to assign these 10 persons to 10 positions, there would be 3628 million alternatives. It would still be possible to select the best one manually, but it would take many hours at best, whereas a computer could do it in a few minutes or less. Matrices much larger than 10 × 10, which would take months or years to solve with a desk calculator, are commonly run on computers.

The computer's power to process huge masses of information and to solve complex problems is difficult to comprehend. John Pfeiffer explains it this way:

> Perhaps the critical fact is that today's fastest models are some one to two million times faster than a man at a desk-type adding machine, which is about the difference between a day and a millennium and means that studies are being undertaken routinely that were unthinkable less than a decade or so ago.[3]

What relevance does this have for the ordinary classroom teacher who generally has little need to solve complex mathematical problems of any kind? The answer is that most of what a computer does is done in mathematical terms. Even an order to a computer to scan literature or retrieve information from a text must be translated via computer languages into numerical terms. The computer will then perform the necessary calculations, translate the answer back into ordinary English, and type it out on a teletypewriter or flash it on a screen.

How much we shall one day put the power of computers to work in education remains to be seen. But computers are certainly here to stay. Many large school systems now have their own computers, and numerous smaller systems are hooked up by telephone lines to university or commercial computer services on which they buy time for administrative functions. The advent of low-cost mini-computers has also greatly increased the feasibility of computers for educational uses.

Using computers for administrative tasks. An important factor to keep in mind as we consider possible computer uses in instruction is that large numbers of educational systems already use computers for a variety of administrative purposes by purchasing, payroll, inventory, personnel, and auditing departments. In addition, computers are widely used to serve a variety of administrative needs that are unique to education. These include the processing of information for student admissions, the continuous updating of student records, the scheduling of classes, the registration of students, and the storage and retrieval of information traditionally found in libraries.

Computers are costly. Thus their purchase or lease can be justified only when the benefits that result are clearly above and beyond those that could reasonably be achieved without them. In the area of administration, however, their cost-effectiveness has been well established. Many computerized information-processing operations actually cost less than the same operations performed manually. Even more important are the many new operations the computer has made possible that could not be achieved without it at any price. The instantaneous processing of election returns and airline reservations are familiar examples. There are hundreds, perhaps thousands, of routine, unspectacular ways in which computerized information processing increases the effectiveness of administrators in government, industry, and some sectors of education.

Thus the availability of computers is not the central question as we think about their uses in instruction. The same computers used for administrative purposes can be used for other purposes as well, though the additional computer time used for instructional programs would have to be paid for. The central question is the legitimacy and feasibility of the educational

[3] John Pfeiffer, *A New Look at Educational Systems Analysis in Our Schools and Colleges* (Racine, Wis.: Western Publishing Co., 1968), p. 37.

uses of computers. Let us take a look at some examples.

Instructional Uses of Computers

There are a variety of legitimate instructional uses for computers. These can be conveniently classified into four groups: drill and practice; tutorial uses and dialogues; simulations and games; and information-handling aids. We shall examine each of these types briefly, plus a fifth and different kind of use, that is, the use of the computer as a subject of instruction itself.

Typically, students using computers sit at specially designed electric typewriters that are connected to the computers by telephone lines. They identify themselves by code numbers and their names, the machines type out questions, they type the answers, and the lessons are under way.

Drill and practice. The following example of a computerized drill comes from an elementary mathematics drill and practice program developed by Patrick Suppes at the Institute for Mathematical Studies in the Social Sciences at Stanford University. The computer, after printing out each problem, positions the student's typewriter to accept the response in a blank. The fact that the computer goes on to a new problem tells the student that a response was correct. In this sample printout, the student's responses are underlined.

This lesson is an example of one of the simpler uses of computers in instruction, but as you can readily see, the availability of such drill and practice exercises on a computer terminal can relieve the teacher of the task of administering such work personally. More important, it eliminates much routine work marking papers and keeping records, because the computer keeps track of each student's performance and can give a summation of his or her work to the teacher at any time.

When students make an error, the computer

```
PLEASE TYPE YOUR NAME
MIKE O'DELL
DRILL NUMBER 509013
(42 + 63)/7 = (42/7 + (63/7)
48 − 38 = 38 +48
WRONG
48 − 38 = 38 − 4
WRONG, ANSWER IS 28
43 − 38 = 38 − 28
76 − (26 − 10) = (76 − 26) + 10
4 × (7 + 13) = (4 × 7) + (4 × 13)
(53 − 20) − 11 = 53 − (20 + 11)
32 + (74 + 18) = (32 + 74) + 18
51 × (36 × 12) = (51 × 36) × 12
17 × (14 + 34) = (17 × 14) + (17 × 34)
362 + 943 = 943 + 362
(5 + 8) × 7 = 5 × 7) + (8 × 7)
(90/10)/3 = 90/(10 × 3)
(72/9)/4 = 72/(9 × 4)
(54 + 18)/6 = (54/6) + (18/__)
TIME IS UP
(54 + 18)/6 = (54/6) + (18/6)
60 − (19 − 12) = (60 − 19) + 12
72 × (43 × 11) = (72 × 43) × 11
(63/7) + (56/7) = (63 + 7)/7
WRONG
(63/7) + (56/7) = (63 + 56)/7
END OF DRILL NUMBER 509013
13 MAY 1966
16 PROBLEMS

                NUMBER    PERCENT
CORRECT           13         81
WRONG              2         12
TIME OUTS          1          6
WRONG
   2
  16
TIME OUTS
  13
222.7 SECONDS THIS DRILL
CORRECT THIS CONCEPT—81 PERCENT, CORRECT TO DATE—
59 PERCENT
4 HOURS, 46 MINUTES, 59 SECONDS OVERALL
GOODBYE MIKE[4]
```

4 Patrick Suppes, Max Jerman, and Dow Brian, *Computer-Assisted Instruction: Stanford's 1965–66 Arithmetic Program* (New York: Academic Press, 1968), p. 29.

immediately calls it to their attention so that they can try again. Depending on the program in the computer, after a predetermined number of wrong answers, students may be referred to a remedial exercise. In the drill shown, however, the computer has been programmed merely to give the correct answer after two wrong answers. In any case, successful students can move ahead to new material as rapidly as their performance warrants. Just as in programmed instruction, they learn at their own pace, get immediate feedback on their efforts, and receive individual tutoring if it is needed. (See Figure 10.2.)

Figure 10.2 In well-designed computer lessons there is a kind of interaction between the lessons and the students that is not unlike that between a teacher and students.

Tutorial and dialogue programs. Tutorial programs differ from drill and practice programs in that the content of a subject is literally taught by the computer. Information may be presented much as it would be in a programmed text. In fact, in designing computer programs of this kind, the same precise analysis of the learning task and specification of objectives that is necessary in designing programmed lessons is required.

A computer, however, may provide various options not usually present in programmed texts. For example, explanations may be given orally via audiotape and visuals may be shown on a cathode ray tube (CRT) very much like the tube in a television set. Students may respond to questions on a typewriter keyboard or by pointing or drawing with a light pen on an electronic screen or CRT in a study carrel. The computer reacts to the students' responses by indicating that they are correct or by "talking" to them in some way (immediate feedback) if it is not. The students then make a further response. Thus a kind of dialogue takes place between the students and the machine.

The Brentwood Tutorial Mathematics Program is one of the better-known examples of computerized tutorial programs. Like the mathematics drill described earlier, it was developed by Patrick Suppes at the Institute for Mathematical Studies in the Social Sciences at Stanford University. It is used to teach mathematics to first-graders. There are some 400 lessons, covering counting, numerals, addition, subtraction, linear measures, set notation, and geometry. Students respond to questions and problems either on a typewriter or by using a light pen to touch one of the answers shown on a CRT. They receive audiotaped instructions through a headset.

If a response is incorrect or students fail to respond within a reasonable time, they receive additional audio instructions. This description of one lesson illustrates how the program works:

> For one problem, a drawing of a car and a drawing of a truck surrounded by set braces and followed by an equal sign were presented on the CRT; this problem was accompanied by the audio message "There are two members in this set." After this message, two more sets, one empty and one containing a train and a steam shovel, each preceded by a box, were displayed below the initial set; the choices were accompanied by the audio instructions "Find another set with two members." At this point a small "p" (for pen) was displayed in the corner of the CRT as a signal to the student to respond. If the student touched his light pen to the box in front of the correct choice, a smiling face was displayed and he heard, "Yes, the sets have the same number of members," and proceeded to the next problem.
>
> If the student did not respond within 20 seconds, he heard "Which set below has two members?" If the student responded incorrectly, he heard the audio message "Point to the box next to the set with two members," and saw a sad face. For most problems in the curriculum, students were allowed three chances to produce the correct answer.[5]

In most of the lessons, the computer keeps track of the number of initially correct responses. When a specified number have been given, students can skip the rest of the problems and go on to the next lesson.

Both explanations and practice problems contain special audio messages heard only by students not performing up to predetermined standards. Furthermore, if students make a certain number of errors during a lesson, the program branches to a remedial lesson that contains the same kinds of problems but develops ideas more slowly and uses a simpler vocabulary. If students fail to understand the remedial lesson, the computer automatically calls a proctor or teacher to assist them.

Computerized tutorial and dialogue programs have been developed in many subjects. The following example (see p. 282) is one of a series used to teach English grammar to intermediate-grade pupils in the Waterford Township schools near Pontiac, Michigan. (See Figure 10.3.) The computer's part of the dialogue is in capital letters. The student responses are underlined.

Simulations and games. Computers also are useful in simulation exercises and games, two instructional methods that we shall discuss in more detail later in the chapter. *Simulations* are representations of real situations with some elements removed for the sake of safety (as in driver or pilot training), because real equipment cannot be used (a cyclotron, for example), or because the length of time involved in a real exercise would be too great (as in genetic or population studies). *Games* are used in many simulated exercises to introduce an element of competition.

Experts at the Huntington Computer Project in New York, for example, have been working for several years on various uses of computer simulations in the classroom. They have experimented with simulations in biology, chemistry, earth science, physics, and social studies. Some simulations are used to enrich existing experiments and other classroom activities; others, however, are used to provide experiences that would be impossible to provide otherwise.

Examples of the latter include a program on evolution, called STERL, which permits students to experiment with the control of pests through a combination of pesticides and the injection of sterilized males in communities of insects. Another program, called POLUT, deals with water pollution. Still another, called EDER1, permits students to explore the con-

[5] Patrick Suppes and Mona Morningstar, "Four Programs in Computer-Assisted Instruction" in Holtzman, *Computer-Assisted Instruction, Testing, and Guidance,* p. 243.

```
OBJECTIVE: YOU WILL BE ABLE TO SELECT THE SUBJECT
FROM A GIVEN SENTENCE.
THE SUBJECT OF A SENTENCE DOES SOMETHING.
EXAMPLE: THE GIRLS PLAYED CARDS. GIRLS IS THE SUB-
JECT BECAUSE THEY ARE DOING SOMETHING. TYPE THE
SUBJECTS IN THESE SENTENCES.
JANE MADE A PIE.
Jane
JANE IS THE SUBJECT BECAUSE SHE IS DOING SOMETHING.
TOMMY SAT ON A TACK.
Tommy
THE SUBJECT OF A SENTENCE NAMES A PERSON, PLACE,
OR THING. IN THE EXAMPLES ABOVE WHAT DID THE SUB-
JECTS NAME: PERSONS, PLACES, OR THINGS?
persons
WHAT IS THE SUBJECT IN THE NEXT SENTENCE?
HIS RED WAGON IS BROKEN.
wagon
WAGON IS A THING. IS THE SUBJECT IN THE NEXT SEN-
TENCE A THING?
COLUMBUS IS THE CAPITAL OF OHIO.
no
WHAT IS IT?
place
A WAY OF FINDING THE SUBJECT IS TO SAY WHO DOES
SOMETHING. WHAT WORD ANSWERS THAT QUESTION IN
THE NEXT SENTENCE?
SALLY SAW HER DOG.
Sally
LOOK AT THE NEXT SENTENCE: THE CLOCK STRUCK THREE.
SINCE CLOCK CANNOT ANSWER THE QUESTION WHO DOES
SOMETHING, SHOULD YOU ASK INSTEAD WHAT DOES
SOMETHING?
yes
TO FIND THE SUBJECT YOU MIGHT ASK WHO OR WHAT IS
DOING SOMETHING.
008 PROBLEMS 008 CORRECT 100 PERCENT 02 MIN.
54 SEC.
THAT IS ALL FOR TODAY. 14:44:48
& C M S P L A PROGRAM
WATERFORD SCHOOLS—ESEA TITLE III
TEAR OFF ON DOTTED LINE[6]
```

[6] *Communications Math Skill Program—Language Arts.* Produced by INDICOM Project, Title III, ESEA, Waterford School District, Pontiac, Mich.

cepts of scarcity, opportunity, and the allocation of resources. The EDER1 program is designed as a game, with nature as the opponent in a Robinson Crusoe environment. The student is placed on an uninhabited island 48 hours before a severe hurricane is due and must use the island's natural resources to secure food, water, and shelter before the hurricane hits.[7]

Simulations and games can give students practice in decision making and allow them to test hypotheses in abstract situations. One familiar example is the prediction of future economic developments. Because a number of economic variables can readily be manipulated on computers, it is possible for students to test out various economic hypotheses.

A simple economic simulation for sixth-graders, for example, involves two games that individual students play against a computer.[8] In the Sumerian game, students play the role of the priest-ruler of a city-state in ancient Mesopotamia. They must decide how to allocate resources, develop crafts, and promote trade. The Sierra Leone Development Project game transforms students into members of the Agency for International Development making decisions on how to allocate funds to help solve the economic problems of a newly emerging nation.[9] Both slides and audiotape are used in these simulations, along with the computer program. Three computer consoles allow three students (or three small groups) to play the game at a time. The games are designed for individualized instruction and thus provide a considerable variety of

[7] L. Braun, *The Digital Computer as a General-Purpose Simulator* (Brooklyn, N.Y.: Huntington Computer Project, Polytechnic Institute of Brooklyn, 1970).

[8] R. L. Wing, "Two Computer-Based Economic Games for Sixth-Graders," in Sarane S. Boocock and E. O. Schild, eds., *Simulation, Games and Learning* (Beverly Hills, Calif.: Sage Publications, 1968).

[9] Both games are available by a special arrangement with the Board of Cooperative Educational Services, 845 Fox Meadow Road, Yorktown Heights, N.Y. 10598.

Figure 10.3 The involvement of students in computerized learning is readily apparent in these pictures.

options, not only in regard to the pace of the proceedings but also in regard to content, the difficulty of problems, and the way things are presented. A study comparing these programs with conventional classroom teaching on the same topics showed that the students working on computers learned about the same amount as the students taught by conventional methods, and in considerably less time.

A higher-level simulation described by Karl Zinn involves a student exploring a simple concept in wildlife management. The setting is a salmon-fishing operation. Zinn explains the game as follows:

> The object of the game is to build up and maintain a population which will maximize the catch taken by the fishery. The size of the run for the coming year is determined by the computer in some way not known to the student, although he does know it depends on the previous year's escapement.[10]

The following printout of a "conversation" between a computer (in capital letters) and a student is accompanied by Zinn's comments, in the right-hand column.

[10] Zinn, *An Evaluative Review of Uses of Computers in Instruction,* pp. 18–19.

CONVERSATION	COMMENTARY
WHICH MANAGEMENT STRATEGY DO YOU WANT TO ADOPT?	The player has the choice of [determining] either [the] escapement or [the] catch.
catch	
CATCH FOR 1969 16,000	The player sets the catch at 16,000 fish.
ESCAPEMENT = 2,000	The computer supplies the size of the escapement and asks about the next year.
CATCH FOR 1970 10,000	
ESCAPEMENT = 1,000	The student notes that when 2,000 escape (1969, above) the next year's run is 11,000 (catch of 10,000 plus 1,000 escaping).
CATCH FOR 1971 5,000	
ESCAPEMENT = 1,000 THE MEN AT THE FISHERY ARE DISTURBED ABOUT THE LOW CATCH	
CATCH FOR 1972 10,000	
NO FISH ESCAPED. LET'S START OVER AGAIN	The student should have kept the catch down until the population had recovered.
WHICH MANAGEMENT STRATEGY DO YOU WANT TO ADOPT?	
escapement	
ESCAPEMENT FOR 1969? 15,000	This time he will try the safer strategy of setting the number of fish which must be permitted to escape to spawn before the fishery can begin to catch.

CATCH = 3,000 THE MEN AT THE FISHERY ARE FURIOUS ABOUT THE LOW CATCH	
ESCAPEMENT FOR 1970? 15,000	The student holds firm because he expects a much bigger run the next year.
CATCH = 11,000	
ESCAPEMENT FOR 1971? 10,000	
CATCH = 15,000	
ESCAPEMENT FOR 1972? 9,000	
CATCH = 21,000	
ESCAPEMENT FOR 1973? 9,000	
CATCH = 19,000	
YOUR TOTAL CATCH FOR THE LAST FIVE YEARS HAS BEEN 68,000 SALMON—13,600 PER YEAR. DO YOU WISH TO DISCUSS THE OPTIMUM STRATEGY NOW?	The student graphs the data so far, infers a relationship between escapement and the run the following year, and is ready to switch to a subprogram which will "discuss" with him the optimum strategy.

Information handling. A fourth general use of computers in instruction is to store information so that it can be called on as needed. Although computers can store and retrieve large masses of information on any subject, we are still some years away from totally computerized libraries.

The use of a computer's "filing capacity," though expensive, may be warranted for special types of information, such as statistics on employment, production, and population, which are continually being updated. The computerized management of library documents is already a reality, and computer programs that manage all the major activities of a library, from ordering materials to searching files, are only a matter of time. Once major libraries, such as the Library of Congress, have been totally computerized, the establishment of data banks for smaller libraries will be a relatively simple matter that can be expected to proceed fairly rapidly.[11]

One of the areas in which the information-handling capacity of computers is being used to advantage is counseling. Computers can store cumulative records of students' IQs, grades, test scores, extracurricular activities, interest inventories, and so on, and match them with a wide range of occupational or educational requirements. For example, the School District of Philadelphia and the Willowbrook High School, a large, comprehensive high school outside Chicago, use computers to give students and counselors information about occupational opportunities in the area, educational and training programs that make it possible to take advantage of them, and other facts helpful in making curriculum choices.

11 Holtzman, *Computer-Assisted Instruction, Testing, and Guidance,* p. 8.

Computers as a Subject of Instruction

The study of computers has become an important part of the curriculum not only in higher education but also in secondary and technical schools. Departments of computer sciences have developed rapidly during the past decade. University students can major in the field, and many do; large numbers of students from other departments also study computer languages and applications so that they can use them in their own fields.

The Cost of Using Computers in Instruction

Computers are expensive. Many people feel that they are too expensive to be used in schools. But education itself is expensive, costing something over $80 billion a year in the United States. What must be considered is not so much the cost of computers as their *cost-effectiveness*—the results achieved per dollar invested compared with other ways of spending money for education.

A 1968 study of costs of traditionally administered instruction (TAI) versus computer-assisted instruction (CAI) showed the cost per student of CAI to be over ten times that of TAI for a class of average size.[12] This wide difference was caused in part by the limited use of computers possible in a typical six-hour school day in schools organized along traditional lines, but it did indicate that unless CAI could be shown to be at least ten times as effective (or efficient) as TAI, a change to CAI was not justifiable at that time. Since then, however, several major developments, including low-cost mini-computers, have altered the cost picture considerably.

A major new factor in the CAI cost picture is the introduction of mini-computers—smaller, slower, limited-capacity computers like the Digital Equipment Corporation's Classic and Wang Laboratories' 2200 that are perfectly adequate for most educational uses. These mini-computers are slow only in comparison with the massive computers used in business and government, and their low initial cost and low maintenance costs have reduced use costs to between 50 and 70 cents per student hour. Sperry-Rand, for example, working with the Chicago school system, has developed a Univac program to help inner-city elementary school children who are at least a year behind in grammar, reading, and arithmetic. The program appears to work effectively at a cost of $1 extra per week per child. Hard figures are still difficult to obtain, but sufficient evidence is available to suggest that costs are no longer a major deterrent to CAI.

Advantages and Limitations of Computerized Instruction

In summing up our discussion of computers, it is helpful to take a look at their pros and cons through the eyes of some representative learning psychologists, educators, educational researchers, and computer specialists.

Some unique contributions of computers. Speaking of the solution of learning problems by using computers, John Feldhusen, an educational psychologist, is clearly an enthusiast of using computers to solve learning problems. He believes that

> CAI teaches at least as well as live teachers or other media, that there is a saving in [the time it takes] to learn, that students respond favorably to CAI, that the computer can be used [to great advantage] in branching and individualizing instruction, that true, natural instructional dialogue is possible, and that the computer will virtually perform miracles in processing performance data.[13]

[12] Felix F. Kopstein and Robert J. Seidel, "Computer-Administered Instruction Versus Traditionally Administered Instruction: Economics," *AV Communication Review* (Summer 1968), p. 163.

[13] John Feldhusen and Michael Szabo, "The Advent of the Educational Heart Transplant, Computer-Assisted Instruction: A Brief Interpretative Review," *Contemporary Education* (April 1969), Indiana State University.

In a report on CAI research and development, Feldhusen discusses the capabilities of CAI in comparison with other media:

> There are some things which CAI is able to do better than other media: (1) Secure, store and process information about the student's performance prior to and/or during instruction . . . . (2) Store large amounts of information and make them available to the learner more rapidly than any other medium. (3) Provide programmed control of several media, such as films, slides, TV, and demonstration equipment. (4) Give the author or teacher an extremely convenient technique for designing and developing a course of instruction. (5) Provide a dynamic interaction between [the] student and [the] instructional program not possible with most other media.[14]

Lawrence Stolurow stresses the potential of CAI in contrast with other media, for individualized instruction:

> Computer-assisted instruction is . . . a potential means of making instruction a truly individualized process. . . . While programed instruction and language laboratories appear to individualize instruction, they actually only take the first baby step in that direction by allowing the student to proceed at his own rate. Mass media approaches have provided an illusion of economy; [there are] hidden . . . costs . . . ; with CAI we could individualize materials electronically rather than by hand.[15]

Writing about the applications of the systems approach to the solution of many of today's educational problems and the role of the computer in that effort, John Pfeiffer points to a generally accepted and important fringe benefit of using computers. This benefit arises from the fact that, before computers can be of any use at all, they must be programmed. Programming requires a prior thinking through of problems and needs with a degree of thoroughness and specificity not commonly associated with educational planning. Pfeiffer concludes that

> there may be an interesting relationship between our increasing emphasis on the need to define objectives and our increasing experience with computers. Computers are notorious for their simple-mindedness, among other things. They demand instructions spelled out in excruciating detail, and dealing with them has probably forced us to become more explicit and exact in dealing with one another. We can be brilliant but rather sloppy thinkers; computers are stupid but accurate. It seems that during the course of time, in the evolving symbiosis between man and machine, we are destined for better or for worse to become somewhat more precise (and, of course, the computer will inevitably become somewhat more intelligent).[16]

Limitations of computers. The cost of computers is their most frequently cited drawback. Nevertheless, many authorities consider misuses or inappropriate uses of computers as far more significant. For instance, the National Council for Educational Technology in England comments:

> It is important not to consider CAI as a learning process which involves the computer solely: [a] "system" could include, for example, teachers, printed material, and linear programed texts. Many experimental . . . CAI [programs] have been ineffective because they have attempted to put the whole process on the computer. . . .[17]

[14] John Feldhusen, "A Position Paper on CAI Research and Development," OE-ERIC Clearing House on Educational Media and Technology, Stanford University, 1969.

[15] Lawrence Stolurow, "Computer Assisted Instruction," in *The Schools and the Challenge of Innovation* (New York: McGraw-Hill, 1969), pp. 270–319.

[16] Pfeiffer, *A New Look at Education,* p. 14.

[17] National Council for Educational Technology (NCET), *Computer-Based Learning Systems: A Programme for Research and Development,* 160 Great Portland Street, London W.1, England, 1969.

There is also some concern that computers may inject an inhuman quality into education. In an article advocating the development of a realistic perspective on technological innovations in education, Anthony Oettinger and Sema Marks comment pointedly on a possible danger on such innovations—particularly those that prove highly efficient and effective:

> If, as is true of all computerized systems of "individualized" instruction now visible as prototypes, as well as of many others based on explicit definitions of "behavioral objectives" (BO's), the intent is to instruct students in such a manner that all will achieve a final level of competency which meets (or surpasses) the same set of minimally acceptable performance criteria, with variation only in [the] style, speed, or level of achievement, the objective cannot be the cultivation of idiosyncrasy. It is, rather, what an industrial engineer might call mass production to narrow specifications with rigid quality control. Each pupil is free to go more or less rapidly exactly where he is told to go.[18]

There are others, however, who disagree, arguing that

> contrary to the skeptical criticism of some alarmists, there is no reason to believe that this new technology will necessarily dehumanize man. There are many things in this world that can be done better by machines than by human beings. The advent of the computer, and the educational technology related to it, clearly points the way to major changes in education that will free the individual, both teacher and student, to interact in more human ways than ever before.[19]

[18] Anthony G. Oettinger and Sema Marks, "Educational Technology—New Myths and Old Realities," *Harvard Educational Review* (Fall 1968), p. 701.

[19] Holtzman, *Computer-Assisted Instruction, Testing, and Guidance,* p. 13.

Sources of Computer Information

Keeping up to date on computer technology and its educational applications can be time-consuming, but it is definitely worthwhile. One continuing source of information, of course, is the publications of professional associations such as the Association for Educational Communications and Technology (AECT), the Association for Educational Data Systems (AEDS), the American Educational Research Association (AERA), and the International Federation for Information Processing (IFIP).[20] The best single source, however, is Karl Zinn and Susan McClintock's *Guide to the Literature on Interactive Uses of Computers for Instruction.*[21] This guide is really a continuing source of sources that Zinn and his associates revise from time to time; it includes, in convenient form, a wide variety of annotated listings of significant reports of projects and conferences, publications, and program sources, as well as helpful analyses of current developments in the educational use of computers. Other sources of information in these areas are listed at the end of the chapter.

SIMULATIONS AND GAMES

A *simulation* is a simplified version of reality in which essential physical or social elements are represented without the hazards, costs, or time constraints normally associated with them. The purpose of simulations is to enable us to understand and function in real situations—flying an airplane, handling irate customers in a store,

[20] AECT and AERA are at 1126 16th St., N.W., Washington, D.C.; AEDS is at 1201 16th St., N.W., Washington, D.C. 20036; the IFIP is at 23 Dorset Square, London N.W.1, England.

[21] Second edition, 1970, Center for Research on Learning and Teaching, University of Michigan. Distributed by the ERIC Clearing House on Information Resources, Syracuse University, Syracuse, N.Y. 13210.

serving on a city council, dealing with discipline problems in a classroom, marketing new products, making investments, and so on. Educational simulations are frequently cast in the form of competitive games to motivate and interest students.

Games are contests played according to rules, where the object is to win. Winners and losers are clearly identified. Skill and chance or some combination of the two are generally key factors. By combining simulation and gaming, many highly effective learning experiences can be developed. Although most simulations and games do not require computers, they constitute a valuable educational application of computers. Computers do not play games in the usual sense, of course; but because of their ability to store and process information with great rapidity, they enable people to simulate situations and play games that might not otherwise be practical.

Types of Educational Simulations and Games

There are four principal types of educational simulations and games: nonsimulation games, planning exercises, interpersonal simulation games, and large-system simulation games.[22]

Nonsimulation games are competitive learning activities in which success is determined by the degree of learning demonstrated. Examples are "Wff 'n Proof," a game designed to teach mathematical logic to children 6 years old and older; "Equations," a series of five games designed to teach basic computational skills from the primary grades on up; and "The Propaganda Game," in which junior and senior high school students learn the techniques used by professionals to mold public opinion.[23] Electric boards like those in Figure 10.4 are also nonsimulation games in a sense, because they provide opportunities for students to train and test themselves and perhaps to compete with others in the process.

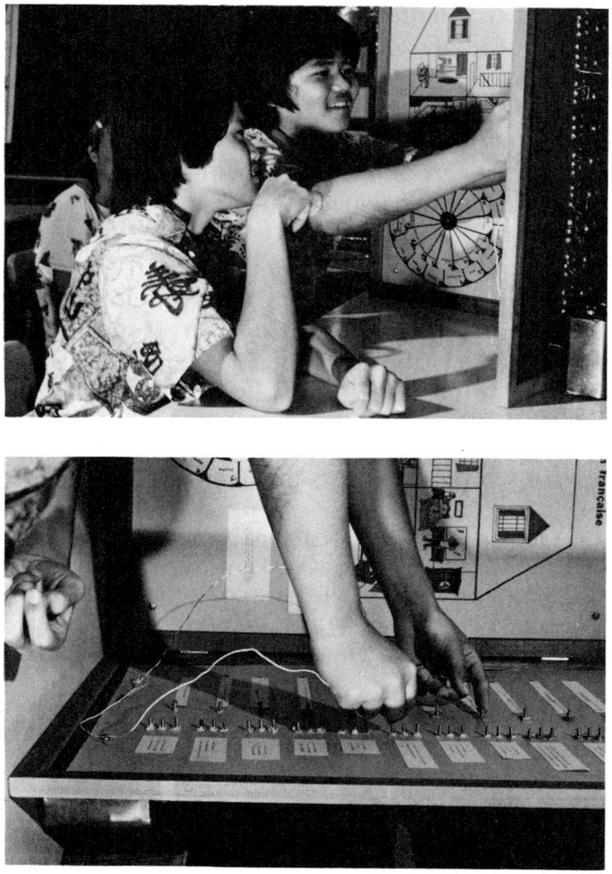

Figure 10.4 Electric boards are simple to construct and can be adjusted for different patterns of response. Students respond to questions mounted on the board by touching an electrical contact to their choice among several possible answers. The correct response causes a bulb to light up.

For more advanced students, instructors may devise original nonsimulation games that focus on basic concepts. For example, in an urban planning game, each student can draw a card that calls for political, economic, or social activity or some combination of the three. He or she

[22] Paul A. Twelker and Kent Layden. *Educational Simulation/Gaming,* ERIC at Stanford, Palo Alto, Calif., 1972.

[23] All three games are produced by Wff 'n Proof, 1111 Maple Ave., Turtle Creek, Pa. 15145.

must then identify the sector (s) involved and outline the action they would take. Points can be allocated for correct responses; the student with the highest score at the end of a specified time wins.

Planning exercises are nonsimulation games that focus on processes rather than content. The participants examine social problems requiring solution and work in committees to develop solutions that are in competition for adoption by the group as a whole on the basis of evaluative criteria which are developed and applied by the group. As an example of a planning exercise, the following is suggested:

> An instructor wishes his class to plan the use of a core area of their own city. Planning teams are formed—each to draw up a comprehensive plan of attack. One group, known as evaluators, represents a cross-section of interests: environmentalists, businessmen, city bureaucrats, community service people, etc. Activity proceeds through the following phases: planning of proposals by the planning teams and evaluation criteria by the evaluators, reporting of proposals, and judging of proposals.[24]

The above example clearly involves a measure of role playing or interpreting the feelings and actions of others. An example is also found in the Democracy (Legislature) game for high school and older students. Students who get into the spirit of the game literally try to "become" senators or representatives and to act and react as they conceive that such persons would. The Democracy game is therefore representative, as well, of the third category of simulation games, namely, interpersonal simulation games.

Interpersonal simulation games are learning activities in which students respond as if they were participating in the interactions being simulated. The interactions are structured by rules or other factors in the game itself and may vary widely. Interpersonal simulation games are designed to give the participants a genuine feel for the dynamics of interpersonal relationships, as well as insight into the problems being simulated.

One example of an interpersonal simulation game is "FLIP" ("Family Life Income Patterns"), a game for junior high school and older students.[25] Participants play family members who must deal with budgeting problems, such as emergency expenditures, desires versus needs, credit management, and the like. Quite naturally the needs and desires of individual family members conflict to some extent from the outset, and the game is designed to encourage cooperative financial management in the best interests of the family as a whole.

Large-system simulation games are the most complex of the educational simulation games. They deal with a wide range of problems and variables, local, national, and international. The participant always plays some role—as a planner, a decision maker, or merely an observer—that will help him or her to understand the factors influencing decisions and group behavior in such large areas as urban planning, international trade, race relations, and disarmament.

One large-system game attempts to demonstrate the principles of controlled growth in metropolitan areas by examining an uncontrolled urban system. Participants analyze current problems and study the projected effects of various solutions—changing political boundaries, shifting the tax structure, setting up a new transportation system, rezoning, and the like. When computers are used, the projected effects, over time, of possible actions can be estimated with some confidence. Tentative models of urban and regional development involving a broad range of political, demographic, agricultural, economic, and social variables have been developed through research and are widely used in government, business, and industry.

[24] Twelker and Layden, *Educational Simulation/Gaming.*

[25] Available from Instructional Simulations, 2147 University Ave., St. Paul, Minn. 55114.

Designing and Evaluating Educational Simulations

Educational simulations and games, like other well-organized learning experiences, must be designed to meet specified objectives. What is required is (1) a systematic analysis of the problem, process, or situation to be taught; (2) the selection of a suitable model (format) for the game; (3) setting up the "parts," or roles, to be played; (4) establishing rules for the game so that it will achieve the specified objectives; (5) determining (and, if necessary, preparing) the materials and information needed by the players; and (6) testing the game with representative groups of students and reworking it until it functions as it should.

Simulations and games for schools and colleges are available for a wide range of subjects and grade levels. *Because it is quite possible for games to be interesting but involve little tangible learning, it is important to ascertain the extent to which they have been validated as educational materials.* Companies that sell educational games should be able to provide data on their value as cognitive learning materials.

On the other hand, cognitive learning is not the only kind of learning that matters. Learning about processes and the risks and rewards of alternative decisions is also important. Games involving social interactions require forms of cooperative activity that are themselves important educational goals. (See Figure 10.5.) About elements such as these, teachers may have to make intuitive judgments or base their selections on testimony of other teachers.

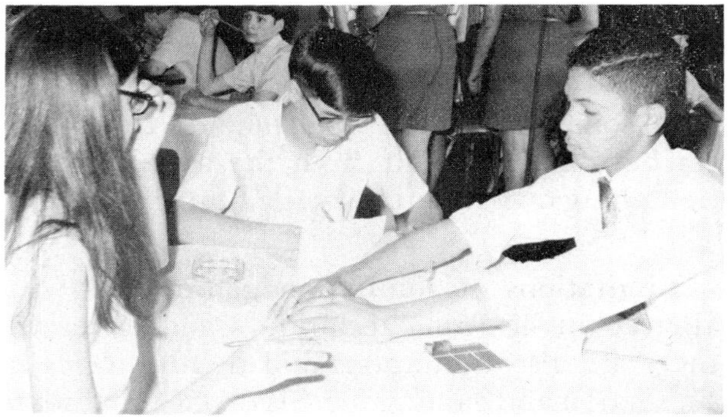

Figure 10.5 One way to increase motivation and participation in games is to hold national tournaments for teams from junior and senior high schools. Here students from three high schools play "Equations" in the Fifth National Academic Games Olympics in New Orleans.

Advantages and Limitations of Simulation/Gaming

Like other teaching materials, simulation exercises should be used so as to maximize their advantages and minimize their limitations. Simulation/gaming has several primary advantages and two chief limitations that must be weighed in any specific situation.

Advantages of simulation/gaming. One of the marked advantages of effective simulations is *increased student motivation and participation.* Students respond with unusual enthusiasm and interest to simulation/gaming because of its relevance to "how things get done" in real life and the social interaction and cooperation it requires. Even culturally impoverished students tend to do very well in educational games and to take very quickly to "operating" in the game environment.

Another benefit of good simulations is the *social interaction* they generate. In educational simulations, players must not only think out their own best moves on the basis of the information they have, but must also persuade their teammates of the effectiveness of those moves. Thus players tend to learn how to operate more effectively within a group. Individuals who get too far out of line, through either overaggressiveness or apathy, tend to be "straightened out" by their peers.

Still another advantage of simulation games

is that *they can often be played by students of different ages and achievement levels.* The slower students tend to learn from the faster ones, sometimes better than they do from their teachers. Both benefit from the social interaction the games require, while learning things.

Limitations of simulation/gaming. As with all teaching-learning techniques and materials, there are also limitations and disadvantages to simulation and gaming. One is the fact that *some games take considerable time* to play. A review of 29 historical games for junior and senior high schools, for example, shows that they take from 1 to 30 hours to play, with an average of approximately 4 to 5 hours for each game. Many primary- and middle-grade games in reading, phonics, and mathematical skills, on the other hand, take only 15 to 20 minutes per exercise. The time required for games must naturally be weighed against the learning that results.

A possible drawback of simulations for some teachers is the fact that these games are *occasionally somewhat complex and must be monitored carefully by the teacher.* Setting up and conducting the games may also require a careful study of the directions that accompany these materials. Again, the time spent on these things must be weighed against the benefits that result.

Research on the effectiveness of simulation and games in most school subjects is still spotty and inconclusive.[26] It is difficult to prove statistically that simulation and games are inherently valuable classroom activities. Nevertheless, experience seems to demonstrate that learning does take place and that there are sufficient beneficial effects in terms of increased motivation and involvement to warrant using simulation and games from time to time. Teachers who use games report their best results when such materials are carefully incorporated in an overall instructional plan. This, of course, should be standard practice with *any* teaching materials or techniques.

Sources of Simulation Games

If you want to try out a simulation game, where can you get one? For what subjects and grade levels are games available? Where can you find out about them? What do they cost?

There are many sources and types of educational games. School supply companies and professional magazines, in which game publishers' advertisements regularly appear, are good sources of information on them. Your school's resource center or library may have some games on hand. There is also a quite comprehensive guide to simulation games published by Didactic Systems, Inc., and updated periodically.[27] The following entry for a game called "The Community" is representative.

THE COMMUNITY
Erwin Rausch

PLAYING DATA

Age Level	High School College Management/ Administrative
Number of Players	Minimum 3, no maximum
Playing Time	2 to 5 hours in 30-minute periods
Preparation Time	1 hour at first only

26 Robert H. Davis, in a review of *Simulation and Gaming in Education* by P. J. Tansey and D. Unwin (New York: Barnes and Noble, 1969), in *Simulation and Games* (December 1970), p. 43; Paul A. Twelker, "Simulation and Media," in P. J. Tansery, ed., *Educational Aspects of Simulation* (New York: McGraw-Hill, 1971).

27 Robert E. Horn (ed.), *The Guide to Simulations/Games for Education and Training,* 3d ed. (Cranford, N.J.: Didactic Systems, 1978, P.O. Box 457, Cranford, N.J., 07016; $23.00.)

MATERIALS

Components	Players' manuals Administrator's manual Worksheets

Supplementary Material "A Guide to Teaching"

COMMENT

THE COMMUNITY is the only game we've encountered which gives students a chance to experience the problems of the local, tax-supported economic systems in which they live. The problems of limited funds and competing priorities with which it deals lie close to the root of our national turmoil; I'd like to see every student playing the game from time to time. THE COMMUNITY is an interactive game, and calls for cooperation as well as competition and conflict; too many economics games—and business games as well—ignore the cooperative aspects of man's admittedly self-oriented interactions. Further, I think that of all economics games THE COMMUNITY makes the most significant use of role-playing to increase learning. Game events are deterministic, with quantitative (zero sum) outcomes. Play is by teams, and calls for rapid thinking, coalition formation, bargaining, and decision making. Results of outside evaluation are available from Didactic Systems.

SUMMARY DESCRIPTION

Roles	The players represent in turn the taxpayers of the community, the employers and employees, the elected officials
Objectives	To earn point credits for achievements and avoid demerits and losses: to build the "best" community
Decisions	Determining wage rates Determining tax rates and allocation of public revenues to public needs Deciding which improvements to approve
Purposes	The game is intended to acquaint students with the public sector of the economy It illustrates the basic problems of selecting and financing public services
Cost	$2.15 for teacher's guide $2.00 for six players, minimum order $10.00 must include teacher's guide
Producer	Didactic Systems, Inc. Box 457 Cranford, NJ 07016

The professional and other journals listed at the end of this chapter provide reviews and listings of recently produced simulation exercises. The quarterly journal *Simulation and Games* and *Simulation/Gaming/News* are particularly good sources for such information.

SUMMARY

Already in use for administrative purposes in many colleges and school systems, computers have many instructional applications as well. Experiments with computerized instruction indicate that (1) learning does take place, frequently more rapidly than when conventional teaching methods are used, and (2) individualized instruction is greatly facilitated. Computers are used in instruction principally for drills, tutorial work and dialogues with students, simulation and gaming, and help in handling information.

The primary attributes of computers are their capacity to record and process huge amounts of information and to perform complex mathematical computations with great speed and accuracy. These attributes make individualized instruction feasible in a variety of forms and free the teacher from substantial amounts of record keeping and processing. *Any* use of computers requires careful programming, in itself probably an educational dividend.

The heavy costs of computers are most often

cited as barriers to their use for instructional purposes, but there are signs that substantial reductions in costs are close at hand. Inappropriate applications of computers are a more fundamental problem from an instructional standpoint. Some educators also fear that computers may inject inhuman qualities into education.

Simulations and games first came into prominence in education in the early 1960s. They entail role-playing in a variety of contexts. They appear to increase student motivation and participation, to encourage social interaction and cooperation among students, to be suitable for wide ranges of age and achievement levels, and to add realism and relevance to learning experiences. Like computers, games can be overused or misused. They may require careful planning and monitoring to be effective. Some games also take considerable time. The potential benefits of simulation and games, however, justify their careful consideration by teachers interested in improving the quality and relevance of instruction.

ACTIVITIES

1. Given a set of six program printouts or descriptions, state what kind of programs they are and why.
2. From a list of 15 statements supplied by your instructor, select 4 that correctly describe advantages of computers, 4 that correctly describe disadvantages, and 4 that are inaccurate or inadequate statements of either strengths or limitations of computerized instruction.
3. Working with a small group of fellow students, investigate and do a report for the class on how computers are used to advantage in handling one of the six pairs of administrative functions that follow: (a) payroll and personnel, (b) purchasing and inventory, (c) budgeting and budget control, (d) student admissions and record keeping, (e) class and classroom scheduling, and (f) program planning and evaluation. Try to visit a computer installation and talk to administrative personnel in the course of your research.
4. Prepare a one-page summary of "probable future computer applications in instruction" and "implications for changes in teachers' roles" given the following assumptions: (a) Computer costs will come down to about the present per-pupil costs of instruction. (b) Available dollars per pupil will increase slowly, if at all. (c) The emphasis on individualized instruction will increase. (d) Public pressure on schools and colleges will continue undiminished. (e) Validated CAI programs will increase in number and quality.
5. Obtain a list of 10 or more learning activities from your instructor; classify each according to appropriateness as specified in Objective 5 and supply justification for your selections. Use a format of three columns headed: "Activity," "Preferable medium," "Reason."
6. Using the definitions and examples in the chapter, describe two or more different kinds of simulation and two or more different kinds of games. Identify and list topics for which each might be of significant value.

REFERENCES

PRINT REFERENCES

Abt, Clark C., *Serious Games* (New York: Viking Press, 1970).

Ahl, David, and James Bailey, "Computers Are for Kids—Not for Geniuses," *School Management* (April 1971), p. 26.

Atkinson, R. C., and H. A. Wilson, *Computer-Assisted Instruction: A Book of Readings* (New York: Academic Press, 1970).

Bacon, W. M., Jr., and M. G. Newkirk, "Uses of Simulation in Teaching History," *Contemporary Education* (Fall 1974), pp. 38–41.

Boocock, Sarane S., and E. O. Schild, eds. *Simula-*

tion Games in Learning (Beverly Hills, Calif.: Sage, 1968).

Campbell, G. M., and L. C. Jansson, "Computer Costs and Capabilities for Instruction and Administration," *NASSP Bulletin* (March 1974), pp. 54–63.

Commission on Instructional Technology. *To Improve Learning: A Report to the President and the Congress of the United States* (Washington, D.C.: U.S. Government Printing Office, 1970).

Crawford, Jack, and Paul A. Twelker, "Affect Through Simulation: The Gamesman Technologist," in *Contributions of Behavioral Science to Instructional Technology, 1, The Affective Domain* (Washington, D.C.: Gryphon House, 1970).

Cruickshank, Donald E., "Notions of Simulations and Games: a Preliminary Inquiry," *Educational Technology* (July 1972), pp. 17–19.

Edwards, Keith J., *The Effect of Ability, Achievement, and Number of Plays on Learning from a Simulation Game* (Johns Hopkins University, 1971). ERIC: Ed 055 309.

Elliott, Paul H., "Computers in Education: Relevance for Occupational Education," *Audiovisual Instruction* (April 1973), pp. 7–13.

Fletcher J. D., P. Suppes and D. T. Jamison, *A Note on the Effectiveness of Computer-Assisted Instruction* (Stanford, Calif.: Stanford University Institute for Mathematical Studies in the Social Sciences, 1972). ERIC: 071 450.

Gilliam, E. M., "Trends in Simulation," *High School Journal* (April 1974), pp. 265–272. Also *Education Digest* (September 1974), pp. 57–59.

Gustafson, Kent L. "Simulation of Interpersonal Relations." *Audiovisual Instruction,* January 1971, pp. 35–37.

Hall, K. A., and others, "Triumph for CAI: Pennsylvania State University," *Phi Delta Kappan* (September 1974), pp. 70–72.

Heines, Jesse M. "Everything You Always Wanted to Know About Computers . . . You Can Teach Yourself," *Educational Technology* (May 1975), pp. 47–50.

Hoffstetter, Fred T., "Music Dream Machines: New Realities for Computer-Based Musical Instruction," *Creative Computing* (March/April 1977), pp. 50–54.

Holloway, W. H., "Improved School Management and Planning: the Promise of Computer Simulation," *Educational Technology* (March 1974), pp. 33–36.

Horn, Robert E. (ed.), *The Guide to Simulations/Games, Third Edition* (Cranford, N.J.: Didactic Systems, 1978.)

Inbar, Michael, and Clarice S. Stoll, *Simulation and Gaming in Social Science* (New York: Free Press, 1972).

Kagan, Norman, "Can Technology Help Us Toward Reliability in Influencing Human Interaction?" *Educational Technology* (February 1973), p. 44.

Kagan, Norman, et al. *Studies in Human Interaction,* Michigan State University, 1967.

Kiser, Michael and Larry Stuart, "Putting Games into English and English into Games," *Media and Methods* (April 1974), pp. 26–29.

Kleiman, C., "Plato Is Alive and Well and Teaching in Chicago," *College Management* (November 1973), pp. 28–30.

Layman's Guide to the Use of Computers, Association for Educational Data Systems, N.E.A., 1971.

Lekan, Helen M., *Index to Computer-Assisted Instruction,* 3rd ed. (New York: Harcourt Brace Jovanovich, 1972). Information on programs in 70 subjects, cross-referenced by subject; central processor, computer language, instructional logic, and source.

Lien, R. L., "Appropriate Use of the Computer for Instructional Purposes," *Educational Technology* (December 1974), pp. 35–39.

Magidson, Errol M., "One More Time: CAI is Not Dehumanizing," *Audiovisual Instruction* (October 1977), pp. 20–21.

Margolin, Joseph B., and Marion R. Misch, eds., *Computers in the Classroom: An Interdisciplinary View of Trends and Alternatives* (East Lansing, Mich.: Spartan Press, 1970).

Moldstad, John, ed., "CAI Current Approaches and Trends," *Viewpoints,* Bulletin of the School of Education, Indiana University (July 1974).

Oettinger, Anthony G., and Nikki Zapol, "Will Information Technologies Help Learning?"

Teachers College Record (Fall 1972). See also Charles A. Wedemeyer, "Commentary on 'Will Information Technologies Help Learning?'" in *Educational Technology* (January 1973), pp. 89–91.

O'Grady, C., "Computers Cannot Take Over; Two Years on By," Report by R. Hooper *Times Educational Supplement* (July 11, 1975).

Okey, James R. and Kenneth Majer, "Individual and Small-Group Learning with Computer-Assisted Instruction," *AV Communication Review* (Spring 1976), pp. 79–89.

Raser, John R., *Simulation and Society: An Exploration of Scientific Gaming* (Boston: Allyn and Bacon, 1969).

Silberman, Henry F., and Robert T. Filep, "Information Systems Applications in Education," in *Annual Review of Information Science and Technology,* vol. III (Chicago, Ill.: Encyclopaedia Britannica, 1968), pp. 357–395.

Silvern, Leonard C., *Systems Engineering of Education VI: Principles of Computer-Assisted Instruction Systems* (Los Angeles, Calif.: Education and Training Consultants Company, 1970).

Simulation and Games (pub. quarterly) by Sage Publications, 275 South Beverly Drive, Beverly Hills, CA 90212.

Simulation/Gaming/News (six issues during the school year, $6 per year), Box 8039, University Station, Moscow, ID 83843.

Stadsklev, Ron, *Simulation Gaming in Social Education* (University, Ala.: Institute of Higher Education Research and Services).

Stolurow, Lawrence M. "Computer-Assisted Instruction," *The Schools and the Challenge of Innovation,* H. T. James, ed. (Washington, D.C.: The Commission for Educational Development, 1969), pp. 270–319.

Strategy and Tactics (pub. bimonthly) by Simulations Publications, Inc., 44 East 23rd Street, New York, NY 10010.

Suppes, Patrick, and B. Albracht, "Computer Confrontation," *Saturday Review of Education* (May 1973), pp. 48–49.

Suppes, Patrick, *Computer-Assisted Instruction at Stanford 1966–68:* data, models, and evaluation of the arithmetic programs by Patrick Suppes and Mona Morningstar and others. (New York: Academic Press, 1972).

Tansey, P. J., and Derick Unwin, *Simulation and Gaming in Education* (New York: Barnes and Noble, 1969).

———, and L. Waters, "Simulation, a Useful and Flexible Tool," *Times Educational Supplement* (July 21, 1972), p. 2983.

Tickton, Sidney G., ed., *To Improve Learning, An Evaluation of Instructional Technology,* vol. I (New York: Bowker, 1970).

———, *To Improve Learning, An Evaluation of Instructional Technology,* vol. II (New York: Bowker, 1971).

Twelker, Paul A., ed., *Instructional Simulation: A Research Development and Dissemination Activity* (Monmouth, Ore.: Teaching Research, 1969).

———, and Kent Layden, *Educational Simulation/Gaming* (ERIC/IR at Syracuse, Syracuse, NY, 1972).

Varenhorst, Barbara B., "Game Theory, Simulations and Group Counselling," *Educational Technology* (February 1973), pp. 40–43.

WFF'N PROOF Newsletter (quarterly on games, $1 per year), 1111 Maple Ave., Turtle Creek, PA 15145.

Zinn, Karl L., *An Evaluative Review of Uses of Computers in Instruction.* Project CLUE, Final Report, USOE Contract No. OEC–5–9–32–509–0032 (Ann Arbor: University of Michigan Press, 1970).

MEDIA REFERENCES

Apollo Reentry Simulation, 16mm film, color, 11 min. NASA.

CAI, 16mm film, color, 17 min. RCA.

Class of '01: The College of Tomorrow, 16mm film, color, 25 min. McGraw-Hill.

Computer Glossary, 16mm film, color, 10 min. EBF.

Computer Glossary, 16mm film, color, 11 min. Eames, 901 Washington Blvd., Venice, CA 90291.

Computer in the Classroom, 16mm film, b/w, 13 min. Rand Corporation.

Computers and the Mind of Men: Managers and Models, 16mm film, b/w, 30 min. NET.

Flight Simulation, 16mm film, color, 20 min. IBM.

Gemini Mission Simulator, 16mm film, color, 9 min. NASA.

Kagan Stimulus Film, I & II, 16mm film, b/w, 56 min. Michigan State University.

Living Machine, 16mm film, b/w, 57 min. NFBC.

Palo Alto Unified School District CAI Programs, slide/tape cassette, 130 slides, 25 min. Palo Alto, CA.

The Process of Communication, 16mm film, b/w, 45 min. Ohio State University.

Sign On/Sign Off, 16mm film, color, 24 min. Pennsylvania State University.

Understanding Computers, color, ¾″ videotape, 10 min. Time-Life.

SOURCE REFERENCES

Computers and Programs

Centurion Industries, Redwood City, CA 94063.

Computing Newsletter for Schools of Business, Cragnor Rd., Colorado Springs, CO 80907.

Control Data Corporation, 8100 34th Ave., South Minneapolis, MN 55420.

Cybernetic Systems, 9615 Acoma S.E., Albuquerque, NM 87123.

Digital Equipment Corporation, 146 Main St., Maynard, MA 01754.

Fed Software Library, Mail Station K–16, Honeywell Information Systems, P.O. Box 6000, Phoenix, AR 85005.

Hewlett-Packard, Inc., 11000 Wolfe Rd., Cupertino, CA 95014.

Honeywell Information Systems, 200 Smith St., Waltham, MA 02154.

IBM, Thomas J. Watson Research Center, P.O. Box 218, Yorktown Heights, NY 10598. (Or call nearest IBM branch office.)

Kentron International, 233 Keawe St., Honolulu, HI 96813.

People's Computer Company, P.O. Box 310, Menlo Park, CA 94025. (Free newsletter.)

Remington Rand, 1290 Ave. of the Americas, New York, NY 10019.

Sperry Univac, P.O. Box 508, Blue Bell, PA 19422.

Wang Laboratories, 836 North St., Tewksbury, MA 01876.

Simulations and Games

A comprehensive bibliography including simulation games was published in the February 1969 issue of *Social Education.*

Abt Associates, Games Control, 55 Wheeler St., Cambridge, MA 02138.

Academic Games Associates, 430 East 33rd St., Baltimore, MD 21218 ("Consumer," "Democracy," "Economic System," "Life Career," and "The Ghetto Game").

American Management Association, 135 West 50th St., New York, NY 10020.

Bobbs-Merrill Co., 4300 West 62nd, Indianapolis, IN 46268.

Bureau of Business Research, The University of Texas at Austin, Austin, TX 78712.

Burroughs Corporation, Burroughs Place, Detroit, MI 48232.

E. M. Babb and L. M. Eisgruber, Dept. of Agri. Econ., Purdue University, Lafayette, IN 47907.

Games Central, 55H Wheeler St., Cambridge, MA 02138.

Handbook of Simulation Gaming in Social Education, Institute of Higher Education Research University, AL 35486.

Indiana University School of Business, Bloomington, IN 47401.

Instructional Simulations, 2147 University Ave., St. Paul, MN 55114.

Interact, P.O. Box 262, Lakeside, CA 92040. (Extensive cultural, political, and economic listings for secondary and upper-elementary social studies and history.)

John Wiley & Sons, 605 Third Ave., New York, NY 10016.

Macmillan Library Services, 866 3rd Ave., New York, NY 10022.

Milton Bradley Company, Educational Division, Springfield, MA 01101.

"Poppin' Swap Nutrition Game," The Pillsbury Company, Minneapolis, MN 55402.

Proctor and Gamble Company, Educational Services Dept., P.O. Box 599, Cincinnati, OH 45201.

Project CONLEX, Lincoln P. Bloomfield, M.I.T., Cambridge, MA 02139.

Rand Corporation, 1700 Main St., Santa Monica, CA 90401.

Remington Rand UNIVAC, 1290 Ave. of the Americas, New York, NY 10019.

Science Research Associates, 529 East Erie St., Chicago, IL 60611. (Economic decision games and inter-nation simulations).

Scott, Foresman & Co., 1900 E. Lake Ave., Glenview, IL 60025.

SIMILE, 218 Twelfth St., P.O. Box 910, Del Mar, CA 92014.

Simulation and Computer Directorate, ICAF, Fort McNair, Washington, DC 20315.

Simulations Publications, 44 E. 23rd St., New York, NY 10010.

Sloan School of Management, M.I.T., Cambridge, MA 02138.

University of California Institute of Urban and Regional Development, Berkeley, CA 94720.

Western Management Science Institute, UCLA, Los Angeles, CA 90024.

11 Multimedia Instructional Development

Objectives

To enable you to do the following:

1. Give examples of instructional development at the national and state level and identify at least six steps in the process that parallel those in the instructional development plan described in Chapter 1.
2. Give three examples of instructional development at the teacher level and identify at least six steps in the process that parallel those in the instructional development plan you have been evolving.
3. Evaluate your own instructional plan by comparing it with other plans, particularly in regard to alternative learning materials and strategies and learner responses.
4. Explain why a knowledge of the wide variety of learning media available today, and their uses, is important for teachers at all levels.

The value of audiovisual learning resources and equipment in education has been fully demonstrated. Teachers who use audiovisual learning experiences in day-to-day instruction are now the rule rather than the exception. Companies that once concentrated solely on the production of print learning materials now create a wide variety of related media to suit the individual learning style of students.

Audiovisual equipment has been improved. It is more durable and easier to operate. Much of it has been simplified and miniaturized. As a result, students can use tape recorders, overhead projectors, 8mm cameras and projectors, lightweight videotape equipment, slide projectors, and the like, to respond to instruction as well as to learn.

Now that we have examined the wide variety of learning resources that can become useful components of an instructional development plan, the time has come to study several actual plans. Seeing how others are using the instructional development approach will help you "put it all together" to achieve your own teaching goals.

Multimedia learning strategies have moved out of the experimental stage into the realm of practical application. The national and state-level programs described below are highly sophisticated applications of the instructional development approach that exceed what any individual teacher can hope to accomplish. The systems strategy on which they are based, however, is very similar to the simplified instructional development plan suggested in Chapter 1. The approach is the same, but on a smaller scale.

INSTRUCTIONAL PLANNING AT THE NATIONAL LEVEL

In 1973 the National Endowment for the Humanities appointed representatives of education, business, and labor to work with the American Revolution Bicentennial Administration in developing a multimedia program to alert schoolchildren, young people, and adults to the state of the nation on its 200th birthday and to create a national dialogue about the fundamental issues confronting the country in 1976. The group developed a calendar of nine topics to be presented in 1975 and 1976. Each topic would be a focus of discussion for a one-month period. It was hoped that the program as a whole would encourage all Americans, adults and children, to explore where the country is, how it got there, and where it is headed.

The plan was introduced to the public in 1974, and the task of creating the materials for the program was assigned to film producers, publishers, and other media experts. Copies of the calendar were distributed to educational, business, and labor organizations. They also appeared as pull-out inserts in national magazines and in spot announcements on television and radio.

Our primary concern, of course, is with what happened in the nation's schools as a result of the program.

The task of preparing and announcing lists of books, films, records, and related learning materials was undertaken by the American Library Association. In addition to special bicentennial radio and television broadcasts, TV documentaries on each of the nine topics were produced by WNET (New York City's Channel 13), a public broadcasting station.

The series, called *Ourstory,* was originally aired over the nation's 250-plus public television stations, but local school districts could secure film or videotape copies for classroom use.[1] Each of the programs in the series is a drama based on actual events in the lives of historically important Americans. Three of the nine programs are described briefly below.

"The Peach Gang" depicts the conflict between Indian and white concepts of justice in the case of Arthur Peach, an 18-year-old indentured servant tried in 1638 for the murder of a Narragansett Indian. As in all the programs in the series, the drama is left unresolved, to encourage viewers to discuss the issues. All the programs have study guides that contain prebroadcast questions and activities and suggestions for follow-up activities. (See Figure 11.1.)

"Eliza" deals with the struggles of a 16-year-old girl whose soldier father gives her the responsibility of managing their 2000-acre plantation while he goes about his military duties. The issue raised in the program is the use and abuse of land.

"The World Turned Upside Down" focuses on a slave's attempt to win his freedom by serving as a spy for the colonists during the American Revolution.

An alternative or corollary radio series, the *American Issues Radio Forum,* also dealt with the calendar of topics drawn up by the bicentennial committee. Documentaries on the issues were presented, and noted scholars in the humanities answered telephone questions of listeners. Broadcast schedules were sent to schools well in advance so that the programs could be incorporated into lesson plans or arrangements could be made to tape-record them for later use.

[1] Because almost all such bicentennial materials were produced with government funds, they are in the public domain and can be obtained by applying to the producing agency or to the National Endowment for the Humanities.

Other materials were also produced and offered, usually without charge, to interested teachers. Weekly articles on the issues were prepared and printed in local newspapers across the country. Related television specials were produced and aired, and a national schedule of school debates was set up. Talking books were prepared and distributed to the blind. The variety of media that can be used to reach individual segments of a wide national audience is almost endless. But what is unique here is the manner in which the bicentennial planners systematically set about arriving at a consensus with respect to the objectives to be met, the communication channels to be used, and the various strategies to be employed to get a meaningful response from millions of Americans. Such a large-scale illustration of the effective use of interrelated media lends validity to the use of comparable techniques in education.

INSTRUCTIONAL PLANNING AT THE STATE LEVEL: THE HAWAIIAN ENGLISH PROJECT

Many state school authorities have undertaken the development of comprehensive curriculum plans based on the use of a wide variety of interrelated learning media. Generally, the goal is to provide alternative learning experiences for students of varying interests, backgrounds, and competence. The Hawaiian English Project, one among 1500 programs funded, was rated significant and effective by the U.S. Office of Education and was one of 12 to receive the Right to Read Award for excellence in helping learners improve their reading skills; it exemplifies the spirit of systematic instructional development and the intelligent use of interrelated media.[2]

[2] For a summary of the three major areas of the program, its specific objectives, and the multimedia learning materials used, apply to Mrs. Grace Fujita, English Project Staff Coordinator, Hawaii Curriculum Project, 1750 Wist Place, Honolulu, Hawaii 96822.

(a)

(b)

(c)

(d)

The Hawaii English Program involves hundreds of teachers, school administrators, supervisors, and parents. It is an optional program, in which more than 60 percent of the state's elementary school children participate.

It focuses on language skills (listening, speaking, reading, writing, and typing), language systems, and literature. The language skills program is in widespread use in grades K–6. The program has now been developed and extended through grades 7 and 8 as a total English program that includes literature, language studies, communication, and the like. Ninety percent of Hawaii Junior High School's English teachers opted independently to use the program materials and suggested teaching strategies when the program was installed in 1978–79.

Objectives of the Language Skills Program

The goals of the language skills program are the result of eight years of analyzing student needs. The overall goal is to help students gain progressively greater control over the way they use language, including reading, speaking, writing, and listening.

Sequences of independent learning experiences lead each child to progress step by step from his or her initial level of competence toward higher levels. Each higher level is an intermediate goal that brings the child closer to the program's terminal goals.

The program's specific objectives include, for example, (1) learning to distinguish between the basic sounds of the English language in reading and speaking, (2) learning to write cursive letters clearly and legibly, (3) developing an interest in learning to read, (4) learning to read, (5) developing an interest in reading widely and comprehensively, (6) learning to listen attentively to sounds and words and to respond correctly to them. Many other subskills are also defined as objectives.

In general, all the specific objectives of the language skills program fit into two basic categories: listening and reading skills and oral and writing skills. The learning materials used by students to attain these overall objectives reflect the various specific objectives of the programs. However, as they are used in the classroom, they are closely interrelated and thus become part of a *total* learning experience.

Materials and Strategies

Curriculum materials. A variety of means are used to convey information about language skills to learners. These materials can be classified according to their nature and the sense primarily employed by learners in responding

Figure 11.1 Television is one of several interrelated channels used by the National Endowment for the Humanities and the American Revolution Bicentennial Administration to celebrate the bicentennial. A series of nine television programs designed for use by the nation's students and other interested groups were produced and are available on 16mm sound films or videotapes. (*a*) In the program "The Peach Gang," Indian and white men's ideas of justice conflict as a Narragansett chief, Canonicus (*b*), confronts a white indentured servant with charges of murdering a member of his tribe. (*c*) In "Eliza," the daughter of Lucas Pinckney meets numerous obstacles as she tries to run her father's plantation in his absence. (*d*) In "The World Turned Upside Down," three officers contemplate the consequences of allowing a runaway slave to serve as an American spy in return for a promise of freedom. Study guides and bibliographies were provided for all the programs in the *Ourstory* series. In addition, radio forums gave listeners a chance to discuss the issues raised with a panel of experts. What are your reactions to such an interrelated use of media?

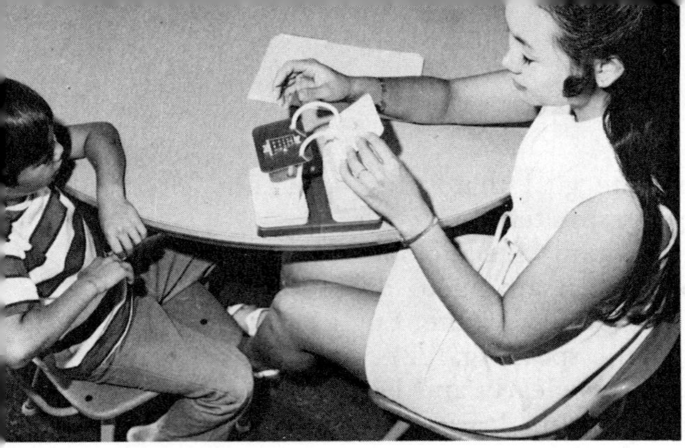

(a)

(c)

(b)

Figure 11.2 (*a*) A teacher and pupil work with a stack of picture-word cards. (*b* and *c*) An audio card reader is used to identify letter sounds. (*d*) This equipment gives pupils visual cues on continuous-loop 8mm film. (*e* and *f*) Tape-recorded books provide an audiovisual learning experience. (*g*) By following cues in the diagrams, children learn typing skills. (*h*) Children learn the alphabet by feeling flocked letters. (*i*) Records sing to children and ask them to sing back. (*j*) Games help develop manipulative and visual skills. What role does the teacher play when such materials are discussed? Could any one teacher hope to arrange such varied and essential self-tutorial or peer-assisted learning experiences working alone with the limited resources of the traditional classroom?

(d)

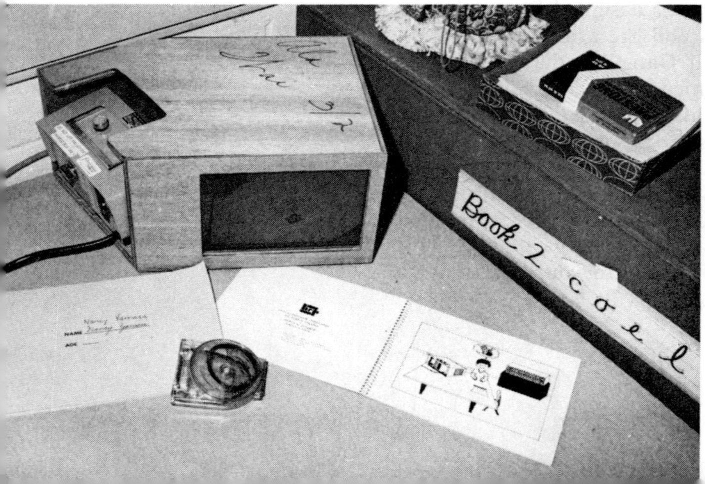

(e)

(*f*)

(*g*)

(*h*)

(*i*)

(*j*)

to them as audio, visual, or tactile. (See Figure 11.2.) They include:

Picture-word cards. A series of punched cards stacked on rods attached to a base. They can be used by two or more children or a teacher and child working together. They are primarily visual materials.

Audio card readers. Audio card readers record and/or play back sounds. They provide primarily audio, but also visual, learning experiences.

Films. Continuous-loop 8mm silent motion picture cartridges are used.

Books. Although basically visual materials, books can provide an audiovisual learning experience when they are used with audiotape of the story.

Typewriters. Typewriters provide primarily visual but also tactile learning experiences.

Paper and/or pencils. These provide primarily visual learning experiences.

Flocked cards. Cards with textured or raised letters or numerals provide a tactile and visual learning experience.

Tape recorders. Tape recorders are sources of audio learning experiences and are also used for audio response to instruction.

Phonographs and records. These are sources of audio learning experiences.

Games. Games such as listening games are used for task-oriented or competitive activities or self-evaluation.

Most of the materials for the program are packaged in individual containers that can be easily handled and stored. There are a great many items in the total package, but the problem of keeping track of them is reduced considerably by giving students the responsibility for putting them away in the proper place after they have been used. Housekeeping skills of this sort are specifically taught.

A detailed teachers' manual for the program discusses (1) its conceptual framework, (2) the learning environment needed, (3) the various subprograms, (4) learner goals, (5) entry and exit behaviors, (6) the learning procedure, (7) additional steps to be taken, and (8) record keeping. All the materials used have been intensively tested and revised as weaknesses have come to light.

Teaching strategies. The Hawaii Language Skills Program is distinctive in that it provides *differentiated* learning opportunities and encourages children to assume greater responsibility for learning. Not surprisingly, these distinctive aspects of the program produced some problems when it was first introduced. When teachers who are accustomed primarily to teaching large groups first face the responsibility of providing differentiated learning experiences for children who are also accustomed primarily to large-group teaching, dilemmas are likely to arise. These transitional problems were dealt with in Hawaii in teacher-training sessions held during the school year and in the summer. At these sessions, teachers observed and practiced ways of arranging learning experiences for individuals and small groups. As a result, they were able to follow the program with confidence and enthusiasm—feelings that "rub off" on children.

Peer teaching is very helpful in encouraging children to assume responsibility for learning. Once they have mastered a skill or technique, children can get a feeling of purpose, and fulfillment from teaching it to others. In other words, both the child who is taught and the one who does the teaching gain from such a system. Helping another to learn gives a child a chance to review what he or she knows in a gamelike situation with an adult purpose. Moreover, children welcome peer instruction as a contrast to carrel-based instruction. Carrels should not be overused; too much carrel-based teaching often has a dampening effect. Some children become bored when they must spend long periods of time by themselves. They miss the human interaction that occurs when they learn from or with others.

The language skills program is organized so that activities for the whole class are interspersed with activities for small groups or individuals. Each three-week unit usually begins with a large-group discussion, with the teacher introducing questions that bring out what is to be learned. How things are to be learned is then discussed. During these planning periods, students listen, ask questions, and select the individualized learning materials they wish to work with. While activities chosen by the children are in progress the teacher provides help and encouragement to those who need it and evaluates the children's work. *Performance* becomes the key criterion in an environment that rewards productive behavior.

Usually, groups are reformed when questions arise that the teacher feels would be of interest to many children when individuals have developed skills that are worthy of being shared with the group. Thus large groups observe small groups and individuals exhibit their accomplishments in reading, singing, typing and handwriting, telling original stories, or dramatizing audiotaped book stories.

Evaluating the Program

The language skills program was evaluated on the basis of the performance of randomly selected students from various grades and schools. The tests used were selected on the basis of objectivity, realiability, and suitability, as well as their cost in terms of time. Variables such as attitudes toward the program were also considered and reported.

Overall, the program appears to have worked phenomenally well during the test period. Of the students polled, 86 percent reported that they liked their lessons and 36 percent said they liked them *very much*. Not everyone liked the same subjects best; 34 percent of the children reported that they liked reading best, 12 percent liked writing, and 6 percent liked listening. Typing was the most popular skill with 45 percent of the children. Some 55 percent of the students reported that they chose their classroom activities themselves, 82 percent of the students reported that they liked to tutor, and 79 percent reported received tutoring.

The numbers of books read by students in the program was used as a measure of reading activity. Over a three-month period, third-graders read an average of 51 books each, second-graders read 10 books each, and kindergartners and first graders read 1 book each. The overall average was 10 books read per pupil, with a range from 0 to 114. A control group of third-grade students not in the program read an average of 8 books each during the test period; a control group of second-graders read 2 books each; and control groups of first-graders and kindergartners read 1 or less than 1 book each. The overall average for the control groups was 2 books read per pupil, with a range from 0 to 30. The books read by both groups were generally comparable; most contained 30 to 100 pages.

In addition, word recognition and comprehension were measured by two standardized tests and three objective tests. Spelling, punctuation and capitalization, and writing skills were measured using three objective tests. *In every case, on every test, the performance of students in the program was superior to that of other students.*[3]

[3] *1973–1974 Evaluation of the Hawaiian English Program*, Elementary School Level, Hawaii Curriculum Project, 1750 Wist Place, Honolulu, Hawaii.

The English Literature and Language Systems Programs

These segments of the Hawaii English Project are in operation through grades 11 and 12. The English literature program was developed in much the same way as the language skills program. It consists of 37 nonsequential, nongraded instructional units that focus on five areas of learner experiences—the world around us, make believe, the social order, adventures, and growing up. All involve the use of alternative media and rely heavily on games and simulations in which the learners take the initiative.

The language systems program is based on learner interaction with 15 self-contained, nongraded, non sequential units on animal and human communication systems. Each unit may take from four to six weeks to complete. Because these units are unique, at least one of the series should be described.

The writing systems unit leads students to compare various kinds of writing systems, particularly those found in the Pacific Basin. Activities such as typesetting, making clay tablets, brush writing, and identifying foreign coins lead students to discover that some systems are based on "words" (ideographic systems such as Egyptian hieroglyphics and Chinese), some on syllables (such as the Japanese Kana), and some on individual sounds (alphabetic systems such as ours). Students also match the major writing systems of the world with the countries that use them. The materials for this unit are packaged in a single *unit-resource box*. They include 35 student activity books and handbooks, 3 card games, 2 filmstrips, 1 film loop, 2 audiocassettes, 9 library research books, 1 foreign coin collection, 7 outline maps of the world, clay, a metal file to be used as a stylus, colored pencils, calligraphy brushes, calligraphers' ink, painting sets, rollers, currency converters, tracing paper, newsprint, blotting paper, and a teacher's manual outlining performance objectives, activities, and hoped-for outcomes. (See Figure 11.3.)

Schools across the nation are doing similar kinds of systematic planning for curriculum development. The basic methods are somewhat more sophisticated than those introduced in Chapter 1, but the principle is the same. An example of the work of one consortium is given below for those of you who may one day wish to assume a leadership role in systems planning in your own school district.

A NINE-STEP INSTRUCTIONAL DEVELOPMENT SYSTEM

Experience has shown that those who undertake instructional development fare best when they follow a procedure that has been tested in actual school situations. The procedure described below has been developed, tested, and refined by a consortium of five universities with strong programs in instructional development and technology.[4] It is the result of a team effort by teachers, administrators, and specialists in various areas. Although the nine steps in the procedure are set forth here in a linear fashion, it should be thought of as a process that can be begun, or entered, at any appropriate point. (See Figure 11.4.)

Stage 1: The Definition Stage

Step 1. Identify the problem. This beginning step is of critical importance in a systems approach. It involves assessment of needs not only in terms of what is perceived to be the status quo and what the ideal situation may be, but also in terms of the underlying causes of the

[4] Indiana University, Michigan State University, Syracuse University, the University of Southern California, and the U.S. International University comprise the University Consortium for Instructional Development and Technology (UCIDT). Initial versions of the Instructional Development Institutes were produced and widely used under grants from the U.S. Office of Education. A new modular IDI is available from UCIDT.

(*a*)

(*b*)

Figure 11.3 (*a*) These interrelated learning materials are all included in one of 15 language systems learning packages for the Hawaii English Próject. They may be used by individuals or small groups of students who wish to learn how one or more language systems evolved. (*b*) This student has elected to investigate Chinese calligraphy. Others in her class have chosen to investigate Indian, Egyptian, and Arabic writing. What kind of órganization, planning, and research is responsible for these materials?

problem. Causes that can be rectified must be identified, and their relative importance or priority must be determined. Defining the problem may require considerable time, because it almost invariably necessitates gathering substantial amounts of information.

Step 2. Analyze the setting. Analyzing the setting of the problem means identifying the human and functional factors involved in any significant change in the existing system. If a new approach is to succeed, it must be supported by those people in a school or school system who serve as decision makers, opinion leaders, and agents of change. It is important to be aware of how they react to new ideas and whether they deal with problems in a creative, a defensive, or an emotional manner. It is important to know what kind of learners you are dealing with and what resources exist in the

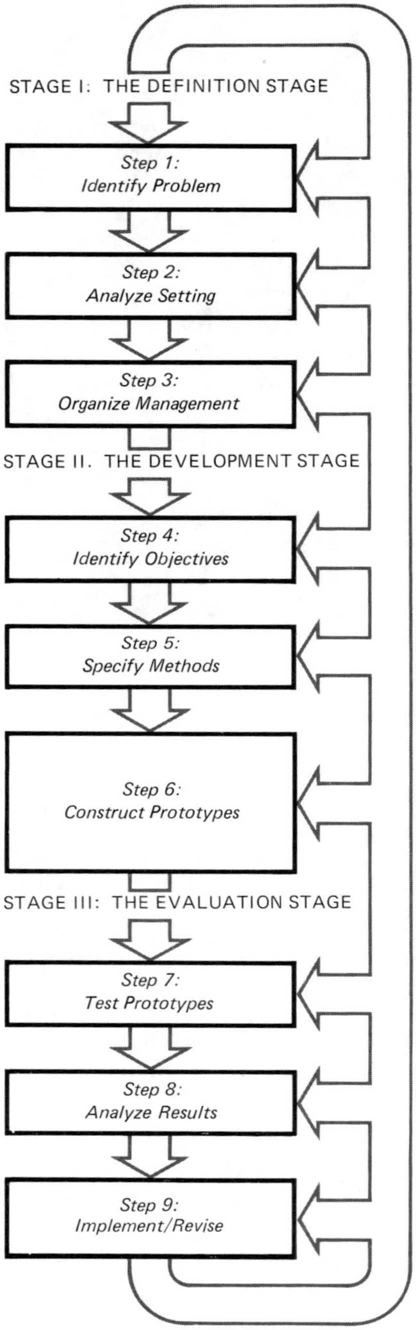

a. Compare status quo to ideal situation.
b. Propose tentative solution.

c. Determine learner characteristics.
d. Inventory school/community resources.

e. Assign responsibilities.
f. Establish lines of communication.
g. Specify planning and control procedures.

h. State terminal performance objectives.
i. State enabling objectives and determine relationships between objectives.
j. Construct performance measures.

k. Specify instructional strategies and media.
l. Specify alternative methods.

m. Prepare a comprehensive description of the instructional design.
n. Specify how instructional design will be evaluated.
o. Review the instructional design and evaluation procedures.
p. Specify procedures for collection and development of instructional materials.
q. Construct and assemble instructional materials.
r. Specify procedures to be used by personnel in trying out instructional prototype.

s. Determine ways of testing materials and strategies.
t. Carry out evaluation as planned.
u. Tabulate and process evaluation data.

v. Determine relationships among results, methods, and objectives.

w. Indicate what kinds of revisions (if any) are suggested by the results of full-scale testing.
x. Determine if the prototype instructional package must be reexamined or if it can be implemented without major revisions.

Figure 11.4 The process of instructional development outlined in the text has numerous substeps and decision points. Each of these entails rather precise tasks that must be done if the system is to function effectively.

school and the community to support a new approach.

Step 3. Organize the management of the program. Whenever people work together on a problem or program, controls must be established to ensure that assigned tasks are carried out, that expert assistance is available when needed, and that ideas, problems, and other developments are communicated to the right people as they occur. In order to ensure that tasks are completed by an agreed time, target dates for finishing each phase of a project must be set up. Typically, the ultimate completion date is established first, and then the dates when other tasks must be accomplished if the final date is to be met.

In short, when a group or team is working on an instructional development problem, the following management considerations are important.

a. Who is given the responsibility *and the authority* to accomplish each task.
b. What instructional alternatives are to be considered and what personnel and material resources can be used to put these into practice.
c. In what sequence objectives are to be met and by what deadlines.

Stage 2: The Development Stage

Step 4. Identify the objectives. Objectives must be spelled out in terms that make it possible to determine rationally whether they have been met. Two kinds of objectives, in particular, are important: *terminal performance objectives* (TOs) and *enabling objectives* (*EOs*), necessary to the attainment of the terminal objectives. Terminal objectives must be spelled out first and then enabling objectives; finally, *performance measures* must be constructed so observers can ascertain definitely whether each objective has been achieved.

Step 5. Specify the methods to be used to accomplish objectives. Once objectives have been established, we reach the point of decision —the point when we must determine which methods and materials to use to attain objectives. The range of instructional methods and materials is extensive, but not unlimited; we have to face up to what is practical in terms of available resources, personnel, equipment, and facilities. Frequently, trade-offs must be made. For example, it might be desirable to introduce computers for individualized instruction, but if a computer system is not available or is out of reach financially, the best practical alternative must be determined. This is the stage at which initial decisions must be made about learning media, based on learners' specific needs. (See Figure 11.5.)

Step 6. Construct prototypes. Once the most effective learning experiences and materials for particular purposes—readings, tapes, films, or whatever—have been determined, prototype materials must be purchased or produced. Ways of evaluating these materials must also be developed.

Stage 3: The Evaluation Stage

Step 7. Test the prototypes. The instructional "package" created in Stage 2 should be tested with a representative group of students. Data should be collected on what works, what doesn't, and why. Probably some materials and instructional strategies will have to be revised before they are tested on a larger scale in Step 8.

Step 8. Analyze the results. A full-scale tryout of an instructional package may reveal the need for further adjustments in the instructional

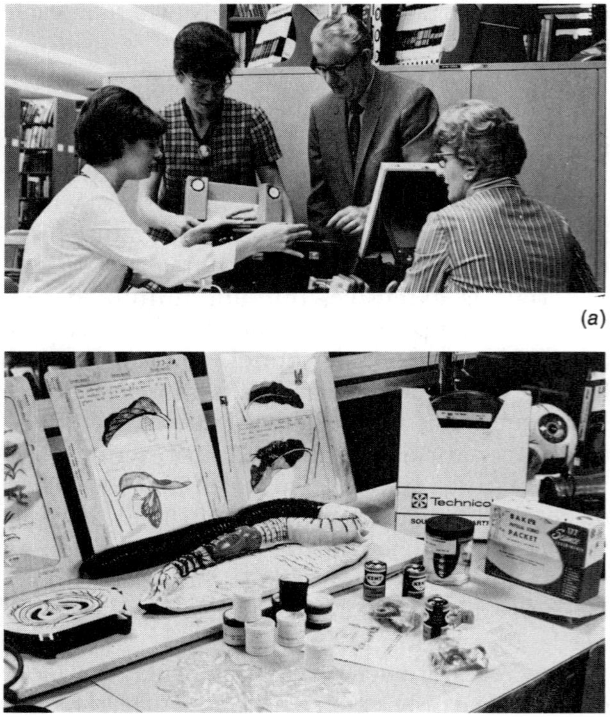

(a)

(b)

Figure 11.5 In instructional development the aim is to arrange appropriate learning experiences. Specific teaching methods and materials can be considered (*a*) in cooperative planning sessions attended by teachers and other members of the school staff. At the same time (*b*) prototype materials can be assessed.

design or in the materials used. It is important to ascertain how well enabling objectives are being met as well as whether terminal objectives have been achieved.

Step 9. Implement or revise the instructional package. The results of the full-scale tryout of methods and materials in Step 8 should be used to decide whether the new system is ready to be put into regular use. In any case, provisions should be made for continued evaluation and modification of the program.

INSTRUCTIONAL PLANNING AT THE TEACHER LEVEL

In the following paragraphs, examples will be given of how classroom teachers, working alone or with one or two other teachers, have pursued the kind of instructional development plan described in Chapter 1.

Example 1: A Voter Education Course for High School Students

With the passage of the Twenty-sixth Amendment in 1971, several million young people between the ages of 18 and 21 received the right to vote. Yet only about 30 percent of this group exercised their right to register, and less than that percentage voted. Many teachers felt that the problem was caused by something that was lacking in the social studies courses offered in high schools. The two teachers, Rhoda Miller and Lily Hatanaka, who planned the course in voter education described here felt that what was needed was a systematic review of the needs of students of voting age and the development of a variety of interesting and meaningful learning experiences to meet these needs.

The basic question was, "What is it that must be taught if the outcome is to be increased interest in the qualifications of candidates for political office and the responsibilities of voters?" In answering this question, the teachers arrived at a slightly expanded statement of objectives. They decided to continue the emphasis on cognitive information. Young voters must be well informed about political processes, political offices, and the responsibilities of officeholders at various levels of government. But they decided also to find a way to make young people become actively involved in political processes in a realistic way.

To achieve cognitive objectives, they would continue to use textbooks, films, political cartoons and editorials, and so on. Deciding how to involve learners (at least those who showed interest in such activities) in the political life and issues of the local community was much more of a challenge.

The teachers first updated and evaluated materials they had used in the past. Those that were of questionable value were discarded. The experiences of other school districts were studied, and voter education programs such as Project 18 and the League of Women Voters' voter education materials were analyzed for cues as to how greater interest in political affairs might be created.[5]

Anticipated learner responses included (in addition to passing tests of cognitive learning):

1. The successful completion of one or more investigative activities: an interview with the political reporter or analyst for a local newspaper, radio station, or television station; an interview with a local political officeholder or candidate; or perhaps a trip to the headquarters of a local political party.
2. A report to the class on one such activity, using visual or other materials.
3. Actual participation in a local election (if possible).

In addition, students would be encouraged to think up learning experiences related to the content of the course and the desired outcomes.

The most critical part of the planning phase for the two teachers was the surveying and evaluation of instructional experiences. Needless to say, this activity was time-consuming.

The following interrelated learning experiences were eventually selected:

1. *The opportunity to participate in the simulation CAMPAIGN.* Those who elect to participate must study and learn the rules of the simulation and accept and learn a role—that of a party worker, a campaign manager, a convention delegate, a convention manager, a media representative, a representative of special interests (labor, education, white-collar workers, business, agriculture, etc.), a pollster, a political analyst, and so on—and be prepared to express an appropriate point of view. On the basis of each participant's role, issues will be created, arguments set forth, and support given or denied as a simulated convention is held. A platform will be formulated, candidates will be nominated, and a political campaign will be conducted. The goal is to give students experience with political variables and the opportunity to evaluate their own and their classmates' behavior in a political situation.[6]

2. *A study of apathy using films and past voter-participation statistics.* For example, the film *Detached Americans* (16mm, sound, b/w, 33 min., Columbia Broadcasting System) was chosen to give students a chance to observe the actions of 39 witnesses to a murder (none stepped forward to testify) and to discuss why they behaved as they did. Students would be encouraged to make some generalizations about apathy in all walks of life.

The film *True Story of an Election* (sound, b/w, 27 min., Churchill Films) was chosen to give students a basis for understanding and appreciating the importance of involvement in the political process.

Films from the series *The Making of the President* (sound, b/w, 20–30 min., Films Incorporated) were chosen to give students an opportunity to discuss, in groups of four to five, the actions of the image makers referred to, to prepare statements attacking or justifying those actions, and to describe how what they have learned will affect their personal involvement in future political campaigns.

[5] *Project 18, Effectively Influencing Political Decisions,* U.S. Office of Education, Washington, D.C. (ERIC ED 071 938), 1972. For information on League of Women Voters' materials, contact your local branch office.

[6] *Campaign,* Instructional Simulations, Inc., 2147 University Ave., St. Paul, Minn. 55414.

3. *A study of the role of the news media,* using editorial cartoons projected on screens for viewing by large groups. Students would be encouraged to bring political cartoons from local newspapers and national magazines and to use them in creating displays on local issues and candidates.

As the semester continued, other topics were introduced and studied using various learning resources:

1. Two filmstrip sets on block voting were used during class and by individual students.
2. Audiocassettes on minority-group voting power were made available for individual study.
3. A videocassette on lobbying in the local legislature was made available by the school district television office.

Several groups of students became interested in exploring additional games placed in the library for use by small groups: *City Hall,* a political simulation in which participants attempt to get their candidate into the mayor's office (Ginn and Company) and *Mr. President,* a team board game in which players take on the roles of the president and vice-president (3-M Company).

Although both teachers and students responded to the cognitive aspects of the course in highly satisfactory manner, it was the students' enthusiastic response to the opportunity to choose specific topics of investigation for themselves that showed the real significance of the new instructional approach. At the beginning of the semester, students had been invited to work on a project of their choice. Not all the students did this—at least not right away. The most usual activity was to interview the real-life counterpart of their personas in the simulation *Campaign* in the community. (See Figure 11.6.) Having already played the interviewee's part for some weeks in class gave the interviewers confidence and served as a conversational ice-breaker. One newscaster interviewed even invited the interviewing student to appear on a television broadcast and to "bring along things to show."

Another response activity worth describing stemmed from the decision of one group of students to organize an in-school campaign against compulsory cafeteria duty (which was required of all students). The group set out to influence and win the support of both "voters" and "legislators." Their campaign activities included:

1. Producing a slide show depicting the menial tasks students were asked to perform. An accompanying tape described the feelings of students who believed that this kind of work was not educational.
2. Producing charts to show how many hours of learning time were lost because of such activities.
3. Producing editorials for the school newspaper with the theme "if students must work during lunch time, shouldn't teachers?"
4. Conducting a survey of other schools' policies about cafeteria duty.

The campaign was very exciting and produced a great deal of student involvement. The students lost, however. The "legislature" failed to act. As one "wiser" student said later, "It was a poor issue. We acted from emotion—not from thought. But, then, we've seen issues like this get support—in fact, we're living with some right now."

The overall evaluation of the project resulted in some changes. It was decided, for example, that the simulation, though it was well received, would work even better if the teacher were letter perfect in his or her role as general manager. When snags occur, decisions must be made instantly or momentum is lost. It was found, too, that not all students are good at

(a)

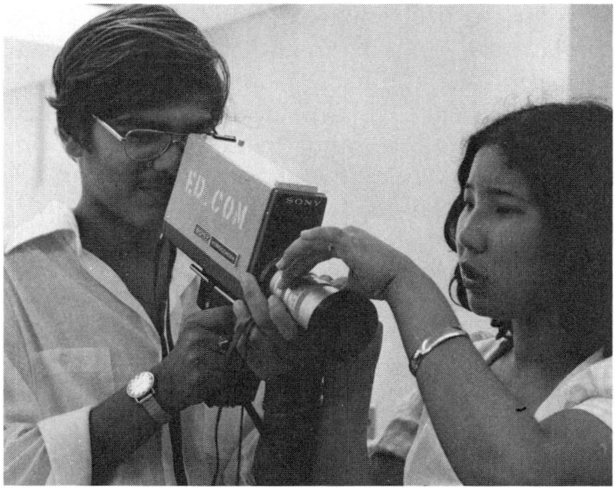

(b)

(c)

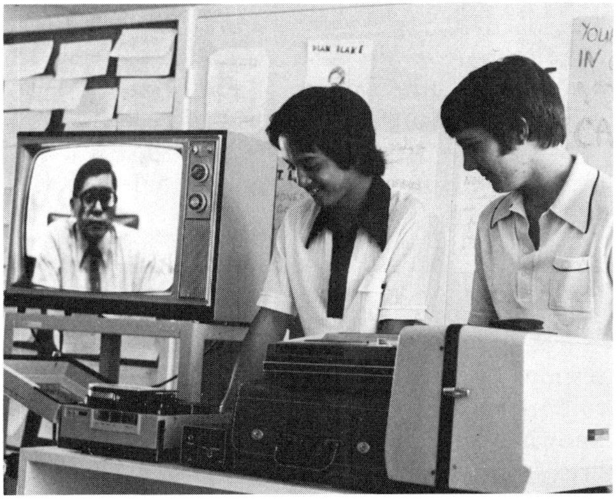

(d)

Figure 11.6 (*a*) This student, and others, played the simulation game *Campaign*. (*b* and *c*) Some students also interviewed three real-life counterparts, using a borrowed video recorder. (*d*) Both the student "reporters" and their classmates were enthusiastic about the televised versions of their real-world political figures. How well would activities like these fit into your instructional plan?

simulations, that more time should be taken to explain roles to players, and that continued participation is a must. Dropouts can ruin the game for their well-motivated teammates. Those who have doubts about the activity should not be encouraged to take part.

Most *Campaign* participants were enthusiastic about the game, but several would have liked to have seen more "dirty tricks" included in the stimulated procedures.

Students judged most of the reading materials to be useful and were able to suggest several additional ones.

The highest rating was given to the 23 sound motion pictures and videotapes used—even if the skirts were the wrong length in several of them. The ideas still came through. Multimedia kits, particularly the *New York Times* kit *The Presidential Series*[7] were popular, as were the study prints and copies of editorials and cartoons shown using an overhead projector.

Most agreed that the various projects were a lot of work, but interesting and valuable.

Example 2: A Primary-Grade Multimedia Experience

Three members of a teaching team shared the responsibility for planning learning experiences for 75 children ages 6 thorugh 9 in what is known as a group-graded room. All the children were considered normal learners, except for a few borderline students. These children would stay with the group unless it became evident that they needed special education.

The overall learning objectives for the group were the usual ones for children their age: mastery of language skills, the acquisition of elementary cognitive information in science and arithmetic; and an elementary grounding in art, music, physical education, personal hygiene, and safety.

[7] New York Times Teaching Resources, Multi-media Division, 488 Madison Ave., New York, N.Y. 10022.

During the preceding year the members of the group had performed normally on standard tests. However, the most intelligent did little better than average, and the least intelligent did disturbingly poorly. During the summer, the three teachers took stock of their situation and planned ways to increase the number and variety of learning experiences available to the children. The basic objectives remained the same; what they sought to change was the organization of the classroom and the number and variety of ways the children could learn and respond to learning.

They would, they decided, keep on using the time-tested learning resources: books, filmstrips, games, audiocassettes, geometric shapes, models, study prints, and the like. But they spent many hours locating and arranging to secure additional materials. They arranged withdrawals of materials from the school and district libraries and drew up a semester-long schedule for using 16mm sound films, film loops, and additional filmstrips. They also gave the district tape depository a list of audiotapes to duplicate for them.

Next, they replanned the layout of the classroom so that all learning resources they had selected would always be available to the students and made room in the class schedules for the opening weeks for some training in housekeeping.

Each teacher agreed to be responsible for cooperative planning and, in addition, to take the initiative in continually diagnosing learner progress and needs, (2) encouraging children to pursue a variety of learning experiences, or (3) helping class members use newfound information and skills in innovative ways.

A typical day's routine included breaking the group up into smaller groups for instruction by the three teachers and, following this, a planning session in which each group was broken up into still smaller groups of one, two, or three pupils who would then elect to pursue one of the 30 or more learning activities for small groups that had been arranged. (See Figure 11.7.) It is with these learning activities that we are particularly concerned here.

The classroom, double the size of an ordinary classroom, was arranged so that there were three open floor areas, each of which could accommodate 25 children. Around these open areas were 30 small activity spaces, formed using work tables or groups of desks with slides, filmstrip, or film projectors or space to do artwork, play games, and the like.

During planning sessions, each group of 25 pupils would assemble around a planning board containing pictures of the 30 activity areas and "keys" in the form of lettered tickets for each area. (See Figure 11.7*a*.) Each child would walk to the board, announce a selection, and wait to see if another child or children would choose the same activity. Mutual interests were usually the basis for the formation of groups. Often the teacher would suggest who might profit by working together and discourage tendencies to form cliques. Mutual interests often brought children of mixed abilities together and resulted in peer teaching. This kind of interaction produced a much greater degree of cooperation and involvement than is found in traditional classrooms and encouraged social relationships.

The role of the three teachers also changed as a result of the new instructional approach. Though organization and the inventory of learning materials had to be almost completely changed four times during the year in order to keep up with the progress and shifting interests of the group, most of this work was done during mid-semester and semester breaks. Thus the teachers still had time during class to observe the children's progress carefully and offer suggestions and encouragement as needed.

As the semester unwound, the daily planning sessions became a popular event. Housekeeping problems occurred less often. The scores of the group on tests of skills and information showed greater variety. However, many of the slower and faster learners made the greatest gains. Several of the borderline students made so much progress that they could be reclassified as normal learners.

Once the classroom had been properly reorganized, discipline problems all but disappeared. This was due largely to the fact that as soon as children completed their tasks as members of the large groups they were free to return to small-group activities. Children who finished first did not have "nothing to do." Some pupils who had volunteered responses became helpers, either "tutoring" other children or trouble shooting—plugging in power lines correctly, untangling earphone cords, cleaning up the terrarium or seedling trays, and so on.

The children also responded in many ways to new learning experiences. They collected specimens, invented arithmetic problems, wrote stories, wrote songs on projectuals and led the group in singing them, prepared simple graphs to show the rate of growth of seedlings, presented recorded book reports, and recommended games, film loops, and other learning resources to one another.

The consensus of the teaching team was that the tasks involved in readying the many activity centers were at first quite demanding. Each time it was done, poor or marginal materials were discarded and new learning alternatives were sought. All agreed, however, that the sense of involvement, self-assurance, and initiative the children developed as a result of the new approach made the work well worthwhile.

Example 3: A Unit on Custer

This example illustrates what one teacher, interacting with people and resources near at hand, can accomplish. One winter day Roy

(a)

ART
CREATIVE STITCHERY

(b)

FABLES
Contractions
A contraction is made up of two words, with one or more letters left out. The apostrophe (') takes the place of the letter or letters that have been left out.
1. I am
2. we will
3. are not
4. it is
5. let us

(c)

Make a cube.

(d)

(e)

(f)

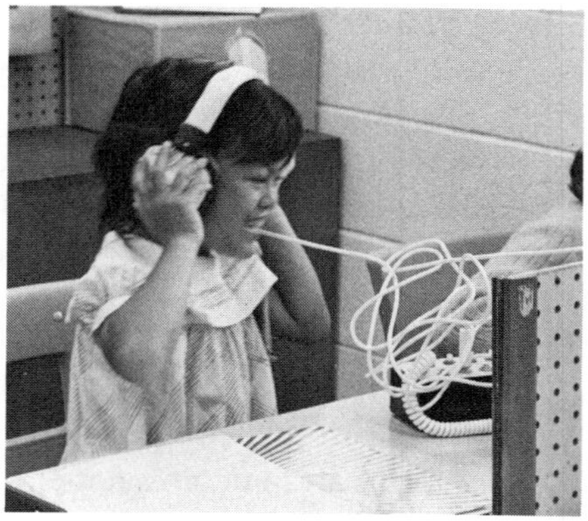

(g)

Shehab's sixth-grade social studies class in the Crescentwood Elementary School in East Detroit began a unit on George Armstrong Custer. It was a new topic, never before studied in that particular school. Before it was over, a city council, a police department, a parks commission, two newspapers, a television station, a radio station, a historical museum, a public library, and the people of two communities were to become involved in the work of the sixth-graders.

Normally, world history and ancient history are taught in the sixth grade in the Detroit school system, and the students *had*, in fact, been studying key historical events and people—from the Roman Empire and Julius Caesar to Churchill, Franklin Roosevelt, and Stalin. As they studied these prominent figures and the times in which they lived, the students began to realize, under the skillful guidance of their teacher, that there are often strongly divergent points of view about important people and events. While seeking a way to impress this idea on his students, Shehab noticed an article in a Detroit newspaper revealing that General George Armstrong Custer had lived for some 11 years in Monroe, Michigan, not far from Detroit, that the public library and the county historical museum in Monroe had a unique exhibit on Custer's life and times, and that a new feature film entitled *Little Big Man*, in which Custer was a major character, was soon to be released.

Materials and strategies. After discussing the article with his students and finding them interested in discovering more about the famous Indian fighter. Shehab secured permission from the principal to develop a new unit on the colorful and controversial general. He then asked Lewis Saks, the system's director of learning resources, to help him and his students find suitable materials to study. The school libraries had little on the subject, but a search of public libraries, university libraries in the area, homes in the community, and the library and historical museum in Monroe turned up a few instructional films and many pictures of the Battle of the Little Big Horn. And, of course, there was the feature film to be shown in a few weeks.

Because one of the primary purposes of the unit was to highlight the fact that there can be conflicting opinions about historical figures, Shehab divided the class in half—one group to search for information and views favoring Custer and the other group to seek material that presented Custer in a less favorable light. Every student became involved, and many undertook special projects such as building a scale model of the battlefield where Custer made his last stand and studies of his careers at West Point and in the Civil War, his reputation as an Indian fighter, and his personal characteristics. (See Figure 11.8.)

As the students became more and more absorbed in what they were doing, many sought

Figure 11.7 These children are at work in their classroom, which, in addition to space for meetings of three groups of 25 students each, includes 30 learning areas for small groups. Each of these 30 spaces contains learning materials and equipment. (*a*) During a daily planning period, each child selects one of the letter "keys" that admit one, two, or three pupils to a given learning area. (*b*) Ten of these areas are shown here. Each allows children to do further work in subjects taught to the group as a whole. (*c*) One of the three members of the teaching team observes a small group working on grammar. (*d*) This girl is pondering the meaning of an arithmetic problem. (*e*) This boy is measuring how much a seedling has grown during three weeks. (*f*) Carrel mates view a sound filmstrip about the western states. (*g*) In one of three recording areas, a pupil is preparing a taped report on her favorite books, despite a problem with a tangled cord. How would these activities fit your instructional plan?

Figure 11.8 Every child has an imagination that can flourish or be turned off, depending on how we nurture it. Who knows what thoughts of the Battle of the Little Big Horn this boy may be having or where they may lead?

additional information on their own, and all looked forward to seeing *Little Big Man*. Permission was secured from parents, the school administration, and the theater management for the students to view the film, which was rated unsuitable for children, and the class went as a group to see it.

By that time the pupils had already learned a good deal about Custer, a fact reflected in the discussions following the film (which was strongly anti-Custer). Many youngsters were able to point out inaccuracies in the film's story line. Many others, particularly those who were seeking evidence on Custer's positive qualities, pointed out that the general as portrayed in the film was quite a different character from the man they had studied. Discussions of the film led to further activities in which a number of controversial points were debated and to questions about why the film took liberties not only with the characterization of Custer, but with numerous historical facts. Quite on their own, the sixth-graders came to the conclusion that the purpose of the film was to entertain and make money rather than to present accurate information.

At this point the members of the class decided they needed more information on Custer. The director of the Monroe County Library and the county director of learning resources were invited to visit the class to discuss the general. Their presentations were greeted with such a variety of questions reflecting an in-depth knowledge of Custer's life that the visitors, impressed, invited the class to visit the Monroe County Library and Historical Museum. The class responded enthusiastically, and began at once to make plans for the visit.

The trip proved to be an exciting and valuable learning experience. Also, thanks to the imagination and initiative of Lewis Saks, who made the arrangements for the trip, it generated considerable interest in both communities. The school bus bringing the students from East Detroit was met at the Monroe city limits by a police escort. The city council gave permission for pictures to be taken from the top of the statue of General Custer in the public square. Local newspapers ran stories on the visiting students, and local radio and television stations interviewed them and used excerpts in their evening newscasts. A motion picture photographer documented the proceedings, and the children themselves took many pictures. Monroe High School history classes sent representatives to observe and report the proceedings.

The students' reaction to the experience was highly positive—in part because of the care with which the plans for the trip had been made, but also because they had learned enough about Custer and the whole problem of differing points of view to be genuinely interested in the subject. They were able to find many new materials on Custer at the Monroe public library, including letters, documents, and official reports. At the museum, they were able to sit at Custer's desk, in his chair, and even in the saddle he used; they also inspected a life insurance policy of Custer's. The children surprised some of the local experts with their questions and with the extent of their knowledge. Some examined official documents—reports of campaigns, including the Battle of the Little Big Horn, records of court martial cases in which Custer was involved, and records of his time at West Point. (See Figure 11.9.)

The more the students learned, the more difficult they found it to decide what to *believe* about the character and the acts of the legendary general. They learned that he was indeed an avid Indian fighter, but they also learned why. They learned that he had indeed gone AWOL during his military career, but, again, that he may have had a reason to do so. On their own they began to draw comparisons with the tangled trials of Lieutenant Calley and others involved in the My Lai incident. They were beginning to learn, in short, the valuable lesson that there are seldom simple or final answers. (See Figure 11.10.)

SUMMARY

Examples of systematic planning for education can be found at the national, state, and local levels. In each case described in the chapter, a combination of media was used in innovative ways to achieve specific educational objectives. Though the information to be communicated, the age of the learners, and the purposes of the programs differed, the basic way of looking at things was similar. It is this kind of goal-oriented, learner-centered, open-ended approach that is basic to instructional development, at any level. Individual teachers may even find some of the instructional strategies and learning activities suggested adaptable to their own purposes.

Our primary purpose here, of course, is to examine the role played by learning media in this kind of instructional approach.

(a) (b)

Figure 11.9 Research can be boring or stimulating. (*a*) Here in the Monroe County Public Library students learn some interesting facts about a famous man. (*b*) The knowledge a child brings to a museum display can make all the difference. These Custer realia would be just relics to many children, but to these young investigators with a background in the subject and a purpose, they are fascinating.

We have seen how national planners used film, videotape, television, radio, and print materials to educate children and adults about national issues during the bicentennial.

We have seen how a statewide plan to improve the language skills of primary, elementary, and high school students was developed and implemented, using tested self-tutorial materials and techniques.

We have seen how two high school teachers set about developing an innovative course in voter education using a variety of learning resources and printed materials.

We have seen how a team of primary school teachers redesigned their instructional approach and the layout of their classroom to provide small groups of children with access to a wide variety of learning media.

We have seen how a sixth-grade social studies teacher used conflicting evidence about a local historical figure—evidence discovered by students themselves from a variety of sources—to show that it is often difficult to make black-and-white judgments about the past.

The innovative use of modern educational technology is an integral part of the systems approach to solving teaching and learning problems. An awareness of the range of that technology, and its applications, is also a tremendous advantage in teaching the technologically oriented children of today.

ACTIVITIES

1. It is now time to try out your own instructional development plan, when the opportunity arises. After this has been done, you will

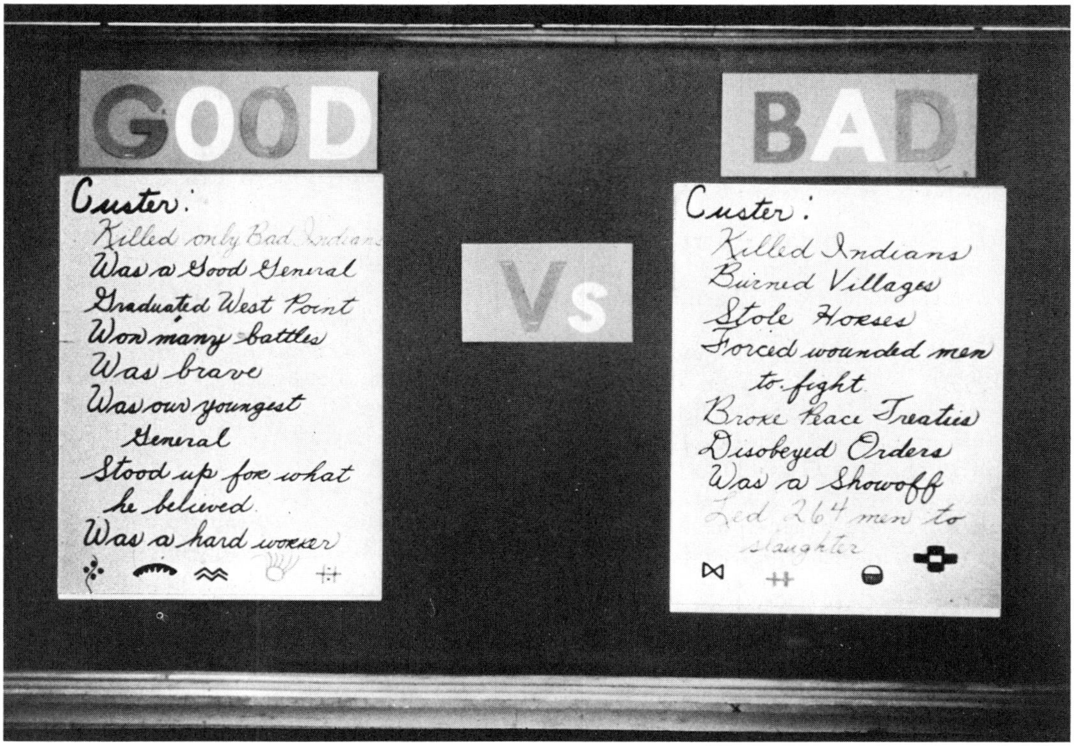

Figure 11.10 What is "truth"? The students who summarized these good and bad "facts" about Custer are not sure, and so they have learned an important lesson.

have a basis for evaluating and revising it. Observe the degree to which hoped-for outcomes are realized, and be alert, too, for valuable outcomes you did not anticipate. Such serendipity may be surprising, but it can happen. It is another of the rewards of creative teaching.

REFERENCES

PRINT REFERENCES

Briggs, L. J., and others, "Methods—Media Selection in Education" (Pittsburgh, Pa.: American Institute for Research, 1967).

Brieve, Fred J., A. T. Johnston, and Ken. M. Young, *Educational Planning* (Worthington, Ohio: Charles A. Jones Publishing Co., 1973).

Crawford, Jack J., *Facilitating Inquiry in the Classroom* (Palo Alto, Calif.: Northwest Educational Regional Laboratory, American Institute for Research in the Behavioral Sciences, 1972).

Davis, Robert H., Lawrence T. Alexander, and Stephen L. Yelon, *Learning System Design: An Approach to the Improvement of Instruction* (New York: McGraw-Hill, 1974).

Hinze, Richard H., King, Arthur R., Krause, Loretta D., and Nunes, Shiho S., "Ten Years of Curriculum Research and Development in Hawaii: Where Have We Been?," *Educational Perspectives,* Journal of the College of Education, University of Hawaii, vol. 16, no. 2, May 1977, pp. 3–30.

Katz, Daniel, and Robert L. Kahn, *Social Psychology of Organization,* ch. 11 (New York: Wiley, 1966).

Kaufman, Roger A., "A Systems Approach to Education: Derivation and Definition," *AV Communication Review* (Winter 1968).

Kaufman, Roger A., *Educational System Planning* (Englewood Cliffs, N.J.: Prentice-Hall, 1972).

MEDIA REFERENCES

AV Forum, tape cassette, monthly report on current topics in instructional technology. AV Forum, 23434 Industrial Park Court, Farmington, MI 48024.

Child of the Future, 16mm film, b/w, 58 min. NFBC, 1963.

Designing Effective Instruction, color slides or tapes. General Programmed Teaching, 424 University Avenue, Palo Alto, CA 94301 (1968). Unit titles follow:
- —Introduction to Basic Principles
- —General Goals, Affective Objectives, Cognitive Objectives
- —Main Components of an Objective
- —Classification of Objectives
- —Criterion Tests
- —Determining Entry Level
- —Entry Level Tests
- —Stimulus and Response
- —One-Way and Two-Way Stimulus—Response Pairs, Single and Multiple Discriminations
- —Content Analysis
- —Stimulus-Response Pairs in Chain Activities
- —Influence of Objectives on Content
- —Developing Objectives and Deriving Content
- —Programmed Lesson Plans and Instructional Media
- —Validation

Essential Ingredient, The, 16mm film, sound, color, 14 min., Florida State Department of Education, 1975.

Galaxy of Motion Picture Documents on Communication Theory and the New Educational Media, 16mm films, color. Ohio State University, 1966 (35 titles).

Individualized Instruction, color slides with tapes. AECT, 1970 (24 titles).

Instructional Development, 16mm film, b/w, 17 min. Indiana University, 1971.

Instructional Development: The People, 16mm film, color, 19 min. Michigan State University, 1971.

Instructional Development: The Process, 16mm film, color, 26 min. Michigan State University, 1972.

Instructional Development: The Results, 16mm film, color, 10 min. Michigan State University, 1971.

Introduction to Feedback, 16mm film, color, 12 min. IBM, 1963.

Make a Mighty Reach, 16mm film, color, 56 min. IDEA, 1967.

Planning and Organizing for Teaching, 35mm filmstrip, sound, b/w, 110 frames. NEA, 1965.

Programming Is a Process, 16mm film, color, 32 min. University of Illinois, 1967.

Systems Engineering of Learning, 35mm filmstrip, sound, color, 114 frames. Educational and Training Consultants Company, 979 Teakwood Road, Los Angeles, CA 90049, 1964.

SOURCE REFERENCES

Learning Systems

Avedex, Inc., 7326 Niles Center Rd., Skokie, IL 60076.

Behavioral Research Laboratories, Ladera Professional Center, P.O. Box 577, Palo Alto, CA 94302.

Califone International, 5922 Bowcroft St., Los Angeles, CA 90016.

Grolier Educational Corporation, 845 Third Ave., New York, NY 10022.

D.C. Heath & Co., 125 Spring St., Lexington, MA 02173. (mini systems)

Philips Audio Video Systems, One Philips Parkway, Montvale, NJ 07645.

UCIDT, 801D Waite Phillips Hall, University of Southern California, Los Angeles, CA 90007. (Instructional Development Institutes.)

Westinghouse Electric Corporation, P.O. Box J, Sea Cliff, NY 11579.

Instructional Kits

Amidon & Associates, 4329 Nicollet Ave. So., Minneapolis, MN 55409.

Behavioral Research Laboratories, Ladera Professional Center, P.O. Box 577, Palo Alto, CA 94302.

BFA Educational Media, 2211 Michigan Ave., P.O. Box 1795, Santa Monica, CA 90406.

Bureau of Dental Health Education, American Dental Association, 211 East Chicago Ave., Chicago, IL 60611.

Cathedral Films, 2921 W. Alameda Ave., Burbank, CA 91505.

Comspace Corporation, 350 Great Neck Rd., Farmingdale, NY 11735.

D.C. Heath and Company, 125 Spring St., Lexington, MA 02173.

Denoyer-Geppert Company, 5235 Ravenswood Ave., Chicago, IL 60640.

Ideal School Supply Company, 11000 So. Lavergne Ave., Oak Lawn, IL 60453.

McGraw-Hill Book Company, Webster Div., 330 W. 42nd St., New York, NY 10036.

Mind/Matter Corporation, P.O. Box 345, Danbury, CT 06810.

See, Inc., 3 Bridge St., Newton, MA 02195.

Shorewood Reproductions, 10 East 53rd St., New York, NY 10022.

Society for Visual Education, 1345 Diversey Pkwy., Chicago, IL 60614.

Teaching Resources Films, 2 Kisco Plaza, Mt. Kisco, NY 10549.

United Scientific Company, 216 South Jefferson St., Chicago, IL 60606.

U.S. Committee for UNICEF, 331 E. 38th St., New York, NY 10016.

Programing Equipment

Arion Corporation, 825 Boone Ave. N., Minneapolis, MN 55427.

General Techniques, 1270 Broadway, New York, NY 10001.

Link Educational Laboratories, P.O. Box 11073, Montgomery, AL 36111.

North American Philips Corporation, Training and Education Systems, 100 E. 42nd St., New York, NY 10017.

V-M Corp., P.O. Box 1247-375 West Main St., Benton Harbor, MI 94022.

Programed instruction

Addison-Wesley Publishing Company, South St., Reading, MA 94025.

Behavioral Research Laboratories, Ladera Professional Center, Box 577, Palo Alto, CA 94302.

Encyclopaedia Britannica Educational Corporation, 425 Michigan Ave., Chicago, IL 60611.

Field Enterprises, Merchandise Mart Plaza, Chicago, IL 60654.

Harcourt Brace Jovanovich, 757 Third Ave., New York, NY 10017.

Hendershot's Bibliography, 4114 Ridgewood, Bay City, MI 48706.

Holt, Rinehart and Winston, 383 Madison Ave., New York, NY 10017.

Kalart Victor Corp., Henius St., Plainville, CN 06062.

McGraw-Hill Book Company, 330 W. 42nd St., New York, NY 10036.

The Macmillan Company, 866 Third Ave., New York, NY 10022.

Sargent-Welch Scientific Company, 7300 N. Linder Ave., Skokie, IL 60076.

John Wiley & Sons, 605 Third Ave., New York, NY 10016.

Index

78 79 80 81 82 9 8 7 6 5 4 3 2 1